£32.95

A GUIDE TO

DB2

FOURTH EDITION

A GUIDE TO

DB2

FOURTH EDITION

A user's guide to the IBM product
IBM DATABASE 2
(a relational database management system
for the MVS environment)
and its major companion products

C. J. DATE

with

COLIN J. WHITE

ADDISON-WESLEY PUBLISHING COMPANY

Reading, Massachusetts • Menlo Park, California • New York
Don Mills, Ontario • Wokingham, England • Amsterdam • Bonn
Sydney • Singapore • Tokyo • Madrid • San Juan • Milan • Paris

Library of Congress Cataloging-in-Publication Data

Date, C. J.
   A guide to DB2 / C. J. Date, with Colin J. White.—4th ed.
     p.   cm.
   Includes bibliographical references and index.
   ISBN 0-201-55821-1
   1. Data base management. 2. IBM Database 2. I. White, Colin J.
  II. Title.
  QA76.9.D3D15995 1993
  005.75′65—dc20   92-5425
                                                CIP

Many of the designations used by manufacturers and sellers to distinguish their products are claimed as trademarks. Where those designations appear in this book, and Addison-Wesley was aware of a trademark claim, the designations have been printed in initial caps or all caps.

The programs and applications presented in this book have been included for their instructional value. They have been tested with care, but are not guaranteed for any particular purpose. The publisher does not offer any warranties or representations, nor does it accept any liabilities with respect to the programs or applications.

1 2 3 4 5 6 7 8 9 10-HA-95949392

To Ted, for obvious reasons

Preface

It is customary when producing a new edition of a book to reprint the prefaces from earlier editions. In the case of this particular book, however, so much has changed since those earlier editions that the previous prefaces are no longer very relevant, and I have therefore decided to drop them from the present edition.

Let me immediately make it clear that when I say that so much has changed, I am not referring so much to changes in the content and structure of the book per se (although such changes there certainly are). Rather, I am referring to changes in the data processing community and the database environment at large. Relational technology has come to be almost universally accepted as the technology of choice—indeed, it quite clearly dominates the database marketplace—and there is no longer any need to defend it against unreasoned attacks. DB2 in particular, as a specific embodiment of that technology, is by now a highly successful product, with almost 7,500 installations at the time of writing (and a projection of over 12,000 by

1995). Thus, the previous prefaces, which tended to adopt a somewhat defensive attitude toward such matters, are no longer fully appropriate.

Let me now turn to an explanation of the book's purpose and scope. The principal subject of the book, DB2 (or "IBM DATABASE 2," to give it its full name), is, as the reader probably knows, an IBM program product for the MVS environment. More specifically, it is a *relational database management system* for MVS, which means that it is a product that allows users in the MVS environment (both end-users and application programmers) to store data in, and retrieve data from, databases that are perceived as collections of *relations* or tables. It provides access to those databases by means of a relational language called SQL ("Structured Query Language"). Thus, the major purpose of the book is to present a detailed (and not wholly uncritical) description of both DB2 in general and the SQL language in particular—what they are, what they are intended for, and how they can be used.

The intended audience for the book includes DP management, end-user management, database specialists (including database and system administrators, database designers, and database application programmers), DP students and teachers, and more generally anyone who wishes to broaden his or her knowledge of the database field by studying a state-of-the-art system. The emphasis throughout is on the *user* (where by "user" I mean, principally, either an end-user or an application programmer); treatment of user-oriented material, such as the SQL language, is very thorough. By contrast, details that are of interest only to system programmers or operators, such as details of system commands, are generally omitted or at best treated only rather sketchily. Readers are assumed to have at least a general appreciation of the overall structure, concepts, and objectives of database systems in general; however, prior knowledge of relational systems per se is not required.

The book is divided into four major parts, together with a set of appendixes:

    I. An Overview of DB2

    II. The DB2 Database Management System

    III. Distributed Database Management

    IV. The DB2 Product Family

Each part in turn is divided into a number of chapters:

- Part I (two chapters) sets the scene by explaining in general terms what relational databases are all about, presenting an overview of the relevant features of DB2, and discussing DB2's internal structure (in particular, showing how it deals with SQL requests from the user).

- Part II (14 chapters) presents a very careful description of DB2 from the user's point of view; in other words, it covers essentially all aspects of the SQL language as supported by DB2, in detail. It also addresses certain database and system administration concerns, such as physical storage structures, the system catalog, and database and system utilities.

- Part III (one long chapter) describes DB2's distributed database support and a variety of related matters.

- Part IV (three chapters) provides an introduction to IBM's AD/Cycle and Information Warehouse "solution frameworks" and explains DB2's role with respect to those frameworks. More specifically, it describes some of the most important DB2 companion products—CSP, QMF, DXT, DPROP, and so on.

In addition, there are seven appendixes, including one on the relational model (which is the theory on which relational systems such as DB2 are based), another on DB2's date and time support, another giving a BNF grammar for SQL data manipulation operations, and so on.

For readers who may be familiar with the previous edition of the book, the major differences from that edition are summarized below:

- The book as a whole is at the level of DB2 Version 2 Release 3 ("DB2 Version 2.3"). The product discussions in Part IV are also all at the most recent release levels.

- Chapter 2 has been completely rewritten to incorporate the new "package" concept that was introduced with Version 2.3. Related changes have also been made to various other parts of the book. *Note*: The function provided by packages was provided (in part) by *plans* prior to Version 2.3, and of course plans are still supported in Version 2.3 for reasons of compatibility. It seems to this writer, however, that there would have been little reason to support plans at all if packages had been available in the first place (i.e., right from the very first release of DB2), and packages are generally to be preferred over plans if there is a choice. Because of this fact (and also because treating packages and plans simultaneously leads to unduly complex explanations), this edition concentrates primarily on packages per se, and relegates consideration of the plan alternative to a series of secondary discussions (later sections and subsections, footnotes, etc.).

- The chapters on embedded SQL have been extensively revised to incorporate a variety of new features of Version 2.3—WITH HOLD, NOFOR, STDSQL, SQLSTATE, and so on.

- The chapter on administration facilities has been completely rewritten, in particular to explain the two new versions of the BIND command (BIND PACKAGE and BIND PLAN).

- The chapter on distributed database has also been completely rewritten (and considerably expanded) to incorporate a discussion of the new Distributed Relational Data Architecture (DRDA) and DB2's support for that architecture. Client/server operation is discussed, and the chapter includes a comparison between the DRDA distributed database support in DB2 Version 2.3 and the proprietary (nonDRDA) support in DB2 Version 2.2.

- The old chapters on QMF, AS, CSP, ADF, DXT, micro-to-mainframe links (HDBV and ECF), and DBRAD have been dropped. In their place is a brand new set of chapters on AD/Cycle and the Information Warehouse. These new chapters cover much of the same ground as the older ones, but the presentation is better structured, and the text now lays more emphasis on those products such as CSP that have emerged as "strategic" within IBM's overall DB2 plan.

- A major feature of DB2 Version 2.3 is its compliance with national and international SQL standards. The appendix on DB2 and the SQL standard has been totally rewritten to reflect this compliance.

- The appendixes "Advantages of DB2" and "Query-By-Example" have been dropped for reasons of space (and relevance, in part).

As usual, of course, I have also taken the opportunity to make a large number of minor improvements and corrections throughout the text.

A NOTE ON THE TEXT

There is one point—some would say a small point, though I would have to disagree—on which the terminology of this book differs from that of the IBM manuals. The IBM manuals very often use the phrase "tables and views," which suggests strongly that views are *not* tables, and suggests further that "tables" means *base* tables specifically. This terminology is unfortunate, because the whole point about a relational system is that "everything is tables"—i.e., tables are the *only* data structure—and base tables and views are both just special cases of this more general construct. In this book, therefore, we will normally use "table" in the general sense, and will say "base table" or "view" explicitly if such is our intended meaning.

Another point I would like to make quite clear right at the outset is the following. The DB2 product has (of course) changed and evolved considerably since its first release. Unfortunately, some of the changes that have been made in the interests of enhanced functionality have had the side-effect of making the product more complex and more difficult to teach and learn. Since the primary objective of this book is only to act as a tutorial introduction to the DB2 product, not to describe it in every last detail, I have deliberately made certain simplifying assumptions in some parts of the text, and I have deliberately ignored some of the finer detail in others. (However, I have not told any deliberate lies!)

There is one final point to be made regarding the text, namely as follows: Certain terms that were used (not always very consistently) in earlier editions of this book have been dropped from this edition. The terms in question are as follows:

record (replaced by "row")

field (replaced by "column")

predicate (replaced by "condition" or "conditional expression")

constant (replaced by "literal")

ACKNOWLEDGMENTS

Although I have dropped the prefaces from earlier editions, it does not seem appropriate to drop the acknowledgments to the numerous friends and colleagues who helped with those editions—so here goes. First and foremost, it is a real pleasure to acknowledge the friendship and support I received from Ted Codd, not only during the writing of the first edition of this book but throughout my professional career up to that time. Like so many other people in this field, I owe my career and very livelihood to the work that Ted originally did in the late sixties and early seventies, and I am delighted to be able to acknowledge that debt in public here. It is only fitting that this book should be dedicated to him.

Second, I would like to thank my coauthor Colin White for his major contribution to every edition since the first. Colin wrote the chapters on related products (Part IV of the present edition) and also contributed to certain other chapters, especially Chapters 2 and 16. His contributions serve to enhance the value and usefulness of the book immeasurably.

I would also like to thank the following people for technical assistance with, and/or constructive criticism of, various earlier editions and drafts of this book: Nagraj Alur, Jnan Dash, Marc Descollonges, Jim Doak, Bob Engles, Sandy Eveland, Rob Goldring, Paul Higginbotham, Roger Miller, Nick Nomm, Roger Reinsch, Walt Roseberry, Phil Shaw, Ueli Wahli, Dan

Wardman, Sharon Weinberg, and George Zagelow. All of these people either currently are or once were members of the DB2 development team at IBM; I am very grateful to all of them, and hope that this book does justice to their efforts.

Turning now to this new edition, a very special vote of thanks must go to Roger Miller, a senior member of the DB2 development team at IBM, who did the most thorough job of reviewing the manuscript that any author could wish for, and helped out in a variety of other ways as well. Thanks too to the other reviewers Nagraj Alur, Bill Bireley, Rob Goldring, and Roberta Rousseau for their constructive and helpful comments. I would also like to acknowledge the assistance Colin and I received from the IBM Santa Teresa Laboratory (the home of DB2). Finally, I cannot do better than repeat the following from the preface to another of my books: I am, as always, grateful to my editor, Elydia Davis, and to the staff at Addison-Wesley for their assistance and their continually high standards of professionalism. It has been, as always, a pleasure to work with them.

Healdsburg, California   C. J. Date
1992

Contents

PART I   AN OVERVIEW OF DB2

PART II   THE DB2 DATABASE MANAGEMENT SYSTEM

███████████

PART III   DISTRIBUTED DATABASE MANAGEMENT

███████████

PART IV   THE DB2 PRODUCT FAMILY

APPENDIXES

PART

I

AN OVERVIEW OF DB2

CHAPTER

◆ 1 ◆

DB2: A Relational System

1.1 INTRODUCTION

"DB2" is an abbreviation for "IBM DATABASE 2." DB2 is a subsystem of the MVS operating system.* More specifically, it is a *database management system* (DBMS) for that operating system. More specifically still, it is IBM's long-awaited, and by now highly successful, *relational* DBMS for MVS; thus, it is a system that allows MVS users to build, access, and maintain relational databases, using the well-known relational language SQL

---

*Version 1 of DB2 ran on both the original MVS/370 system product ("Multiple Virtual Systems/370") and the extended version MVS/XA ("MVS/Extended Architecture"). Version 1 has since been superseded by Version 2, which runs on MVS/XA and the newer MVS/ESA ("MVS/Enterprise Systems Architecture"). The current release of DB2, and the primary subject of this book, is Version 2 Release 3 ("Version 2.3").

3

("Structured Query Language"). IBM's product line prior to DB2 included a nonrelational (actually hierarchic) DBMS for MVS, namely IMS, and a relational DBMS for VM and VSE, namely SQL/DS, but did not include a relational offering for MVS. (We shall have more to say about IMS and SQL/DS later.) In June 1983, however, the MVS relational product DB2 was finally announced. The purpose of this book is to describe that product.

What does it mean for a system to be relational? To answer this question properly, it would unfortunately be necessary to discuss a good deal of preliminary material first. Since any such discussion would be out of place at this early point in the book, we defer it for now (see Section 1.2 and Appendix A for more detail); however, we give a rough-and-ready answer to the question without that discussion, in the hope that such an answer will help to allay any apprehensions the reader may be feeling at the outset. Briefly, a relational system is a system in which:

(a) The data is perceived by the user as tables (and nothing but tables); and

(b) The operators at the user's disposal (e.g., for query) are operators that generate new tables from old. For example, there will be one operator to extract a subset of the rows of a given table, and another to extract a subset of the columns—and of course a row subset and a column subset of a table can both in turn be regarded as tables themselves.

Fig. 1.1 illustrates these two points. Part (a) of the figure shows the data, a single table, named CELLAR, with three columns and four rows. Part (b) shows two sample queries, one involving a row-subsetting operation and the other a column-subsetting operation, together with the corresponding result in each case.

The two queries shown in part (b) of the figure are in fact examples of the SELECT statement of the Structured Query Language SQL mentioned earlier. SQL (usually pronounced "sequel," though the official pronunciation is "ess-cue-ell") is the database language supported, not only by DB2, but also by IBM's SQL/DS, OS/2 Extended Edition Database Manager, and SQL/400 products, and also by numerous products from vendors other than IBM.

Aside: SQL is also an official standard language; it was adopted by the American National Standards Institute (ANSI) in 1986 and by the International Organization for Standardization (ISO) in 1987 as, respectively, a national and an international standard for relational systems. Later, in 1989, that ANSI/ISO standard was enhanced to include certain integrity features. Another dialect of SQL was adopted by IBM itself in 1987 as part of its own "Systems Application Architecture"

(a) Given table: CELLAR

WINE	YEAR	BOTTLES
Zinfandel	84	10
Chardonnay	90	6
Cabernet	84	12
Riesling	90	9

(b) Operators (examples):

1. Row subset:

```
SELECT WINE, YEAR, BOTTLES
FROM    CELLAR
WHERE   YEAR = 90 ;
```

WINE	YEAR	BOTTLES
Chardonnay	90	6
Riesling	90	9

2. Column subset:

```
SELECT WINE, BOTTLES
FROM    CELLAR ;
```

WINE	BOTTLES
Zinfandel	10
Chardonnay	6
Cabernet	12
Riesling	9

Fig. 1.1   Data structure and operators in a relational system (examples)

(SAA) standard; that standard also was extended later (1991) to include certain additional features. The DB2 dialect of SQL is broadly compliant with, but not identical to, the 1986–1987–1989 ANSI/ISO standard and the 1987–1991 IBM SAA standard. See Appendix E for further discussion. *End of aside.*

The purpose of this book, then, is to provide an in-depth tutorial and reference text on a specific relational system, DB2 (also on its principal companion products—see Part IV). It is intended for end-users, application programmers, database administrators, and more generally anyone who wishes to obtain an understanding of the major concepts of the DB2 system. It is not intended as a substitute for the system manuals provided by IBM; but it *is* intended as a comprehensive, convenient (single-volume) guide to the use of the product. As stated in the Preface, the emphasis is definitely on the user, and therefore on product externals rather than internals, although various internal aspects are discussed from time to time. The reader is assumed to have an overall appreciation of the structure and objectives of database systems in general, but not necessarily any specific knowledge of relational systems in particular. All applicable relational concepts are introduced in the text as they are needed. In addition, Appendix A provides a more formal summary of those concepts, for purposes of reference.

In this preliminary chapter, we present a brief overview of the DB2 product. In particular, we give some idea as to what is involved in creating and accessing data in a DB2 database, and we briefly discuss the DB2 database language SQL. These topics, and of course many others, are amplified in subsequent chapters.

1.2 RELATIONAL DATABASES

DB2 databases are relational. *A relational database is a database that is perceived by its users as a collection of tables (and nothing but tables).* An example (the suppliers-and-parts database) is shown in Fig. 1.2.

S

S#	SNAME	STATUS	CITY
S1	Smith	20	London
S2	Jones	10	Paris
S3	Blake	30	Paris
S4	Clark	20	London
S5	Adams	30	Athens

SP

S#	P#	QTY
S1	P1	300
S1	P2	200
S1	P3	400
S1	P4	200
S1	P5	100
S1	P6	100
S2	P1	300
S2	P2	400
S3	P2	200
S4	P2	200
S4	P4	300
S4	P5	400

P

P#	PNAME	COLOR	WEIGHT	CITY
P1	Nut	Red	12	London
P2	Bolt	Green	17	Paris
P3	Screw	Blue	17	Rome
P4	Screw	Red	14	London
P5	Cam	Blue	12	Paris
P6	Cog	Red	19	London

Fig. 1.2 The suppliers-and-parts database (sample values)

As you can see, the database consists of three tables, namely S, P, and SP.

- Table S represents *suppliers*. Each supplier has a supplier number (S#), unique to that supplier; a supplier name (SNAME), not necessarily unique; a rating or status value (STATUS); and a location (CITY). For the sake of the example, we assume that each supplier is located in exactly one city.

- Table P represents *parts* (more accurately, kinds of part). Each kind of part has a part number (P#), which is unique; a part name (PNAME), not necessarily unique; a color (COLOR); a weight (WEIGHT); and a location where parts of that type are stored (CITY). For the sake of the example, again, we assume that each kind of part comes in exactly one color and is stored in a warehouse in exactly one city.

- Table SP represents *shipments*. It serves in a sense to connect the other two tables together. For example, the first row of table SP in Fig. 1.2 connects a specific supplier from table S (namely, supplier S1) with a specific part from table P (namely, part P1); in other words, it represents a shipment of parts of kind P1 by the supplier called S1 (and the shipment quantity is 300). Thus, each shipment has a supplier number (S#), a part number (P#), and a quantity (QTY). For the sake of the example, once again, we assume that there can be at most one shipment at any given time for a given supplier and a given part; thus, for a given shipment, the combination of S# value and P# value is unique with respect to the set of shipments currently appearing in the SP table.

A couple of minor points concerning this example:

- First, of course, the database is extremely simple, much more simple than any real database that you are likely to encounter in practice. Nevertheless, it is adequate to illustrate most of the points that we need to make in this book, and we will use it as the basis for most (not all) of the examples in the following chapters. You should therefore take a little time to familiarize yourself with it now.

- Second, there is nothing wrong with using more descriptive names such as SUPPLIERS, PARTS, and SHIPMENTS in place of the rather terse names S, P, and SP; indeed, descriptive names are generally to be recommended in practice. But in the case of the suppliers-and-parts database specifically, the three tables are referenced so frequently in the chapters that follow that very short names seemed desirable. Long names tend to become irksome with much repetition.

Much more important, the example also illustrates a number of technical matters that deserve explicit discussion:

- First, note that *all data values are atomic*. That is, at every row-and-column position in every table there is always exactly one data value, never a list of multiple values. Thus, for example, in table SP (considering the first two columns only, for simplicity), we have

S#	P#
.	.
S2	P1
S2	P2
.	.
S4	P2
S4	P4
S4	P5
.	.
.	.

instead of

S#	P#
.	.
S2	P1, P2
.	.
S4	P2, P4, P5
.	.
.	.

A column such as P# in the second version of this table represents what is sometimes called a "repeating group." A repeating group is a column that contains *multiple data values* (with, typically, different numbers of values in different rows), instead of just one value in each row. *Relational databases do not allow repeating groups.* The second version of the table above would not be permitted in a relational system.

- Second, note that the entire information content of the database is represented as *explicit data values*. This method of representation (as explicit values in column positions within rows of tables) is the *only* method available in a relational database. Specifically, there are no "links" or pointers connecting one table to another.* For example, there is a connection (as already pointed out) between the S1 row of table S and the P1 row of table P, because supplier S1 supplies part P1; but that connection is represented, not by pointers, but by the existence of a row in table SP in which the S# value is S1 and the P# value is P1. In nonrelational systems (such as IMS), by contrast, such information is typically represented by some kind of physical link or pointer that is explicitly visible to the user. Some consequences of this difference will be discussed later in the book.

- Third, note that each of the tables in the example has a *unique identifier*—that is, a set of columns whose value in any given row is unique, in the sense that the value in question does not appear in the same position in any other row in the table. For example, values of the S# column of table S are unique in this sense; such values can accordingly be used to pinpoint individual supplier rows within the table. The unique identifier for table S is thus the set of columns {S#}. Likewise, the unique identifier for table P is the set {P#}, and the unique identifier for table SP is the set {S#,P#}.

---

*This sentence does not mean that there cannot be pointers *at the physical storage level*—there certainly can, and indeed there certainly will. But all such pointers are *concealed from the user.* We are concerned here purely with the logical level of the system. See the further discussion of this point in the next section.

Note: When the "set" contains just a single column, as in the case of tables S and P, we usually drop the set braces and say simply that the unique identifier is just that column; thus, we would typically say that (e.g.) the unique identifier for table S is just S#. But the reader should not lose sight of the fact that, strictly, such unique identifiers are always *sets* of columns.

The formal relational term for such a unique identifier is *primary key*. DB2 does not fully enforce the primary key discipline (that is, it does not actually require every table to have a primary key), but users are nevertheless *strongly* recommended to follow such a discipline in practice. We will do so throughout this book. See Chapter 11 for further discussion.

At this point the reader may be wondering why a database such as that in Fig. 1.2 is called "relational" anyway. The answer is simple: "Relation" is just a mathematical term for a table (to be precise, a table of a certain specific kind—details to follow in Chapter 4). Thus, for example, we can say that the database of Fig. 1.2 consists of three *relations*. For the most part, in fact, we will take "relation" and "table" as synonymous in this book. Relational systems have their origin in the mathematical theory of relations; of course, this does not mean that you need to be a mathematician in order to use a relational system, but it does mean that there is a respectable body of theoretical results that can be applied to practical problems of database usage, such as the problem of database design.

If it is true that a relation is just a table, then why not simply call it a table and have done with it? The answer is that we very often do (and in this book we usually will). However, it is worth taking a moment to understand why the term "relation" was introduced in the first place. Briefly, the explanation is as follows. Relational systems are based on what is called *the relational model of data*. The relational model, in turn, is an abstract theory of data that is based in part on the mathematical theory mentioned earlier. The principles of the relational model were originally laid down in 1969-70 by one man, Dr. E. F. Codd, at that time a researcher in IBM. It was late in 1968 that Codd, a mathematician by training, first realized that the discipline of mathematics could be used to inject some solid principles and rigor into a field—database management—that, prior to that time, was all too deficient in any such qualities. Codd's ideas were first widely published in a now classic paper, "A Relational Model of Data for Large Shared Data Banks" (*Communications of the ACM 13*, No. 6, June 1970). Since that time, those ideas (by now almost universally accepted) have had a wide-ranging influence on just about every aspect of database technology, and indeed on other fields as well, such as the field of artificial intelligence and natural language processing.

Now, the relational model as originally formulated by Codd very deliberately made use of certain terms—such as the term "relation" itself—that were not familiar in data processing circles at that time, even though the concepts in some cases were. The trouble was, many of the more familiar terms were very fuzzy. They lacked the precision necessary to a formal theory of the kind that Codd was proposing. For example, consider the term "record." At different times that single term can mean either a record *instance* or a record *type*; a *COBOL-style* record (which allows repeating groups) or a *flat* record (which does not); a *logical* record or a *physical* record; a *stored* record or a *virtual* record; and so on. The formal relational model therefore does not use the term "record" at all; instead, it uses the term "tuple" (short for "*n*-tuple"), which was given a precise definition by Codd when he first introduced it. We do not give that definition here; for our purposes, it is sufficient to say that the term "tuple" corresponds approximately to the notion of a *flat logical record instance* (just as the term "relation" corresponds approximately to the notion of a table). If you wish to study some of the more formal literature on relational database systems, you will of course have to familiarize yourself with the formal terminology, but in this book we are not trying to be very formal, and we will stick for the most part to terms that are reasonably familiar. (One formal term we will use somewhat, however, is the term "primary key" mentioned earlier in this section.)

Fig. 1.3 shows the terms we will be using most heavily (table, row, column, also primary key). For interest it also gives the corresponding formal term in each case.

Formal relational term	Informal equivalent(s)
relation	table
tuple	row, (logical) record
attribute	column, field
primary key	unique identifier

Fig. 1.3   Some terminology

1.3 THE SQL LANGUAGE

As already explained, DB2—in common with most other relational products, from IBM and other vendors—supports the language SQL ("Structured Query Language"). This language is used to formulate relational operations, i.e., operations that define and manipulate data in relational form. In this section, we present a brief introduction to the SQL language.

First the definitional operations. Fig. 1.2 (the suppliers-and-parts database) of course represents that database as it might appear at some particular instant in time; it is a *snapshot* of the database. Fig. 1.4, by contrast, shows the *structure* of that database; it shows how the database might be defined or described, using SQL "data definition" statements.*

```
CREATE TABLE S
    ( S#       CHAR(5)   NOT NULL,
      SNAME    CHAR(20)  NOT NULL,
      STATUS   SMALLINT  NOT NULL,
      CITY     CHAR(15)  NOT NULL,
    PRIMARY KEY ( S# ) ) ;

CREATE TABLE P
    ( P#       CHAR(6)   NOT NULL,
      PNAME    CHAR(20)  NOT NULL,
      COLOR    CHAR(6)   NOT NULL,
      WEIGHT   SMALLINT  NOT NULL,
      CITY     CHAR(15)  NOT NULL,
    PRIMARY KEY ( P# ) ) ;

CREATE TABLE SP
    ( S#       CHAR(5)   NOT NULL,
      P#       CHAR(6)   NOT NULL,
      QTY      INTEGER   NOT NULL,
    PRIMARY KEY ( S#, P# ),
    FOREIGN KEY ( S# ) REFERENCES S,
    FOREIGN KEY ( P# ) REFERENCES P ) ;
```

Fig. 1.4 The suppliers-and-parts database (data definition)

As you can see, the definition includes one CREATE TABLE statement for each of the three tables. The CREATE TABLE statement is, as already indicated, an example of a SQL data definition statement. Each CREATE TABLE statement specifies the name of the table to be created, the names and data types of the columns of that table, the set of columns that constitute the primary key, and a variety of additional information. In the example, that additional information includes (a) a NOT NULL specification for every column (explained in Chapter 3, Section 3.6) and (b) in the case of table SP, a couple of "foreign key" specifications (explained in Chapter 11).

---

*Throughout this book we show SQL statements, commands, etc., in upper case, for clarity. In practice it is usually more convenient to enter such statements and commands in lower case. DB2 will generally accept both.

It is not our purpose at this juncture to describe the CREATE TABLE statement in detail; that detailed description appears later, in Chapter 4. One point that does need to be stressed right at the outset, however, is that CREATE TABLE is an *executable statement*. (In fact, every statement in the SQL language is executable, except for a few that are used in embedded SQL only—see Chapters 12 and 14.) If the three CREATE TABLEs in Fig. 1.4 were to be entered at a terminal, exactly as shown, the system would actually build the three tables, then and there. Initially, of course, those tables would be empty—that is, they would each contain just the row of column headings, no data rows as yet. However, we could subsequently go on to insert such data rows—possibly via the SQL INSERT statement, to be discussed in Chapter 7—and, in just a few minutes' work, we could have a (probably small, but still useful and usable) database at our disposal, and could start doing some useful things with it.* So this simple example illustrates right away one of the advantages of relational systems in general, and DB2 in particular: They are very easy to use (ease of "getting on the air" is of course just one aspect of ease of use in general). As a result, they can make users very productive. We shall see many other advantages later.

Note: Although it really has nothing to do with the subject of this section (namely, the SQL language), it is worth mentioning in passing that DB2 is specifically designed to be easy to install as a *system*—by which we mean that, not only is it easy (as indicated above) to "install" or create a new DB2 database at any time, but it is also easy to install the overall DB2 system in the first place. In other words, the process of building the necessary library data sets, specifying the required system parameters, defining certain system defaults, etc., is deliberately made as simple as possible. Sample programs are provided to verify that system installation has been performed correctly. The overall procedure should typically take from one to two working days.

To continue with the example: Having created our three tables, and loaded some data into them, we can now start doing useful work with them, using SQL *data manipulation* statements. One of the things we can do is *data retrieval*, which is specified in SQL by means of the SELECT statement. Fig. 1.5 illustrates the use of that statement.

A particularly significant feature of most relational systems, including in particular DB2, is that the same relational language (usually SQL) is available at *two different interfaces*, namely an interactive interface (DB2I—"DB2 Interactive"—in the case of DB2) and an application programming interface. The two interfaces are both illustrated in Fig. 1.5:

---

*In the interests of accuracy, it should be mentioned that no rows can actually be inserted into a table until an index has been created on that table's primary key (assuming, of course, that the table in question does have a declared primary key). See Chapter 11 for further discussion.

(a) Interactive (DB2I):

```
SELECT  CITY
FROM    S
WHERE   S# = 'S4' ;
```

Result:

CITY
London

(b) Embedded in PL/I (could be COBOL, FORTRAN, etc.):

```
EXEC SQL SELECT  CITY
         INTO    :XCITY
         FROM    S
         WHERE   S# = 'S4' ;
```

Result:

XCITY
London

Fig. 1.5 A retrieval example

- Fig. 1.5(a) shows an example of the interactive interface, DB2I. Here the user has typed the SELECT statement at a terminal, and DB2 has responded—through its DB2I component—by displaying the result ("London") directly at that terminal.

- Fig. 1.5(b) shows essentially the same SELECT statement embedded in an application program written in one of the DB2-supported "host" programming languages (PL/I, in the example). In this second case the statement will be executed when the program is executed, and the result ("London") will be returned, not to a terminal, but to the program variable XCITY (by virtue of the INTO clause in the SELECT; XCITY is just an input area within the program).

Thus, SQL is both an *interactive query language* and a *database programming language*. Furthermore, this remark applies to the entire SQL language; that is, any SQL statement that can be entered at a terminal can alternatively be embedded in a program. Note in particular that the remark applies even to statements such as CREATE TABLE; you can create tables from within an application program, if it makes sense in your application to do so (and if you are authorized to perform such operations). SQL statements can be used (in DB2) with any of the following host languages: C, COBOL, FORTRAN, PL/I, and System/370 Assembler Language* (see Chapters 2 and 12 for further discussion).

Note: Interactive SQL and embedded SQL do differ from each other on certain points of detail, of course. For example, each embedded SQL statement must be prefixed with EXEC SQL in order to distinguish it from the surrounding host language statements (see Fig. 1.5(b) for an illustra-

---

*Certain IBM language products (e.g., APL2, BASIC) also provide interfaces to DB2 via the "dynamic SQL" facilities discussed in Chapter 14.

tion). Likewise, the embedded version of the SELECT statement needs an INTO clause to designate the input area, as we have seen, and the host language variable named in that clause has a colon prefix in order to distinguish it from a database column. So of course it is not 100 percent true to say that the SELECT statement is the same at both interfaces. But it is broadly true, if we overlook the minor differences of detail.

We are now in a position to understand how DB2 looks to the user. By "user" here we mean either an end-user at an online terminal or an application programmer writing in one of the DB2-supported host languages such as PL/I. (We note in passing that the term "user" will be used consistently throughout this book with either or both of these two meanings.) As already explained, each such user will be using SQL to operate on tables. See Fig. 1.6.

The first point to be made concerning the figure is that there will normally be many users, of both kinds, all operating on the same data at the same time. DB2 will automatically apply the necessary controls (basically locking—see Chapter 13) to ensure that those users are all protected from one another; i.e., DB2 will guarantee that one user's updates cannot cause another user's operations to produce an incorrect result.

Next, note that tables, like users, also come in two kinds. The two kinds of tables are called *base tables* and *views*.

- A base table is a "real" table—i.e., a table that "physically exists," in the sense that there exist physically stored records, and possibly physical indexes, in one or more MVS files (actually VSAM linear data sets), that directly represent that table in storage. Tables S, P, and SP in Fig. 1.4 are all base tables.

- By contrast, a view is a "virtual" table—i.e., a table that does not "physically exist," but looks to the user as if it did. Views can be thought of as different ways of looking at the base tables. As a trivial example, a given user might have a view of the suppliers base table S in which only those suppliers in London are visible. Views are defined in terms of the underlying base tables in a manner to be explained in Chapter 9.

Note: The foregoing characterization of base tables (as tables that "physically exist") is certainly the way such tables are usually thought of. Strictly speaking, however, that characterization is both incorrect and potentially misleading, even seriously so. A more accurate definition is as follows: *A base table is a named table that is not defined in terms of other named tables* (see Chapter 4 for further discussion). In fact, it is *not* required that base tables "physically exist" in the sense explained above, although in DB2 they always do.

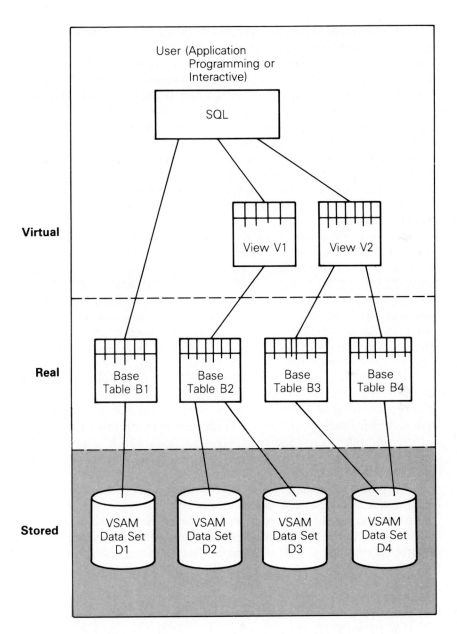

Fig. 1.6   DB2 as perceived by an individual user

And even when a table does "physically exist," it is important to understand that it is still not *physically stored* as a table—i.e., as a set of physically adjacent stored records, with each stored record consisting simply of a direct copy of a row of the table. There are numerous differences of detail between the table per se and its storage representation (see Chapter 15). The point is, however, that users can always think of such tables as physically existing, without having to concern themselves with how they are actually implemented in storage. Indeed, the whole point of a relational database is to allow users to deal with data in the form of tables per se, instead of in terms of the storage representation of such tables. To repeat from Section 1.2, a relational database is a database that is *perceived by its users* as a collection of tables. It is *not* just a database in which data is physically stored as tables.

Like base tables, views can also be created at any time. The same is true of indexes. (The CREATE TABLE statement already discussed is for creating "real" or base tables. There is an analogous CREATE VIEW statement for creating views or "virtual" tables, and an analogous CREATE INDEX statement for creating indexes. All of these statements will be discussed in detail in later chapters.) Similarly, base tables, and views and indexes, can all be "dropped" (that is to say, destroyed) at any time, using DROP TABLE or DROP VIEW or DROP INDEX. With regard to indexes, however, note carefully that although the user—that is, *some* user, probably a "database administrator" (see Chapter 10)—is responsible for creating and destroying them, users are *not* responsible for saying when those indexes should be used. Indexes are never mentioned in SQL data manipulation statements such as SELECT. The decision as to whether or not to use a particular index in responding to, say, a particular SELECT operation is made by the system, not by the user. We shall have more to say on this topic in the next chapter.

The primary user interface to DB2 is the SQL language. We have already indicated (a) that SQL can be used in both interactive and embedded environments, and (b) that it provides both data definition and data manipulation operations. (In fact, as we shall see later, it provides certain "data control" operations as well.) The major data definition operations—

```
CREATE TABLE
CREATE VIEW
CREATE INDEX

DROP TABLE
DROP VIEW
DROP INDEX
```

—have already been touched on. The major data manipulation operations (in fact, the only ones, if we temporarily disregard some embedded-only features) are

```
SELECT
INSERT
UPDATE
DELETE
```

We give examples (Fig. 1.7) of SELECT and UPDATE to illustrate an additional point, namely the fact that SQL data manipulation statements typically operate on *entire sets of rows*, instead of just on one row at a time. Given the sample data of Fig. 1.2, the SELECT statement in Fig. 1.7(a) returns a set of four values, not just a single value; and the UPDATE statement in Fig. 1.7(b) changes two rows, not just one. In other words, SQL is a *set-level language*.

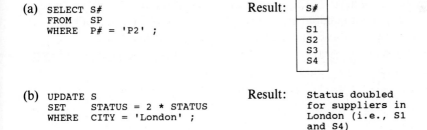

(a) `SELECT  S#`   Result:
     `FROM    SP`
     `WHERE   P# = 'P2' ;`

S#
S1
S2
S3
S4

(b) `UPDATE S`   Result: status doubled
     `SET     STATUS = 2 * STATUS`   for suppliers in
     `WHERE   CITY = 'London' ;`   London (i.e., S1
                                      and S4)

Fig. 1.7 SQL data manipulation examples

Set-level languages such as SQL are sometimes described as "nonprocedural," on the grounds that users specify *what*, not *how* (i.e., they say what data they want without specifying a procedure for getting it). The process of "navigating" around the physical database to locate the desired data is performed automatically by the system, not manually by the user. (For this reason, relational systems are sometimes described as "automatic navigation" systems.) However, "nonprocedural" is not really a very satisfactory term, because procedurality and nonprocedurality are not absolutes. The best that can be said is that some language *A* is either more or less procedural than some other language *B*. Perhaps a better way of putting matters is to say that languages like SQL are at *a higher level of abstraction* than languages like COBOL and PL/I.* With a language like SQL, in other words, the system handles more of the details than it does with a language

---

*Or languages like the database languages of nonrelational systems, come to that. For example, DL/I, the language of IMS, operates essentially one "row" (the IMS term is "segment") at a time.

like COBOL. Fundamentally, it is this *raising of the level of abstraction* that is responsible for the increased productivity that relational systems such as DB2 can provide.

1.4 SUMMARY

This brings us to the end of this preliminary chapter, in which we have sketched some of the most significant features of DB2, IBM's relational database management system for the MVS operating system. We have seen in outline what it means for a system to be relational; we have discussed the relational (tabular) data structure; and we have described some of the operators available in SQL for operating on data in that tabular form. In particular, we have touched on the three categories of SQL statement (data definition, data manipulation, and data control), and given examples from the first two of those categories. We remind the reader that:

- All SQL statements are executable (except for a few that are used in embedded SQL only);

- Every SQL statement that can be entered at a terminal can also be included in a program, and (in the case of DB2) that program can be written in C, COBOL, FORTRAN, PL/I, or Assembler Language;

- SQL data manipulation statements (SELECT, UPDATE, etc.) are all set-level.

In the next chapter we will examine the internal structure and principal components of DB2, and briefly discuss the environments in which DB2 runs.

EXERCISES

1.1 What does it mean to say that DB2 is a relational system?

1.2 Given the sample data of Fig. 1.2, show the effect of each of the following SQL statements.

```
(a) SELECT  SNAME
    FROM    S
    WHERE   STATUS = 30 ;

(b) SELECT  S#, P#
    FROM    SP
    WHERE   QTY > 200 ;

(c) UPDATE  SP
    SET     QTY = QTY + 300
    WHERE   QTY < 300 ;
```

(d) DELETE
```
    FROM    SP
    WHERE   QTY = 500
    OR      QTY < 200 ;
```
(e) INSERT
```
    INTO    SP (S#, P#, QTY)
    VALUES  ('S3','P1',500) ;
```

1.3 What is DB2I?

1.4 What is a repeating group?

1.5 Define the terms *relation* and *relational database.*

1.6 (a) Give a possible CREATE TABLE statement for the CELLAR table of Fig. 1.1. (b) Write an *embedded* PL/I-SQL statement to retrieve the number of bottles of 1984 Zinfandel from that table.

1.7 Define the terms *base table* and *view.*

1.8 What do you understand by the term "automatic navigation"?

1.9 Define the term *primary key.*

ANSWERS TO SELECTED EXERCISES

1.1 A relational system is a system in which the data is perceived as tables (and nothing but tables), and the operators available to the user are operators that generate new tables from old.

1.2 (a)

SNAME
Blake
Adams

(b)

S#	P#
S1	P1
S1	P3
S2	P1
S2	P2
S4	P4
S4	P5

(c)

S#	P#	QTY
S1	P2	500
S1	P4	500
S1	P5	400
S1	P6	400
S3	P2	500
S4	P2	500

(Only altered rows shown.)

(d) Rows (S1,P5,100) and (S1,P6,100) are deleted from table SP.

(e) Row (S3,P1,500) is inserted into table SP.

1.3 DB2I—"DB2 Interactive"—is the DB2 component that (among other things) allows SQL statements to be entered and executed interactively. For more information, see Chapter 16.

1.4 A repeating group is (conceptually) a column of a table that contains multiple data values per row (different numbers of values in different rows). Repeating groups are not permitted in a relational database. *Note*: An explanation of, and justification for, this apparent restriction can be found in the book *An Introduction to Database Systems: Volume I*, by C. J. Date (5th edition, Addison-Wesley, 1990).

1.5 A relation is a table (without repeating groups!). A relational database is a database that is perceived by its users as a collection of relations. *Note*: More precise definitions are given in Appendix A.

1.6 (a)
```
CREATE TABLE CELLAR
        ( WINE      CHAR(16)  NOT NULL,
          YEAR      INTEGER   NOT NULL,
          BOTTLES   INTEGER   NOT NULL,
        PRIMARY KEY ( WINE, YEAR ) ) ;
```

(b)
```
EXEC SQL SELECT BOTTLES
         INTO   :XBOTT
         FROM   CELLAR
         WHERE  WINE = 'Zinfandel'
         AND    YEAR = 84 ;
```

1.7 A base table is a "real" table; it has some direct storage representation (at least in DB2). A view is a "virtual" table; it does not have any direct storage representation of its own. A view is like a *window* into the underlying base tables, through which the data (or some subset of the data) in those underlying tables can be observed, possibly in some rearranged structure.

1.8 "Automatic navigation" means that the system assumes the responsibility of searching through the physical database to locate the data the user has requested. Users specify what they want, not how to get to what they want.

1.9 Informally, a primary key is just a unique identifier for a table. For example, the primary key for the parts table P is P#; given a P# value Px, that value Px can be used to identify an individual part row, and to distinguish that row from all others appearing in the P table. A more formal definition of the term is given in Chapter 11.

CHAPTER

◆ 2 ◆

System Structure and Operating Environments

2.1 MAJOR COMPONENTS

The internal structure of DB2 is quite complex, as is only to be expected of a state-of-the-art system that provides all of the functions typically found in a modern DBMS. The product thus contains a very large number of internal components. From a high-level point of view, however, it can be regarded as having just four *major* components, each of which divides up into numerous subcomponents. The four major components* are as follows (refer to Fig. 2.1):

---

*Each of the four components runs in a separate MVS address space. This fact notwithstanding, the entire DB2 system can be started or stopped with a single operator command.

21

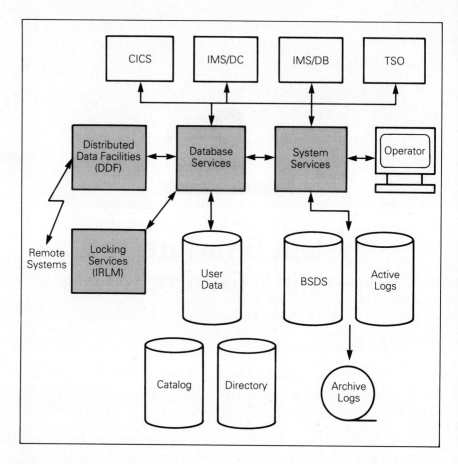

Fig. 2.1 DB2 structure

1. The *system services* component, which supports system operation, operator communication, logging, and similar functions

2. The *locking services* component, which provides the necessary controls for managing concurrent access to data

3. The *database services* component, which supports the definition, retrieval, and update of user and system data

4. The *distributed data facility* component, DDF (added in DB2 Version 2.2), which provides DB2's distributed database support

For tutorial reasons, we will simply ignore most aspects of DB2's distributed database capability (including in particular the DDF component)

until we reach Part III of this book. Of the other three components, only the database services component is directly relevant to the user—the other two, although of course crucial to the overall functioning of the system, are for the most part "transparent to the user." In this chapter, therefore, we will just give a quick overview of the first two components, in Sections 2.2 and 2.3, respectively; we will then go on to discuss the database services component in more detail in Sections 2.4–2.7. Finally, in Section 2.8, we will explain the various MVS environments in which DB2 operates.

2.2 SYSTEM SERVICES

The system services component handles all system-wide tasks, including:

- Controlling connections to other MVS subsystems (CICS, IMS/DC, IMS/DB, and TSO).* See Section 2.8 for more information on using DB2 in conjunction with each of these subsystems.

- Handling system startup and shutdown and operator communication.

- Managing the *system log*. The system log is a set of predefined disk data sets that are used to record information for recovering user and system data in the event of a failure. When an active log data set becomes full (or upon operator command), DB2 switches to a new data set and copies the old one to an *archive* log data set on disk or tape. When the active log data sets are all full, they are recycled (i.e., DB2 starts using the first one again). Dual copies of both the active and the archive log can be maintained to allow DB2 to recover data if an error occurs on (one copy of) the log itself. Information regarding the log data sets themselves is recorded in a duplexed system data set known as the *Boot Strap Data Set* (BSDS). Utilities are provided for maintaining and listing the BSDS.

- Gathering system-wide statistics, performance, auditing, and accounting information. This information is collected by the DB2 *Instrumentation Facility* and either (a) written to a System Management Facility (SMF) or Generalized Trace Facility (GTF) data set or (b) passed to a performance monitor program (several third-party vendors provide such programs). A separate product, the DB2 Performance Monitor (DB2PM), is provided for producing batch reports and interactive graphics from this data set. The DB2 Instrumentation Facility also pro-

---

*In the MVS/ESA environment, the IMS/DC and IMS/DB products have been upgraded to "IMS/ESA Transaction Manager" and "IMS/ESA Database Manager," respectively. In this book we will continue to use the older terms, but the reader should understand that those terms are meant to include the new MVS/ESA products as well.

vides an interface to permit users or third-party vendors to write their own (possibly online) performance monitors.

2.3   LOCKING SERVICES

Locking services are provided by an MVS subsystem called the IMS Resource Lock Manager (IRLM). Despite the "IMS" in its name, the IRLM does not really have anything to do with IMS per se; on the contrary, it is a general-purpose lock manager—it is used to control concurrent access to DB2 data, regardless of whether IMS is present in the system or not.* The DB2 locking scheme is described in more detail in Chapter 13.

2.4   DATABASE SERVICES

The primary purpose of the database services component is to support the definition, retrieval, and update of database data—in other words, to implement the functions (or at least the principal functions) of the SQL language. The necessary support is provided by a series of five subcomponents, namely as follows:

> Precompiler
>
> Bind
>
> Runtime Supervisor[†]
>
> Data Manager
>
> Buffer Manager

Together, these components support (a) the preparation of application programs for execution and (b) the subsequent execution of those programs. The functions of the individual components, in outline, are as follows.

- Precompiler

    The Precompiler is a preprocessor for the host programming languages (PL/I, COBOL, etc.). Its function is to analyze a host language source

---

*What is more, the IRLM does not provide any coordination between DB2 locking and IMS locking, either—which implies that two transactions, one holding some IMS data and requesting some DB2 data and the other holding some DB2 data and requesting some IMS data, can deadlock with each other without the deadlock being detected (such a situation is resolved by a timeout mechanism instead). See Chapter 13 for a discussion of deadlock.

[†]The IBM manuals do not use the term "Runtime Supervisor"; instead, they refer to something called the *Relational Data System* or RDS. However, the term "RDS" applies to more than just what we call the Runtime Supervisor—for instance, it includes the Bind component. We prefer our term because it is more specific.

module, stripping out all the SQL statements it finds and repla
them by host language CALL statements. (At run time those CA
will pass control—indirectly—to the Runtime Supervisor.) From
SQL statements it encounters, the Precompiler constructs a *Database
Request Module* (DBRM), which becomes input to the Bind component, discussed next.

- Bind

The function of the Bind component is twofold: It is used to "bind" a
given DBRM to produce what is called a *package*, and it is used to
"bind together" a list of packages to produce what is called an *application plan*, or simply *plan*.* We consider each of these functions in turn.

First, packages. If a DBRM is thought of as a "SQL source module" (which is effectively what it is), then the package produced by
binding that DBRM can be thought of as the corresponding *object*
module. In other words, a package consists of a set of internal control
structures, representing the compiled form of the original SQL statements in the corresponding DBRM. DB2 is thus a *compiling system*:
Bind performs a compiling function for SQL statements, much as the
host language compiler provides a compiling function for the host language statements in which those SQL statements are embedded. We
will return to this point later, in Sections 2.5 and 2.6.

> *Aside*: The first release of DB2 genuinely did compile SQL state-
> ments into actual machine code. As mentioned above, however,
> DB2 now compiles such statements into a set of internal control
> structures (in effect a higher-level intermediate language), not into
> machine code per se; those control structures are then used to drive
> a set of generalized I/O routines within the Data Manager. This
> change to the internal design of DB2 was made for maintainability
> reasons. It is not very important from the user's perspective, how-
> ever, and for simplicity we will continue to regard Bind as compil-
> ing SQL statements into "code," even though that code is no
> longer true machine code per se. *End of aside.*

One last point concerning packages: Each package is assigned to exactly
one *collection* when it is created (i.e., when it is bound). Collections
are essentially just a means of giving a name to a logically related set
of packages; they do not really have any physical existence of their

---

*The Bind component changed significantly in DB2 Version 2.3, when packages were first
introduced. Here we are describing the most recent version, i.e., Bind as of Version 2.3. Later
in this chapter, in Section 2.7, we will give a brief summary of the differences between that
most recent version and previous versions, and explain some of the reasons for the changes.

own, unlike packages per se which certainly do (packages are physically stored in the DB2 *directory*—see the remarks on this latter topic at the end of the present section). Typically (but not necessarily), all of the packages used in a given application would be assigned to the same collection. Collections provide a useful "level of indirection" between packages and plans, as will be made clear in Section 2.7.

Turning now to plans: Essentially, the plan for a given application consists simply of a list of the packages (more precisely, a list of the *names* of the packages) needed to execute that application. Bind produces such a plan by "binding together" the specified packages.* The packages concerned are specified either by individual package name or by collection name (meaning, in this latter case, all packages in the specified collection).

- Runtime Supervisor

  The Runtime Supervisor is resident in main memory when the application program is executing. Its job is to oversee that execution. When the application program requests some database operation to be performed (loosely speaking, when it wishes to execute some SQL statement), control goes first to the Runtime Supervisor, which uses control information in the application plan to request the appropriate operations on the part of the Data Manager.

- Data Manager

  You can think of the Data Manager as a *very sophisticated access method*. It performs all of the normal access method functions—search, retrieval, update, index maintenance, and so on. Broadly speaking, the Data Manager is the component that manages the physical database(s). It invokes other system components as necessary in order to perform detailed functions such as locking, logging, I/O operations, etc., during the performance of its basic task.

- Buffer Manager

  The Buffer Manager is the component responsible for physically transferring data between external storage and (virtual) memory. It employs sophisticated techniques such as read-ahead buffering and look-aside buffering to get the best performance out of the buffer pools under its care and to minimize the amount of physical I/O actually performed.

Fig. 2.2 summarizes the foregoing in the form of a control flow diagram. In the next section we will take a more detailed look at the principal

---

*And/or DBRMs. See Section 2.7.

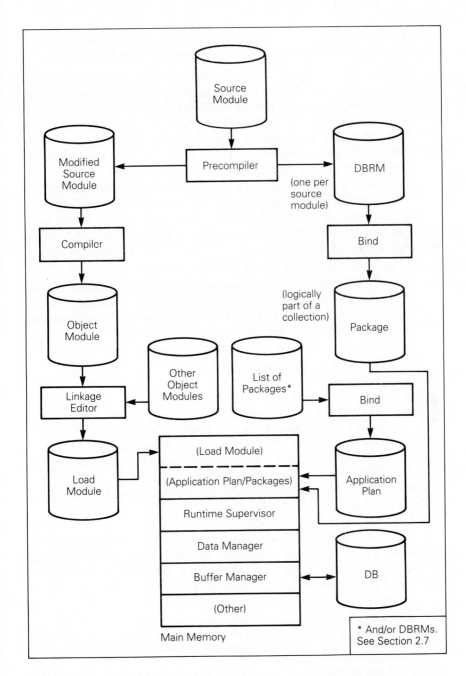

Fig. 2.2 DB2 application program preparation and execution (overview)

steps in that diagram. To conclude the present section, we briefly mention a couple of additional functions of the database services component:

- *System data*: The database services component also maintains certain control and descriptor information regarding (e.g.) database tables and their columns, database backup operations, database indexes, and so forth. This information is divided into two groups, which are kept in the *catalog* and the *directory*, respectively. From the user's point of view, the difference between the two is as follows: The catalog consists of regular tables, just like user data, and is accessible by means of SQL data retrieval statements, which can be used (e.g.) to produce reports for use by database administrators (see Chapter 8 for more information on the catalog); the directory cannot be accessed via SQL and is intended purely for DB2's own internal use. (In fact, the directory and catalog contain much the same information, but the directory version is in control block form for efficiency reasons.)

- *Utilities*: The database services component also includes a set of utilities for performing such functions as database loading and database reorganization. A list of such utilities and a sketch of the functions they perform is given in Chapter 16.

2.5 DETAILED CONTROL FLOW

In this section we consider in detail what is involved in preparing and executing a DB2 application program. First, we consider an example of a PL/I program *P* (more accurately, PL/I source module *P*) that includes one or more SQL statements. *Note*: We take PL/I for definiteness. The overall process is of course essentially the same for the other host languages (C, COBOL, FORTRAN, Assembler Language).

Before *P* can be compiled by the PL/I compiler, it must be *precompiled* by the DB2 Precompiler.* See Fig. 2.3.

As explained in the previous section, the DB2 Precompiler removes all SQL statements it finds in *P* and replaces them by PL/I CALL statements.† (Those CALLs are directed to the DB2 Language Interface module—see below.) It uses the SQL statements to build a *Database Request Module* (DBRM) for *P*, which it stores away as a member of an MVS partitioned

---

*If *P* also includes any CICS statements (of the form EXEC CICS . . . ;), then it must also be processed by the CICS Preprocessor. The DB2 Precompiler and the CICS Preprocessor can be run in either order, but (for reasons beyond the scope of this text) it is usually better in practice to run the DB2 Precompiler first.

†It leaves a copy of each SQL statement in the modified source module in the form of a comment.

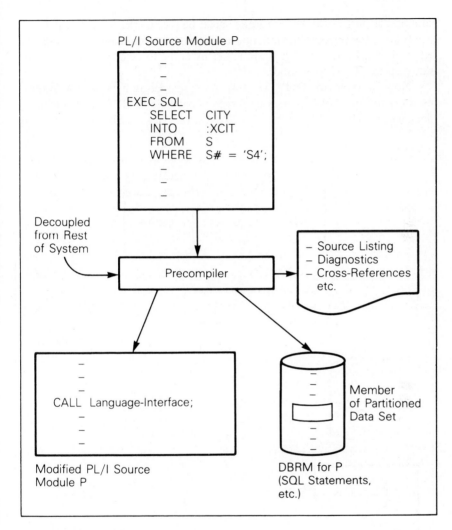

PL/I Source Module P

```
        EXEC SQL
             SELECT   CITY
             INTO     :XCIT
             FROM     S
             WHERE    S# = 'S4';
```

Decoupled
from Rest
of System

Precompiler

– Source Listing
– Diagnostics
– Cross-References
   etc.

```
CALL  Language-Interface;
```

Modified PL/I Source
Module P

Member
of Partitioned
Data Set

DBRM for P
(SQL Statements,
etc.)

Fig. 2.3 Precompilation

data set. The DBRM contains an edited form of the original SQL statements, together with certain additional information. The Precompiler also
produces a source listing, showing the original source code, diagnostics,
cross-reference information, etc.

Next, the modified PL/I source module is compiled and link-edited in
the normal way (except that the DB2 *Language Interface* module, which is

supplied as part of the DB2 product, must be part of the input to the Linkage Editor; the purpose of that module is basically to make PL/I, COBOL, etc., all "look the same" to DB2). Let us agree to refer to the output of this step as "PL/I load module *P*."

Now we come to Bind (Fig. 2.4). As explained in Section 2.4, Bind is used (a) to bind DBRMs into packages ("package bind") and (b) to bind packages into plans ("plan bind"). We discuss package bind first, ignoring

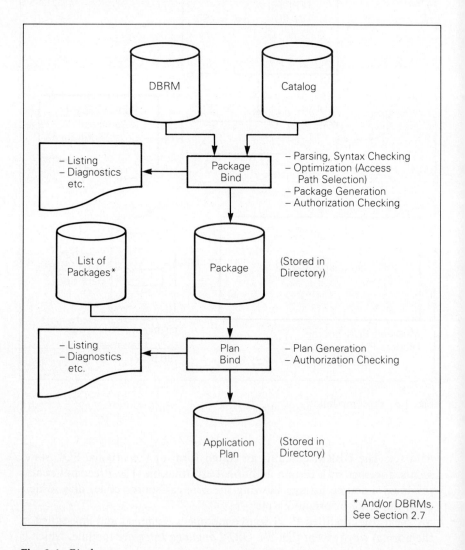

Fig. 2.4 Bind

plan bind totally until further notice (i.e., we take "bind" to mean package bind specifically, until further notice).

We have already indicated that Bind is really a *compiler*. In fact, it is an *optimizing* compiler: Its aim is to convert high-level database requests (in effect, SQL statements) into optimized internal form. Its input is a DBRM; its output (i.e., the compiled form of that DBRM) is a *package*, and is stored away in the DB2 directory (see the end of the previous section for a brief description of the directory). The major functions of Bind, then, are as follows.

- Syntax Checking

  Bind examines the SQL statements in the input DBRM, parses them, and reports on any syntax errors it finds. *Note*: Such checks are necessary, even though the Precompiler has already performed similar checks, because the Precompiler is decoupled from the rest of DB2: It can run even when DB2 is not available—it can even run on a different machine—and its output is not automatically protected. Thus, Bind cannot assume that its input is valid Precompiler output—the user might have constructed an invalid "DBRM" via some other mechanism.

- Optimization

  Bind includes an *optimizer* as an important subcomponent. The function of the optimizer is to choose, for each SQL statement it processes,* an optimal access strategy for implementing that statement. Remember that data manipulation statements such as SELECT specify only what data the user wants, not how to get to that data; the *access path* for getting to that data will be chosen by the optimizer. Programs are thus independent of such access paths (for further discussion of this important point, see later in this section).

  As an example of the foregoing, consider the SELECT statement shown in the PL/I source module *P* in Fig. 2.3. Even in that very simple case, there are at least two ways of performing the desired retrieval:

  1. By doing a physical sequential scan of (the stored version of) table S until the row for supplier S4 is found;

  2. If there is an index on the S# column of that table—which there probably will be[†]—then by using that index and hence going directly to the S4 row.

---

*More accurately, each SQL *manipulative* statement.

[†]Recall that S# is the primary key for table S. The primary key of a base table must always be supported by a UNIQUE index in DB2. For details, see Chapters 4 and 11.

The optimizer will choose which of these two strategies to adopt. In general, the optimizer will make its choice on the basis of such considerations as the following:

- Which tables are referenced in the SQL statement (there may be more than one)
- How big those tables are
- What indexes exist
- How selective those indexes are
- How the data is physically clustered on the disk
- The form of the WHERE clause in the request

and so on. Bind will then generate code that is *tightly bound* to (i.e., highly dependent on) the optimizer's choice of strategy. For example, if the optimizer decides to make use of an index called X, then the generated package will include explicit references to index X.

The question arises: Where does the optimizer get its information from? For example, how does it know how big the tables are, or what indexes exist? The answer is that this information is kept in the catalog, in the form of "database statistics." A special utility, RUNSTATS, is provided for gathering such statistics and storing them in the catalog for the optimizer's use. Refer to Chapter 16 for more details regarding RUNSTATS.

- Package Generation

  This is the process of actually building the package.

- Authorization Checking

  Bind also checks authorization; more specifically, it checks that the user who is to be the owner of the bound package (a) is allowed to perform the operations requested in the DBRM to be bound, and (b) is also allowed to assign packages to the applicable package collection. We will examine authorization in detail in Chapter 10.

Now we turn to the second of Bind's two general functions, plan bind. The input to this process is a list of packages and/or package collections;* the output is the bound application plan, and is stored in the DB2 directory. Plan bind (like package bind) also does some authorization checking: Specifically, it checks that the user who is to be the owner of the bound plan is authorized to execute all of the applicable packages. Again, we will examine authorization in detail in Chapter 10.

---

*And/or DBRMs (see Section 2.7).

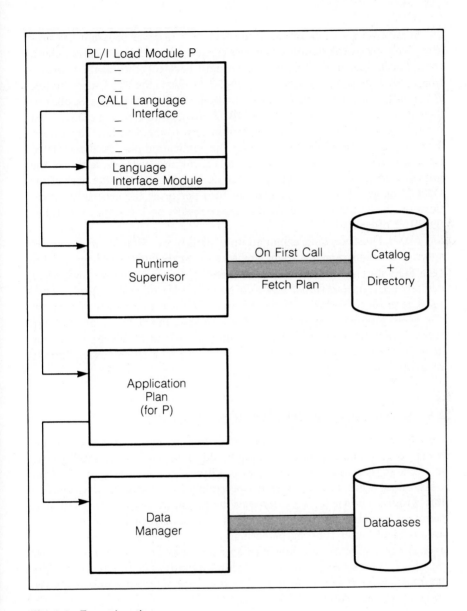

Fig. 2.5 Execution time

Finally we get to execution time. Since the original program has now effectively been broken into two pieces (load module and application plan), those two pieces must somehow be brought back together again at execution time. This is how it works (see Fig. 2.5). First, the PL/I load module *P* is loaded into memory; it starts to execute in the usual way. Sooner or later it reaches the first call to the DB2 Language Interface module. That module gets control and passes control in turn to the Runtime Supervisor. The Runtime Supervisor then retrieves the application plan (and associated packages) from the DB2 directory, loads them into memory, and uses the information they contain to request the desired function on the part of the Data Manager. The Data Manager in turn performs the necessary operations on the actual stored data and passes results back (as appropriate) to the PL/I program.

Note: The foregoing explanation is slightly oversimplified in one respect. DB2 plans and packages are actually *segmented* (one segment for each SQL statement in the original program), and the Runtime Supervisor actually retrieves *individual segments* one at a time on an "as needed" basis. The purpose of this refinement is to economize on memory utilization; if a given program contains 50 SQL statements, but only ten of them are actually executed on a given run, then only 20 percent of the compiled code actually needs to be fetched into memory on that particular run (loosely speaking).

2.6 AUTOMATIC RECOMPILATION

Our discussions so far have glossed over one extremely important point, which we now explain. First, as already indicated, DB2 is a compiling system: Database requests are *compiled* (by Bind) into internal form. By contrast, many other database systems—certainly all prerelational systems, to this writer's knowledge—are *interpretive* in nature. Now, compilation is certainly advantageous from the point of view of performance; it will nearly always yield better runtime performance than will interpretation.* However, it suffers from the following significant drawback: *It is possible that decisions made by the "compiler" (actually Bind) at compilation time are no longer valid at execution time.* The following simple example will serve to illustrate the problem:

---

*This claim is (obviously) especially true for repetitive transactions, i.e., transactions that are executed over and over again in a production environment. What is perhaps not so obvious is that compiling can provide a significant performance advantage in the ad hoc query environment also. For further discussion of this point, see later in this section.

1. Suppose program *P* is compiled (bound) on Monday, and Bind decides to use an index—say index *X*—in its strategy for *P*. Then the compiled version of *P* will include explicit references to *X*, as explained earlier.

2. On Tuesday, some suitably authorized user issues the statement

   ```
   DROP INDEX X ;
   ```

3. On Wednesday, some suitably authorized user tries to execute the program *P*. What happens?

What does happen is the following. When an index is dropped, DB2 examines the catalog to see which packages (if any) are dependent on that index. Any such packages it finds it marks "invalid." When the Runtime Supervisor retrieves such a package for execution, it sees the "invalid" marker, *and therefore invokes Bind to produce a new package*—i.e., to choose some different access strategy and then to recompile the original SQL statements (which have been kept in the catalog) in accordance with that new strategy. Assuming the recompilation is successful, the new package effectively replaces the old one, and the Runtime Supervisor continues with that new package. Thus the entire recompilation process is "transparent to the user"; the only effect that might be observed is a slight delay in the execution of certain SQL statements (possibly some change in overall program performance also, of course; the point is, however, that there should be no effect on program *logic*).

Note carefully that the automatic recompilation we are talking about here is a *SQL* recompilation, not a *PL/I* recompilation. It is not the PL/I program per se that is invalidated by the dropping of the index, only certain SQL statements embedded within that program.

We can now see how it is possible for programs to be independent of physical access paths—more specifically, how it is possible to create and drop such paths without at the same time having to rewrite programs. As stated earlier, SQL data manipulation statements such as SELECT and UPDATE never include any explicit mention of such paths. Instead, they simply indicate what data the user is interested in; and it is DB2's responsibility (actually Bind's responsibility) to choose a path for getting to that data, and to change to another path if the old one no longer exists. We say that systems like DB2 provide a high degree of *physical data independence*: Users and user programs are not dependent on the physical structure of the stored database. The advantage of such a system—a highly significant advantage—is that it is possible to make changes in the physical database (e.g., for performance reasons) *without having to make any corresponding changes in application programs*. In a system without such independence, application programmers have to devote some significant portion of their time—a figure of 50 percent is quite typical—to making changes to existing programs that are necessitated merely by changes to the physical database. In a system like DB2, by contrast, those programmers can concentrate on "real work"—i.e., on the production of new applications.

One further point concerning the foregoing: Our example was in terms of a dropped *index*, and perhaps that is the commonest case in practice. However, a similar sequence of events occurs when other objects (not just indexes) are dropped—likewise when authorizations are revoked (see Chapter 10). Thus, for example, dropping a table will cause all packages that refer to that table to be flagged as invalid.* Of course, the automatic recompilation will work in this case only if another table has been created with the same name as the old one by the time the recompilation is done (and maybe not even then, if there are significant differences between the old table and the new one).

Let us return to indexes specifically for a moment. Given the fact that DB2 does automatic recompilations if an existing index is dropped, the reader might be wondering whether it will also do such recompilations if a new index is created. The answer is no, it will not. The reason for this state of affairs is that there can be no guarantee in such a case that recompiling will actually be profitable; recompilation might simply mean a lot of unnecessary work (existing compiled code might already be using an optimum strategy). The situation is different with DROP—a program will simply not work if it relies on a nonexistent object (index or otherwise), so recompiling is mandatory in this case. Hence, if you create a new index, and you have some existing DBRM that you suspect might benefit from that new index, then it is your responsibility to request an explicit recompilation for that DBRM. See Chapter 16 for further discussion.

We conclude this section by noting that SQL is *always* compiled in DB2, never interpreted, even when the statements in question are submitted interactively (e.g., via DB2I). Performance tests have indicated that, even in the interactive case, compilation almost always results in better overall performance than interpretation. The advantage of compilation is that the process of physically accessing the required data is done by compiled code—that is, by code that is tightly tailored to the specific request, not by generalized, interpretive code. The disadvantage, of course, is that there is

---

*In the interests of accuracy, we should explain that—partly for reasons of compatibility with earlier DB2 releases—dropping an object or revoking an authorization will sometimes invalidate entire plans, not just individual packages. (Prior to DB2 Version 2.3, in fact, plans were the *only* things that could be invalidated, since packages did not even exist.) Throughout this book, therefore, whenever we talk about "packages" being invalidated, the reader should understand that what we really mean is "packages and/or plans." See Section 2.7 for further discussion.

a cost in doing the compilation, i.e., in producing that tightly tailored code. But the advantage almost always outweighs the disadvantage, sometimes dramatically so. It is only when the query is extremely simple that the cost of doing the compilation might be greater than the potential savings. An example of such a simple query might be "Retrieve the supplier row for supplier S1"—that is, a request for a single, specific row, given a value that identifies that row uniquely. Notice that this query does not really exploit the set-level facilities of SQL at all.

2.7 PACKAGES AND PLANS

(*Note*: This section is probably best omitted on a first reading.)

As mentioned earlier in this chapter, the package concept was first introduced into DB2 in Version 2.3. Previously, the two principal activities performed by Bind ("package bind" and "plan bind") were collapsed into a single process, in which all of the DBRMs for a given application were simultaneously compiled into optimized code *and* bound together into the required application plan. This scheme, however, suffered from a number of disadvantages, the following among them:

- If an individual DBRM needed to be recompiled for any reason (e.g., because some index had been dropped), the *entire plan* had to be recompiled and rebound.

- If multiple plans involved the same DBRM, that same DBRM had to be compiled multiple times—and, if that DBRM ever needed to be recompiled, then all relevant plans had to be recompiled and rebound in their entirety.

- Adding a new DBRM to an existing plan required (again) a recompilation and rebind of the entire plan.

- Partly as a consequence of the foregoing points, bind and (especially) rebind times were becoming unacceptably high in some DB2 installations, and availability was suffering as a result.

There were also difficulties—the details are beyond the scope of this early part of the book—having to do with application maintenance, and application version control, and performance, and security, and system administration, and distributed database, and flexibility (or rather lack thereof).

The package concept was introduced to remedy such deficiencies. In Version 2.3, to review, a *package* is the compiled form of a DBRM, and a *plan* is essentially just a list of packages (or rather, package names). In Version 2.3, therefore:

- If a given DBRM needs to be recompiled, all that has to be done is an appropriate package bind—it is *not* necessary to recompile the entire plan. Indeed, it may not be necessary to do a new plan bind to incorporate the new package either.

- If multiple plans involve the same DBRM, that DBRM can now be compiled *once*, and the corresponding package referenced multiple times in multiple plan binds.

It is even possible (in effect) to add a new package to an existing plan without having to do a new plan bind, thanks to the concept of package *collections*. As explained in Section 2.4, each package belongs to exactly one collection. When a plan is bound, the input to the bind operation can be specified as any combination of packages and/or collections (and/or DBRMs—see below). And specifying a collection is equivalent to specifying all of the packages in that collection—*including* packages that may be added to the collection after the plan bind is done. The collection thus effectively serves as a level of indirection between the packages and the plan; whatever packages are in the collection at the time the plan is executed are considered to be part of the plan for the purposes of that particular execution.

Collections also provide a means whereby a given plan can access different (but similar) tables at different times. Suppose, for example, that two users, A and B say, both own a table called T, and suppose those tables are "the same shape," in the sense that they have the same column names (and corresponding columns have the same data types). Suppose moreover that D is a DBRM that refers to the table name T. Then it is possible to compile two distinct packages from D, one that accesses the table belonging to A and one that accesses the table belonging to B. If those two packages are placed in two distinct collections, and if those two collections are then bound together into the same plan, then it is possible (by selecting the appropriate collection at run time) for the plan to access whichever of the two tables is desired.*

We will have more to say regarding packages and plans elsewhere in this book—in particular, in our discussions of distributed database in Part III. (In fact, the new distributed database capabilities introduced in DB2 Version 2.3 *rely* on the package concept, as we will see.)

---

*Selecting the collection at run time is done by means of a new SQL statement, SET CURRENT PACKAGESET (see Chapter 3). "Package set" is another term for "collection." The terminology in this area was already bad, in this writer's opinion, since it started with a word ("collection") with a very general meaning and gave it a meaning that was highly specific (indeed, the same criticism applies to both "package" and "plan" as well, not to mention "bind" itself); perhaps that was why it was deemed necessary, after first introducing the term, *immediately* to introduce a synonym for it—although (again in this writer's opinion) the existence of two different terms for one new concept merely serves to increase confusion.

In closing, it should be clear by now why the "plan bind" operation permits DBRMs as input as well as—or indeed, instead of—packages. The reason is, of course, that prior to Version 2.3 of DB2, DBRMs were the only *possible* input. For compatibility with earlier releases, therefore, it was necessary in Version 2.3 to continue to support such a possibility. And this in turn is the reason why (as mentioned in a footnote earlier in the chapter) dropping an object, or revoking an authorization, may sometimes invalidate entire plans instead of just individual packages.

2.8 OPERATING ENVIRONMENTS

We close this chapter with a brief discussion of the various environments in which DB2 operates. DB2 applications fall into a number of different categories:

1. IMS batch (also known as DL/I batch)
2. IMS online (also known as IMS/DC)
3. CICS
4. TSO online
5. TSO batch
6. CAF

(refer to Fig. 2.6). We explain the differences among these various categories as follows.

1. An IMS batch DB2 application is a conventional IMS batch application that accesses DB2 data (via SQL statements) as well as IMS data (via DL/I database calls). DB2 itself serves as the necessary *transaction manager* in such an environment.* *Note*: The reader is warned that the term "transaction" has different interpretations in different systems. See Chapter 13 for an explanation of the interpretation used in this book. For readers who may already be familiar with IMS, we should perhaps stress the point that we are *not* using the normal IMS interpretation.

2. An IMS online DB2 application is an outline application† that is invoked from an IMS terminal and uses the data communications (DC)

---

*Despite this fact, the necessary "commit" and "rollback" functions must be requested by means of IMS DL/I calls, not by means of the SQL statements COMMIT and ROLLBACK. Refer to Chapter 13 for an explanation of such matters.

†For the benefit of readers familiar with IMS, we note that IMS batch message processing (BMP), message processing (MPP), and fast path (IFP) are all supported.

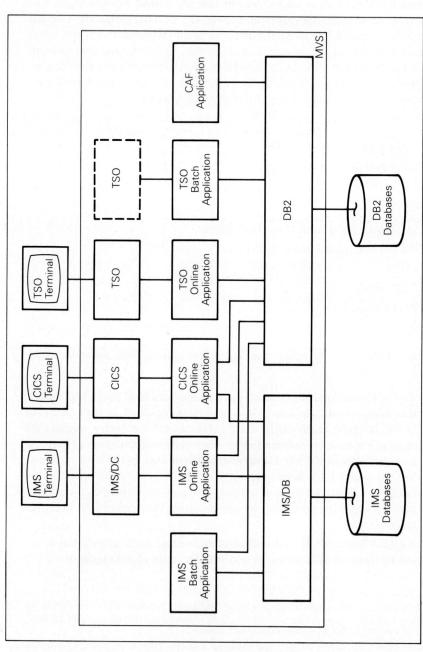

Fig. 2.6   DB2 operating environments

facilities of IMS (i.e., DL/I DC calls) to exchange messages with that terminal. Like an IMS batch DB2 application, an IMS online DB2 application can access both DB2 data and IMS data. (Unlike other DB2 applications, it can also access IMS Fast Path data.) The combination of DB2 with IMS/DC acts as a *full-function database/data communications* (DB/DC) *system*; this time IMS acts as the transaction manager (again, see Chapter 13).

3. A CICS DB2 application is an online application that is invoked from a CICS terminal and uses the facilities of CICS to exchange messages with that terminal. Like an IMS batch or IMS/DC DB2 application, a CICS DB2 application can access both DB2 data and IMS data (also VSAM data). The combination of DB2 with CICS also acts as a full-function DB/DC system, with CICS acting as the transaction manager (once again, see Chapter 13).

4. TSO is an MVS component and product that enables programs to be invoked and executed interactively from a TSO terminal. In particular, it allows DB2 to be invoked from such a terminal. If DB2 is invoked in this manner, and if DB2 in turn invokes a user application, then that application is said to be a "TSO online" DB2 application. Such an application can operate on DB2 data but not on IMS data. DB2 itself serves as the transaction manager in this case. *Note*: The application can use ISPF, GDDM, and TSO screen management facilities to communicate with the terminal.

5. TSO (or more precisely the TSO Terminal Monitor Program, TMP) can also execute as a batch job. If it does, and if it then invokes DB2, and if DB2 in turn then invokes a user application, then that application is said to be a "TSO batch" DB2 application (refer to Section 16.2 in Chapter 16 for more details regarding this possibility). A TSO batch DB2 application, like a TSO online DB2 application, can operate on DB2 data but not on IMS data. Again DB2 itself serves as the transaction manager in this case.

6. It is also possible for a "pure" MVS application (i.e., an application running directly under MVS instead of under IMS, CICS, or TSO) to operate on DB2 data, thanks to a feature known as the DB2 Call Attach Facility, CAF. CAF is intended for users who for some reason need more direct control of the environment than the cases discussed above can provide. Generalized applications provided by third-party software vendors often use the facilities of CAF. As another example, the IBM-provided "generalized application" QMF—discussed in Part IV of this book—is also implemented via CAF. The details of CAF are beyond the scope of this text.

7. Finally, all DB2 application types—IMS batch, IMS online, CICS, TSO online, TSO batch, and CAF—can execute concurrently. They can even share the same DB2 databases (and the same IMS databases, where applicable, and where permitted by IMS itself and/or MVS).

For the reader who may be unfamiliar with MVS and/or IMS and/or CICS and/or TSO, we offer the following words of encouragement: It is not *necessary* to be familiar with these products in order to understand the capabilities of DB2. All that is necessary is to understand that an application that uses the facilities of DB2 must operate either

(a) "stand alone" as a pure MVS application using the Call Attach Facility, or

(b) under the control of exactly one of IMS, CICS, or TSO.

It is also important to realize that the various categories are not interchangeable. That is, a DB2 application that is designed to run under (e.g.) IMS/DC cannot be moved to (e.g.) the CICS environment without some coding changes. However, the changes in question have to do with the portions of the application that interact with the transaction manager, not the portions that perform database operations; the database operations are the same in all cases.

EXERCISES

2.1 Name the major components of DB2.

2.2 Draw a diagram showing the overall process of program preparation and program execution in DB2.

2.3 List the principal functions of Bind.

2.4 Define *physical data independence*. Explain how DB2 provides such independence. Why is physical data independence desirable?

2.5 Summarize the various DB2 operating environments.

ANSWERS TO SELECTED EXERCISES

2.1 The major DB2 components are the system services, locking services, database services, and distributed data facility components. The database services component, in turn, divides into the Precompiler, Bind, Runtime Supervisor, Data Manager, and Buffer Manager components.

2.2 See Fig. 2.2 in Section 2.5.

2.3 Bind has two broad functions, "package bind" and "plan bind." Package bind is the process of compiling a DBRM into a corresponding package, and plan bind is the process of binding a list of packages (and/or DBRMs) together into an application plan. Package bind in turn involves four principal functions: syntax checking, optimization, package generation, and authorization checking. We elaborate on the optimization function slightly, since it is so critical. Optimization is the process of deciding a strategy for implementing database requests (i.e., SQL statements). The optimizer's choice of strategy is based in part on information contained in the catalog (the so-called "database statistics") regarding physical storage structure, availability of indexes, data value distributions, etc.

2.4 Physical data independence means that users and user programs do not depend on the physical structure of the database. User requests (i.e., SQL statements) are formulated purely in terms of the logical structure (i.e., in terms of tables and columns); the choice of physical access paths to implement those requests is made by the system (actually by the optimizer), not by the user. As a result, the physical structure of the database can be changed—e.g., for performance reasons—without requiring any user programs to be rewritten.

2.5 See Fig. 2.6 in Section 2.8.

PART

II

THE DB2
DATABASE
MANAGEMENT SYSTEM

C H A P T E R

◆ 3 ◆

Basic Objects and Operators

3.1 INTRODUCTION

In this chapter we describe the basic scalar (i.e., elementary) objects and operators supported by DB2. The basic data object is the *scalar value*; for example, the object appearing at the intersection of a given row and a given column of a given table is a scalar value. Each scalar value is of some particular scalar *data type*. For each such data type, there is also an associated format for writing *literals* of that type. Scalar data types and literals are discussed in Sections 3.2 and 3.3, respectively.

Scalar objects can be operated upon by means of certain *scalar operators*. For example, two numeric values can be added together by means of the scalar arithmetic operator "+", and can be tested for equality by means of the scalar comparison operator "=". In addition, DB2 provides certain *scalar functions* (e.g., the substring function SUBSTR), which can also be regarded as scalar operators. Scalar objects and operators can be combined to form *scalar expressions*. The operators available for each data

47

type, and the corresponding scalar expressions, are discussed in Section 3.4. Section 3.5 then discusses the general operations of *assignment* and *comparison*. Finally, Section 3.6 considers the problem of *missing information*.

Note: "Scalar value," "scalar operator," and "scalar expression" are not official DB2 terms. We use them because they are more descriptive and more precise than the official terms, which are simply "value," "operator," and "expression," respectively. On the other hand, "scalar function" *is* an official DB2 term; it is used in order to distinguish such functions from the "aggregate" (or column) functions to be described in Chapter 6.

3.2 DATA TYPES

DB2 supports the following scalar data types.

Numeric Data

INTEGER	Four-byte binary integer, 31 bits and sign
SMALLINT	Two-byte binary integer, 15 bits and sign
DECIMAL(p,q)	Packed decimal number, p digits and sign ($0 < p < 32$), with assumed decimal point q digits from the right ($0 < = q < = p$), occupying $(p+1)/2$ or $(p+2)/2$ bytes, according as p is odd or even
FLOAT(p)	Floating point number n, say, represented by a binary fraction f of p binary digits precision ($-1 < f < +1$, $0 < p < 54$) and a binary integer exponent e ($-65 < e < +64$), such that $n = f * (16 ** e)$

Notes:

1. The symbol "**" stands for exponentiation. The approximate range of magnitudes for n is $5.4E-79$ to $7.2E+75$ (see the discussion of float literals in Section 3.3 for an explanation of this notation).

2. Although we use the symbol "**" in our explanations, note that DB2 does not in fact support any such operator (see Section 3.4).

3. If $p < 22$ the number n is single precision and occupies four bytes, otherwise it is double precision and occupies eight bytes.

String Data

CHARACTER(n) Fixed length string of exactly n 8-bit characters ($0 < n < 255$), occupying n bytes

VARCHAR(n) Varying length string of up to n 8-bit characters ($0 < n$), occupying $n+2$ bytes (two bytes for a hidden length field)

Note: The maximum value of n depends on a number of factors, but in general must be less than the page size for the table space containing the table (see Chapter 15)

GRAPHIC(n) Fixed length string of exactly n 16-bit characters ($0 < n < 128$), occupying $2n$ bytes

VARGRAPHIC(n) Varying length string of up to n 16-bit characters ($0 < n$), occupying $2n+2$ bytes (two bytes for a hidden length field)

Note: The maximum value of n depends on a number of factors, but in general must be less than half the page size for the table space containing the table (see Chapter 15)

Date/Time Data

DATE Date, represented as a sequence of eight unsigned packed decimal digits (*yyyymmdd*), occupying four bytes; permitted values are legal dates in the range January 1st, 1 A.D., to December 31st, 9999 A.D.

TIME Time, represented as a sequence of six unsigned packed decimal digits (*hhmmss*), occupying three bytes; permitted values are legal times in the range midnight to midnight, i.e., 000000 to 240000

TIMESTAMP "Timestamp" (combination of date and time, accurate to the nearest microsecond), represented as a sequence of 20 unsigned packed decimal digits (*yyyymmddhhmmssnnnnnn*), occupying ten bytes; permitted values are legal timestamps in the range 00010101000000000000 to 99991231240000000000

Notes:

1. The following abbreviations and alternative spellings are permitted:

INT	for	INTEGER
DECIMAL(p)	for	DECIMAL(p,0)
DECIMAL	for	DECIMAL(5)
DEC	for	DECIMAL
NUMERIC	for	DECIMAL
FLOAT	for	FLOAT(53)
REAL	for	FLOAT(21)
DOUBLE PRECISION	for	FLOAT(53)
CHARACTER	for	CHARACTER(1)
CHAR	for	CHARACTER
LONG VARCHAR	for	VARCHAR(n), where n is the maximum that DB2 will allow
GRAPHIC	for	GRAPHIC(1)
LONG VARGRAPHIC	for	VARGRAPHIC(n), where n is the maximum that DB2 will allow

2. The GRAPHIC and VARGRAPHIC data types are intended for dealing with double-byte character sets—i.e., character sets with more than 256 distinct characters (e.g., Kanji), in which each character is represented by a 16-bit encoding. *Note*: It is in fact possible to mix 8- and 16-bit characters within the same string, but the details are beyond the scope of this book.

3. If the length n is greater than 254 for VARCHAR or 127 for VARGRAPHIC (or if LONG VARCHAR or LONG VARGRAPHIC is specified explicitly), the value is a "long string" and is subject to severe restrictions. Long strings are intended for the handling of free-format data such as text, rather than simple formatted data such as a part number or a supplier city. Long string values can be used in assignment operations, either to the database (INSERT or UPDATE) or from the database (SELECT); however, they cannot be used in any operation that would involve a long string comparison. Thus, for example, long strings cannot be indexed, nor can they be referenced in a WHERE clause (except with LIKE) or a GROUP BY clause or an ORDER BY clause, and so on. (See Chapters 5 and 6 for an explanation of these last two clauses.) For completeness, we list the restrictions here. A long string cannot appear in any of the following contexts:

- PRIMARY KEY
- FOREIGN KEY

- CREATE INDEX
- any function (except LENGTH and SUBSTR)
- DISTINCT
- WHERE (except in a LIKE condition)
- GROUP BY
- HAVING (except in a LIKE condition)
- ORDER BY
- UNION (unless ALL is specified)

4. From this point on, we will reserve the term "character string" to mean data of type CHAR or VARCHAR, the term "graphic string" to mean data of type GRAPHIC or VARGRAPHIC, and the unqualified term "string" to mean data of both string types generically.

5. The character string data types CHAR and VARCHAR (and LONG VARCHAR) can optionally include the additional specification FOR BIT DATA—for example:

```
READING  CHAR(32)  FOR BIT DATA
```

FOR BIT DATA means that data values within the column in question—READING, in the example—are to be considered as uninterpreted byte strings.* In particular, if such a value is included as part of a message transmitted between the DB2 system (which uses the standard IBM EBCDIC character code) and some other system, say a PC, that uses some different character code (say ASCII), then character code conversion is *not* to be performed on that value.

3.3 LITERALS

The various kinds of literal value supported in DB2 are as follows:

integer	Written as a signed or unsigned decimal integer, with no decimal point†
	Examples: 4 -95 +364 0
decimal	Written as a signed or unsigned decimal number, with a decimal point
	Examples: 4. -95.7 +364.05 0.007

---

*It might have been clearer to introduce a new BYTE(*n*) data type. Note too that FOR BIT DATA definitely means "byte string," not "bit string" (and certainly not "Boolean").

†If the integer is too large in absolute magnitude for data type INTEGER, it is treated as a decimal literal instead (even though it does not have a decimal point).

float	Written as a decimal or integer literal, followed by the letter E, followed by an integer literal

Examples: `4E3`   `-95.7E46`   `+364E-5`   `0.7E1`

Note: The expression xEy represents the value $x * (10 ** y)$

character string	Written *either* as a sequence of characters enclosed in single quotes* *or* as a sequence of pairs of hexadecimal digits (representing the EBCDIC encodings of the characters concerned), enclosed in single quotes and preceded by the letter X

Examples:
```
'123 Main St.'
'PIG'
X'F1F2F340D481899540E2A34B'
X'D7C9C7'
```

(the 1st and 3rd of these examples represent the same value, as do the 2nd and 4th)

graphic string	Written as a sequence of double-byte characters preceded by the "shift out" character X'0E' and followed by the "shift in" character X'0F', the whole enclosed in single quotes and preceded by the letter G or the letter N[†]

Example: `G'<.....>'`

(the shift out and shift in characters have been shown as "<" and ">", respectively; ". . . . ." represents the required sequence of graphic characters)

date	Written as a character string literal of the form *mm/dd/ yyyy*, enclosed in single quotes (but see "Notes on Date/ Times" below)

Examples:
```
'1/18/1941'
'12/25/1989'
```

time	Written as a character string literal of the form *hh:mm* AM or *hh:mm* PM, enclosed in single quotes (but see "Notes on Date/Times" below)

Examples:
```
'10:00 AM'
'9:30 PM'
```

---

*As usual, a single quote must be represented as two consecutive single quotes within a character string literal.

[†]This is the normal format. The format in PL/I contexts is slightly different. See the IBM manuals for details.

timestamp   Written as a character string literal of the form *yyyy-mm-dd-hh.mm.ss.nnnnnn*, enclosed in single quotes (but see "Notes on Date/Times" below)

Examples: `'1990-4-28-12.00.00.000000'`
`'1944-10-17-18.30.45'`

Notes on Date/Times:

1. Strictly speaking there is no such thing as a date literal. Instead, there are *character string representations of date values*. If a character string value—in particular, a character string literal—appears in a context that requires a date value, then that character string will be interpreted as a date value, provided of course that it is of the appropriate form (a conversion error will occur if it is not). We will use the term "date string" to refer to a character string that represents a valid date.

2. The remarks of the previous paragraph apply to times and timestamps also, mutatis mutandis. We will use the terms "time string" and "timestamp string" to refer to character strings that represent valid time and timestamp values.

3. Several different character string representations of dates and times are supported: US style, European style, etc. A variety of methods (installation options, Precompiler options, etc.) are available for specifying the style to be used in any particular context. The examples above all use US style. See Appendix B for further discussion.

4. We remark that a peculiarity of US-style time strings in DB2 is that they do not include a seconds component, as can be seen from the discussion of "time literals" above. Nevertheless, the internal representation of a time value always does include such a component.

5. Leading zeros can be omitted from the month and day portions of a date or timestamp string and from the hours portion of a time or timestamp string. The seconds portion (including the preceding colon or period) can be omitted entirely from a time string (in fact, it must be so omitted from a US-style time string); an implicit specification of zero is assumed. Trailing zeros can be omitted from the microseconds portion of a timestamp string; the microseconds portion (including the preceding period) can also be omitted entirely, in which case an implicit specification of zero is assumed.

6. The full DB2 support for dates and times is quite complex. For this reason we defer a detailed account of that support to an appendix (Appendix B).

Data Types of Literals

Literal data types are as indicated below:

integer	INTEGER
decimal	DECIMAL(p,q), where p and q are the actual precision and scale specified
float	FLOAT(53)
character string	VARCHAR(n), where n is the actual length specified
graphic string	VARGRAPHIC(n), where n is the actual length specified

Note in particular that string literals are always taken to be varying length. Also, all literals are assumed to have the NOT NULL property (see Section 3.6).

3.4 SCALAR OPERATORS AND FUNCTIONS

DB2 provides a number of builtin scalar operators and functions that can be used in the construction of scalar expressions. We summarize those operators and functions below, for purposes of reference. *Note*: For a discussion of the builtin *aggregate* functions, see Chapter 6. For more details on the functions having to do with dates and times, see Appendix B.

- Numeric operators

  DB2 supports the usual numeric operators $+$, $-$, $*$, and $/$, all with the obvious meanings. *Note*: The operators $+$ and $-$ can be used with dates, times, and timestamps as well as with numbers (again, see Appendix B for details).

- Concatenation

  The concatenation operator $\|$ can be used to concatenate two character strings or two graphic strings.* It is written as an infix operation; e.g., the expression INITIALS $\|$ LASTNAME can be used to concatenate the values of INITIALS and LASTNAME (in that order).

- CHAR

  Converts a date, time, timestamp, or decimal number to its character string representation.

---

*The operator can also be written as CONCAT.

- DATE

  Converts a scalar value to a date.

- DAY

  Extracts the day portion of a date or timestamp (or "date duration" or "timestamp duration"—see Appendix B).

- DAYS

  Converts a date or timestamp to a number of days.

- DECIMAL

  Converts a number to decimal representation (with specified precision).

- DIGITS

  Converts a number (decimal or integer) to character string representation. (Note that there is some overlap between this function and the CHAR function discussed above. Note too that—strangely—there is no converse function to convert a character string representation of a number into the corresponding numeric value.)

- FLOAT

  Converts a number to floating point representation.

- HEX

  Converts a scalar value to a character string representing the internal hexadecimal encoding of the value.

- HOUR

  Extracts the hours portion of a time or timestamp (or "time duration" or "timestamp duration"—see Appendix B).

- INTEGER

  Converts a number to integer representation.

- LENGTH

  Computes the length of a scalar value in bytes (or double-bytes, for graphic data).

- MICROSECOND

  Extracts the microseconds portion of a timestamp (or "timestamp duration"—see Appendix B).

- MINUTE

  Extracts the minutes portion of a time or timestamp (or "time duration" or "timestamp duration"—see Appendix B).

- MONTH

  Extracts the month portion of a date or timestamp (or "date duration" or "timestamp duration"—see Appendix B).

- SECOND

  Extracts the seconds portion of a time or timestamp (or "time duration" or "timestamp duration"—see Appendix B).

- SUBSTR

  Extracts a substring of a string. For example, the expression SUBSTR (SNAME,1,3) extracts the first three characters of the specified supplier name.

- TIME

  Converts a scalar value to a time.

- TIMESTAMP

  Converts either (a) a single scalar value, or (b) a pair of scalar values (representing a date and time respectively), to a timestamp.

- VALUE

  Converts a null into a nonnull value (see Section 3.6).

- VARGRAPHIC

  Converts a character string into a graphic string.

- YEAR

  Extracts the year portion of a date or timestamp (or "date duration" or "timestamp duration"—see Appendix B).

Special Registers

DB2 also supports a number of "special registers" (this term is taken from COBOL; "zero-argument builtin scalar functions" would perhaps be more accurate, or at least more descriptive). The special registers currently defined are USER, CURRENT SQLID, CURRENT SERVER, CURRENT PACKAGESET, CURRENT DATE, CURRENT TIME, CURRENT TIMESTAMP, and CURRENT TIMEZONE. A reference to a special register returns a scalar value, as follows:

- USER

  Returns the "primary authorization ID." See Chapter 10 for an illustration of the use of USER.

- CURRENT SQLID

  Returns the "current authorization ID." Again, see Chapter 10 for further discussion.

- CURRENT SERVER

  Returns the ID of the "current server." See Part III for further discussion.

- CURRENT PACKAGESET

  Returns the ID of the "collection" currently in use (see Chapter 2).

- CURRENT DATE

  Returns the current date, i.e., the date "today."

- CURRENT TIME

  Returns the current time, i.e., the time "now."

- CURRENT TIMESTAMP

  Returns the current timestamp, i.e., the date "today" concatenated with the time "now."

- CURRENT TIMEZONE

  Returns a "time duration" (see Appendix B) representing (typically) the displacement of the local time zone from Greenwich Mean Time.* Note that the value returned by each of CURRENT DATE, CURRENT TIME, and CURRENT TIMESTAMP is based on a reading of the local clock, incremented in each case by the value of CURRENT TIMEZONE.

  For examples of the use of the various date/time special registers, see Appendix B once again.

Scalar Expressions

As indicated at the beginning of this section, the scalar operators and functions can be used (in conjunction with scalar operands and arguments) to construct scalar expressions. A scalar expression is an expression whose operands are simple scalar values and whose value in turn is another such

---

*We note in passing that in the standards world, at least, the term Greenwich Mean Time (GMT) has recently been dropped, and GMT-based times have been replaced by "UTC" times (where UTC stands for "Universal Coordinated Time").

scalar value.* Generally speaking, such expressions can appear wherever a *literal* of the appropriate type is permitted—for example, as operands in SELECT, WHERE, and HAVING clauses (see Chapters 5–7)—though, regrettably, there are many exceptions to this simple general rule. Such exceptions are noted later at appropriate points in the book.

There are six types of scalar expression, characterized according to the data type of the value they represent: numeric, character string, graphic string, date, time, and timestamp expressions. We give examples here of the first two types only; graphic string expressions are syntactically similar to character string expressions, and date, time, and timestamp expressions are discussed in Appendix B. Note that (as several of the examples below suggest) parentheses can always be used in an expression to force a desired order of evaluation. Note too that the aggregate functions discussed in Chapter 6 can also be used within certain scalar expressions, since they each return a scalar value; two examples, using the aggregate functions AVG and MIN respectively, are shown below.

Numeric expressions:

```
STATUS
WEIGHT * 454
SALARY + COMMISSION + BONUS
( QTY + 1500 )  / 75.2
( LENGTH ( SNAME ) - 1 ) * 2
50 - ( AVG ( QTY ) / 100 )
```

Character string expressions:

```
PNAME
INITIALS || LASTNAME
SUBSTR ( SNAME, 1, 3 )
'NNNN' || SUBSTR ( DIGITS ( QTY ), 8, 2 )
MIN ( COLOR )
USER
```

3.5 ASSIGNMENTS AND COMPARISONS

Assignments

Assignment operations are performed when values are retrieved from the database (e.g., via SELECT) or stored into the database (e.g., via UPDATE). In general, an assignment involves assigning the value of some scalar expression (the *source*) to some scalar object (the *target*). The data

---

*For details regarding the data type, precision, etc., of the result of a scalar expression, the reader is referred to the IBM manuals.

type of the source and the data type of the target must be *compatible*. Compatibility is defined as follows:

1. All numbers are compatible with one another.

2. All character strings are compatible with one another.

3. All graphic strings are compatible with one another.

4. All dates are compatible with one another. Dates and character strings are also compatible with one another.

5. All times are compatible with one another. Times and character strings are also compatible with one another.

6. All timestamps are compatible with one another. Timestamps and character strings are also compatible with one another.

7. In Cases 4, 5, and 6 above, the character string in question must be a valid date string or time string or timestamp string (as applicable), unless it is being assigned to, in which case its value is irrelevant. See Appendix B for further discussion.

8. There are no other instances of compatibility.

Note 1: The target of an assignment in an INSERT or UPDATE operation must be represented by an *unqualified* name (see Chapters 4 and 5 for a discussion of qualified and unqualified names).

Note 2: In a string assignment, the source can be a substring of a given string (specified by means of the SUBSTR function), but the target cannot. Likewise, in a date/time assignment, the source can be—for example—the days component of a given date/time (specified by means of the DAY function), but the target cannot.

Comparisons

Comparisons are performed under many circumstances—for example, when DB2 is eliminating duplicate values (see the discussion of DISTINCT in Chapter 5). A comparison is also one kind of *condition* or *conditional expression* (though not the only kind); conditional expressions are used in WHERE and HAVING clauses (see Chapters 5–7). Comparisons can be regarded as a special kind of scalar expression, but a scalar expression that evaluates to a truth value instead of to one of the DB2-supported data types. The general form of a comparison is

```
comparand   operator   comparand
```

where:

(a) The two comparands must be *compatible* (as that term is defined under "Assignments" above). In other words, the comparands must be scalar expressions of the same type—i.e., both numeric or both character string or . . . (etc.). The data types of the two expressions are not required to be absolutely identical, but for performance reasons it is usually a good idea if they are.

(b) The operator is any of the following: =, ¬= (not equals), <, ¬<, <=, >, ¬>, >=.*

Comparisons are evaluated as follows:

- Numbers compare algebraically (negative values are considered to be smaller than positive values, regardless of their absolute magnitude).

- Strings (character or graphic) compare in accordance with their internal byte encoding. If two strings of different lengths are to be compared, the shorter is conceptually padded at the right with blanks to make it the same length as the other before the comparison is done.

- Dates and times and timestamps compare in accordance with the obvious chronologic ordering. See Appendix B for further discussion.

Examples:

```
WEIGHT * 454 > 1000
SUBSTR (PNAME,1,1) = 'C'
REVIEW_DATE < CURRENT DATE
SUM (QTY) > 500
```

The last of these examples makes use of an aggregate function (SUM). Again, see Chapter 6 for a discussion of aggregate functions.

3.6   MISSING INFORMATION

To complete this chapter on basic objects and operators, it is necessary to say something regarding missing information. The problem of missing information is one that is frequently encountered in the real world. For example, historical records sometimes include such entries as "Date of birth unknown"; meeting agendas often show a speaker as "To be announced"; and police records may include the entry "Present whereabouts unknown." Hence it is desirable to have some way of dealing with such situations in our formal database systems.

---

*DB2 also allows "not equals" to be written as < > (for reasons of compatibility with the SQL standard).

SQL systems like DB2 represent such missing information by means of special markers called *nulls* (or by nonnull "default values"; we ignore this latter possibility for the moment). For example, we might say, loosely, that the weight of some part is null. What we mean by such a statement is, more precisely, that (a) we know that the part exists, and of course (b) it does have a weight, but (c) we do not know what that weight is. In other words, we do not know a genuine weight value that can sensibly be put in the WEIGHT slot in the row for the part in question. Instead, therefore, we *mark* that slot as "null," and we interpret that mark to mean, precisely, that we do not know what the real value is.

Informally, we usually think of such a slot as "containing a null," or of the corresponding value as "being null," and we will tend to use such terms in this book (because they are the terms most often used in SQL contexts). But the foregoing discussion should serve to show that such a manner of speaking *is* only informal, and indeed not very accurate. That is why the expression "null value" (which is heard very frequently) is deprecated: The whole point about nulls is precisely that they are not values. In particular, a null is not the same as (e.g.) a blank or a zero.

In general, any column can contain nulls *unless* the definition of that column explicitly specifies NOT NULL (see Chapter 4). If a given column is allowed to contain nulls, and a row is inserted into the table and no value is provided for that column, DB2 will automatically place a null in that position.

- Suppose, for example, that NOT NULL is specified for column P# in table P.* The effect of this specification is to guarantee that every row in table P will always contain a genuine (i.e., nonnull) P# value; in other words, a value must always be provided for column P# when a row is inserted into the P table, and updating an existing P# value to null will not be allowed.

- Suppose also, by contrast, that NOT NULL is *not* specified for column WEIGHT in that same table. Then WEIGHT might be null in some P row; in other words, it is possible to insert a P row without providing a WEIGHT value, and updating an existing WEIGHT value to null will be allowed.

    Aside: In DB2, a column that can accept nulls is physically represented in the stored database by two columns, the data column itself and a hidden indicator column, one byte wide, that is stored as a prefix

---

*In fact, NOT NULL *must* be specified for column P#, because it is the primary key for table P. See Chapters 4 and 11.

to the actual data column. An indicator column value of binary ones indicates that the corresponding data column value is to be ignored (i.e., taken as null); an indicator column value of binary zeros indicates that the corresponding data column value is to be taken as genuine. But the indicator column is always (of course) "transparent to the user." *End of aside.*

The specification NOT NULL in a column definition can optionally be extended to include the additional specification WITH DEFAULT. NOT NULL WITH DEFAULT means that the column in question cannot contain nulls, but that it is nevertheless still legal to omit a value for the column on INSERT. If a row is inserted and no value is provided for some column to which NOT NULL WITH DEFAULT applies, DB2 automatically places one of the following nonnull default values in that position:

- Zero for numeric columns

- Blanks for fixed length string columns

- Empty (zero-length string) for varying length string columns

- The value of CURRENT DATE or CURRENT TIME or CURRENT TIMESTAMP, as appropriate, for date, time, or timestamp columns (except as explained in Appendix B)

Nonnull default values are genuine, legal data values (unlike nulls).

To return to nulls per se: Let us consider the effect of nulls on scalar expressions. Consider, for example, the numeric expression

```
WEIGHT * 454
```

where WEIGHT represents the weight of some part, P*x* say. What if the weight of part P*x* happens to be null?—what then is the value of the expression? The answer is that it also is considered to be null. In general, in fact, *any* scalar numeric expression is considered to evaluate to null if any of the operands of that expression is itself null. Thus, e.g., if WEIGHT happens to be null, then all of the following expressions also evaluate to null:

```
WEIGHT + 454      454 + WEIGHT      + WEIGHT
WEIGHT - 454      454 - WEIGHT      - WEIGHT
WEIGHT * 454      454 * WEIGHT
WEIGHT / 454      454 / WEIGHT
```

This state of affairs is justified by the intended interpretation of null as "value unknown"; after all, if WEIGHT is unknown, then obviously WEIGHT * 454 is unknown too.*

---

*Perhaps "justified" should be in quotes here. Note, for example, that according to that "justification" the expression WEIGHT − WEIGHT, which should clearly yield zero, actually (and incorrectly) yields null in SQL.

Analogous considerations apply to string expressions and to date, time, and timestamp expressions. *Note*: It is worth mentioning that aggregate functions such as SUM do *not* behave in accordance with the foregoing rules but instead simply ignore any nulls in their argument (except for the COUNT function). See Chapter 6 for further discussion.

Comparisons are also affected by the presence of nulls. Let A and B be two expressions that are compatible for comparison purposes (see Section 3.5). If A evaluates to null or B evaluates to null *or both*, then (in the context of a WHERE or HAVING clause) each of the comparisons

```
A = B      A ¬= B      A <> B
A < B      A ¬< B      A >= B
A > B      A ¬> B      A <= B
```

evaluates, not to *true* or *false*, but to the *unknown* truth value. The justification for this rule (again) is the intended interpretation of null as "value unknown": If the value of A is unknown, then clearly it is *unknown* whether, e.g., A > B. Note in particular, therefore, that two nulls are not considered to be equal to one another—that is, the comparison "null = null" evaluates to *unknown*.*

The concept of nulls thus leads us into what is called a *three-valued logic*, in which the three truth values are *true*, *false*, and *unknown*. The three-valued logic truth tables for AND, OR, and NOT are shown below (t = *true*, f = *false*, u = *unknown*):

AND	t u f
t	t u f
u	u u f
f	f f f

OR	t u f
t	t t t
u	t u u
f	t u f

NOT	
t	f
u	u
f	t

Suppose, for example, that A = 3, B = 4, and C is null. Then the following expressions have the indicated truth values:

```
A > B AND B > C  :  false
A > B OR  B > C  :  unknown
A < B OR  B < C  :  true
NOT ( A = C )    :  unknown
```

Two special comparison operators, IS NULL and IS NOT NULL, are provided to test for the presence or absence of nulls. For example:

---

*At least, this is the case in the context of a WHERE or HAVING clause. However, two nulls *are* considered to be equal (equivalently, to be duplicates of each other) for purposes of indexing (UNIQUE—see Chapter 4) and duplicate elimination (DISTINCT—see Chapter 5) and ordering (ORDER BY—see Chapter 5) and grouping (GROUP BY—see Chapter 6) and union (UNION—see Chapter 6). The whole question of the effect of nulls on comparisons is discussed further in Chapter 5.

```
C IS NULL       :   true
A IS NULL       :   false
B IS NOT NULL   :   true
```

(assuming A, B, and C are still as above).

The scalar function VALUE (mentioned briefly in Section 3.4) can be useful in dealing with nulls. Suppose for the sake of the example that nulls are permitted for the CITY column in table P. Then the query

```
SELECT  P#, VALUE ( CITY, 'City unknown' )
FROM    P ;
```

will return the character string "City unknown" for any part for which the city is given as null in the database. In general, VALUE takes a sequence of arguments of compatible data types, and returns either the value of the first nonnull argument in the sequence, or null if the arguments are all null.

One final point: In certain contexts—but *not* in general scalar expressions, and not in a SELECT clause—the special zero-argument function NULL can be used to represent null.* For instance:

```
UPDATE P
SET     WEIGHT = NULL
WHERE   P# = 'P4' ;
```

Author's note: It is this writer's very firm opinion that nulls and three-valued logic are far more trouble than they are worth and should be *totally avoided*—they display very strange and inconsistent behavior and are a rich source of error and confusion (as perhaps our discussions have already sufficiently suggested). Please note too that these remarks apply to any system that supports SQL-style nulls, not just to DB2 specifically. Extensive discussion of the problems that can arise can be found in three books:

- *Relational Database: Selected Writings* (1986)
- *Relational Database Writings 1985-1989* (1990)
- *Relational Database Writings 1989-1991* (1992)

all by C. J. Date (the last joint with Hugh Darwen) and published by Addison-Wesley. In this book, therefore, we will generally specify either NOT NULL or NOT NULL WITH DEFAULT for all columns, unless we are trying to illustrate some specific point involving nulls.

---

*DB2 does not actually consider NULL to be a "zero-argument function" (nor is it a literal or "special register"), because it cannot appear in all contexts in which such objects can appear. Exactly what DB2 does consider it to be is not at all clear.

EXERCISES

3.1 List the DB2 data types.

3.2 List the various kinds of literal value supported by DB2.

3.3 What is a "special register"? List the special registers supported by DB2.

3.4 Assignment and comparison operations require their operands to be *compatible*. Define "compatible."

3.5 Suppose A = 1, B = 2, C = −1, and D is null. Give the truth values for the following expressions:

    (a)   A < B AND B > C

    (b)   A > B OR B < C

    (c)   A ¬= B AND (B < C OR C < A)

    (d)   (A - C) ¬< B

    (e)   (A - D) ¬> B

    (f)   A = B OR A < B OR A > B

    (g)   A = D OR A < D OR A > D

    (h)   D = A OR D = D

    (i)   NOT (D > A)

    (j)   A > B AND NOT (A > B)

    (k)   A IS NULL OR B IS NULL OR C IS NULL

    (l)   A IS NOT NULL AND D IS NULL

ANSWERS TO SELECTED EXERCISES

3.1 INTEGER
SMALLINT
DECIMAL(*p*,*q*)
FLOAT(*p*)

CHARACTER(*n*)	—optionally FOR BIT DATA
VARCHAR(*n*)	—also LONG VARCHAR
GRAPHIC(*n*)	
VARGRAPHIC(*n*)	—also LONG VARGRAPHIC

DATE
TIME
TIMESTAMP

3.2 DB2 supports integer, decimal, float, character string, and graphic string literals. It also supports "date," "time," and "timestamp" literals—that is, character string literal representations of date, time, and timestamp values.

3.3 A special register is a zero-argument builtin scalar function. The special registers in DB2 are USER, CURRENT SQLID, CURRENT SERVER, CURRENT PACKAGESET, CURRENT DATE, CURRENT TIME, CURRENT TIMESTAMP, and CURRENT TIMEZONE.

3.4 See Section 3.5.

3.5 (a) True

   (b) False

   (c) True

   (d) True

   (e) Unknown

   (f) True

   (g) Unknown

   (h) Unknown

   (i) Unknown

   (j) False

   (k) False

   (l) True

C H A P T E R

4

Data Definition

4.1 INTRODUCTION

In this chapter we examine the SQL data definition statements of DB2 in some detail. It is convenient to divide those statements into two broad classes, which we may very loosely characterize as *logical* and *physical*—"logical" having to do with objects that are genuinely of interest to users, such as base tables and views, and "physical" having to do with objects that are primarily of interest to the system, such as disk volumes. Needless to say, matters are not really as clearcut as this simple classification would suggest—some "logical" statements include parameters that are really "physical" in nature, and vice versa, and some statements do not fit neatly into either category. But the classification is convenient as an aid to understanding, and we will stay with it for now. The present chapter is concerned only with "logical" data definition.

The principal logical data definition statements are listed below:

```
CREATE TABLE       CREATE VIEW       CREATE INDEX
ALTER TABLE
DROP TABLE         DROP VIEW         DROP INDEX
```

(*Note*: Strictly speaking, the CREATE and DROP INDEX statements are "physical," not "logical"; however, they are needed to support certain "logical" facilities, as we shall see in Section 4.3. There is also an ALTER INDEX statement, but it falls totally into the "physical" category.) We defer discussion of CREATE and DROP VIEW to Chapter 9; the remaining statements above are the subject of the present chapter. Note that there is no ALTER VIEW statement.

4.2 BASE TABLES

As indicated in the Preface, a base table is an important special case of the more general concept "table." Let us therefore begin by making that more general concept a little more precise. Here then is a definition: A *table* in a relational system consists of a row of *column headings*, together with zero or more rows of *data values* (different numbers of data rows at different times). For a given table:

- The column heading row specifies one or more columns (giving, among other things, a data type for each).

- Each data row contains exactly one scalar value* for each of the columns specified in the column heading row. Furthermore, all the values in a given column are of the same data type, namely the data type specified in the column heading row for that column.

Two points arise in connection with the foregoing definition.

1. Note that there is no mention of *row ordering*. Strictly speaking, the rows of a relational table are considered to be unordered. (The rows of a relation constitute a mathematical *set*, and sets in mathematics do not have any ordering.) It is possible, as we shall see in Chapter 5, to *impose* an order on those rows when they are retrieved in response to a query, but such an ordering should be regarded as nothing more than a convenience for the user—it is not intrinsic to the notion of a table per se.

---

*Some might argue that "exactly one" here should be "at most one," owing to the possibility of nulls.

2. In contrast to the first point, the columns of a table *are* considered to
    be ordered, left to right.* For example, in the suppliers table S (see Fig.
    1.2 in Chapter 1), column S# is the first column, column SNAME is
    the second column, and so on. In practice, however, there are very few
    situations in which that left-to-right ordering is significant, and even
    those can be avoided with a little discipline. Such avoidance is to be
    recommended, as we shall explain later.

    Aside: Of course, rows and columns do have a physical ordering in
    the stored version of the table on the disk; what is more, those physical
    orderings can and do have a very definite effect on system perform-
    ance. The point is, however, that those physical orderings are (in most
    situations, and ideally in all situations) "transparent to the user." *End
    of aside*.

To turn now to base tables specifically: A base table is an *autonomous,
named* table. By "autonomous," we mean that the table exists in its own
right—unlike (e.g.) a view, which does not exist in its own right but is derived from one or more base tables (it is merely an alternative way of looking at those base tables). By "named," we mean that the table is explicitly
given a name via an appropriate CREATE statement—unlike (e.g.) a table
that is merely constructed as the result of a query, which does not have any
explicit name of its own and has only ephemeral existence (for examples of
such unnamed tables, see the two result tables in Fig. 1.1 in Chapter 1).

CREATE TABLE: Format 1

We are now in a position to discuss the CREATE TABLE statement in
detail. First, we remind the reader that CREATE TABLE creates a *base*
table specifically. The statement comes in two formats. Format 1 (the more
fundamental of the two) takes the general form:

```
CREATE TABLE base-table
  ( column-definition [, column-definition ] ...
  [, primary-key-definition ]
  [, alternate-key-definition [, alternate-key-definition ] ... ] )
  [, foreign-key-definition [, foreign-key-definition ] ... ] )
  [ other parameters ] ;
```

where a "column-definition", in turn, takes the form:

```
column data-type [ NOT NULL [ WITH DEFAULT | UNIQUE ] ]
```

---

*At least, they are considered to be so ordered in systems like DB2 that are based on SQL,
although such ordering is properly not part of the relational model.

Note: Square brackets are used in syntactic definitions throughout this book to indicate that the material enclosed in those brackets is optional (i.e., may be omitted). An ellipsis (...) indicates that the immediately preceding syntactic unit may optionally be repeated one or more times. Material in capitals must be written exactly as shown; material in lower case must be replaced by specific values chosen by the user.

To revert to CREATE TABLE: the optional specifications NOT NULL and NOT NULL WITH DEFAULT have already been explained in Chapter 3 (Section 3.6); we defer explanation of the optional specification NOT NULL UNIQUE to Chapter 11. Likewise, we also defer detailed discussion of "primary-key-definition," "alternate key definition," and "foreign-key-definition" to Chapter 11; note, however, that although the primary key definition is in fact optional in DB2, we will always include such a definition in our examples in this book. The optional "other parameters" are mostly to do with physical storage matters and are discussed (very briefly) in Chapter 15.

Here is an example (the CREATE TABLE statement for table S, now shown complete):

```
CREATE TABLE S
    ( S#      CHAR(5)   NOT NULL,
      SNAME   CHAR(20)  NOT NULL WITH DEFAULT,
      STATUS  SMALLINT  NOT NULL WITH DEFAULT,
      CITY    CHAR(15)  NOT NULL WITH DEFAULT,
      PRIMARY KEY ( S# ) ) ;
```

The effect of this statement is to create a new, empty base table called *xyz*.S, where *xyz* is the name by which the user issuing the CREATE TABLE statement is known to the system (see Chapter 10). Entries describing the table are made in the DB2 catalog. User *xyz* can refer to the table by its full name *xyz*.S or by the abbreviated name S; other users must refer to it by its full name.* The table has four columns, called *xyz*.S.S#, *xyz*.S.SNAME, *xyz*.S.STATUS, and *xyz*.S.CITY, and having the indicated data types; column *xyz*.S.S# is the primary key (note that the primary key must be explicitly declared to be NOT NULL). User *xyz* can refer to the columns of the table by their full names or by the abbreviated names S.S#, S.SNAME, S.STATUS, and S.CITY; other users must always use the *xyz* qualifier. For user *xyz* (only), the "S." portion can be omitted also if no ambiguity results. In general, the rules concerning names are as follows: User names, such as *xyz*, must be unique across the entire DB2 system; (unqualified) table names must be unique within user; and (unqualified) column names

---

*At this early point in the book we deliberately ignore DB2's *alias* and *synonym* capabilities. See Chapter 8.

must be unique within table. "Table" here refers to both base tables and views; that is, a view cannot have the same name as a base table.

Aside: While we are on the subject of names, let us get a few other points out of the way. First, SQL keywords (CREATE, TABLE, SE-LECT, etc.) cannot be used as names in any context in which the keyword in question would have its special SQL meaning. Second, the first character of any name must be "alphabetic" (A–Z or one of the special characters #, $, @), the remainder if any must be "alphabetic," numeric (0–9), or the underscore character. Third, table and column names are limited to a maximum of 18 characters, user names to a maximum of 8 characters. Finally, we should mention for completeness that DB2 also supports "delimited" names and names that are composed of double-byte characters. The details of these last two possibilities are beyond the scope of this book, however. *End of aside*.

Once the table has been created (and a UNIQUE index created on its primary key—see Section 4.3), data can be entered into it via the SQL INSERT statement (see Chapter 7) or via the DB2 load utility (see Chapter 16).

CREATE TABLE: Format 2

Format 2 of CREATE TABLE allows the user to create a base table that is "the same shape as" some existing named table (base table or view):

```
CREATE TABLE base-table LIKE table
[ other parameters ] ;
```

The optional "other parameters" are exactly as for Format 1. Here is an example:

```
CREATE TABLE SCOPY LIKE S ;
```

Table "base-table" inherits its column definitions—but nothing else—from "table." In the example, therefore, it is as if table SCOPY were defined as follows:

```
CREATE TABLE SCOPY
     ( S#      CHAR(5)   NOT NULL,
       SNAME   CHAR(20)  NOT NULL WITH DEFAULT,
       STATUS  SMALLINT  NOT NULL WITH DEFAULT,
       CITY    CHAR(15)  NOT NULL WITH DEFAULT ) ;
```

Note in particular that "base-table" does *not* inherit any primary, alternate, or foreign key definitions from "table" (and if "table" has any column UNIQUE specifications, it does not inherit those either). What is more, DB2 does not permit any such specifications to be stated explicitly either.

ALTER TABLE

Just as a new base table can be created at any time, via CREATE TABLE, so an existing base table can be *altered* at any time by the addition of a new column at the right, via ALTER TABLE:

```
ALTER TABLE base-table
        ADD column data-type [ NOT NULL WITH DEFAULT ] ;
```

For example:

```
ALTER TABLE S
      ADD DISCOUNT SMALLINT ;
```

This statement adds a DISCOUNT column to the S table. All existing S rows are extended from four columns to five; the value of the new fifth column is null in every case (it would have been zero if NOT NULL WITH DEFAULT had been specified; note that the unqualified specification NOT NULL—i.e., with the further specification WITH DEFAULT omitted—is not allowed in ALTER TABLE). Note also, incidentally, that the expansion of existing rows just described is not physically performed at the time the ALTER TABLE is executed; all that happens at that time is that the description of those rows in the catalog changes. Thereafter, for a given row in the ALTERed table:

1. The next time it is read from the disk, DB2 appends the additional null or nonnull default value before passing it to the user;
2. The next time it is written to the disk, DB2 writes the physically expanded version (unless the additional value is still null or the nonnull default value, in which case the expansion still does not occur).

But from the user's perspective, it is as if the rows *were* all physically expanded at ALTER TABLE time. There is no way to tell the difference.

ALTER TABLE also allows primary and foreign (but not alternate) key specifications to be added to or removed from a given base table (see Chapter 11). *Note:* Other types of alteration are possible also, but they are not nearly so important as the ones we have mentioned; we leave the details to the IBM manuals. Note in particular that ALTER TABLE does *not* support any kind of change to the width or data type of an existing column, and neither does it support the removal of an existing column.

DROP TABLE

An existing base table can be destroyed at any time by means of the DROP TABLE statement:

```
DROP TABLE base-table ;
```

The specified base table is removed from the system (more precisely, the description of that table is removed from the catalog). All indexes and views defined on that base table are automatically dropped also. (All foreign key specifications that refer to that base table are also automatically dropped. See Chapter 11.)

4.3 INDEXES

Like base tables, indexes are created and dropped using SQL data definition statements. However, CREATE INDEX and DROP INDEX (also ALTER INDEX and certain data control statements) are the *only* statements in the SQL language that refer to indexes at all; other statements—in particular, data manipulation statements such as SELECT—deliberately do not include any such references. The decision as to whether or not to use some particular index in responding to a particular SQL request is made not by the user but by DB2 (actually by the optimizer subcomponent of Bind), as explained in Chapter 2.

CREATE INDEX takes the general form:

```
CREATE [ UNIQUE ] INDEX index
     ON base-table ( column [ order ] [, column [ order ] ] ... )
     [ other parameters ] ;
```

The optional "other parameters" have to do with physical storage matters, as in CREATE TABLE. Each "order" specification is either ASC (ascending) or DESC (descending); if neither ASC nor DESC is specified, then ASC is assumed by default. The left-to-right sequence of naming columns in the CREATE INDEX statement corresponds to major-to-minor ordering in the usual way. For example, the statement

```
CREATE INDEX X ON T ( P, Q DESC, R ) ;
```

creates an index called X on (base) table T in which entries are ordered by ascending R-value within descending Q-value within ascending P-value. The columns P, Q, and R need not be contiguous, nor need they all be of the same data type, nor need they be all fixed length or all varying length.

Once created, an index is automatically maintained by the Data Manager to reflect updates on the table, until such time as the index is dropped.

The UNIQUE option in CREATE INDEX specifies that no two rows in the indexed base table will be allowed to take on the same value for the indexed column or column combination at the same time. In the case of the suppliers-and-parts database, for example, we would have to specify the following UNIQUE indexes in order to enforce uniqueness for the primary keys (see Chapter 11 for further discussion):

```
CREATE UNIQUE INDEX XS  ON S  ( S# ) ;
CREATE UNIQUE INDEX XP  ON P  ( P# ) ;
CREATE UNIQUE INDEX XSP ON SP ( S#, P# ) ;
```

Now DB2 will reject any attempt to introduce a duplicate value (via an INSERT or UPDATE operation) into column S.S# or column P.P# or the column combination SP.(S#,P#).

Indexes, like base tables, can be created and dropped at any time. Note, however, that an attempt to create a UNIQUE index on a nonempty table that already violates the uniqueness constraint will fail. Note also that (as mentioned in Section 3.6) two nulls are considered to be equal to each other for UNIQUE indexing purposes. Thus, if a given column has "nulls allowed" (i.e., if NOT NULL is not specified in the column definition), a UNIQUE index on that column will permit *at most one* null to appear in the column at any given time.

Any number of indexes can be built on a single base table. Here is another index for table S:

```
CREATE INDEX XSC ON S ( CITY ) ;
```

UNIQUE has not been specified in this case, because multiple suppliers can be located in the same city.

The statement to drop an index is

```
DROP INDEX index ;
```

The index is destroyed (i.e., its description is removed from the catalog). If an existing package depends on that dropped index, then, as explained in Chapter 2, that package will automatically be recompiled the next time it is invoked. Refer back to Chapter 2 if you need to refresh your memory regarding this process.*

4.4 DISCUSSION

The fact that data definition statements can be executed at any time makes DB2 a very flexible system. In older database products, prior to the

---

*Recall in particular from Chapter 2 that dropping an index may sometimes cause entire plans to be invalidated (and subsequently recompiled), not just individual packages.

advent of relational systems, the addition of a new type of object, such as a new type of record (row) or a new type of field (column) or a new index, was an operation not to be undertaken lightly: Typically it involved bringing the entire system to a halt*, unloading the database, revising and recompiling the database definition, and finally reloading the database in accordance with that revised definition. In such a system, it becomes highly desirable to get the database definition (and therefore, much more significantly, the database *design*) *complete* and *correct* once and for all, before starting to load and use the data—which means that

(a) the job of getting the system installed and operational can quite literally take months or even years of highly specialized people's time, and

(b) once the system is running, it can be difficult and costly, perhaps prohibitively so, to remedy early design errors.

In DB2, by contrast, it is possible to create and load just a few base tables and then to start using those tables immediately. Later, new base tables and new columns can be added in a piecemeal fashion, without having any effect on existing users of the database. It is also possible to experiment with the effects of having or not having particular indexes, again without affecting existing users at all (other than in performance, of course). Moreover, as we shall see in Chapter 9, it is even possible under certain circumstances to rearrange the structure of the database—e.g., to move a column from one base table to another—and still not affect the logic of existing programs. In a nutshell, it is not necessary to go through the total database design process before any useful work can be done with the system, nor is it necessary to get everything right the first time. The system is *forgiving*.

Caveat: The foregoing should *not* be taken to mean that database design is unnecessary in a system like DB2. Of course database design is still needed. However:

- It doesn't all have to be done at once.
- It doesn't have to be perfect first time.
- Logical and physical design can be tackled separately.
- If requirements change, then the design can change too, in a comparatively painless manner.

---

*We remark in passing that many modern installations simply cannot afford to bring the system to a halt—they require nonstop (24-hour-a-day) operation. For such an installation, the comparative inflexibility of older systems is a major drawback, possibly a complete showstopper.

- Many new applications—typically small-scale applications, involving, for example, personal or departmental databases—become feasible in a system like DB2 that would simply never have been considered under an older (nonrelational) system, because those older systems were just too complicated to make such applications economically worthwhile (in particular, the upfront costs in those systems were prohibitive).

EXERCISES

4.1 Fig. 4.1 shows some sample data values for a database containing information concerning suppliers (S), parts (P), and projects (J). Suppliers, parts, and projects are uniquely identified by supplier number (S#), part number (P#), and project number (J#), respectively. The significance of an SPJ (shipment) row is that the specified supplier supplies the specified part to the specified project in the specified quantity (and the combination S#-P#-J# uniquely identifies such a row). Write a suitable set of CREATE TABLE statements for this database. *Note*: This database will be used in numerous exercises in subsequent chapters.

S

S#	SNAME	STATUS	CITY
S1	Smith	20	London
S2	Jones	10	Paris
S3	Blake	30	Paris
S4	Clark	20	London
S5	Adams	30	Athens

P

P#	PNAME	COLOR	WEIGHT	CITY
P1	Nut	Red	12	London
P2	Bolt	Green	17	Paris
P3	Screw	Blue	17	Rome
P4	Screw	Red	14	London
P5	Cam	Blue	12	Paris
P6	Cog	Red	19	London

J

J#	JNAME	CITY
J1	Sorter	Paris
J2	Punch	Rome
J3	Reader	Athens
J4	Console	Athens
J5	Collator	London
J6	Terminal	Oslo
J7	Tape	London

SPJ

S#	P#	J#	QTY
S1	P1	J1	200
S1	P1	J4	700
S2	P3	J1	400
S2	P3	J2	200
S2	P3	J3	200
S2	P3	J4	500
S2	P3	J5	600
S2	P3	J6	400
S2	P3	J7	800
S2	P5	J2	100
S3	P3	J1	200
S3	P4	J2	500
S4	P6	J3	300
S4	P6	J7	300
S5	P2	J2	200
S5	P2	J4	100
S5	P5	J5	500
S5	P5	J7	100
S5	P6	J2	200
S5	P1	J4	100
S5	P3	J4	200
S5	P4	J4	800
S5	P5	J4	400
S5	P6	J4	500

Fig. 4.1 The suppliers-parts-projects database

4.2 Write a set of CREATE INDEX statements for the database of Exercise 4.1 to enforce the required primary key uniqueness constraints.

4.3 What are the main advantages of indexes? What are the main disadvantages?

4.4 "Uniqueness" of a column or column combination is a logical property, but it is enforced in DB2 by means of an index, which is a physical construct. Discuss.

ANSWERS TO SELECTED EXERCISES

4.1 `CREATE TABLE S`
```
      ( S#        CHAR(5)    NOT NULL,
        SNAME     CHAR(20)   NOT NULL WITH DEFAULT,
        STATUS    SMALLINT   NOT NULL WITH DEFAULT,
        CITY      CHAR(15)   NOT NULL WITH DEFAULT,
      PRIMARY KEY ( S# ) ) ;

CREATE TABLE P
      ( P#        CHAR(6)    NOT NULL,
        PNAME     CHAR(20)   NOT NULL WITH DEFAULT,
        COLOR     CHAR(6)    NOT NULL WITH DEFAULT,
        WEIGHT    SMALLINT   NOT NULL WITH DEFAULT,
        CITY      CHAR(15)   NOT NULL WITH DEFAULT,
      PRIMARY KEY ( P# ) ) ;

CREATE TABLE J
      ( J#        CHAR(4)    NOT NULL,
        JNAME     CHAR(10)   NOT NULL WITH DEFAULT,
        CITY      CHAR(15)   NOT NULL WITH DEFAULT,
      PRIMARY KEY ( J# ) ) ;

CREATE TABLE SPJ
      ( S#        CHAR(5)    NOT NULL,
        P#        CHAR(6)    NOT NULL,
        J#        CHAR(4)    NOT NULL,
        QTY       INTEGER,
      PRIMARY KEY ( S#, P#, J# ) ) ;
```

Note: We allow column SPJ.QTY to accept nulls purely because it is required to do so by a later exercise—not for any really good reason.

4.2
```
CREATE UNIQUE INDEX SX   ON S   ( S# ) ;
CREATE UNIQUE INDEX PX   ON P   ( P# ) ;
CREATE UNIQUE INDEX JX   ON J   ( J# ) ;
CREATE UNIQUE INDEX SPJX ON SPJ ( S#, P#, J# ) ;
```

4.3 The advantages of indexes are as follows:

(a) They can speed up direct access based on a given value for the indexed column or column combination. Without the index, a sequential scan would be required.

(b) They can speed up sequential access based on the indexed column or column combination. Without the index, a sort would be required.

(c) In DB2 in particular, UNIQUE indexes serve to enforce uniqueness constraints (especially primary key uniqueness constraints).

The disadvantages are as follows:

(a) They take up space in the database. The space taken up by indexes can easily exceed that taken up by the data itself in a heavily indexed database.

(b) While an index may well speed up retrieval operations, it will at the same time slow down update operations. Any INSERT or DELETE on the indexed table or UPDATE on the indexed column or column combination will require an accompanying update on the index.

4.4 An unfortunate state of affairs. DB2 is not quite as data independent as it ought to be. (Of course, it is true that enforcement via an index will provide better performance on a large table than enforcement via a sequential scan would; however, (a) the index should not be *required*, and (b) it would be desirable to provide alternative "efficient" enforcement mechanisms, such as hashing, in addition.)

· 5 ·

Data Manipulation I: Retrieval Operations

5.1 INTRODUCTION

SQL provides four data manipulation statements: SELECT, INSERT, UPDATE, and DELETE. This chapter and the next are concerned with the SELECT statement; Chapter 7 is concerned with the other three statements. The aim in all three chapters is to be reasonably comprehensive but *not* to replace the relevant IBM manuals. As usual, all examples are based on the suppliers-and-parts database. Also, we assume until further notice that all statements are entered interactively; the special considerations that apply to embedded SQL are ignored until Chapter 12.

Note: Many of our examples, especially those in the next chapter, are quite complex. The reader should not infer that it is SQL itself that is complex. Rather, the point is that common operations are so simple in SQL (and indeed in most relational languages) that examples of such operations tend to be rather uninteresting, and do not illustrate the full power of the language. Of course, we do show some simple examples first (Section 5.2). Section 5.3 is concerned with a slightly more complicated—but extremely important—facility known as *join*.

5.2   SIMPLE QUERIES

We start with a simple example—the query "Get supplier numbers and status for suppliers in Paris," which can be expressed in SQL as follows:

```
SELECT S#, STATUS
FROM    S
WHERE   CITY = 'Paris' ;
```

Result:

S#	STATUS
S2	10
S3	30

The example illustrates the commonest form of the SQL SELECT statement—"*SELECT* specified values *FROM* a specified table *WHERE* some specified condition is true." Notice that the result of the query is another table—a table that is derived in some way from the given tables in the database. In other words, the user in a relational system like DB2 is always operating in the simple tabular framework, a very attractive feature of such systems.

The fact that, as just noted, the result of any query is another table is referred to as the *closure* property of relational systems, and it is very important. In general, a closed system is a collection (possibly infinite) of all objects of a certain type, say OBJS, and a corresponding collection of operators, say OPS, such that:

(a) The operators in OPS apply to the objects in OBJS, and

(b) The result of applying any such operator to any such object(s) is another object in OBJS.

The practical significance of this point (in the case of relations specifically) is as follows: Since the result of one SELECT operation is another relation, it is possible, at least in principle, to apply another SELECT operation to that result (provided, of course, that that result has been saved somewhere). It also means, again in principle, that SELECT operations can be nested. See Sections 6.2 and 7.2 and Chapter 9 for illustrations and further discussion of these points.

Incidentally, we could equally well have formulated the original query using *qualified column names* throughout:

```
SELECT S.S#, S.STATUS
FROM   S
WHERE  S.CITY = 'Paris' ;
```

The use of qualified names is often clearer, and sometimes essential, as we shall see in Section 5.3 and elsewhere.

For reference, we show below the general form of the SELECT statement (ignoring the possibility of UNION, which is discussed in the next chapter).

```
  SELECT [ ALL | DISTINCT ] scalar-expression(s)
  FROM   table(s)
[ WHERE  conditional-expression ]
[ GROUP  BY column(s) ]
[ HAVING conditional-expression ]
[ ORDER  BY column(s) ] ;
```

We now proceed to illustrate the major features of this statement by means of a rather lengthy series of examples. *Note*: The GROUP BY and HAVING clauses are discussed in Chapter 6. All of the remaining clauses are at least introduced in this chapter, though the more complex aspects of those clauses are also deferred to Chapter 6.

5.2.1 Simple Retrieval. Get part numbers for all parts supplied.

```
SELECT P#
FROM   SP ;
```

Result:

P#
P1
P2
P3
P4
P5
P6
P1
P2
P2
P2
P4
P5

Notice the duplication of part numbers in this result. DB2 does not eliminate duplicate rows from the result of a SELECT statement unless the user explicitly requests it to do so via the keyword DISTINCT, as in the next example.

5.2.2 Retrieval with Duplicate Elimination. Get part numbers for all parts supplied, with redundant duplicates eliminated.

```
SELECT DISTINCT P#
FROM    SP ;
```

Result:

P#
P1
P2
P3
P4
P5
P6

Note: It just so happens in this particular example that each row contains a single scalar value; the effect of the DISTINCT specification is therefore to eliminate duplicate *scalar values*. In general, however, DISTINCT means "eliminate duplicate *rows*." See Example 5.3.5 in the next section for an example of the use of DISTINCT with rows containing more than one scalar value.

The alternative to DISTINCT is ALL. ALL is assumed if neither DISTINCT nor ALL is specified explicitly.

5.2.3 Retrieval of Computed Values. For all parts, get the part number and the weight of the part in grams (part weights are given in table P in pounds).

```
SELECT P#, 'Weight in grams =', WEIGHT * 454
FROM    P ;
```

Result:

P#		
P1	Weight in grams =	5448
P2	Weight in grams =	7718
P3	Weight in grams =	7718
P4	Weight in grams =	6356
P5	Weight in grams =	5448
P6	Weight in grams =	8626

The SELECT clause (also the WHERE and HAVING clauses, q.v.) can include general scalar expressions, involving, e.g., scalar operators such as plus and minus and scalar functions such as SUBSTR, instead of or as well as simple column names. Note, however, that simple column names are the only SELECT-expressions that give rise to named columns in the result; all other result columns are unnamed, as the example illustrates.

*5.2.4 Simple Retrieval ("SELECT *").* Get full details of all suppliers.

```
SELECT *
FROM    S ;
```

Result: A copy of the entire S table.

The star or asterisk is shorthand for a list of all column names in the table(s) named in the FROM clause, in the left-to-right order in which those columns appear in the relevant table(s). The SELECT statement shown is thus equivalent to:

```
SELECT S#, SNAME, STATUS, CITY
FROM   S ;
```

The star notation is convenient for interactive queries, since it saves keystrokes. However, it is potentially dangerous in embedded SQL (i.e., SQL within an application program), because the meaning of "*" may change if the SELECT statement is recompiled and some definitional change has occurred in the interim. In this book we will use "SELECT *" only in contexts where it is safe to do so (basically ad hoc queries only), and we recommend that actual users of DB2 do likewise.

Incidentally, it is possible to qualify the "*" by the name of the relevant table. For example, the following is legal:

```
SELECT S.*
FROM   S ;
```

5.2.5 *Qualified Retrieval.*   Get supplier numbers for suppliers in Paris with status > 20.

```
SELECT S#
FROM   S
WHERE  CITY = 'Paris'
AND    STATUS > 20 ;
```

Result:

S#
S3

The *conditional expression* (or just *condition*) following WHERE can consist of a simple *comparison* (see Chapter 3 for a definition of this term), or it can consist of multiple comparisons and/or other kinds of conditional expressions all combined together using the Boolean operators AND, OR, and NOT, and parentheses if required to indicate a desired order of evaluation. Other kinds of condition are discussed in numerous subsequent examples.*

5.2.6 *Retrieval with Ordering.*   Get supplier numbers and status for suppliers in Paris, in descending order of status.

---

*The IBM manuals use the term "predicate" for what we are here calling conditions or conditional expressions.

```
SELECT  S#, STATUS
FROM    S
WHERE   CITY = 'Paris'
ORDER   BY STATUS DESC ;
```

Result:

S#	STATUS
S3	30
S2	10

In general, the result table is not guaranteed to be in any particular order. Here, however, the user has specified that the result is to be arranged in a particular sequence before being displayed. Ordering may be specified in the same manner as in CREATE INDEX (see Section 4.3)—that is, as

```
column [ order ] [, column [ order ] ] ...
```

where, as before, "order" is either ASC or DESC, and ASC is the default. Each "column" must identify a column of the *result table*. Thus, for example, the following is ILLEGAL:*

```
SELECT  S#
FROM    S
ORDER   BY CITY ;                        -- illegal !!!
```

It is also possible to identify columns in the ORDER BY clause by column *number* instead of column name—i.e., by the ordinal (left-to-right) position of the column in question within the result table. This feature makes it possible to order a result on the basis of a result column that does not have a name. For example, to order the result of Example 5.2.3 by ascending part number within ascending gram weight:

```
SELECT  P#, 'Weight in grams =', WEIGHT * 454
FROM    P
ORDER   BY 3, P# ;
```

The "3" refers to the third column of the result table. Result:

P#		
P1	Weight in grams =	5448
P5	Weight in grams =	5448
P4	Weight in grams =	6356
P2	Weight in grams =	7718
P3	Weight in grams =	7718
P6	Weight in grams =	8626

---

*Incidentally, note the *comment* in this example. SQL comments are permitted only if the Precompiler option STDSQL(86) is in effect (see Appendix E). They are introduced by a double hyphen and terminated by end-of-line. They can appear wherever a blank separator can appear.

5.2.7 Retrieval Using BETWEEN. Get parts whose weight is in the range 16 to 19 inclusive.

```
SELECT  P#, PNAME, COLOR, WEIGHT, CITY
FROM    P
WHERE   WEIGHT BETWEEN 16 AND 19 ;
```

Result:

P#	PNAME	COLOR	WEIGHT	CITY
P2	Bolt	Green	17	Paris
P3	Screw	Blue	17	Rome
P6	Cog	Red	19	London

The BETWEEN condition is really just shorthand for a condition involving two individual comparisons "ANDed" together. The foregoing SELECT statement is equivalent to the following:

```
SELECT  P#, PNAME, COLOR, WEIGHT, CITY
FROM    P
WHERE   WEIGHT >= 16
AND     WEIGHT <= 19 ;
```

NOT BETWEEN can also be specified—for example,

```
SELECT  P#, PNAME, COLOR, WEIGHT, CITY
FROM    P
WHERE   WEIGHT NOT BETWEEN 16 AND 19 ;
```

Result:

P#	PNAME	COLOR	WEIGHT	CITY
P1	Nut	Red	12	London
P4	Screw	Red	14	London
P5	Cam	Blue	12	Paris

Like the BETWEEN condition, the NOT BETWEEN condition can be regarded merely as shorthand for another condition that does not use NOT BETWEEN. *Exercise*: Show the "expanded form" of the foregoing example.

5.2.8 Retrieval Using IN. Get parts whose weight is any one of the following: 12, 16, 17.

```
SELECT  P#, PNAME, COLOR, WEIGHT, CITY
FROM    P
WHERE   WEIGHT IN ( 12, 16, 17 ) ;
```

Result:

P#	PNAME	COLOR	WEIGHT	CITY
P1	Nut	Red	12	London
P2	Bolt	Green	17	Paris
P3	Screw	Blue	17	Rome
P5	Cam	Blue	12	Paris

IN, like BETWEEN, is really just shorthand. An IN condition is logically equivalent to a condition involving a sequence of individual comparisons all "ORed" together. For example, the foregoing SELECT statement is equivalent to the following:

```
SELECT P#, PNAME, COLOR, WEIGHT, CITY
FROM   P
WHERE  WEIGHT = 12
OR     WEIGHT = 16
OR     WEIGHT = 17 ;
```

NOT IN is also available:

```
SELECT P#, PNAME, COLOR, WEIGHT, CITY
FROM   P
WHERE  WEIGHT NOT IN ( 12, 16, 17 ) ;
```

Result:

P#	PNAME	COLOR	WEIGHT	CITY
P4	Screw	Red	14	London
P6	Cog	Red	19	London

Like IN, NOT IN is really just shorthand. *Exercise*: Show the "expanded form" of the foregoing example.

5.2.9 Retrieval Using LIKE.   Get all parts whose names begin with the letter C.

```
SELECT P#, PNAME, COLOR, WEIGHT, CITY
FROM   P
WHERE  PNAME LIKE 'C%' ;
```

Result:

P#	PNAME	COLOR	WEIGHT	CITY
P5	Cam	Blue	12	Paris
P6	Cog	Red	19	London

Note, incidentally, that the following SELECT would have produced the same result:

```
SELECT P#, PNAME, COLOR, WEIGHT, CITY
FROM   P
WHERE  SUBSTR ( PNAME, 1, 1 ) = 'C' ;
```

However, not all LIKE conditions can be reformulated in terms of SUBSTR in this manner. In general, a LIKE condition takes the form

```
scalar-expression LIKE literal [ ESCAPE character ]
```

where "scalar-expression" represents a value of type string (CHARACTER, VARCHAR, GRAPHIC, or VARGRAPHIC), and "literal" must be of a compatible data type. For a given row, the condition evaluates to *true* if the specified value conforms to the pattern defined by "literal." Provided no

ESCAPE clause is specified, characters within "literal" are interpreted as follows:

- The _ character (break or underscore) stands for *any single character.*
- The % character (percent) stands for *any sequence of n characters* (where *n* may be zero).
- All other characters simply stand for themselves.

In the example, therefore, the SELECT statement will retrieve rows from table P for which the PNAME value begins with the letter C and has any sequence of zero or more characters following that C.

Here are some more examples of LIKE:

`ADDRESS LIKE '%Berkeley%'`	— will evaluate to *true* if ADDRESS contains the string 'Berkeley' anywhere inside it
`S# LIKE 'S__'`	— will evaluate to *true* if S# is exactly 3 characters long and the 1st is an S
`PNAME LIKE '%c___'`	— will evaluate to *true* if PNAME is 4 characters long or more and the last but three is a c
`STRING LIKE '\_%'` `ESCAPE '\'`	— will evaluate to *true* if STRING begins with an underscore character (see below)

In this last example, the backslash character "\" has been specified as the escape character, which means that the special interpretation given to the literal characters "_" and "%" can be disabled if desired by preceding such characters with a backslash character.

NOT LIKE is also available. For example:

`CITY NOT LIKE '%E%'`	— will evaluate to *true* if CITY does not contain an E

5.2.10 Retrieval Involving NULL. Suppose for the sake of the example that column S.STATUS has "nulls allowed," and supplier S5 has a status of null, rather than 30. Get supplier numbers for suppliers with status greater than 25.

```
SELECT  S#
FROM    S
WHERE   STATUS > 25 ;
```

Result:

S#
S3

Supplier S5 does not qualify. As explained in Chapter 3, whenever one of the operands of a comparison is null, then, regardless of the comparison operator involved, the result of the comparison is *never* considered to be *true*—even if the other operand is also null. In other words, if STATUS happens to be null, then none of the following comparisons evaluates to *true*:*

```
STATUS >   25
STATUS <=  25
STATUS =   25
STATUS ¬=  25
STATUS =   NULL        -- This is illegal syntax. See below.
STATUS ¬=  NULL        -- So is this.
STATUS >   NULL        -- So is this.
STATUS <=  NULL        -- So is this.
```

Thus, if we issue the query

```
SELECT  S#
FROM    S
WHERE   STATUS <= 25 ;
```

and compare the result with that of the previous query, supplier S5 will not appear in either of them. The result is:

S#
S1
S2
S4

As mentioned in Chapter 3 (Section 3.6), a special comparison operator of the form

```
IS [ NOT ] NULL
```

is provided for testing for the presence [or absence] of nulls. For example:

```
SELECT  S#
FROM    S
WHERE   STATUS IS NULL ;
```

---

*As explained in Chapter 3, they all evaluate to the *unknown* truth value. The SELECT statement retrieves rows for which the WHERE condition evaluates to *true*, not to *false* and not to *unknown*.

Result:

S#
S5

Note that the syntax is "STATUS IS NULL," not "STATUS = NULL." The syntax "STATUS = NULL" is illegal, because *nothing*—not even null itself—is considered to be equal to null (in the context of a WHERE or HAVING clause).

We note in conclusion that it is not possible to SELECT NULL; that is, the symbol NULL is not allowed in a SELECT clause. For example, the following is ILLEGAL:

```
SELECT  P#, 'Weight =', NULL          -- illegal !!!
FROM    P
WHERE   WEIGHT IS NULL ;
```

5.3 JOIN QUERIES

The ability to "join" two or more tables is one of the most powerful features of relational systems. In fact, it is the availability of the join operation, almost more than anything else, that distinguishes relational from nonrelational systems (see Appendix A). So what is a join? Loosely speaking, it is *a query in which data is retrieved from more than one table.* Here is a simple example.

5.3.1 Simple Equijoin. Get all combinations of supplier and part information such that the supplier and part in question are located in the same city (i.e., are "colocated," to coin an ugly but convenient term).

```
SELECT  S.*, P.*
FROM    S, P
WHERE   S.CITY = P.CITY ;
```

Notice that the column references in the WHERE clause here *must* be qualified by the names of the containing tables (for otherwise they would be ambiguous). Result:

S#	SNAME	STATUS	S.CITY	P#	PNAME	COLOR	WEIGHT	P.CITY
S1	Smith	20	London	P1	Nut	Red	12	London
S1	Smith	20	London	P4	Screw	Red	14	London
S1	Smith	20	London	P6	Cog	Red	19	London
S2	Jones	10	Paris	P2	Bolt	Green	17	Paris
S2	Jones	10	Paris	P5	Cam	Blue	12	Paris
S3	Blake	30	Paris	P2	Bolt	Green	17	Paris
S3	Blake	30	Paris	P5	Cam	Blue	12	Paris
S4	Clark	20	London	P1	Nut	Red	12	London
S4	Clark	20	London	P4	Screw	Red	14	London
S4	Clark	20	London	P6	Cog	Red	19	London

We have shown the two CITY columns in this result explicitly as S.CITY and P.CITY, to avoid ambiguity.

Explanation: It is clear from the English language statement of the problem that the required data comes from two tables, namely S and P. In the SQL formulation of the query, therefore, we first name both those tables in the FROM clause, and we then express the connection between them (i.e., the fact that the CITY values must be equal) in the WHERE clause. To understand how this works, imagine yourself looking at two rows, one row from each of the two tables—say the two rows shown here:

S#	SNAME	STATUS	CITY		P#	PNAME	COLOR	WEIGHT	CITY
S1	Smith	20	London		P1	Nut	Red	12	London

▲ _____ identical _____ ▲

From these two rows you can see that supplier S1 and part P1 are indeed "colocated." These two rows will generate the result row

S#	SNAME	STATUS	S.CITY	P#	PNAME	COLOR	WEIGHT	P.CITY
S1	Smith	20	London	P1	Nut	Red	12	London

because they satisfy the condition in the WHERE clause (i.e., S.CITY = P.CITY). Similarly for all other pairs of rows having matching CITY values. Notice that supplier S5 (located in Athens) does not appear in the result, because there are no parts stored in Athens; likewise, part P3 (stored in Rome) also does not appear in the result, because there are no suppliers located in Rome.

The result of this query is said to be a *join* of tables S and P over matching CITY values. The term "join" is also used to refer to the operation of constructing such a result. The condition S.CITY = P.CITY is said to be a *join condition*.

A number of further points arise in connection with this example, some major, some minor.

- There is no requirement that the columns in a join condition be identically named, though they very often will be.

- There is no requirement that the comparison operator in a join condition be equality, though it very often will be. Examples of where it is not are given below (Example 5.3.2 and latter part of Example 5.3.6). If it is equality, then the join is called an *equijoin*.

- The WHERE clause in a join-SELECT can include other conditions in addition to the join condition itself. Example 5.3.3 below illustrates this possibility.

- It is of course possible to SELECT just specified columns from a join, instead of necessarily having to SELECT all of them. Examples 5.3.4–5.3.6 below illustrate this possibility.

- The expression

```
SELECT  S.*, P.*
FROM    S, P
  .....        ;
```

can be further abbreviated to simply

```
SELECT  *
FROM    S, P
  .....        ;
```

Alternatively, of course, it can be expanded to

```
SELECT  S#, SNAME, STATUS, S.CITY,
        P#, PNAME, COLOR, WEIGHT, P.CITY
FROM    S, P
  .....        ;
```

In this formulation, S.CITY and P.CITY in the SELECT clause *must* be referred to by their qualified names, as shown, because the unqualified name CITY would be ambiguous.

- The equijoin by definition must produce a result containing two identical columns. If one of those two columns is eliminated, what is left is called the *natural* join. To construct the natural join of S and P over cities in SQL, we could write:

```
SELECT  S#, SNAME, STATUS, S.CITY,        -- or P.CITY,
        P#, PNAME, COLOR, WEIGHT
FROM    S, P
WHERE   S.CITY = P.CITY ;
```

Natural join is far and away the single most useful form of join—so much so, that we often use the unqualified term "join" to refer to this case specifically.

- It is also possible to form a join of three, four, ..., or any number of tables. Example 5.3.5 below shows a join involving three tables.

- The following is an alternative (and helpful) way to think about how joins may conceptually be constructed. First, form the *Cartesian product* of the tables listed in the FROM clause. The Cartesian product of a set of *n* tables is the table consisting of all possible rows *r*, such that *r* is the concatenation of a row from the first table, a row from the second table, ..., and a row from the *n*th table. For example, the Cartesian product of table S and table P (in that order) is the following table (let us call it CP):

S#	SNAME	STATUS	S.CITY	P#	PNAME	COLOR	WEIGHT	P.CITY
S1	Smith	20	London	P1	Nut	Red	12	London
S1	Smith	20	London	P2	Bolt	Green	17	Paris
S1	Smith	20	London	P3	Screw	Blue	17	Rome
S1	Smith	20	London	P4	Screw	Red	14	London
S1	Smith	20	London	P5	Cam	Blue	12	Paris
S1	Smith	20	London	P6	Cog	Red	19	London
S2	Jones	10	Paris	P1	Nut	Red	12	London
.	.	.	.	.	.	.	.	.
.	.	.	.	.	.	.	.	.
.	.	.	.	.	.	.	.	.
S5	Adams	30	Athens	P6	Cog	Red	19	London

The complete table contains 5 * 6 = 30 rows.

Now eliminate from this Cartesian product all those rows that do not satisfy the join condition. What is left is the required join. In the case at hand, we eliminate from CP all those rows in which S.CITY is not equal to P.CITY; and what is left is exactly the join shown earlier.

By the way, it is perfectly possible (though perhaps unusual) to formulate a SQL query whose result is a Cartesian product. For example:

```
SELECT S.*, P.*
FROM   S, P ;
```

Result: Table CP as shown above.

5.3.2 Greater-Than Join.
Get all combinations of supplier and part information such that the supplier city follows the part city in alphabetical order.

```
SELECT S.*, P.*
FROM   S, P
WHERE  S.CITY > P.CITY ;
```

Result:

S#	SNAME	STATUS	S.CITY	P#	PNAME	COLOR	WEIGHT	P.CITY
S2	Jones	10	Paris	P1	Nut	Red	12	London
S2	Jones	10	Paris	P4	Screw	Red	14	London
S2	Jones	10	Paris	P6	Cog	Red	19	London
S3	Blake	30	Paris	P1	Nut	Red	12	London
S3	Blake	30	Paris	P4	Screw	Red	14	London
S3	Blake	30	Paris	P6	Cog	Red	19	London

5.3.3 Join Query with an Additional Condition. Get all combinations of supplier information and part information where the supplier and part concerned are colocated, but omitting suppliers with status 20.

```
SELECT  S.*, P.*
FROM    S, P
WHERE   S.CITY = P.CITY
AND     S.STATUS ¬= 20 ;
```

Result:

S#	SNAME	STATUS	S.CITY	P#	PNAME	COLOR	WEIGHT	P.CITY
S2	Jones	10	Paris	P2	Bolt	Green	17	Paris
S2	Jones	10	Paris	P5	Cam	Blue	12	Paris
S3	Blake	30	Paris	P2	Bolt	Green	17	Paris
S3	Blake	30	Paris	P5	Cam	Blue	12	Paris

5.3.4 Retrieving Specified Columns from a Join. Get all supplier-number/part-number combinations such that the supplier and part in question are colocated.

```
SELECT  S.S#, P.P#
FROM    S, P
WHERE   S.CITY = P.CITY ;
```

Result:

S#	P#
S1	P1
S1	P4
S1	P6
S2	P2
S2	P5
S3	P2
S3	P5
S4	P1
S4	P4
S4	P6

5.3.5 Join of Three Tables. Get all pairs of city names such that a supplier located in the first city supplies a part stored in the second city. For example, supplier S1 supplies part P1; supplier S1 is located in London, and part P1 is stored in London; so (London,London) is a pair of cities in the result.

```
SELECT  DISTINCT S.CITY, P.CITY
FROM    S, SP, P
WHERE   S.S# = SP.S#
AND     SP.P# = P.P# ;
```

Result:

S.CITY	P.CITY
London	London
London	Paris
London	Rome
Paris	London
Paris	Paris

As an exercise, the reader should decide which particular supplier/part combinations give rise to which particular result rows in this example.

5.3.6 *Joining a Table with Itself.*   Get all pairs of supplier numbers such that the two suppliers concerned are colocated.

```
SELECT FIRST.S#, SECOND.S#
FROM   S FIRST, S SECOND
WHERE  FIRST.CITY = SECOND.CITY ;
```

This query involves a join of table S with itself (over matching cities), as we now explain. Suppose for a moment that we had two separate copies of table S, the "first" copy and the "second" copy. Then the logic of the query is as follows: We need to be able to examine all possible pairs of supplier rows, one from the first copy of S and one from the second, and to retrieve the two supplier numbers from such a pair of rows when the city values are equal. We therefore need to be able to reference two supplier rows at the same time. In order to distinguish between the two references, we introduce two *range variables* FIRST and SECOND, each of which "ranges over" table S. At any particular time, FIRST represents some row from the "first" copy of table S, and SECOND represents some row from the "second" copy.* The result of the query is found by examining all possible pairs of FIRST/SECOND values and checking the WHERE condition in every case:

S#	S#
S1	S1
S1	S4
S2	S2
S2	S3
S3	S2
S3	S3
S4	S1
S4	S4
S5	S5

We can tidy up this result by extending the WHERE clause as follows:

---

*Of course, DB2 does not really construct two physical copies of the table. Our explanation is purely conceptual in nature. Note also that the IBM manuals use the term "correlation name" in place of the more orthodox (and more descriptive) term "range variable."

```
SELECT  FIRST.S#, SECOND.S#
FROM    S FIRST, S SECOND
WHERE   FIRST.CITY = SECOND.CITY
AND     FIRST.S# < SECOND.S# ;
```

The effect of the condition FIRST.S# < SECOND.S# is twofold: (a) It eliminates pairs of supplier numbers of the form (x,x); (b) it guarantees that the pairs (x,y) and (y,x) will not both appear. Result:

S#	S#
S1	S4
S2	S3

This is the first example we have seen in which the explicit use of range variables has been necessary. However, it is never wrong to introduce range variables, even when they are not explicitly required, and sometimes they can help to make the statement clearer. (They can also save writing, if table names are on the lengthy side.) In general, a range variable is a variable that ranges over some specified table—i.e., a variable whose only permitted values are the rows of that table. In other words, if range variable R ranges over table T, then, at any given time, R represents some row r of T. For example, the query "Get supplier number and status for suppliers in Paris" (the example from the beginning of Section 5.2) could be expressed as follows:

```
SELECT  SX.S#, SX.STATUS
FROM    S SX
WHERE   SX.CITY = 'Paris' ;
```

The range variable here is SX, and it ranges over table S. The SELECT statement can be paraphrased:

"For each possible value of the range variable SX, retrieve the S# and STATUS components of that value, if and only if the CITY component has the value Paris."

As a matter of fact, SQL *always* requires queries to be formulated in terms of range variables. If no such variables are specified explicitly, then SQL assumes the existence of *implicit* variables with the same name(s) as the corresponding table(s). For example, the query

```
SELECT  *
FROM    S ;
```

is treated by SQL as if it had been expressed as follows:

```
SELECT  S.*
FROM    S S ;
```

This latter formulation arguably makes it a little clearer that the symbol "S" in the expression "S.*" really means *range variable* S, not *table* S.

5.4 SUMMARY

We have now come to the end of the first of our two chapters on the SELECT statement. We have illustrated:

- The SELECT clause itself, including the use of general scalar expressions and "SELECT *"
- The use of DISTINCT to eliminate duplicate rows, including the use of DISTINCT with a join
- The FROM clause (with one or more tables), including the use of range variables
- The use of ORDER BY to order the result
- The WHERE clause, including:
  - simple comparisons
  - the Boolean operators AND, OR, NOT
  - the special operators [NOT] BETWEEN, [NOT] IN, [NOT] LIKE
  - the special operator IS [NOT] NULL
  - join conditions

In the next chapter we will consider some more complex features of the SELECT statement—to be specific, subqueries, the existential quantifier, quantified comparisons, aggregate functions, and the UNION operator.

EXERCISES

All of the following exercises are based on the suppliers-parts-projects database (see the exercises in Chapter 4). In each one, you are asked to write a SELECT statement for the indicated query. For convenience we repeat the structure of the database below:

```
S      ( S#, SNAME, STATUS, CITY )
       PRIMARY KEY ( S# )
P      ( P#, PNAME, COLOR, WEIGHT, CITY )
       PRIMARY KEY ( P# )
J      ( J#, JNAME, CITY )
       PRIMARY KEY ( J# )
SPJ    ( S#, P#, J#, QTY )
       PRIMARY KEY ( S#, P#, J# )
```

Simple Queries

5.1 Get full details of all projects.

5.2 Get full details of all projects in London.

5.3 Get supplier numbers for suppliers who supply project J1, in supplier number order.

5.4 Get all shipments where the quantity is in the range 300 to 750 inclusive.

5.5 Get a list of all part-color/part-city combinations, with duplicate color/city pairs eliminated.

5.6 Get all shipments where the quantity is nonnull.

5.7 Get project numbers and cities where the city has an "o" as the second letter of its name.

Joins

5.8 Get all supplier-number/part-number/project-number triples such that the indicated supplier, part, and project are all colocated.

5.9 Get all supplier-number/part-number/project-number triples such that the indicated supplier, part, and project are not colocated.

5.10 Get all supplier-number/part-number/project-number triples such that no two of the indicated supplier, part, and project are located in the same city.

5.11 Get part numbers for parts supplied by a supplier in London.

5.12 Get part numbers for parts supplied by a supplier in London to a project in London.

5.13 Get all pairs of city names such that a supplier in the first city supplies a project in the second city.

5.14 Get part numbers for parts supplied to any project by a supplier in the same city as that project.

5.15 Get project numbers for projects supplied by at least one supplier not in the same city.

5.16 Get all pairs of part numbers such that some supplier supplies both the indicated parts.

ANSWERS TO SELECTED EXERCISES

The following answers are not necessarily the only ones possible.

5.1
```
SELECT J#, JNAME, CITY
FROM   J ;
```

Or:
```
SELECT *
FROM   J ;
```

```
5.2   SELECT  J#, JNAME, CITY
      FROM    J
      WHERE   CITY = 'London' ;

Or:   SELECT  *
      FROM    J
      WHERE   CITY = 'London' ;

5.3   SELECT  DISTINCT S#
      FROM    SPJ
      WHERE   J# = 'J1'
      ORDER   BY S# ;

5.4   SELECT  S#, P#, J#, QTY
      FROM    SPJ
      WHERE   QTY >= 300
      AND     QTY <= 750 ;

Or:   SELECT  S#, P#, J#, QTY
      FROM    SPJ
      WHERE   QTY BETWEEN 300 AND 750 ;

5.5   SELECT  DISTINCT COLOR, CITY
      FROM    P ;

5.6   SELECT  S#, P#, J#, QTY
      FROM    SPJ
      WHERE   QTY IS NOT NULL ;
```

The foregoing is the "official" answer. However, the following will also work (why?):

```
      SELECT  S#, P#, J#, QTY
      FROM    SPJ
      WHERE   QTY = QTY ;

5.7   SELECT  J#, CITY
      FROM    J
      WHERE   CITY LIKE '_o%' ;

Or:   SELECT  J#, CITY
      FROM    J
      WHERE   SUBSTR ( CITY, 2, 1 ) = 'o' ;

5.8   SELECT  S#, P#, J#
      FROM    S, P, J
      WHERE   S.CITY = P.CITY
      AND     P.CITY = J.CITY ;

5.9   SELECT  S#, P#, J#
      FROM    S, P, J
      WHERE   NOT
              ( S.CITY = P.CITY AND P.CITY = J.CITY ) ;

Or:   SELECT  S#, P#, J#
      FROM    S, P, J
      WHERE   S.CITY ¬= P.CITY
      OR      P.CITY ¬= J.CITY ;

5.10  SELECT  S#, P#, J#
      FROM    S, P, J
      WHERE   S.CITY ¬= P.CITY
      AND     P.CITY ¬= J.CITY
      AND     J.CITY ¬= S.CITY ;
```

5.11 SELECT DISTINCT P#
```
     FROM    SPJ, S
     WHERE   SPJ.S# = S.S#
     AND     CITY = 'London' ;
```

5.12 SELECT DISTINCT P#
```
     FROM    SPJ, S, J
     WHERE   SPJ.S# = S.S#
     AND     SPJ.J# = J.J#
     AND     S.CITY = 'London'
     AND     J.CITY = 'London' ;
```

5.13 SELECT DISTINCT S.CITY, J.CITY
```
     FROM    S, SPJ, J
     WHERE   S.S# = SPJ.S#
     AND     SPJ.J# = J.J# ;
```

5.14 SELECT DISTINCT P#
```
     FROM    SPJ, S, J
     WHERE   SPJ.S# = S.S#
     AND     SPJ.J# = J.J#
     AND     S.CITY = J.CITY ;
```

5.15 SELECT DISTINCT J.J#
```
     FROM    SPJ, S, J
     WHERE   SPJ.S# = S.S#
     AND     SPJ.J# = J.J#
     AND     S.CITY ¬= J.CITY ;
```

5.16 SELECT SPJX.P#, SPJY.P#
```
     FROM    SPJ SPJX, SPJ SPJY
     WHERE   SPJX.S# = SPJY.S#
     AND     SPJX.P# > SPJY.P# ;
```

· **6** ·

Data Manipulation II: Retrieval Operations (continued)

6.1 INTRODUCTION

In this chapter we complete our treatment of the SQL SELECT statement. The plan of the chapter is as follows:

- Section 6.2 introduces the concept of *subqueries* or *nested SELECTs*. As a matter of historical interest, we remark that it was the fact that one SELECT could be nested inside another that was the original justification for the "Structured" in the name "Structured Query Language"; however, later additions to the language have made nested SELECTs per se very much less important than they used to be.

- Section 6.3 is concerned with the *existential quantifier* EXISTS, a feature that (in this writer's opinion) ranks with join as one of the most important and fundamental features of the entire SQL language—though not perhaps the most easy to understand.

- Section 6.4 describes the use of the so-called *quantified comparison operators* with subqueries.

- Section 6.5 discusses the *aggregate functions* COUNT, SUM, AVG, etc.; in particular, it describes the use of the GROUP BY and HAVING clauses in connection with those functions. *Note*: The official DB2 term for "aggregate function" is "column function."

- Section 6.6 discusses the UNION operator.

- Finally, in an attempt to tie together a number of the ideas introduced in this and the previous chapter, Section 6.7 presents an example of a very complex SELECT and shows in principle how that SELECT might be processed by DB2.

As you can see, the chapter is rather long, and you may wish to omit some of the more complicated portions on a first reading. However, you should read at least the first part of each section on your first pass through. One of the reasons for the length of the chapter is that SQL is a very redundant language, in the sense that it frequently provides several different ways of formulating the same query. Since we are trying to be reasonably comprehensive in our coverage of that language, the chapter necessarily contains a certain amount of redundancy also.

6.2 SUBQUERIES

In this section we discuss *subqueries* or *nested SELECTs*. Loosely speaking, a subquery is a SELECT–FROM–WHERE expression that is nested inside another such expression.* Subqueries are typically used to represent the set of values to be searched by means of an IN condition, as the following example illustrates.

6.2.1 Simple Subquery. Get supplier names for suppliers who supply part P2.

```
SELECT  SNAME
FROM    S
WHERE   S# IN
      ( SELECT  S#
        FROM    SP
        WHERE   P# = 'P2' ) ;
```

---

*A subquery can also include GROUP BY and HAVING clauses. ORDER BY and UNION are illegal, however.

Result:

SNAME
Smith
Jones
Blake
Clark

Explanation: The system evaluates the overall query—conceptually, at any rate—by evaluating the nested subquery first. That subquery returns the set of supplier *numbers* for suppliers who supply part P2, namely the set {S1,S2,S3,S4}. The original query is thus equivalent to the following simpler query:

```
SELECT  SNAME
FROM    S
WHERE   S# IN
        ( 'S1', 'S2', 'S3', 'S4' ) ;
```

Hence the result is as shown earlier.

The implicit name qualification in this example merits some additional discussion. Observe in particular that the "S#" to the left of the IN is implicitly qualified by "S", whereas the "S#" in the subquery is implicitly qualified by "SP". In general, the rules for determining the implicit qualifier for an unqualified column name are quite complex (they take up over a page and a half of the IBM manual!), but in essence they involve searching the FROM clauses one by one, starting with the one most immediately part of the query or subquery in which the unqualified reference appears and moving outward, and stopping as soon as a table name (or range variable name—see Examples 6.2.3–6.2.5 below) is found that has an associated column with the appropriate name.

In the example, this process works as follows. The fact that there are two unqualified references to "S#" (one to the left of the IN and one in the nested subquery) means that DB2 has to perform two separate searches. The first stops when it finds table S in the outer FROM clause; the second stops when it finds table SP in the FROM clause of the nested subquery. Thus the original query is equivalent to the following query (in which all assumed qualifications are shown explicitly):

```
SELECT  S.SNAME
FROM    S
WHERE   S.S# IN
        ( SELECT  SP.S#
          FROM    SP
          WHERE   SP.P# = 'P2' ) ;
```

It is always possible to override the implicit assumptions with explicit qualifications (see Examples 6.2.3–6.2.5 below). In fact, many people feel that explicit qualification should *always* be used, even when it is strictly unnecessary, simply as a matter of good discipline. A good rule of thumb is: When in doubt, qualify.

There is one more (important) point to make before we move on to our next subquery example: The original problem—"Get supplier names for suppliers who supply part P2"—can equally well be expressed as a *join* query, as follows:

```
SELECT  S.SNAME
FROM    S, SP
WHERE   S.S# = SP.S#
AND     SP.P# = 'P2' ;
```

Explanation: The join of S and SP over supplier numbers consists of a table of 12 rows (one for each row in SP), in which each row consists of the corresponding row from SP extended with SNAME, STATUS, and CITY values for the supplier identified by the S# value in that row. Of these twelve rows, four are for part P2; the final result is thus obtained by extracting the SNAME values from those four rows.

The two formulations of the original query—one using a subquery, one using a join—are equally correct. It is purely a matter of taste as to which formulation a given user might prefer. At least, this statement is true in principle; unfortunately, there is no guarantee that the two formulations will *perform* equally well. In fact, the IBM manuals suggest that the subquery formulation will almost never perform better than the join formulation and may very well perform worse, and hence that subqueries should generally be avoided. This fact is somewhat ironic, given that subqueries were the principal justification for the SQL language in the first place.

*6.2.2 **Subquery with Multiple Levels of Nesting.***   Get supplier names for suppliers who supply at least one red part.

```
SELECT  SNAME
FROM    S
WHERE   S# IN
      ( SELECT  S#
        FROM    SP
        WHERE   P# IN
              ( SELECT  P#
                FROM    P
                WHERE   COLOR = 'Red' ) ) ;
```

Result:

SNAME
Smith
Jones
Clark

Explanation: The innermost subquery evaluates to the set {P1,P4,P6}. The next outermost subquery evaluates in turn to the set {S1,S2,S4}. Last, the outermost "subquery" evaluates to the final result shown. In general, subqueries can be nested to any depth.

To make sure you understand this example, try the following exercises:

(a) Rewrite the query with all name qualifications shown explicitly.

(b) Write an equivalent join formulation of the same query.

6.2.3   *Correlated Subquery*.   Get supplier names for suppliers who supply part P2 (same as Example 6.2.1).

We show another solution to this problem in order to illustrate another point.

```
SELECT  SNAME
FROM    S
WHERE   'P2' IN
      ( SELECT  P#
        FROM    SP
        WHERE   S# = S.S# ) ;
```

Explanation: In the last line here, the unqualified reference to S# is implicitly qualified by SP; the other reference is *explicitly* qualified by S. This example differs from the preceding ones in that the inner subquery cannot be evaluated once and for all before the outer query is evaluated, because that inner subquery depends on a *variable*, namely S.S#, whose value changes as the system examines different rows of table S. Conceptually, therefore, evaluation proceeds as follows:

(a) The system examines some row of table S; let us suppose this is the row for S1. The variable S.S# thus currently has the value S1, so the system evaluates the inner subquery

```
    ( SELECT  P#
      FROM    SP
      WHERE   S# = 'S1' )
```

to obtain the set {P1,P2,P3,P4,P5,P6}. Now it can complete its processing for S1; it will select the SNAME value for S1, namely Smith, if and only if P2 is in this set (which of course it is).

(b) Next the system moves on to repeat this kind of processing for another row of table S, and so on, until all such rows have been dealt with.

A subquery such as the one in this example is said to be a *correlated* subquery. A correlated subquery is one whose value depends upon some variable that receives its value in some outer query; such a subquery therefore has to be evaluated repeatedly (once for each value of the variable in question), instead of once and for all. We show another example of a correlated subquery below (Example 6.2.5); several further examples are given in Sections 6.3–6.5.

Some people like to use explicit range variables in conjunction with correlated subqueries, in order to make the correlation clearer (see Example 5.3.6 in Chapter 5 if you need to refresh your memory concerning range variables). For example:

```
SELECT  SX.SNAME
FROM    S SX
WHERE   'P2' IN
      ( SELECT P#
        FROM    SP
        WHERE   S# = SX.S# ) ;
```

The range variable in this example is SX, introduced in the FROM clause and then used as an explicit qualifier in the WHERE clause in the subquery (and in the outer SELECT clause). The operation of the overall statement can now be more clearly (and more accurately) explained as follows:

- SX is a variable that ranges over the rows of table S (i.e., a variable that, at any given time, represents some row of table S).
- For each possible value of SX in turn, do the following:
  1. evaluate the subquery to obtain a set, *p* say, of part numbers;
  2. add the current value of SX.SNAME to the overall result set, if and only if P2 is in the set *p*.

In the previous version of this query, the symbol "S" was really performing two different functions: It stood for the suppliers base table itself (of course), and it also stood for a variable that ranged over the rows of that base table. As already stated, many people find it clearer to use two different symbols to distinguish between the two different functions.

It is never wrong to introduce a range variable, and sometimes it is essential (see Example 6.2.5 below).

6.2.4 Subquery and Outer Query Referring to Same Table.   Get supplier numbers for suppliers who supply at least one part supplied by supplier S2.

```
SELECT  DISTINCT S#
FROM    SP
WHERE   P# IN
      ( SELECT P#
        FROM    SP
        WHERE   S# = 'S2' ) ;
```

Result:

S#
S1
S2
S3
S4

Notice here that references to SP in the subquery do not mean the same thing as references to SP in the outer query. The two SP's are really *two different variables*. Explicit range variables can be used to make this fact explicit:

```
SELECT DISTINCT SPX.S#
FROM    SP SPX
WHERE   SPX.P# IN
      ( SELECT SPY.P#
        FROM    SP SPY
        WHERE   SPY.S# = 'S2' ) ;
```

Equivalent join query:

```
SELECT DISTINCT SPX.S#
FROM    SP SPX, SP SPY
WHERE   SPX.P# = SPY.P#
AND     SPY.S# = 'S2' ;
```

Notice that at least one explicit range variable *must* be introduced in this latter formulation (why?).

6.2.5 Correlated Subquery and Outer Query Referring to Same Table.

Get part numbers for all parts supplied by more than one supplier. (Another solution to this problem is given later as Example 6.5.9.)

```
SELECT DISTINCT SPX.P#
FROM    SP SPX
WHERE   SPX.P# IN
      ( SELECT SPY.P#
        FROM    SP SPY
        WHERE   SPY.S# ¬= SPX.S# ) ;
```

Result:

P#
P1
P2
P4
P5

The operation of this query can be explained as follows: "For each row in turn, say SPX, of table SP, extract the P# value, if and only if that P# value appears in some row, say SPY, of table SP whose S# value is *not* equal to the S# value in row SPX." Note again that at least one explicit range variable *must* be used in this query.

6.2.6 Subquery with Scalar Comparison Operator.

Get supplier numbers for suppliers who are located in the same city as supplier S1.

```
SELECT  S#
FROM    S
WHERE   CITY =
        ( SELECT CITY
          FROM    S
          WHERE   S# = 'S1' ) ;
```

Result:

S#
S1
S4

Sometimes the user may know that a given subquery should return exactly one value, as in this example. In such a case a simple scalar comparison operator (such as =, >, etc.) can be used in place of the more usual IN. However, an error will occur if the subquery in fact returns more than one value and IN has not been used. An error will *not* occur if the subquery returns no values at all; instead, the comparison is treated exactly as if the subquery had returned a null.* In other words, if *x* is a scalar variable, then the comparison

```
x   scalar-comparison-operator ( subquery )
```

(where "subquery" returns an empty set) evaluates, not to *true* or *false*, but to the *unknown* truth value. See Chapter 5, Example 5.2.10, and Chapter 3 for more discussion of the unknown truth value.

Note, incidentally, that the comparison in the foregoing example must be written as shown, with the subquery following the comparison operator. In other words, the following is ILLEGAL:

```
SELECT  S#
FROM    S
WHERE  (SELECT CITY
        FROM    S
        WHERE   S# = 'S1') = CITY ;            -- illegal !!!
```

Note also that, although subqueries in general can include GROUP BY and HAVING clauses (see Section 6.5), those clauses are not permitted when the subquery appears in conjunction with a simple scalar comparison operator such as =, >, etc.

6.3 THE EXISTENTIAL QUANTIFIER

6.3.1 Query Using EXISTS.   Get supplier names for suppliers who supply part P2 (same as Examples 6.2.1 and 6.2.3).

---

*This *is* the way SQL works, even though the treatment is logically incorrect.

```
SELECT  SNAME
FROM    S
WHERE   EXISTS
      ( SELECT  *
        FROM    SP
        WHERE   S# = S.S#
        AND     P# = 'P2' ) ;
```

Explanation: EXISTS here represents the *existential quantifier,* a notion borrowed from formal logic. Let *x* be some arbitrary variable. In logic, then, the *existentially quantified condition*

```
EXISTS x ( condition-involving-x )
```

evaluates to *true* if and only if "condition-involving-*x*" evaluates to *true* for some value of the variable *x*. For example, suppose *x* stands for any integer in the range 1 to 10 (i.e., *x* ranges over the set of integers from 1 to 10). Then the expression

```
EXISTS x ( x < 5 )
```

evaluates to *true*. By contrast, the expression

```
EXISTS x ( x < 0 )
```

evaluates to *false*.

In SQL, an existentially quantified condition is represented by an expression of the form "EXISTS (SELECT . . . FROM . . .)". Such an expression evaluates to *true* if and only if the result of evaluating the subquery represented by the "SELECT . . . FROM . . ." is nonempty—in other words, if and only if there exists a row in the FROM table of the subquery satisfying the WHERE condition of that subquery. (In practice, that subquery will almost certainly be of the correlated variety.)

To see how this works out in the example at hand, consider each SNAME value in turn and see whether it causes the existence test to evaluate to *true*. Suppose the first SNAME value is Smith, so that the corresponding S# value is S1. Is the set of SP rows having S# equal to S1 and P# equal to P2 empty? If the answer is no, then there exists an SP row with S# equal to S1 and P# equal to P2, and so Smith should be one of the values retrieved. Similarly for each of the other SNAME values.

Although this first example merely shows another way of formulating a query for a problem that we already know how to handle in SQL (using either join or IN), in general EXISTS is one of the most fundamental, and most important, features of the entire SQL language. In fact, any query that can be expressed using IN can alternatively be formulated using

EXISTS;* however, the converse is not true. See Example 6.3.3 below for an illustration.

Caveat: We have already said that EXISTS in SQL evaluates to *true* if its subquery argument returns a nonempty set. If instead that argument set is empty, it evaluates to *false*. Note, therefore, that it never returns the *unknown* truth value. In other words, EXISTS in SQL is not a faithful representation of the existential quantifier of formal logic (more precisely, formal logic with nulls—i.e., three-valued logic, as briefly described in Chapter 3). As a consequence, EXISTS in SQL needs to be treated with a considerable degree of circumspection—for otherwise it is, regrettably, all too easy to misinterpret queries and results, and hence to make *wrong business decisions*. The details are beyond the scope of this text; suffice it to say that everything works correctly so long as there are no nulls involved, a fact that in itself is an eloquent argument in favor of avoiding nulls altogether (as already suggested in Section 3.6). See the book *Relational Database Writings 1985-1989*, by C. J. Date (Addison-Wesley, 1990) for explanations and further discussion.

6.3.2   Query Using NOT EXISTS.   Get supplier names for suppliers who do not supply part P2 (inverse of Example 6.3.1).

```
SELECT  SNAME
FROM    S
WHERE   NOT EXISTS
      ( SELECT  *
        FROM    SP
        WHERE   S# = S.S#
        AND     P# = 'P2' ) ;
```

Result:

SNAME
Adams

The query may be paraphrased: "Select supplier names for suppliers such that there does not exist a shipment relating them to part P2." Notice how easy it is to convert the solution to the previous problem (Example 6.3.1) into this solution.

Incidentally, the parenthesized subquery in an EXISTS expression does not necessarily have to involve the "SELECT *" form of SELECT; it may, for example, be of the form "SELECT column . . .". In practice, however, it very often will be of the "SELECT *" form, as our examples have already suggested.

---

*Except for the caveat in the paragraph immediately following.

6.3.3 *Query Using NOT EXISTS.* Get supplier names for suppliers who supply all parts.

There are two quantifiers commonly encountered in logic, EXISTS and *FORALL*. FORALL is the *universal* quantifier. In logic, the *universally quantified condition*

```
FORALL x ( condition-involving-x )
```

evaluates to *true* if and only if "condition-involving-*x*" evaluates to *true* for all values of the variable *x*. For example, if (again) the variable *x* stands for any integer in the range 1 to 10, then the expression

```
FORALL x ( x < 100 )
```

evaluates to *true*, whereas the expression

```
FORALL x ( x < 5 )
```

evaluates to *false*.

FORALL is fundamentally what is needed to express the query at hand; what we would like to say is something like "Select supplier names where, FORALL parts, there EXISTS a shipment saying that the supplier supplies the part." Unfortunately, SQL does not directly support FORALL. However, any condition involving FORALL can always be converted into an equivalent condition involving EXISTS instead, by virtue of the following identity:

```
FORALL x ( p )  ≡  NOT ( EXISTS x ( NOT ( p ) ) )
```

Here *p* is any condition involving the variable *x*. For example, suppose once again that *x* stands for any integer in the range 1 to 10. Then the expression

```
FORALL x ( x < 100 )
```

(which of course evaluates to *true*) is equivalent to the expression

```
NOT ( EXISTS x ( NOT ( x < 100 ) ) )
```

("there does not exist an *x* such that it is not the case that *x* is less than 100"—i.e., "there is no *x* such that *x* is greater than or equal to 100"). Likewise, the expression

```
FORALL x ( x < 5 )
```

(which is *false*) is equivalent to the expression

```
NOT ( EXISTS x ( NOT ( x < 5 ) ) )
```

("there does not exist an *x* such that it is not the case that *x* is less than 5"—i.e., "there is no *x* such that *x* is greater than or equal to 5").

As another example, suppose the variables *x* and *y* represent real numbers. Then the expression

```
FORALL x ( EXISTS y ( y > x ) )
```

(which is *true*) is equivalent to

```
NOT ( EXISTS x ( NOT ( EXISTS y ( y > x ) ) ) )
```

("there is no real number *x* such that there is no real number *y* such that *y* is greater than *x*"). Incidentally, this example illustrates the important point that if the expression involves both FORALL and EXISTS, then the order of quantifiers matters. For consider: As we have just seen, the expression FORALL *x* (EXISTS *y* (*y* > *x*)) is *true*. However, the expression EXISTS *y* (FORALL *x* (*y* > *x*)) ("there is a real number *y* such that, for all real numbers *x*, *y* is greater than *x*"—i.e., "there exists a number greater than all other numbers"), which is obtained from the first expression by simply inverting the order of the quantifiers, is *false*.

Turning now to the problem at hand, we can convert the expression "Supplier names where, FORALL parts, there EXISTS a shipment saying that the supplier supplies the part" into the equivalent expression "Supplier names where NOT EXISTS a part such that NOT EXISTS a shipment saying that the supplier supplies the part." Hence the SQL formulation is:

```
SELECT  SNAME
FROM    S
WHERE   NOT EXISTS
      ( SELECT *
        FROM    P
        WHERE   NOT EXISTS
              ( SELECT *
                FROM    SP
                WHERE   S# = S.S#
                AND     P# = P.P# ) ) ;
```

Result:

SNAME
Smith

The query may be paraphrased: "Select supplier names for suppliers such that there does not exist a part that they do not supply." In general, the easiest way to tackle complicated queries such as this one is probably to write them in a "pseudoSQL" form with FORALL quantifiers first, and then convert them, more or less mechanically, into real SQL involving NOT EXISTS instead.

6.3.4 *Query Using NOT EXISTS.* Get supplier names for suppliers who supply at least all those parts supplied by supplier S2.

One way to tackle this rather complex problem is to break it down into a set of simpler problems and deal with them one at a time. Thus we can first discover the set of part numbers for parts supplied by supplier S2:

```
SELECT  P#
FROM    SP
WHERE   S# = 'S2' ;
```

Result:

P#
P1
P2

Using CREATE TABLE and INSERT (to be discussed in Chapter 7), it is possible to save this result in a table in the database, say table TEMP. Then we can go on to discover the set of supplier names for suppliers who supply all parts listed in TEMP (very much as in Example 6.3.3):

```
SELECT  SNAME
FROM    S
WHERE   NOT EXISTS
      ( SELECT *
        FROM    TEMP
        WHERE   NOT EXISTS
              ( SELECT *
                FROM    SP
                WHERE   SP.S# = S.S#
                AND     SP.P# = TEMP.P# ) ) ;
```

Result:

S#
S1
S2

Table TEMP can now be dropped.

It is often a good idea to handle complex queries in this step-at-a-time manner, for ease of understanding. However, it is also possible to express the entire query as a single SELECT, eliminating the need for TEMP entirely:

```
SELECT  SNAME
FROM    S
WHERE   NOT EXISTS
      ( SELECT *
        FROM    SP SPY
        WHERE   S# = 'S2'
        AND     NOT EXISTS
              ( SELECT *
                FROM    SP SPZ
                WHERE   SPZ.S# = S.S#
                AND     SPZ.P# = SPY.P# ) ) ;
```

6.3.5   Query Using Implication.   Get supplier names for suppliers who supply at least all those parts supplied by supplier S2 (same as previous example).

We use this example again to illustrate another very useful concept, that of *logical implication*. The original problem can be rephrased as follows: "Get supplier names for suppliers Sx (say) such that, FORALL parts Py, *IF* supplier S2 supplies part Py, *THEN* supplier Sx supplies part Py also." The expression

```
IF p THEN q
```

(where p and q are conditions) is a *logical implication condition*. It is defined to be equivalent to the expression

```
NOT ( p )   OR   q
```

In other words, the implication "IF p THEN q" (also read as "p IMPLIES q") is *false* if and only if q is *false* and p is *true*, as the truth table below indicates:

p	q	IF p THEN q
t	t	t
t	f	f
f	t	t
f	f	t

Note: The value of "IF p THEN q" if p or q is *unknown* is left as an exercise for the reader.

Many problems are very naturally expressed in English in terms of implication (see the exercises at the end of this chapter for several examples). SQL does not support implication directly, but the foregoing definition shows how any condition involving implication can easily be converted into another that does not. For example, let p be the condition "Supplier S2 supplies part Py," and let q be the condition "Supplier Sx supplies part Py." Then the condition

```
IF p THEN q
```

is equivalent to the condition

```
NOT ( supplier S2 supplies part Py )
OR  ( supplier Sx supplies part Py )
```

or, in SQL terms,

```
NOT EXISTS
  ( SELECT *
    FROM   SP SPY
    WHERE  SPY.S# = 'S2' )
```

```
OR  EXISTS
  ( SELECT *
    FROM    SP SPZ
    WHERE   SPZ.S# = Sx
    AND     SPZ.P# = SPY.P# )
```

Hence the condition

```
FORALL Py ( IF p THEN q )    ,
```

which is equivalent to

```
NOT EXISTS Py ( NOT ( IF p THEN q ) )    ,
```

that is, to

```
NOT EXISTS Py ( NOT ( NOT ( p ) OR q ) )    ,
```

becomes

```
NOT EXISTS Py ( p AND NOT ( q ) )    ,
```

or, in SQL terms,

```
NOT EXISTS
  ( SELECT *
    FROM    SP SPY
    WHERE   SPY.S# = 'S2'
    AND     NOT EXISTS
          ( SELECT *
            FROM    SP SPZ
            WHERE   SPZ.S# = Sx
            AND     SPZ.P# = SPY.P# ) )
```

Hence the overall query becomes

```
SELECT SNAME
FROM   S
WHERE  NOT EXISTS
      ( SELECT *
        FROM    SP SPY
        WHERE   SPY.S# = 'S2'
        AND     NOT EXISTS
              ( SELECT *
                FROM    SP SPZ
                WHERE   SPZ.S# = S.S#
                AND     SPZ.P# = SPY.P# ) ) ;
```

which is as shown before, under Example 6.3.4. Thus the notion of implication provides the basis for a systematic approach to a certain class of (rather complicated) queries and their conversion into an equivalent SQL form. Exercises 6.12–6.18 at the end of the chapter provide practice in that approach.

6.4   QUANTIFIED COMPARISONS

Note: We include this topic primarily for completeness. The fact is, the quantified comparison operators are almost—but unfortunately not quite—entirely superfluous; furthermore, they are confusing and (in this writer's opinion) dangerously error-prone, as we shall see.

A *quantified comparison* is a conditional expression of the form

```
comparand  quantified-comparison-operator  ( subquery )
```

where the "quantified-comparison-operator" consists of a scalar comparison operator (=, ¬=, >, etc.) followed by either ANY or ALL.* Here is an example of the use of a quantified comparison.

6.4.1   Query Using Quantified Comparison.   Get part names for parts whose weight is greater than that of every blue part.

```
SELECT PNAME
FROM   P
WHERE  WEIGHT >ALL
     ( SELECT WEIGHT
       FROM   P
       WHERE  COLOR = 'Blue' ) ;
```

Result:

PNAME
Cog

Explanation: The nested subquery returns the set of weights for blue parts, namely the set {17,12}. The outer SELECT then returns the name of the only part whose weight is greater than every value in this set, namely part P6. In general, of course, the final result might contain any number of part names (including zero).

In general, the quantified comparison operators are defined as follows. We consider the ANY case first. Let the comparison be of the form

```
x  $ANY  ( SELECT y FROM ... )
```

where the symbol "$" stands for any one of the operators =, ¬=, < >, <, ¬<, > =, >, ¬>, or < =. Then the overall expression evaluates to *true* if the expression

```
x  $  ( y )
```

---

*For reasons of compatibility with the SQL standard, DB2 allows SOME as an alternative spelling for ANY.

evaluates to *true* for at least one value *y* in the result of evaluating the parenthesized subquery; it evaluates to *false* if the expression

```
x   $   ( y )
```

evaluates to *false* for every value *y* in the result of evaluating that subquery (or if that result is empty); and it evaluates to *unknown* otherwise. *Note*: The reader may already have realized that the IN operator that we discussed in some detail in Section 6.2 is in fact a quantified comparison operator; indeed, it is just a different spelling for =ANY.

Now the ALL case. The expression

```
x   $ALL   ( SELECT y FROM ... )
```

evaluates to *true* if the expression

```
x   $   ( y )
```

evaluates to *true* for every value *y* in the result of evaluating the parenthesized subquery (or if that result is empty); it evaluates to *false* if the expression

```
x   $   ( y )
```

evaluates to *false* for at least one value *y* in the result of evaluating that subquery; and it evaluates to *unknown* otherwise.

To return for a moment to the example ("Get part names for parts whose weight is greater than that of every blue part"): Here is another candidate SQL formulation of the query.

```
SELECT  PNAME
FROM    P PX
WHERE   NOT EXISTS
      ( SELECT *
        FROM    P
        WHERE   COLOR = 'Blue'
        AND     WEIGHT > PX.WEIGHT ) ;
```

("get part names for parts such that there does not exist a blue part with a greater weight"). On the face of it, this alternative formulation looks as if it should be logically equivalent to the previous one (involving >ALL), and indeed so it is, *unless* both of the following are true: (a) There exists at least one blue part with a null weight; (b) there does not exist a blue part with a nonnull weight. Unfortunately, if conditions (a) and (b) both apply, we fall foul once again of the fact that EXISTS in SQL is not a faithful representation of the existential quantifier of three-valued logic. Once again, the details are beyond the scope of this text (though the reader might like to work out what happens in the case at hand under the two formulations); suffice it to say (once again) that everything works correctly so long as there are no nulls involved.

The next example shows why the foregoing lack of true equivalence between the two candidate formulations is so unfortunate.

6.4.2 Query Using Quantified Comparison.   Get supplier numbers for suppliers whose city is not equal to any part city. *Warning*: The following "solution" is INCORRECT.

```
SELECT S#
FROM    S
WHERE   CITY  ¬=ANY                  -- incorrect !!!
      ( SELECT CITY
        FROM    P ) ;
```

Result:

S#
S1
S2
S3
S4
S5

In other words, the SELECT statement shown does *not* select supplier numbers for suppliers whose city is "not equal to any" part city. Refer back to the definition of the quantified comparison operators if you do not see why! The problem is, of course, that the natural intuitive interpretation of ¬=ANY as "not equal to any" is both incorrect and very misleading— or, to put it another way, "any" in an expression such as "not equal to any" would usually be taken to mean *all*, in colloquial English.* The "equivalent" EXISTS formulation makes the correct interpretation clear:

```
SELECT S#
FROM    S
WHERE   EXISTS
      ( SELECT P.CITY
        FROM    P
        WHERE   P.CITY  ¬= S.CITY ) ;
```

("select supplier numbers for suppliers such that there exists some part city that is different from the supplier city"). The trouble is, of course, that the EXISTS formulation is *not* guaranteed to be equivalent to the ¬=ANY formulation in the presence of nulls. The moral is obvious: If you decide to avoid nulls, then you can ignore the quantified comparison operators entirely, always using EXISTS formulations instead.

To close this section, here is a correct formulation of the original query

---

*Analogous criticisms apply to every one of the ANY and ALL operators, of course.

("Get supplier numbers for suppliers whose city is not equal to any part city"):

```
SELECT S#
FROM   S
WHERE  CITY ¬=ALL
     ( SELECT CITY
       FROM    P ) ;
```

Result:

"Equivalent" EXISTS formulation:

```
SELECT S#
FROM   S
WHERE  NOT EXISTS
     ( SELECT P.CITY
       FROM    P
       WHERE   P.CITY = S.CITY ) ;
```

6.5 AGGREGATE FUNCTIONS

Although quite powerful in many ways, the SELECT statement as so far described is still inadequate for many practical problems. For example, even a query as simple as "How many suppliers are there?" cannot be expressed using only the constructs introduced up till now. SQL therefore provides a number of special *aggregate* (or *column*) *functions* to enhance its basic retrieval power. The aggregate functions currently available are COUNT, SUM, AVG, MAX, and MIN.* Apart from the special case of "COUNT(*)" (see below), each of these functions operates on the collection of scalar values in one column of some table—possibly (in fact, probably) a *derived* table, i.e., a table constructed in some way from the given base tables—and produces a single scalar value, defined as follows, as its result:

COUNT — number of values in the column

SUM   — sum of the values in the column

AVG   — average of the values in the column

---

*EXISTS is also considered as an aggregate function, but it differs from the functions discussed in the present section in that it returns a truth value (*true* or *false*), not a value of one of the recognized DB2 data types—i.e., it is not a *computational* function (so far as SQL is concerned). EXISTS also differs from the other aggregate functions in that it uses a different syntactic style (actually a more logical style).

MAX   — largest value in the column

MIN   — smallest value in the column

For SUM and AVG, the argument must be numeric. In general, the argument may optionally be preceded by the keyword DISTINCT, to indicate that redundant duplicate values are to be eliminated before the function is applied (the alternative to DISTINCT is ALL; ALL is assumed if neither DISTINCT nor ALL is specified explicitly). For MAX and MIN, however, DISTINCT is irrelevant and should be omitted.

Aggregate functions are unfortunately subject to numerous rules and restrictions, as follows:

1. For COUNT, DISTINCT *must* be specified; the special function COUNT(*)—DISTINCT not allowed—is provided to count all rows in a table without any duplicate elimination.

2. Regardless of whether DISTINCT is specified, the argument may consist of a general scalar expression such as WEIGHT * 454. However, that expression cannot in turn involve any aggregate functions.

3. Within any given query or subquery, DISTINCT can appear at most once at a given level of nesting (i.e., excluding any subqueries that may appear nested within the given query or subquery). For example, the following is ILLEGAL:

```
SELECT SUM ( DISTINCT QTY ),
       AVG ( DISTINCT QTY )            -- illegal !!!
FROM   SP
.....  ;
```

and so is this:

```
SELECT DISTINCT ...                    -- illegal !!!
FROM   ...
GROUP  BY ...
HAVING SUM ( DISTINCT ... ) ... ;
```

However, the following is legal:

```
SELECT DISTINCT ...
FROM   ...
WHERE  ... IN
     ( SELECT DISTINCT ...
       .....   ) ;
```

4. Any nulls in the argument column are always eliminated before the function is applied, regardless of whether DISTINCT is specified, *except* for the case of COUNT(*), where nulls are handled just like non-null values. *Note*: The scalar function VALUE (see Section 3.6) can be

used to convert nulls into nonnull values, if desired, before the aggregate function is applied.

5. If the argument happens to be an empty set, COUNT returns a value of zero; the other functions all return null. Again, the VALUE function can be used to convert such a null into some nonnull value.

Now for some specific examples of the use of aggregate functions.

6.5.1 Aggregate Function in the SELECT Clause. Get the total number of suppliers.

```
SELECT  COUNT(*)
FROM    S ;
```

Result:

5

Note that the result is still a table, but a table with just one row and one (unnamed) column.

6.5.2 Aggregate Function in the SELECT Clause, with DISTINCT. Get the total number of suppliers currently supplying parts.

```
SELECT  COUNT (DISTINCT S#)
FROM    SP ;
```

Result:

4

6.5.3 Aggregate Function in the SELECT Clause, with a Condition. Get the number of shipments for part P2.

```
SELECT  COUNT(*)
FROM    SP
WHERE   P# = 'P2' ;
```

Result:

4

6.5.4 Aggregate Function in the SELECT Clause, with a Condition. Get the total quantity of part P2 supplied.

```
SELECT  SUM (QTY)
FROM    SP
WHERE   P# = 'P2' ;
```

Result:

1000

Note: Unless the query includes a GROUP BY or HAVING clause (at the same level of nesting), a SELECT clause that includes any aggregate function references must consist *entirely* of such references. Thus, for example, the following is ILLEGAL:

```
SELECT P#, SUM (QTY)                -- illegal !!!
FROM    SP
WHERE   P# = 'P2' ;
```

See Examples 6.5.7–6.5.9 below for an explanation of the GROUP BY and HAVING clauses.

6.5.5 *Aggregate Function in a Subquery.*
Get supplier numbers for suppliers with status value less than the current maximum status value in the S table.

```
SELECT S#
FROM    S
WHERE   STATUS <
      ( SELECT MAX (STATUS)
        FROM    S ) ;
```

Result:

S#
S1
S2
S4

6.5.6 *Aggregate Function in Correlated Subquery.*
Get supplier number, status, and city for all suppliers whose status is greater than or equal to the average for their particular city.

```
SELECT S#, STATUS, CITY
FROM    S SX
WHERE   STATUS >=
      ( SELECT AVG (STATUS)
        FROM    S SY
        WHERE   SY.CITY = SX.CITY ) ;
```

Result:

S#	STATUS	CITY
S1	20	London
S3	30	Paris
S4	20	London
S5	30	Athens

It is not possible to include the average status for each city in this result (why not?).

6.5.7 *Use of GROUP BY.* Example 6.5.6 showed how it is possible to compute the total quantity supplied for some specific part. Suppose, by contrast, that it is desired to compute the total quantity supplied for *each* part: i.e., for each part supplied, get the part number and the total shipment quantity for that part.

```
SELECT  P#, SUM (QTY)
FROM    SP
GROUP   BY P# ;
```

Result:

P#	
P1	600
P2	1000
P3	400
P4	500
P5	500
P6	100

Explanation: The GROUP BY operator causes the table represented by the FROM clause to be rearranged into partitions or *groups*, such that within any one group all rows have the same value for the GROUP BY column.* In the example, table SP is grouped so that one group contains all the rows for part P1, another contains all the rows for part P2, and so on. The SELECT clause is then applied to each group of the partitioned table (rather than to each row of the original table). Each expression in the SELECT clause must be *single-valued per group*; e.g., it can be (one of) the column(s) named in the GROUP BY clause, or a literal, or an aggregate function such as SUM that operates on all values of a given column within a group and reduces those values to a single value.

Note that GROUP BY does not imply ORDER BY; to guarantee that the result in the foregoing example appears in P# order, the clause ORDER BY P# would have to be specified as well (after the GROUP BY clause).

A table can be grouped by any combination of its columns. See Section 6.7 for an illustration of grouping over more than one column.

6.5.8 *Use of WHERE with GROUP BY.* For each part supplied, get the part number and the total and maximum quantity supplied of that part, excluding shipments from supplier S1.

```
SELECT  P#, SUM (QTY), MAX (QTY)
FROM    SP
WHERE   S# ¬= 'S1'
GROUP   BY P# ;
```

---

*Of course, this does not mean that the table is physically rearranged in the database. Our explanation is purely conceptual in nature.

Result:

P#		
P1	300	300
P2	800	400
P4	300	300
P5	400	400

Rows that do not satisfy the WHERE clause are eliminated before any grouping is done.

6.5.9 Use of HAVING.   Get part numbers for all parts supplied by more than one supplier (same as Example 6.2.5).

```
SELECT  P#
FROM    SP
GROUP   BY P#
HAVING  COUNT(*) > 1 ;
```

Result:

P#
P1
P2
P4
P5

HAVING is to groups what WHERE is to rows; thus, if HAVING is specified, GROUP BY should have been specified also.* In other words, HAVING is used to eliminate groups just as WHERE is used to eliminate rows. Comparands in a HAVING clause must be single-valued per group; in practice, such comparands will almost always involve aggregate functions, as in the example above (note that such comparands are not legal in a WHERE clause).

We have already shown (in Example 6.2.5) that this query can be formulated without GROUP BY (and without HAVING), using a correlated subquery. However, the formulation of Example 6.2.5 is really based on a somewhat different perception of the logic involved in answering the question. It is also possible to formulate a query using essentially the *same* logic as in the GROUP-BY/HAVING version, but without making explicit use of GROUP BY and HAVING at all:

```
SELECT  DISTINCT P#
FROM    SP SPX
WHERE   1 <
        ( SELECT  COUNT(*)
          FROM    SP SPY
          WHERE   SPY.P# = SPX.P# ) ;
```

---

*Actually it is possible—though very unusual—to omit the GROUP BY, in which case the entire table is treated as a single group.

The following version (using table P in place of SPX) may perhaps be clearer:

```
SELECT  P#
FROM    P
WHERE   1 <
        ( SELECT  COUNT (S#)
          FROM    SP
          WHERE   P# = P.P# ) ;
```

Yet another formulation uses EXISTS, as follows:

```
SELECT  P#
FROM    P
WHERE   EXISTS
        ( SELECT *
          FROM    SP SPX
          WHERE   SPX.P# = P.P#
          AND     EXISTS
                  ( SELECT *
                    FROM    SP SPY
                    WHERE   SPY.P# = P.P#
                    AND     SPY.S# ¬= SPX.S# ) ) ;
```

All of these alternative versions are in some respects preferable to the GROUP-BY/HAVING version, in that they are at least logically cleaner, and they specifically do not require those additional language constructs. It is certainly not clear from the original statement of the problem—"Get part numbers for all parts supplied by more than one supplier"—that grouping per se is what is needed to answer the question (and indeed it is not needed). Nor is it immediately obvious that a HAVING condition is required rather than a WHERE condition. The GROUP-BY/HAVING version begins to look more like a procedural prescription for *solving* the problem, instead of just a straightforward logical statement of what the problem *is*. On the other hand, there is no denying that the GROUP-BY/HAVING version is the most succinct. Then again, there are some problems of this same general nature for which GROUP BY and HAVING are simply not adequate, so that one of the alternative approaches *must* be used; see Exercise 6.26 for an example of such a problem. And note too that GROUP BY suffers from the severe restriction that it works only to one level; it is not possible to break a table into groups, then to break each of those groups into lower-level groups, and so on, and then to apply some aggregate function, say SUM or AVG, at each level of grouping.*

---

*This effect ("groups within groups," etc.) can be achieved through various frontend subsystems such as QMF, however. See Part IV of this book.

6.6 UNION

The union of two sets is the set of all elements belonging to either or both of the original sets. Since a relation is a set (a set of rows), it is possible to construct the union of two relations; the result will be a set consisting of all rows appearing in either or both of the original relations. However, if that result is itself to be another relation and not just a heterogeneous mixture of rows, the two original relations must be *union-compatible*; that is, the rows in the two relations must be "the same shape" (loosely speaking). In DB2, two tables are union-compatible, and the UNION operator can be applied to them, if and only if:

(a) They have the same number of columns, *m* say;

(b) For all *i* ($i = 1,2,...,m$), the *i*th column of the first table and the *i*th column of the second table are compatible in the sense of Section 3.5.

Here is an example.

6.6.1 Query Involving UNION.   Get part numbers for parts that either weigh more than 16 pounds or are supplied by supplier S2 (or both).

```
SELECT  P#
FROM    P
WHERE   WEIGHT > 16

UNION

SELECT  P#
FROM    SP
WHERE   S# = 'S2' ;
```

Result:

```
P1
P2
P3
P6
```

Several points arise from this simple example.

▪ Redundant duplicates are always eliminated from the result of a UNION unless the UNION operator explicitly includes the ALL qualifier (see below). Thus, in the example, part P2 is selected by both of the two constituent SELECTs, but it appears only once in the final result. By contrast, the statement

```
SELECT  P#
FROM    P
WHERE   WEIGHT > 16

UNION   ALL
```

```
SELECT  P#
FROM    SP
WHERE   S# = 'S2' ;
```

will return part numbers P1, P2, P2 (again), P3, and P6.

- The primary reason for including UNION ALL in the language is that there are many situations in which a union is required and the user *knows* that there will not be any duplicates in the result. In such a case, any attempt by the system to eliminate duplicates will simply impose an undesirable (and unnecessary) performance penalty. Examples illustrating this point appear below.*

- Any number of SELECTs can be UNIONed together. We might extend the original example (version with ALL omitted) to include part numbers for red parts by inserting

```
UNION

SELECT  P#
FROM    P
WHERE   COLOR = 'Red'
```

before the final semicolon. *Note*: The same effect could also be achieved by adding the clause

```
OR      COLOR = 'Red'
```

to the first of the original SELECTs.

- Parentheses can be used if desired to force a particular order of evaluation if multiple UNIONs are involved. Note that, for example, the expressions x UNION ALL (y UNION z) and (x UNION ALL y) UNION z are not equivalent (in general). Parentheses are unnecessary, however, if either all of the UNIONs specify ALL or none of them does.

- Any ORDER BY clause in the query must appear as part of the final SELECT only, and must identify ordering columns by their ordinal position (i.e., by number), not by name.

- The ability to include literals in a SELECT clause is frequently useful in connection with UNION. For example, to indicate which of the two WHERE conditions each individual part in the result happens to satisfy:

---

*Note that with UNION (in contrast to the SELECT clause and the aggregate functions) there is no explicit DISTINCT option as an alternative to ALL. Note too that if there were such an alternative the default would have to be DISTINCT, not ALL, for compatibility with earlier DB2 releases.

```
SELECT  P#, 'weight > 16 lb'
FROM    P
WHERE   WEIGHT > 16

UNION   ALL

SELECT  P#, 'supplied by S2'
FROM    SP
WHERE   S# = 'S2'

ORDER   BY 2, 1 ;
```

Result:

P1	supplied by S2
P2	supplied by S2
P2	weight > 16 lb
P3	weight > 16 lb
P6	weight > 16 lb

We have specified UNION ALL in this version of the problem because it is obvious now that there will be no duplicates to eliminate. (Of course, it would be nice if the optimizer could deduce this fact for itself.)

- The reader may be wondering whether DB2 also supports any analogs of the INTERSECTION and DIFFERENCE operators (since union, intersection, and difference are commonly treated together in discussions of set theory). The intersection of two sets is the set of all elements belonging to both of the original sets; the difference of two sets is the set of all elements belonging to the first of the original sets and not to the second. DB2 does not support these two operators directly, but each of them can be simulated by means of the EXISTS function. For details, the reader is referred to Appendix B.

One important use for UNION (more precisely, UNION ALL) is in the construction of what is called an *outer join*. As explained in Chapter 5, the ordinary (natural) join of two tables does not include a result row for any row in either of the two original tables that has no matching row in the other. For example, the ordinary join of tables S and P over cities does not include any result row for supplier S5 or for part P3, because no parts are stored in Athens and no suppliers are located in Rome (see Example 5.3.1). In a sense, therefore (a very imprecise sense, we hasten to add), the ordinary join may be considered to *lose information* for such unmatched rows. Sometimes, however, it may be desirable to be able to preserve that information. Consider the following example.

6.6.2 Using UNION ALL to Construct an Outer Join.   For each supplier, get the supplier number, name, status, and city, together with part numbers for all parts supplied by that supplier. If a given supplier supplies no parts at all, then show the information for that supplier in the result concatenated with a blank part number.

```
SELECT  S.*, SP.P#
FROM    S, SP
WHERE   S.S# = SP.S#

UNION   ALL

SELECT  S.*, 'xx'
FROM    S
WHERE   NOT EXISTS
      ( SELECT *
        FROM    SP
        WHERE   SP.S# = S.S# ) ;
```

Result:

S#	SNAME	STATUS	CITY	P#
S1	Smith	20	London	P1
S1	Smith	20	London	P2
S1	Smith	20	London	P3
S1	Smith	20	London	P4
S1	Smith	20	London	P5
S1	Smith	20	London	P6
S2	Jones	10	Paris	P1
S2	Jones	10	Paris	P2
S3	Blake	30	Paris	P2
S4	Clark	20	London	P2
S4	Clark	20	London	P4
S4	Clark	20	London	P5
S5	Adams	30	Athens	xx

Explanation: The first twelve result rows as shown correspond to the first of the two SELECTs, and represent the ordinary natural join of S and SP over supplier numbers (except that the QTY column is not included). The final result row corresponds to the second of the two SELECTs, and preserves information for supplier S5, who does not supply any parts. The overall result is the *outer* natural join of S and SP over S#—again, ignoring QTY. (The ordinary join, by contrast, is sometimes referred to as an *inner* join.)

Note that UNION ALL can always be used (instead of UNION, unqualified) in constructing an outer join; it will be more efficient than the ordinary UNION, since there cannot possibly be any duplicates to eliminate.

One final comment on this example: Outer join is extremely important in practice, and it is a pity that systems do not provide clean, direct support for it (this is a criticism of most relational products, not just of DB2). It should not be necessary to have to indulge in circumlocutions of the kind illustrated in the example.

6.7 CONCLUSION

We have now covered all of the features of the SQL SELECT statement
that we intend to illustrate in this book. To conclude the chapter, we present
a very contrived example that shows how many (by no means all) of those
features can be used together in a single query. We also give a conceptual
algorithm for the evaluation of SQL queries in general.

6.7.1 A Comprehensive Example.   For all red and blue parts such that
the total quantity supplied is greater than 350 (excluding from the total all
shipments for which the quantity is less than or equal to 200), get the part
number, the weight in grams, the color, and the maximum quantity supplied
of that part; and order the result by descending part number within ascending values of that maximum quantity.

```
SELECT P.P#, 'Weight in grams =', P.WEIGHT * 454, P.COLOR,
            'Max shipped quantity =', MAX (SP.QTY)
FROM    P, SP
WHERE   P.P# = SP.P#
AND     P.COLOR IN ('Red','Blue')
AND     SP.QTY > 200
GROUP   BY P.P#, P.WEIGHT, P.COLOR
HAVING  SUM (SP.QTY) > 350
ORDER   BY 6, P.P# DESC ;
```

Result:

P#			COLOR		
P1	Weight in grams =	5448	Red	Max shipped quantity =	300
P5	Weight in grams =	5448	Blue	Max shipped quantity =	400
P3	Weight in grams =	7718	Blue	Max shipped quantity =	400

Explanation: The clauses of a SELECT statement are executed in the
order suggested by that in which they must be written*—with the sole exception of the SELECT clause itself, which is applied between the HAVING
clause (if any) and the ORDER BY clause (if any). In the example, therefore, we can imagine the result being constructed as follows.

---

*Please note that (once again) our explanation is purely conceptual in nature. DB2 does *not*
actually execute queries in the manner described (which would be intolerably inefficient in
practice). Instead, it chooses some other more efficient method—a method that is, however,
guaranteed to produce the same final result as the conceptual method described. Indeed,
choosing such a "more efficient method" is precisely one of the functions of the optimizer
(see Chapter 2).
    Note also that if the query involves any UNIONs, the individual SELECT-FROM-
WHERE (etc.) blocks representing the UNION operands are evaluated first in accordance
with the conceptual method described (excluding the ORDER BY if any), the results are then
UNIONed together, and finally the ORDER BY is applied.

1. *FROM*. The FROM clause is evaluated to yield a new table that is the Cartesian product of tables P and SP.

2. *WHERE*. The result of Step 1 is reduced by the elimination of all rows that do not satisfy the WHERE clause. In the example, rows not satisfying the condition

   ```
   P.P# = SP.P# AND P.COLOR IN ('Red','Blue') AND SP.QTY > 200
   ```

   are eliminated.

3. *GROUP BY*. The result of Step 2 is grouped by values of the column(s) named in the GROUP BY clause. In the example, those columns are P.P#, P.WEIGHT, and P.COLOR. *Note*: In theory P.P# alone would be sufficient as the grouping column, since P.WEIGHT and P.COLOR are themselves single-valued per part number. However, DB2 is not aware of this latter fact, and will raise an error condition if P.WEIGHT and P.COLOR are omitted from the GROUP BY clause, because they *are* included in the SELECT clause.

4. *HAVING*. Groups not satisfying the condition

   ```
   SUM (SP.QTY) > 350
   ```

   are eliminated from the result of Step 3.

5. *SELECT*. Each group in the result of Step 4 generates a single result row, as follows. First, the part number, weight, color, and maximum quantity are extracted from the group. Second, the weight is converted to grams. Third, the two character string literals "Weight in grams =" and "Max shipped quantity =" are inserted at the appropriate points in the row.

6. *ORDER BY*. The result of Step 5 is ordered in accordance with the specifications of the ORDER BY clause to yield the final result.

It is of course true that the query shown above is quite complex—but think how much work it is doing. A conventional program to do the same job in a language such as COBOL could easily be nine pages long instead of just nine lines as above, and the work involved in getting that program operational would be significantly greater than that needed to construct the SQL version shown. In practice, of course, most queries will be much simpler than this one anyway.

EXERCISES

As in the previous chapter, all of the following exercises are based on the suppliers-parts-projects database (see the exercises in Chapter 4). In each one, you are asked to write a SELECT statement for the indicated query (except for numbers 6.15–18 and 6.26, q.v.). For convenience we repeat the structure of the database below:

```
S      ( S#, SNAME, STATUS, CITY )
       PRIMARY KEY ( S# )
P      ( P#, PNAME, COLOR, WEIGHT, CITY )
       PRIMARY KEY ( P# )
J      ( J#, JNAME, CITY )
       PRIMARY KEY ( J# )
SPJ    ( S#, P#, J#, QTY )
       PRIMARY KEY ( S#, P#, J# )
```

Within each section, the exercises are arranged in approximate order of increasing difficulty. You should try at least some of the easy ones in each group. Numbers 6.12–6.18 are quite difficult.

Subqueries

6.1 Get project names for projects supplied by supplier S1.

6.2 Get colors of parts supplied by supplier S1.

6.3 Get part numbers for parts supplied to any project in London.

6.4 Get project numbers for projects using at least one part available from supplier S1.

6.5 Get supplier numbers for suppliers supplying at least one part supplied by at least one supplier who supplies at least one red part.

6.6 Get supplier numbers for suppliers with a status lower than that of supplier S1.

6.7 Get supplier numbers for suppliers supplying some project with part P1 in a quantity greater than the average shipment quantity of part P1 for that project. (*Note*: This exercise requires the AVG function.)

EXISTS

6.8 Repeat Exercise 6.3 to use EXISTS in your solution.

6.9 Repeat Exercise 6.4 to use EXISTS in your solution.

6.10 Get project numbers for projects not supplied with any red part by any London supplier.

6.11 Get project numbers for projects supplied entirely by supplier S1.

6.12 Get part numbers for parts supplied to all projects in London.

6.13 Get supplier numbers for suppliers who supply the same part to all projects.

6.14 Get project numbers for projects supplied with at least all parts available from supplier S1.

For the next four exercises (6.15–6.18), convert the SQL SELECT statement shown back into an English equivalent.

```
6.15  SELECT DISTINCT J#
      FROM    SPJ SPJX
      WHERE   NOT EXISTS
            ( SELECT *
              FROM    SPJ SPJY
              WHERE   SPJY.J# = SPJX.J#
              AND     NOT EXISTS
                    ( SELECT *
                      FROM    SPJ SPJZ
                      WHERE   SPJZ.P# = SPJY.P#
                      AND     SPJZ.S# = 'S1' ) ) ;

6.16  SELECT DISTINCT J#
      FROM    SPJ SPJX
      WHERE   NOT EXISTS
            ( SELECT *
              FROM    SPJ SPJY
              WHERE   EXISTS
                    ( SELECT *
                      FROM    SPJ SPJA
                      WHERE   SPJA.S# = 'S1'
                      AND     SPJA.P# = SPJY.P# )
              AND     NOT EXISTS
                    ( SELECT *
                      FROM    SPJ SPJB
                      WHERE   SPJB.S# = 'S1'
                      AND     SPJB.P# = SPJY.P#
                      AND     SPJB.J# = SPJX.J# ) ) ;

6.17  SELECT DISTINCT J#
      FROM    SPJ SPJX
      WHERE   NOT EXISTS
            ( SELECT *
              FROM    SPJ SPJY
              WHERE   EXISTS
                    ( SELECT *
                      FROM    SPJ SPJA
                      WHERE   SPJA.P# = SPJY.P#
                      AND     SPJA.J# = SPJX.J# )
              AND     NOT EXISTS
                    ( SELECT *
                      FROM    SPJ SPJB
                      WHERE   SPJB.S# = 'S1'
                      AND     SPJB.P# = SPJY.P#
                      AND     SPJB.J# = SPJX.J# ) ) ;

6.18  SELECT DISTINCT J#
      FROM    SPJ SPJX
      WHERE   NOT EXISTS
            ( SELECT *
              FROM    SPJ SPJY
              WHERE   EXISTS
                    ( SELECT *
                      FROM    SPJ SPJA
                      WHERE   SPJA.S# = SPJY.S#
                      AND     SPJA.P# IN
                            ( SELECT P#
                              FROM    P
                              WHERE   COLOR = 'Red' )
                      AND     NOT EXISTS
                            ( SELECT *
                              FROM    SPJ SPJB
                              WHERE   SPJB.S# = SPJY.S#
                              AND     SPJB.J# = SPJX.J# ) ) ) ;
```

Quantified Comparisons

6.19 Get names of parts whose weight is less than that of every part in Paris.

6.20 Get names of projects whose city is not equal to any supplier city or part city.

Aggregate Functions

6.21 Get the total number of projects supplied by supplier S1.

6.22 Get the total quantity of part P1 supplied by supplier S1.

6.23 For each part being supplied to a project, get the part number, the project number, and the corresponding total quantity.

6.24 Get project numbers for projects whose city is first in the alphabetic list of such cities.

6.25 Get project numbers for projects supplied with part P1 in an average quantity greater than the greatest quantity in which any part is supplied to project J1.

6.26 Get supplier numbers for suppliers supplying every project with part P1 in a quantity greater than the average quantity in which part P1 is supplied to that project.

Union

6.27 Construct an ordered list of all cities in which at least one supplier, part, or project is located.

6.28 Show the result of the following SELECT:

```
SELECT  P.COLOR
FROM    P
UNION
SELECT  P.COLOR
FROM    P ;
```

6.29 Construct the outer natural join of projects and shipments over project numbers.

6.30 Construct the outer natural join of parts and projects over cities.

6.31 Construct a table showing complete supplier, part, and project information (together with shipment quantity) for each shipment, together with "preserved" information for every supplier, part, and project that does not appear in the shipment table.

ANSWERS TO SELECTED EXERCISES

The following answers are not necessarily the only ones possible.

```
6.1   SELECT  DISTINCT JNAME
      FROM    J
      WHERE   J# IN
              ( SELECT  J#
                FROM    SPJ
                WHERE   S# = 'S1' ) ;
```

```
6.2    SELECT  DISTINCT COLOR
       FROM    P
       WHERE   P# IN
             ( SELECT  P#
               FROM    SPJ
               WHERE   S# = 'S1' ) ;

6.3    SELECT  DISTINCT P#
       FROM    SPJ
       WHERE   J# IN
             ( SELECT  J#
               FROM    J
               WHERE   CITY = 'London' ) ;

6.4    SELECT  DISTINCT J#
       FROM    SPJ
       WHERE   P# IN
             ( SELECT  P#
               FROM    SPJ
               WHERE   S# = 'S1' ) ;

6.5    SELECT  DISTINCT S#
       FROM    SPJ
       WHERE   P# IN
             ( SELECT  P#
               FROM    SPJ
               WHERE   S# IN
                     ( SELECT  S#
                       FROM    SPJ
                       WHERE   P# IN
                             ( SELECT  P#
                               FROM    P
                               WHERE   COLOR = 'Red' ) ) ) ;

6.6    SELECT  S#
       FROM    S
       WHERE   STATUS <
             ( SELECT  STATUS
               FROM    S
               WHERE   S# = 'S1' ) ;

6.7    SELECT  DISTINCT S#
       FROM    SPJ SPJX
       WHERE   P# = 'P1'
       AND     QTY >
             ( SELECT  AVG(QTY)
               FROM    SPJ SPJY
               WHERE   P# = 'P1'
               AND     SPJY.J# = SPJX.J# ) ;

6.8    SELECT  DISTINCT P#
       FROM    SPJ
       WHERE   EXISTS
             ( SELECT  *
               FROM    J
               WHERE   J# = SPJ.J#
               AND     CITY = 'London' ) ;

6.9    SELECT  DISTINCT SPJX.J#
       FROM    SPJ SPJX
       WHERE   EXISTS
             ( SELECT  *
               FROM    SPJ SPJY
               WHERE   SPJY.P# = SPJX.P#
               AND     SPJY.S# = 'S1' ) ;
```

```
6.10  SELECT  J#
      FROM    J
      WHERE   NOT EXISTS
            ( SELECT  *
              FROM    SPJ
              WHERE   J# = J.J#
              AND     P# IN
                    ( SELECT  P#
                      FROM    P
                      WHERE   COLOR = 'Red' )
              AND     S# IN
                    ( SELECT  S#
                      FROM    S
                      WHERE   CITY = 'London' ) ) ;

6.11  SELECT  DISTINCT J#
      FROM    SPJ SPJX
      WHERE   NOT EXISTS
            ( SELECT  *
              FROM    SPJ SPJY
              WHERE   SPJY.J# = SPJX.J#
              AND     SPJY.S# ¬= 'S1' ) ;

6.12  SELECT  DISTINCT P#
      FROM    SPJ SPJX
      WHERE   NOT EXISTS
            ( SELECT  *
              FROM    J
              WHERE   CITY = 'London'
              AND     NOT EXISTS
                    ( SELECT  *
                      FROM    SPJ SPJY
                      WHERE   SPJY.P# = SPJX.P#
                      AND     SPJY.J# = J.J# ) ) ;

6.13  SELECT  DISTINCT S#
      FROM    SPJ SPJX
      WHERE   EXISTS
            ( SELECT  P#
              FROM    SPJ SPJY
              WHERE   NOT EXISTS
                    ( SELECT  J#
                      FROM    J
                      WHERE   NOT EXISTS
                            ( SELECT  *
                              FROM    SPJ SPJZ
                              WHERE   SPJZ.S# = SPJX.S#
                              AND     SPJZ.P# = SPJY.P#
                              AND     SPJZ.J# = J.J# ) ) ) ;
```

This rather complex SELECT statement may be paraphrased: "Get all suppliers (SPJX.S#) such that there exists a part (SPJY.P#) such that there does not exist any project (J.J#) such that the supplier does not supply the part to the project"—in other words, suppliers such that there exists some part that they supply to all projects. Note the use of "SELECT P# FROM . . ." and "SELECT J# FROM . . ." in two of the EXISTS references; "SELECT *" would not be incorrect, but "SELECT P#" (for instance) seems a fraction closer to the intuitive formulation—there must exist a *part* (identified by a part number), not just a row in the shipments table.

6.14
```
SELECT DISTINCT J#
FROM    SPJ SPJX
WHERE   NOT EXISTS
      ( SELECT P#
        FROM    SPJ SPJY
        WHERE   SPJY.S# = 'S1'
        AND     NOT EXISTS
              ( SELECT *
                FROM    SPJ SPJZ
                WHERE   SPJZ.P# = SPJY.P#
                AND     SPJZ.J# = SPJX.J# ) ) ;
```

6.15 Get project numbers for projects that use only parts that are available from supplier S1.

6.16 Get project numbers for projects that are supplied by supplier S1 with some of every part that supplier S1 supplies.

6.17 Get project numbers for projects such that at least some of every part they use is supplied to them by supplier S1.

6.18 Get project numbers for projects that are supplied by every supplier who supplies some red part.

6.19
```
SELECT PNAME
FROM    P
WHERE   WEIGHT <ALL
      ( SELECT WEIGHT
        FROM    P
        WHERE   CITY = 'Paris' ) ;
```

6.20
```
SELECT JNAME
FROM    J
WHERE   CITY ¬=ALL
      ( SELECT CITY
        FROM    S )
AND     CITY ¬=ALL
      ( SELECT CITY
        FROM    P ) ;
```

Note the following "solution" is *not* correct (why not?):

```
SELECT JNAME
FROM    J
WHERE   CITY ¬=ALL
      ( SELECT CITY
        FROM    S
        UNION
        SELECT CITY
        FROM    P ) ;
```

6.21
```
SELECT COUNT (DISTINCT J#)
FROM    SPJ
WHERE   S# = 'S1' ;
```

6.22
```
SELECT SUM (QTY)
FROM    SPJ
WHERE   P# = 'P1'
AND     S# = 'S1' ;
```

6.23
```
SELECT P#, J#, SUM(QTY)
FROM    SPJ
GROUP   BY P#, J# ;
```

```
6.24  SELECT  J#
      FROM    J
      WHERE   CITY =
            ( SELECT  MIN(CITY)
              FROM    J ) ;

6.25  SELECT  J#
      FROM    SPJ
      WHERE   P# = 'P1'
      GROUP   BY J#
      HAVING  AVG(QTY) >
            ( SELECT  MAX(QTY)
              FROM    SPJ
              WHERE   J# = 'J1' ) ;

6.26  SELECT  DISTINCT S#
      FROM    SPJ SPJX
      WHERE   NOT EXISTS
            ( SELECT  *
              FROM    J
              WHERE   NOT EXISTS
                    ( SELECT  *
                      FROM    SPJ SPJY
                      WHERE   SPJY.S# = SPJX.S#
                      AND     SPJY.P# = 'P1'
                      AND     SPJY.J# = J.J#
                      AND     SPJY.QTY >
                            ( SELECT  AVG (QTY)
                              FROM    SPJ SPJZ
                              WHERE   SPJZ.J# = J.J#
                              AND     SPJZ.P# = 'P1' ) ) ) ;

6.27  SELECT  CITY FROM S
      UNION
      SELECT  CITY FROM P
      UNION
      SELECT  CITY FROM J
      ORDER   BY 1 ;
```

6.28
```
┌──────────┐
│          │
├──────────┤
│ Red      │
│ Green    │
│ Blue     │
└──────────┘
```

```
6.29  SELECT  J.*, SPJ.S#, SPJ.P#, SPJ.QTY
      FROM    J, SPJ
      WHERE   J.J# = SPJ.J#
      UNION   ALL
      SELECT  J.*, 'xx', 'xx', 0
      FROM    J
      WHERE   NOT EXISTS
            ( SELECT  *
              FROM    SPJ
              WHERE   SPJ.J# = J.J# ) ;

6.30  SELECT  P.*, J#, JNAME
      FROM    P, J
      WHERE   P.CITY = J.CITY
      UNION   ALL
```

```
      SELECT  P.*, 'xx', 'xx'
      FROM    P
      WHERE   NOT EXISTS
            ( SELECT *
              FROM   J
              WHERE  J.CITY = P.CITY )
      UNION   ALL
      SELECT  'xx', 'xx', 'xx', 0, J.CITY, J.J#, J.JNAME
      FROM    J
      WHERE   NOT EXISTS
            ( SELECT *
              FROM   P
              WHERE  P.CITY = J.CITY ) ;
```

6.31
```
      SELECT  S.*, P.*, J.*, SPJ.QTY
      FROM    S, P, J, SPJ
      WHERE   S.S# = SPJ.S#
      AND     P.P# = SPJ.P#
      AND     J.J# = SPJ.J#
      UNION   ALL
      SELECT  S.*,'xx','xx','xx', 0,'xx','xx','xx','xx', 0
      FROM    S
      WHERE   NOT EXISTS
            ( SELECT *
              FROM   SPJ
              WHERE  SPJ.S# = S.S# )
      UNION   ALL
      SELECT  'xx','xx', 0,'xx', P.*,'xx','xx','xx', 0
      FROM    P
      WHERE   NOT EXISTS
            ( SELECT *
              FROM   SPJ
              WHERE  P.P# = SPJ.P# )
      UNION   ALL
      SELECT  'xx','xx', 0,'xx','xx','xx','xx', 0,'xx', J.*, 0
      FROM    J
      WHERE   NOT EXISTS
            ( SELECT *
              FROM   SPJ
              WHERE  SPJ.J# = J.J# ) ;
```

CHAPTER

◆ 7 ◆

Data Manipulation III: Update Operations

7.1 INTRODUCTION

In the last two chapters we considered the SQL retrieval statement (SELECT) in considerable detail. Now we turn our attention to the update statements INSERT, UPDATE, and DELETE. *Note*: The term "update" unfortunately has two distinct meanings in SQL—it is used generically to refer to all three operations as a class, and also specifically to refer to the UPDATE operation per se. We will distinguish between the two meanings in this book by always using lower case when the generic meaning is intended and upper case when the specific meaning is intended.

Like the SELECT statement, the three update statements operate on both base tables and views. However, for reasons that are beyond the scope of this chapter, *not all views are updatable*. If the user attempts to perform an update operation on a nonupdatable view, DB2 will simply reject the operation, with some appropriate message to the user. For the purposes of the present chapter, therefore, let us assume that all tables to be updated are base tables, and defer the question of views (and of updating views, in particular) to Chapter 9.

The next three sections discuss the three update operations in detail. The syntax of those operations follows the same general pattern as that already shown for the SELECT operation; for convenience, an outline of that general syntax for the operation in question is given at the beginning of the relevant section.

7.2   INSERT

The INSERT statement has the general form

```
INSERT
INTO    table [ ( column [, column ] ... ) ]
VALUES ( literal [, literal ] ... ) ;
```

or

```
INSERT
INTO    table [ ( column [, column ] ... ) ]
subquery ;
```

In the first format, a row is INSERTed into "table" having the specified values for the specified columns; the ith literal in the list of literals corresponds to the ith column in the list of columns. In the second format, "subquery" is evaluated and a copy of the result (multiple rows, in general) is INSERTed into "table"; the ith column of that result corresponds to the ith column in the list of columns. In both cases, omitting the list of columns is equivalent to specifying a list of all columns in the table (see Example 7.2.2 below).

7.2.1   Single-Row INSERT.   Add part P7 (city Athens, weight 24, name and color at present unknown) to table P.

```
INSERT
INTO    P ( P#, CITY, WEIGHT )
VALUES ( 'P7', 'Athens', 24 ) ;
```

A new part row is created with the specified part number, city, and weight, and with blank values for the name and color columns (since no other value has been explicitly specified, and we assume that NOT NULL WITH DEFAULT applies to those columns). In general, the effect of omitting a value for some column in INSERT depends on the way that column was defined in the CREATE (or ALTER) TABLE statement:

- NOT NULL WITH DEFAULT: The column is set to the appropriate nonnull default value (see Chapter 3).

- NOT NULL: The INSERT fails (the database remains unchanged).
- Otherwise: The column is set to null.

Note that the left-to-right order in which columns are named in the INSERT statement does not have to be the same as the left-to-right order in which they appear in the table.

7.2.2 Single-Row INSERT, with Column Names Omitted. Add part P8 (a sprocket, color pink, weight 14, city Nice) to table P.

```
INSERT
INTO    P
VALUES ('P8', 'Sprocket', 'Pink', 14, 'Nice' ) ;
```

Omitting the list of columns is equivalent to specifying a list of all columns in the table, in the left-to-right order in which they appear in the table. As with "SELECT *", this shorthand may be convenient for interactive SQL; however, it is potentially dangerous in embedded SQL (i.e., SQL within an application program), because the assumed list of columns may change if the INSERT statement is recompiled and the definition of the table has changed in the interim. In practice, we recommend always specifying the list of columns explicitly in an embedded SQL context.

7.2.3 Single-Row INSERT. Insert a new shipment with supplier number S20, part number P20, and quantity 1000.

```
INSERT
INTO    SP ( S#, P#, QTY )
VALUES ('S20', 'P20', 1000 ) ;
```

Since by definition the three update operations change the state of the database, there is always the possibility that they may change it in some incorrect way and thereby violate the integrity of the data. The example illustrates this point: The database would clearly be incorrect if the INSERT were executed, because it would now include a shipment for a nonexistent supplier and a nonexistent part. In fact, the example illustrates a very specific kind of integrity violation, namely a *referential* integrity violation. Referential integrity is discussed in detail in Chapter 11.

7.2.4 INSERT . . . SELECT. For each part supplied, get the part number and the total quantity supplied of that part (as in Example 7.4.7), and save the result in the database.

```
CREATE TABLE TEMP
     ( P#       CHAR(6) NOT NULL,
       TOTQTY   INTEGER,
      PRIMARY KEY ( P# ) ) ;

CREATE UNIQUE INDEX XTEMP ON TEMP ( P# ) ;
```

```
INSERT
INTO    TEMP ( P#, TOTQTY )
        SELECT P#, SUM(QTY)
        FROM    SP
        GROUP   BY P# ;
```

The SELECT is executed, just like an ordinary SELECT, but the result, instead of being returned to the user, is inserted into table TEMP. Now the user can do anything he or she pleases with that result—query it further, print it, even update it; none of those operations will have any effect whatsoever on the original data. Eventually, when it is no longer required, table TEMP can be dropped:

```
DROP TABLE TEMP ;
```

The foregoing example illustrates very nicely why the closure property of relational systems (discussed in Section 5.2) is so important: The overall procedure works precisely because the result of a SELECT is another table. It would *not* work if the result was something other than a table.

Incidentally, it is not necessary for the target table to be initially empty for an INSERT . . . SELECT operation, though for the foregoing example it is. If it is not, the new rows are simply added to those already present.

7.3 UPDATE

The UPDATE statement has the general form

```
UPDATE table
SET     column = scalar-expression
     [, column = scalar-expression ] ...
[ WHERE   condition ] ;
```

All rows in "table" that satisfy "condition" are UPDATEd in accordance with the assignments ("column = scalar-expression") in the SET clause. The "scalar-expressions" are (at their most complex) simple scalar expressions involving columns of "table" and/or scalar functions and/or literals (no aggregate functions allowed). For each row to be UPDATEd (i.e., each row that satisfies "condition," or all rows if the WHERE clause is omitted), references in the "scalar-expressions" to columns within that row stand for the values of those columns before any of the assignments have been executed.

7.3.1 Single-Row UPDATE.   Change the color of part P2 to yellow, increase its weight by 5, and set its city to "unknown" (i.e., null; we assume for the sake of the example that column P.CITY is allowed to accept nulls).

```
UPDATE P
SET     COLOR = 'Yellow',
        WEIGHT = WEIGHT + 5,
        CITY = NULL
WHERE   P# = 'P2' ;
```

7.3.2 *Multiple-Row UPDATE.* Double the status of all suppliers in London.

```
UPDATE S
SET     STATUS = 2 * STATUS
WHERE   CITY = 'London' ;
```

7.3.3 *UPDATE with a Subquery.* Set the shipment quantity to zero for all suppliers in London.

```
UPDATE SP
SET     QTY = 0
WHERE   'London' =
      ( SELECT CITY
        FROM   S
        WHERE  S.S# = SP.S# ) ;
```

7.4 DELETE

The DELETE statement has the general form

```
DELETE
FROM    table
[ WHERE  condition ] ;
```

All rows in "table" that satisfy "condition" (or all rows, if the WHERE clause is omitted) are DELETEd.

7.4.1 *Single-Row DELETE.* Delete supplier S5.

```
DELETE
FROM    S
WHERE   S# = 'S5' ;
```

7.4.2 *Multiple-Row DELETE.* Delete all shipments with quantity greater than 300.

```
DELETE
FROM    SP
WHERE   QTY > 300 ;
```

7.4.3 *Multiple-Row DELETE.* Delete all shipments.

```
DELETE
FROM    SP ;
```

SP is still a known table ("DELETE all rows" is not a DROP), but it is now empty.

7.4.4 DELETE with a Subquery.   Delete all shipments for suppliers in London.

```
DELETE
FROM     SP
WHERE    'London' =
         ( SELECT  CITY
           FROM    S
           WHERE   S.S# = SP.S# )  ;
```

7.5 CONCLUSION

This brings us to the end of our detailed discussion of the four data manipulation statements of SQL, namely SELECT, INSERT, UPDATE, and DELETE. Most of the complexity of those statements (what complexity there is) resides in the SELECT statement; once you have a reasonable understanding of SELECT, the other statements are fairly straightforward, as you can see. In practice, of course, the SELECT statement is usually pretty straightforward as well.

Despite the foregoing, however, the update operations do suffer from one minor problem that is worth calling out explicitly, namely as follows: If the WHERE clause in UPDATE or DELETE includes a subquery, then the FROM clause in that subquery must not refer to the table that is the target of that UPDATE or DELETE. Likewise, in the subquery form of INSERT (INSERT . . . SELECT), the FROM clause in that subquery must not refer to the table that is the target of that INSERT. So, for example, to delete all suppliers whose status is lower than the average, the following will *not* work:

```
DELETE
FROM     S
WHERE    STATUS <
         ( SELECT  AVG (STATUS)
           FROM    S )  ;                       -- illegal !!!
```

Instead, it is necessary to proceed one step at a time, as follows:

```
SELECT  AVG (STATUS)
FROM    S ;
```

Result:

22

Hence:

```
DELETE
FROM     S
WHERE    STATUS < 22  ;
```

The reasons for the foregoing restrictions are not inherent but are merely a consequence of the way the operators are implemented in DB2.

Aside: In DB2 Version 2 there are additional restrictions that apply to the update operations in certain circumstances. See Chapter 11 for further discussion. *End of aside*.

In conclusion, we point out that the fact that there are only four data manipulation operations in SQL is one of the reasons for the ease of use of that language (less to learn, less to remember, etc.). And the fact that there *are* only four such operations is a consequence of the simplicity of the relational data structure. As we pointed out in Chapter 1, all data in a relational database is represented in exactly the same way, namely as values in column positions within rows of tables. Since there is only one way to represent anything, we need only one operator for each of the four basic functions (retrieve, change, insert, delete). By contrast, systems based on a more complex data structure fundamentally require $4n$ operations, where n is the number of ways that data can be represented in that system. In CODASYL-based systems, for example, where data can be represented either as records (rows) or as "links" between records, we typically find a STORE operation to create a record and a CONNECT operation to create a link; an ERASE operation to destroy a record and a DISCONNECT operation to destroy a link; a MODIFY operation to change a record and a RECONNECT operation to change a link; and so on. (Actually, CODASYL systems usually provide more than two ways of representing data, and hence more than two sets of operations, but records and links are the two most important.)

EXERCISES

As usual, all of the following exercises are based on the suppliers-parts-projects database:

```
S      ( S#, SNAME, STATUS, CITY )
       PRIMARY KEY ( S# )
P      ( P#, PNAME, COLOR, WEIGHT, CITY )
       PRIMARY KEY ( P# )
J      ( J#, JNAME, CITY )
       PRIMARY KEY ( J# )
SPJ    ( S#, P#, J#, QTY )
       PRIMARY KEY ( S#, P#, J# )
```

Write INSERT, DELETE, or UPDATE statements (as appropriate) for each of the following problems.

7.1 Change the color of all red parts to orange.

7.2 Delete all projects for which there are no shipments.

7.3 Increase the shipment quantity by 10 percent for all shipments by suppliers that supply a red part.

7.4 Insert a new supplier (S10) into table S. The name and city are Smith and New York, respectively; the status is not yet known.

7.5 Construct a table containing a list of part numbers for parts that are supplied either by a London supplier or to a London project.

7.6 Construct a table containing a list of project numbers for projects that are either located in London or are supplied by a London supplier.

7.7 Add 10 to the status of all suppliers whose status is currently less than that of supplier S4.

ANSWERS TO SELECTED EXERCISES

As usual the following solutions are not necessarily unique. Also, note that some of the solutions involve the creation of a temporary result table. We have specified a primary key for each such table as a matter of good discipline; but it should be pointed out that the integrity checking implied by those primary keys will certainly lead to some performance overhead (see Chapter 11). As a consequence, an installation might decide that it is acceptable *not* to specify a primary key for such comparatively short-lived tables.

7.1
```
UPDATE  P
SET     COLOR = 'Orange'
WHERE   COLOR = 'Red' ;
```

7.2
```
DELETE
FROM    J
WHERE   J# NOT IN
        ( SELECT J#
          FROM   SPJ ) ;
```

7.3
```
CREATE TABLE REDS
       ( S#   CHAR(5) NOT NULL,
         PRIMARY KEY ( S# ) ) ;

CREATE UNIQUE INDEX X3 ON REDS ( S# ) ;

INSERT INTO REDS ( S# )
       SELECT DISTINCT S#
       FROM    SPJ, P
       WHERE   SPJ.P# = P.P#
       AND     COLOR = 'Red' ;

UPDATE SPJ
SET    QTY = QTY * 1.1
WHERE  S# IN
       ( SELECT S#
         FROM   REDS ) ;

DROP TABLE REDS ;
```

Note that the following single-statement "solution" is illegal (why?).

```
     UPDATE SPJ
     SET    QTY = QTY * 1.1
     WHERE  S# IN
          ( SELECT DISTINCT S#
            FROM    SPJ, P
            WHERE   SPJ.P# = P.P#
            AND     P.COLOR = 'Red' ) ;
```

7.4
```
     INSERT
     INTO   S ( S#, SNAME, CITY )
     VALUES ('S10', 'Smith', 'New York' ) ;
```

7.5
```
     CREATE TABLE LP
          ( P# CHAR(6) NOT NULL,
            PRIMARY KEY ( P# ) ) ;

     CREATE UNIQUE INDEX X5 ON LP ( P# ) ;

     INSERT INTO LP ( P# )
             SELECT DISTINCT P#
             FROM    SPJ
             WHERE   S# IN
                   ( SELECT S#
                     FROM   S
                     WHERE  CITY = 'London' )
             OR      J# IN
                   ( SELECT J#
                     FROM   J
                     WHERE  CITY = 'London' ) ;
```

7.6
```
     CREATE TABLE LJ
          ( J#  CHAR(4) NOT NULL,
            PRIMARY KEY ( J# ) ) ;

     CREATE UNIQUE INDEX X6 ON LJ ( J# ) ;

     INSERT INTO LJ ( J# )
             SELECT J#
             FROM   J
             WHERE  CITY = 'London'
             OR     J# IN
                  ( SELECT DISTINCT J#
                    FROM    SPJ
                    WHERE   S# IN
                          ( SELECT S#
                            FROM   S
                            WHERE  CITY = 'London' ) ) ;
```

Note: The following "solution" is illegal (why?).

```
 INSERT INTO LJ ( J# )
         SELECT J#
         FROM   J
         WHERE  CITY = 'London'
         UNION
         SELECT DISTINCT J#
         FROM   SPJ
         WHERE  'London' =
               ( SELECT CITY
                 FROM   S
                 WHERE  S.S# = SPJ.S# ) ;
```

7.7 SELECT STATUS
      FROM   S
      WHERE   S# = 'S4' ;

Result:

STATUS
20

Hence:

UPDATE S
SET   STATUS = STATUS + 10
WHERE   STATUS < 20 ;

CHAPTER

◆ **8** ◆

The Catalog

8.1 INTRODUCTION

We have mentioned the catalog several times in this book already (see Chapters 2 and 4). The catalog in DB2 is a system database that contains information (*descriptors*) concerning various objects that are of interest to DB2 itself. Examples of such objects are base tables, views, indexes, databases, application plans, packages, access privileges, and so on. Descriptor information is essential if the system is to be able to do its job properly. For example, the optimizer component of Bind uses catalog information about indexes (as well as other information) to choose an access strategy, as explained in Chapter 2. Likewise, the authorization subsystem (see Chapter 10) uses catalog information about access privileges to grant or deny specific user requests.

A significant advantage of a relational system like DB2 is that *the catalog in such a system itself consists of relations* (or tables—*system* tables, so called to distinguish them from ordinary user tables). As a result, users can interrogate the catalog using the standard facilities of their normal query language (SQL, in the case of DB2)—a very nice feature of such systems.

In DB2 specifically, the catalog currently consists of some 38 system tables.* It is not our purpose here to give an exhaustive description of the catalog; rather, we wish merely to give a basic—and deliberately somewhat simplified—introduction to its structure and content, and to give some idea as to how the information in the catalog can be helpful to the user as well as to the system. The only catalog tables we mention at this point are the following:

- SYSTABLES

  This catalog table contains a row for every named table (base table or view) in the entire DB2 system.[†] For each such table, it gives the table name (NAME), the name of the user who created the table (CREATEDBY), the name of the user who owns the table (CREATOR), the number of columns in the table (COLCOUNT), and many other items of information. The primary key is the combination (CREATOR, NAME). *Note*: It is possible, as we shall see in Chapter 10, for the "creator" and the "owner" of a table to be different; this is why SYSTABLES gives both. The terminology is rather confusing, however—the CREATOR column shows the table *owner*, the CREATEDBY column shows the actual *creator*. The reasons for this confusion are historical and need not concern us here.

- SYSCOLUMNS

  This catalog table contains a row for every column of every table in the DB2 system. For each such column, it gives the column name (NAME), the name of the table of which that column is a part (TBNAME), the name of the owner of that table (TBCREATOR), the data type of the column (COLTYPE), and many other things besides. The primary key is the combination (TBCREATOR, TBNAME, NAME).

- SYSINDEXES

  This catalog table contains a row for every index in the system. For each such index, it gives the index name (NAME), the name of the user who created the index (CREATEDBY), the name of the owner of the

---

*The catalog is *not* the same across different SQL implementations, because the catalog for a particular system necessarily contains a great deal of information that is specific to that system. Indeed, the catalog is typically not even the same from release to release, since the addition of new functionality to the system typically requires the addition of new descriptors to the catalog. Appendix D contains a brief summary of the DB2 catalog tables as of Version 2 Release 3.

[†]It also contains a row for each *alias* (see Section 8.4).

index (CREATOR), the name of the indexed table (TBNAME), the name of the owner of that table (TBCREATOR), and so on. The primary key is the combination (CREATOR, NAME).

By way of example, Fig. 8.1 shows the catalog structure for the suppliers-and-parts database (in outline; of course, almost all the details have been omitted).

SYSTABLES

NAME	CREATEDBY	CREATOR	COLCOUNT	...
S	CJDATE	CJDATE	4	...
P	CJDATE	CJDATE	5	...
SP	CJDATE	CJDATE	3	...

SYSCOLUMNS

NAME	TBNAME	TBCREATOR	COLTYPE	...
S#	S	CJDATE	CHAR	...
SNAME	S	CJDATE	CHAR	...
STATUS	S	CJDATE	SMALLINT	...
CITY	S	CJDATE	CHAR	...
P#	P	CJDATE	CHAR	...
PNAME	P	CJDATE	CHAR	...
COLOR	P	CJDATE	CHAR	...
WEIGHT	P	CJDATE	SMALLINT	...
CITY	P	CJDATE	CHAR	...
S#	SP	CJDATE	CHAR	...
P#	SP	CJDATE	CHAR	...
QTY	SP	CJDATE	INTEGER	...

SYSINDEXES

NAME	CREATEDBY	CREATOR	TBNAME	TBCREATOR	...
XS	CJDATE	CJDATE	S	CJDATE	...
XP	CJDATE	CJDATE	P	CJDATE	...
XSP	CJDATE	CJDATE	SP	CJDATE	...
XSC	CJDATE	CJDATE	S	CJDATE	...

Fig. 8.1   Catalog structure for the suppliers-and-parts database (in outline)

8.2   QUERYING THE CATALOG

As indicated in Section 8.1, a nice feature of the catalog in a relational system like DB2 is that it can be queried by means of ordinary SQL retrieval operations (SELECT statements), just as ordinary tables can. For example, to find out what tables contain an S# column:

```
SELECT TBNAME, TBCREATOR
FROM   SYSIBM.SYSCOLUMNS
WHERE  NAME = 'S#' ;
```

Result:

TBNAME	TBCREATOR
S	CJDATE
SP	CJDATE

The owner (CREATOR) for the catalog tables is considered to be SYSIBM. Thus, to refer to a catalog table such as SYSCOLUMNS, you will need to use SYSIBM as a prefix for the table name (as in the FROM clause in this example); otherwise, DB2 will assume that you are referring to a table of your own (i.e., the default prefix is your own system-known name, as explained in Chapter 4).

Another example: What columns does the suppliers table have?

```
SELECT  NAME
FROM    SYSIBM.SYSCOLUMNS
WHERE   TBNAME = 'S'
AND     TBCREATOR = 'CJDATE' ;
```

Result:

NAME
S#
SNAME
STATUS
CITY

And one more example: How many tables has user CJDATE created?

```
SELECT  COUNT(*)
FROM    SYSIBM.SYSTABLES
WHERE   CREATEDBY = 'CJDATE' ;
```

(Actually, this query will count *aliases* as well as tables. See Section 8.4.)

A user who is not familiar with the structure of the database can use queries such as these to discover that structure. For example, a user who wishes to query the suppliers-and-parts database (say), but does not have any detailed knowledge as to exactly what tables exist in that database and exactly what columns they contain, can use catalog queries to obtain that knowledge first before going on to formulate the data queries per se. In a traditional (prerelational) system, those initial queries would typically have to be directed to the system *dictionary* instead of to the database. Indeed, the DB2 catalog can be regarded as a rudimentary dictionary (rudimentary, in that it contains only information that is directly needed by DB2, whereas a full-scale dictionary typically contains much additional information, such as report definitions, graph definitions, terminal descriptions, etc.). The important difference—and a significant ease-of-use benefit for DB2—is that in DB2 the catalog and the database are queried through *the same interface*, namely SQL; in traditional systems, by contrast, the dictionary and the database have always been distinct and have been accessed through different interfaces. It is interesting to speculate as to whether the DB2 catalog will ever be extended to provide a full-fledged dictionary function.

A couple of final remarks to close this section:

1. After the foregoing was first written, IBM announced a new "Repository" product for DB2 (and other IBM system software products). The Repository is a true dictionary product. Unfortunately, it is *not* an extension of the DB2 catalog—on the contrary, it is a separate product and is accessed through a distinct interface of its own. More information regarding the Repository is given in Part IV of this book.

2. As part of DB2 Version 2.3, IBM introduced a new "Catalog Visibility" tool, which effectively provides a screen-based frontend to the catalog. This tool permits certain simple catalog queries to be formulated without the direct use of SQL, and displays the results of those queries in a more readable form than the normal SELECT statement does. See Chapter 16 for more information.

8.3 UPDATING THE CATALOG

We have seen how the catalog can be queried by means of the SQL SELECT statement. However, the catalog *cannot* be updated using the SQL INSERT, UPDATE, and DELETE statements, and DB2 will reject any attempt to do so.* The reason is, of course, that allowing such operations would potentially be very dangerous: It would be far too easy to destroy information (inadvertently or otherwise) in the catalog so that DB2 would no longer be able to function correctly. Suppose, for example, that the following operation were allowed:

```
DELETE
FROM    SYSIBM.SYSCOLUMNS
WHERE   NAME = 'S#'
AND     TBNAME = 'S'
AND     TBCREATOR = 'CJDATE' ;
```

Its effect would be to remove the row

```
( S#, S, CJDATE, CHAR, ... )
```

from the SYSCOLUMNS table. *As far as DB2 is concerned, the S# column in the S table would now no longer exist*—i.e., DB2 would no longer have

---

*This statement is not quite 100 percent true under DB2 Version 2. In Version 2, suitably authorized users *are* allowed to use the SQL UPDATE statement to update certain "statistics" columns in the catalog, for reasons that are beyond the scope of this chapter. See Chapter 16 for more information. We will ignore this special case for the remainder of this chapter.

any knowledge of that column. Thus, attempts to access data on the basis of values of that column—e.g.,

```
SELECT CITY
FROM    S
WHERE   S# = 'S4' ;
```

—would fail (the system would produce some error message, such as "Undefined column"). Perhaps worse, attempts to update supplier rows could go disastrously wrong—for example, inserting a new row might cause the supplier number to be taken as the supplier name, the supplier name as the status, and so on.

For reasons such as these, INSERT, UPDATE, and DELETE operations are (as already stated) not permitted against tables in the catalog. Instead, it is the *data definition* statements (CREATE TABLE, CREATE INDEX, etc.) that perform such updates. For example, the CREATE TABLE statement for table S causes (a) an entry to be made for S in the SYSTABLES table and (b) a set of four entries, one for each of the four columns of the S table, to be made in the SYSCOLUMNS table. (It also causes a number of other things to happen too, which are however of no concern to us here.) Thus CREATE is in some ways the analog of INSERT for the catalog. Likewise, DROP is the analog of DELETE, and ALTER is the analog of UPDATE.

> *Aside*: The catalog also includes entries for the catalog tables themselves, of course. However, those entries are not created by explicit, user-written CREATE TABLE operations. Instead, they are created automatically by DB2 itself as part of the system installation procedure. In effect, they are "hard-wired" into the system. *End of aside.*

Although (as we have just seen) the regular SQL updating statements cannot normally be used to update the catalog, there are two SQL statements, namely COMMENT and LABEL, that do perform a kind of limited catalog updating function. We discuss each in turn.

COMMENT

The catalog tables SYSTABLES and SYSCOLUMNS each include a column—not shown in Fig. 8.1—called REMARKS, which can be used (in any particular row) to contain a text string that describes in some way the object identified by the rest of that row. The COMMENT statement is used to enter such descriptions into the REMARKS column in these two tables. The following examples illustrate the two basic formats of that statement.

```
COMMENT ON TABLE S IS
        'Each row represents one supplier' ;
```

The specified string is stored in the REMARKS position in the row for table S in the SYSTABLES table, replacing any value previously stored at that position. The table being COMMENTed on can be either a base table or a view.

```
COMMENT ON COLUMN P.CITY IS
        'Location of (unique) warehouse storing this part' ;
```

The specified string is stored in the REMARKS position in the row for column P.CITY in the SYSCOLUMNS table, replacing any value previously stored at that position. The column being COMMENTed on can be a column of either a base table or a view.

Note: It is also possible to COMMENT ON aliases (see Section 8.4 below). Comments can be retrieved via the regular SQL SELECT statement.

LABEL

The tables SYSTABLES and SYSCOLUMNS each also include a column— again not shown in Fig. 8.1—called LABEL, which can be used (in any particular row) to contain a text string that is to be used in reports involving the object identified by the rest of that row. The LABEL statement is used to enter such strings into the LABEL column in these two tables. The following examples illustrate the two basic formats of that statement.

```
LABEL ON TABLE S IS 'Supplier' ;

LABEL ON COLUMN P.CITY IS 'Warehouse location' ;
```

One reason for introducing such labels is that they can be longer than regular DB2 names (maximum 30 characters instead of 18). Labels, like comments, can be applied to both base tables and views (or to columns thereof), also to aliases (see Section 8.4 below). They can be retrieved via the regular SQL SELECT statement or by DESCRIBE (see Chapter 14).

8.4 ALIASES AND SYNONYMS

It is convenient to close this chapter with a brief discussion of *aliases and synonyms*, although the topic does not really have much to do with the catalog per se (except for the fact that aliases and synonyms, like most other objects, are recorded in the catalog—aliases in SYSTABLES, and synonyms in another catalog table called SYSSYNONYMS). We consider aliases first.

Briefly, an alias is an alternative name for a table (base table or view). In particular, you can define an alias for a table that was created by some other user and for which you would otherwise have to use a fully qualified name. For example, suppose some user ALPHA creates a base table called SAMPLE:

```
CREATE TABLE SAMPLE ... ;
```

As we already know, another user BETA can refer to this table by the qualified name ALPHA.SAMPLE—for instance,

```
SELECT *
FROM   ALPHA.SAMPLE ;
```

Alternatively, user BETA can issue:

```
CREATE ALIAS ZTEST FOR ALPHA.SAMPLE ;
```

and can now refer to ALPHA's table by the simple unqualified name ZTEST—for instance,

```
SELECT *
FROM   ZTEST ;
```

The foregoing capability is particularly useful in a distributed database context, where (e.g.) user BETA and table ALPHA.SAMPLE can be at two different sites; indeed, aliases were first introduced (in DB2 Version 2.2) in connection with DB2's distributed database support. See Part III of this book for further discussion of this possibility. Aliases can also serve to provide a useful level of indirection between application programs and data tables, so that the same program can access different tables on different occasions. For example, aliases could be used to direct a given program to one set of data tables for testing purposes and a different set for production use.

To return to the example: Another user GAMMA can also use user BETA's alias ZTEST to refer to user ALPHA's SAMPLE table. For instance:

```
SELECT *
FROM   BETA.ZTEST ;
```

Note the qualified reference BETA.ZTEST in this example.

There is also a DROP ALIAS statement—syntax:

```
DROP ALIAS alias ;
```

For example:

```
DROP ALIAS ZTEST ;
```

Dropping a table (base table or view) causes all aliases for that table to be dropped automatically.

Now we turn to synonyms. A synonym, like an alias, is an alternative name for a table; the principal differences are that (a) a synonym, unlike an alias, is private to the user who creates it, and (b) a synonym, unlike an alias, cannot refer to a remote table. Let us consider the ALPHA–BETA–GAMMA example again, but using synonyms instead of aliases. If user BETA executes the following statement—

```
CREATE SYNONYM ZTEST FOR ALPHA.SAMPLE ;
```

—then user BETA can refer to user ALPHA's SAMPLE table as simply ZTEST. For instance:

```
SELECT *
FROM    ZTEST ;
```

However, user BETA and table ALPHA.SAMPLE must be at the same site in order for the foregoing to work. Also, as already mentioned, the name ZTEST is completely private to user BETA. Thus, another user GAMMA might also have a synonym ZTEST, distinct from user BETA's; furthermore, user GAMMA's ZTEST might refer to table ALPHA.SAMPLE or to any other table (just so long as the table in question is not at a remote site).

There is also a DROP SYNONYM statement—syntax:

```
DROP SYNONYM synonym ;
```

Dropping a table (base table or view) causes all synonyms for that table to be dropped automatically.

Author's note: The reader might very well be wondering why DB2 provides both synonyms and aliases, given that the two mechanisms are so apparently similar—not to mention the fact that *both* would have been unnecessary, in this writer's opinion, if the view mechanism (to be discussed in Chapter 9) had been properly exploited. The justification (such as it is) for providing them both is mainly historical, not technical, and detailed explanations would be out of place here; suffice it to say that aliases provide basically all of the functionality of synonyms and more besides, and hence that there would seem to be little reason ever to use synonyms instead of aliases, except perhaps for reasons of compatibility with the past. For more details, the reader is referred to the IBM manuals.

EXERCISES

8.1 Sketch the details of the catalog for the suppliers-parts-projects database.

Now write SELECT statements for the following queries (numbers 8.2–8.8).

8.2 Which tables include a CITY column?

8.3 How many columns are there in the shipments table?

8.4 List the names of all catalog tables.

8.5 List the names of all users that have created a table with a CITY column, together with the names of the tables concerned.

8.6 List the names of all users that have created at least one table, together with the number of tables created in each case.

8.7 Which tables have at least one index?

8.8 Which tables have more than one index?

8.9 Write statements to do the following:

(a) Create an appropriate comment on the SPJ table.

(b) Change that comment to "Ignore previous comment".

(c) Create an appropriate comment on the P# column of the SPJ table.

(d) Create an appropriate comment on the XS index.

(e) Create an appropriate label for the P# column of the SPJ table.

(f) Create an appropriate alias for the SYSCOLUMNS table.

(g) Drop that alias.

ANSWERS TO SELECTED EXERCISES

As usual the following solutions are not necessarily unique.

8.2
```
SELECT  TBNAME, TBCREATOR
FROM    SYSIBM.SYSCOLUMNS
WHERE   NAME = 'CITY' ;
```

8.3
```
SELECT  COLCOUNT
FROM    SYSIBM.SYSTABLES
WHERE   NAME = 'SPJ'
AND     CREATEDBY = ... ;
```

8.4
```
SELECT  NAME
FROM    SYSIBM.SYSTABLES
WHERE   CREATOR = 'SYSIBM' ;
```

8.5
```
SELECT  CREATEDBY, NAME
FROM    SYSIBM.SYSTABLES
WHERE   NAME IN
        ( SELECT TBNAME
          FROM    SYSIBM.SYSCOLUMNS
          WHERE   NAME = 'CITY' ) ;
```

8.6
```
SELECT  CREATEDBY, COUNT(*)
FROM    SYSIBM.SYSTABLES
GROUP   BY CREATEDBY ;
```

8.7
```
SELECT  TBNAME, TBCREATOR
FROM    SYSIBM.SYSINDEXES ;
```

8.8
```
SELECT TBNAME, TBCREATOR
FROM    SYSIBM.SYSINDEXES
GROUP   BY TBNAME, TBCREATOR
HAVING COUNT (*) > 1 ;
```

8.9

(a)   `COMMENT ON TABLE SPJ IS 'Appropriate comment' ;`

(b)   `COMMENT ON TABLE SPJ IS 'Ignore previous comment' ;`

(c)   `COMMENT ON COLUMN SPJ.P# IS 'Appropriate comment' ;`

(d)   Trick question! It is not possible to COMMENT ON an index.

(e)   `LABEL ON COLUMN SPJ.P# IS 'Part shipped' ;`

(f)   `CREATE ALIAS COLS FOR SYSIBM.SYSCOLUMNS ;`

(g)   `DROP ALIAS COLS ;`

CHAPTER

◆ 9 ◆

Views

9.1 INTRODUCTION

Recall from Chapter 1 that (named) tables come in two kinds, base tables and views. A base table is a named table that is not defined in terms of other tables; in other words, it is an autonomous table, one that "exists in its own right." A view, by contrast, is a named table that is *not* autonomous and does not "exist in its own right" (although it behaves in some ways as if it did). To be more precise, a view is a named table that is represented, not by its own, physically separate, distinguishable stored data, but rather by its *definition* in terms of other named tables (base tables and/or other views). Here is an example:

```
CREATE VIEW GOOD_SUPPLIERS
    AS SELECT S#, STATUS, CITY
        FROM    S
        WHERE   STATUS > 15 ;
```

When this CREATE VIEW is executed, the subquery following the AS keyword—which is in fact the definition of the view—is *not* executed; instead, it is simply saved in the catalog (in a table called SYSVIEWS) under the specified name GOOD_SUPPLIERS. To the user, however, it is now as if there really were a table in the database called GOOD_SUPPLIERS, with rows and columns as shown in the unshaded portions (only) of Fig. 9.1 below. In other words, the name GOOD_SUPPLIERS denotes a *virtual table*, viz. the table that would result if the subquery in the view definition were actually executed.

Note carefully, however, that although we say that the name GOOD_SUPPLIERS denotes "the table that would result if the subquery in the view definition were actually executed," we do not mean to suggest that it refers to a separate copy of the data—i.e., we do not mean to suggest that the subquery really is executed and a result table retrieved. On the contrary, GOOD_SUPPLIERS is effectively just a *window* into the real table S. Furthermore, that window is *dynamic*: Changes to S will be automatically and instantaneously visible through that window (provided, of course, that those changes lie within the unshaded portion of S); likewise, changes to GOOD_SUPPLIERS will automatically and instantaneously be applied to the real table S (see Section 9.4, later), and hence of course be visible through the window.

Aside: Despite the foregoing, DB2 occasionally does execute the subquery and retrieve a separate copy of the data, for reasons beyond the scope of the present section (see Section 9.3 for further discussion). However, this fact does not materially affect the discussions of the present section. *End of aside*.

Now, depending on the user's level of sophistication (and perhaps also on the application concerned), the user may or may not realize that GOOD_SUPPLIERS really is a view; some users may be aware of that fact (and of the fact that there is a real table S underneath), others may genuinely believe that GOOD_SUPPLIERS is a "real" table in its own right.

GOOD_SUPPLIERS	S#	SNAME	STATUS	CITY
	S1	Smith	20	London
	S2	Jones	10	Paris
	S3	Blake	30	Paris
	S4	Clark	20	London
	S5	Adams	30	Athens

Fig. 9.1 GOOD_SUPPLIERS as a view of base table S (unshaded portions)

Either way, it makes little difference: The point is, users can operate on GOOD_SUPPLIERS just as if it were a real table (with certain exceptions, to be discussed later). For instance, here is an example of a retrieval operation (SELECT statement) against GOOD_SUPPLIERS:

```
SELECT *
FROM    GOOD_SUPPLIERS
WHERE   CITY ¬= 'London' ;
```

As you can see, this SELECT certainly looks just like a normal SELECT on a conventional base table. The system (actually Bind) handles such an operation by converting it into an equivalent operation on the underlying base table (or base tables, plural—see Section 9.2). In the example, the equivalent operation is

```
SELECT S#, STATUS, CITY
FROM    S
WHERE   CITY ¬= 'London'
AND     STATUS > 15 ;
```

This new statement can now be compiled and executed in the usual way. The conversion is done by (in effect) *merging* the SELECT issued by the user with the SELECT that was saved in the catalog when the view was defined. From the catalog, the system knows that "FROM GOOD_SUPPLIERS" really means "FROM S"; it also knows that any selection from GOOD_SUPPLIERS must be further qualified by the WHERE condition "STATUS > 15"; and it also knows that "SELECT *" (from GOOD_SUPPLIERS) really means "SELECT S#, STATUS, CITY" (from S). Hence it is able to translate the original SELECT on the virtual table GOOD_SUPPLIERS into an equivalent SELECT on the real table S—equivalent, in the sense that the effect of executing that SELECT on the real table S is as if there really were a table called GOOD_SUPPLIERS and the original SELECT were executed on that.

Update operations are treated in a similar manner. For example, the operation.

```
UPDATE GOOD_SUPPLIERS
SET    STATUS = STATUS + 10
WHERE  CITY = 'Paris' ;
```

will be converted into

```
UPDATE S
SET    STATUS = STATUS + 10
WHERE  CITY = 'Paris'
AND    STATUS > 15 ;
```

INSERT and DELETE operations are handled analogously.

9.2   VIEW DEFINITION

The general syntax of CREATE VIEW is

```
CREATE VIEW view [ ( column [, column ] ... ) ]
    AS subquery
[ WITH CHECK OPTION ] ;
```

As usual, the subquery cannot include either UNION or ORDER BY;*
apart from these restrictions, however, any SELECT that can appear as a
standalone statement can also appear in a CREATE VIEW statement. Here
are some examples.

```
1. CREATE VIEW REDPARTS ( P#, PNAME, WT, CITY )
       AS SELECT P#, PNAME, WEIGHT, CITY
          FROM   P
          WHERE  COLOR = 'Red' ;
```

The effect of this statement is to create a new view called *xyz*.RED-
PARTS, where *xyz* is the system-known name for the user issuing the
CREATE VIEW statement. User *xyz* can refer to the view as simply
REDPARTS; other users can refer to it as *xyz*.REDPARTS (alternatively,
of course, they can introduce an alias or synonym for it, as discussed in
Chapter 8). The view has four columns, called P#, PNAME, WT, and
CITY, corresponding respectively to the four columns P#, PNAME,
WEIGHT, and CITY of the underlying base table P. If column names are
not specified explicitly in the CREATE VIEW, then the view inherits column names from the source of the view in the obvious way (in the example,
the inherited names would be P#, PNAME, WEIGHT, and CITY). Column
names *must* be specified explicitly (for all columns of the view) if

(a) any column of the view is derived from a function, an operational ex-
    pression, or a literal (and so has no name that can be inherited), or if

(b) two or more columns of the view would otherwise have the same name.

See the next two examples for illustrations of these two cases.

```
2. CREATE VIEW PQ ( P#, TOTQTY )
       AS SELECT P#, SUM (QTY)
          FROM   SP
          GROUP  BY P# ;
```

In this example, there is no name that can be inherited for the second
column, since that column is derived from a function; hence column names
must be specified explicitly, as shown. Notice that this view is not just a
simple row-and-column subset of the underlying base table (unlike the view

---

*UNION and ORDER BY can be used in retrieval operations against the view, of course.

REDPARTS discussed above and the view GOOD_SUPPLIERS discussed in the previous section). It might be regarded instead as a kind of statistical summary of that underlying table.

```
3. CREATE VIEW CITY_PAIRS ( SCITY, PCITY )
        AS SELECT DISTINCT S.CITY, P.CITY
           FROM    S, SP, P
           WHERE   S.S# = SP.S#
           AND     SP.P# = P.P# ;
```

The meaning of this particular view is that a pair of city names (x,y) will appear in the view if and only if a supplier located in city x supplies a part stored in city y. For example, supplier S1 supplies part P1; supplier S1 is located in London and part P1 is stored in London; and so the pair (London,London) appears in the view. Notice that the definition of this view involves a join, so that this is an example of a view that is derived from multiple underlying tables.

```
4. CREATE VIEW LONDON_REDPARTS
        AS SELECT P#, WT
           FROM    REDPARTS
           WHERE   CITY = 'London' ;
```

Since the definition of a view can be any valid subquery, and since a subquery can select data from views as well as from base tables, it is perfectly possible to define a view in terms of other views, as in this example.

```
5. CREATE VIEW GOOD_SUPPLIERS
        AS SELECT S#, STATUS, CITY
           FROM    S
           WHERE   STATUS > 15
           WITH CHECK OPTION ;
```

The clause "WITH CHECK OPTION" indicates that UPDATE and INSERT operations against the view are to be checked to ensure that the UPDATEd or INSERTed row satisfies the view-defining condition (STATUS > 15, in the example). The CHECK option is described in more detail in Section 9.4.

The syntax of DROP VIEW is

```
DROP VIEW view ;
```

The specified view is dropped (i.e., its definition is removed from the catalog). Any views defined in terms of that view are automatically dropped too. Here is an example:

```
DROP VIEW REDPARTS ;
```

If a base table is dropped, all views defined on that base table (or on views of that base table, etc.) are automatically dropped too.

There is no ALTER VIEW statement. Altering a base table (via ALTER TABLE) has no effect on any existing views.

9.3   RETRIEVAL OPERATIONS

We have already explained in outline (in Section 9.1) how retrieval operations on a view are converted into equivalent operations on the underlying base table(s). Usually that conversion process is quite straightforward and works perfectly well.* Occasionally, however, it does *not* work. In particular, it can fail if the user tries to treat a view column as a conventional column and that view column is derived from something other than a simple column of the underlying base table—for example, if it is derived from a function. Consider the following example.

View definition:

```
CREATE VIEW PQ ( P#, TOTQTY )
     AS SELECT P#, SUM (QTY)
        FROM    SP
        GROUP   BY P# ;
```

(this is the "statistical summary" view, Example 2 from Section 9.2).

Attempted query:

```
SELECT AVG (TOTQTY)
FROM    PQ ;
```

If we apply the simple merging process described in Section 9.1 to combine this query with the view definition stored in the catalog, we obtain something like the following:

```
SELECT AVG (SUM (QTY))
FROM    SP
GROUP   BY P# ;
```

And this is not a valid SELECT statement, because SQL does not allow aggregate functions to be nested in this fashion. Instead, therefore, what DB2 does is *materialize the view*—that is, it effectively executes the following sequence of operations:

```
CREATE TABLE TEMPPQ ( P# ..., TOTQTY ... ) ;

INSERT INTO TEMPPQ ( P#, TOTQTY )
       SELECT P#, SUM (QTY)
       FROM    SP
       GROUP   BY P# ;
```

---

*In theory it should *always* work, but this is an area where (regrettably) SQL fails to behave in full accordance with relational theory, as will be seen.

```
SELECT AVG (TOTQTY)
FROM    TEMPPQ ;

DROP TABLE TEMPPQ ;
```

The CREATE TABLE and the INSERT are the statements that perform the view materialization; the SELECT corresponds to the user's original query (but it will work correctly now, because there is now no question of nesting aggregate functions); finally, the DROP destroys the materialized view after the query has been done.

Fig. 9.2 summarizes the situations in which DB2 will perform view materialization instead of the simple merging process described earlier. *Note*: The figure is based on one given in the IBM manuals; we remark, however, that it does not seem to cover all cases (that is, it looks as if there are still some view retrievals that will fail, despite the manuals' claim to the contrary). See Exercise 9.6 at the end of the chapter.

view defn involves: retrieval involves:	DISTINCT	GROUP BY	aggregate	aggregate (DISTINCT)
DISTINCT	X			X
GROUP BY	X	X	X	X
aggregate (ALL/DISTINCT)	X	X	X	X
join view to another table	X	X	X	X
not all view cols in SELECT		X		

Fig. 9.2 Cases in which views are materialized

9.4 UPDATE OPERATIONS

We have already stated (in Chapter 7) that *not all views are updatable*. We are now in a position to be able to amplify that statement. *Note*: Before going any further, we should stress the point that DB2—like most other systems at the time of writing—does not in fact handle the updating of views in a very systematic manner. In what follows, therefore, we first consider the question of view updating from a somewhat theoretical standpoint, then go on to discuss the more directly practical question of how

DB2 actually behaves. The whole subject of view updating in general is discussed in much more detail (but rather formally) in the book *Relational Database: Selected Writings*, by C. J. Date (Addison-Wesley, 1986).

First, consider the two views GOOD_SUPPLIERS and CITY_PAIRS defined earlier in this chapter. For convenience, we repeat their definitions below:

```
CREATE VIEW GOOD_SUPPLIERS
    AS SELECT S#, STATUS, CITY
       FROM    S
       WHERE   STATUS > 15 ;

CREATE VIEW CITY_PAIRS ( SCITY, PCITY )
    AS SELECT DISTINCT S.CITY, P.CITY
       FROM    S, SP, P
       WHERE   S.S# = SP.S#
       AND     SP.P# = P.P# ;
```

Of these two views, GOOD_SUPPLIERS is logically updatable, while CITY_PAIRS is logically not. It is instructive to examine why this is so. In the case of GOOD_SUPPLIERS:

(a) We can INSERT a new row into the view—say the row (S6,40,Rome)— by actually inserting the corresponding row (S6,*bbbb*,40,Rome) into the underlying base table. *Note*: We are using *bbbb* here to represent a string of blanks.

(b) We can DELETE an existing row from the view—say the row (S1,20,London)—by actually deleting the corresponding row (S1,Smith,20,London) from the underlying base table.

(c) We can UPDATE an existing column in the view—say to change the city for supplier S1 from London to Rome—by actually making that same change in the corresponding column in the underlying base table.

We will refer to a view such as GOOD_SUPPLIERS, which is derived from a single base table by simply eliminating certain rows and certain columns of that table, *while preserving that table's primary key*, as a *key-preserving-subset* view. (Remember from Chapter 1 that the primary key is basically just a unique identifier.) Such views are inherently updatable, as the foregoing discussion shows by example.

Now consider the view CITY_PAIRS (which is certainly not a key-preserving-subset view). As explained earlier, one of the rows in that view is the row (London,London). Suppose it were possible to DELETE that row. What would such a DELETE signify?—i.e., what updates (DELETEs or otherwise) on the underlying data would such a DELETE correspond to? The only possible answer has to be "We don't know"; there is simply no way (in general) that we can go down to the underlying base tables and make an appropriate set of updates there. In fact, such an "appropriate set of updates" does not even exist; there is *no* set of updates (in general) that could be applied to the underlying data that would have *precisely* the effect of removing the row (London,London) from the view while leaving everything else in the view unchanged. In other words, *the original DELETE is an inherently unsupportable operation.* Similar arguments can be made to show that INSERT and UPDATE operations are also inherently not supportable on this view.

Thus we see that some views are inherently updatable, whereas others are inherently not. *Note the word "inherently" here.* It is not just a question of some systems being able to support certain updates while others cannot. *No* system can consistently support updates on a view such as CITY_PAIRS unaided (by "unaided" we mean "without help from some human user"). As a consequence of this fact, it is possible to classify views as indicated by the Venn diagram shown in Fig. 9.3 (overleaf).

Note carefully from the figure that although key-preserving-subset views (such as GOOD_SUPPLIERS) are always theoretically updatable, *not all theoretically updatable views are key-preserving-subset views.* In other words, there are some views that *are* theoretically updatable that are *not* key-preserving-subset views. The trouble is, although we know that such views exist, we do not know precisely which ones they are; it is still (in part) a research problem to pin down precisely what it is that characterizes such views.

Now, although it is true that DB2 does support the concept of a primary key, it is unfortunately the case that that support was added only in Version 2—it was not included in Version 1 of the product at all. As a result, DB2's view-updating mechanism does not operate in terms of key-preserving-subset views. Instead, it operates in terms of what we will call *row-and-column-subset* views. A row-and-column-subset view is a view that is derived from a single base table by simply eliminating certain rows and certain columns of that table. A row-and-column-subset view may or may not be a key-preserving-subset view. (More precisely, all key-preserving-subset views are row-and-column-subset views, but the converse is not true.) For the purposes of this book, therefore, the important point is the following:

In DB2, only row-and-column-subset views can be updated.

(Actually even this statement is still not 100 percent accurate. We will make it more precise in a moment.) DB2 is not alone in this regard, by the way; very few products currently support update operations on views that are not row-and-column-subsets, and *no* product currently supports update operations on all views that are known to be updatable.

The fact that not all views are updatable is frequently expressed as

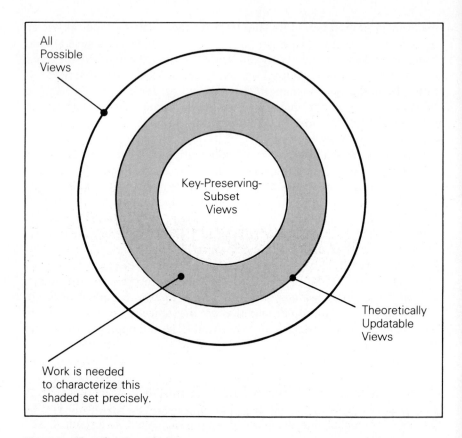

Fig. 9.3 Classification of views

"You cannot update a join." That statement is *not* an accurate character-ization of the situation, nor indeed of the problem: There are some views that are not joins that are not updatable, and there are some views that are joins that are (theoretically) updatable—although not updatable in DB2. But it is true that joins represent the "interesting case," in the sense that it would be very convenient to be able to update a view whose definition in-volved a join. Now, it may well be the case that such views will indeed be updatable in some future DB2 release; but we are concerned here only with what DB2 will currently allow. Let us now make it clear exactly what that is. In DB2, a view that is to accept updates must be derived from a single base table. Moreover:

(a) If a column of the view is derived from an expression involving a scalar operator or a scalar function or a literal, then INSERT operations are not allowed, and UPDATE operations are not allowed on that column. However, DELETE operations are allowed.

(b) If a column of the view is derived from an aggregate function, then the view is not updatable.

(c) If the definition of the view involves either GROUP BY or HAVING at the outermost level, then the view is not updatable.

(d) If the definition of the view involves DISTINCT at the outermost level, then the view is not updatable.

(e) If the definition of the view includes a nested subquery and the FROM clause in that subquery refers to the base table on which the view is defined, then the view is not updatable.

(f) If the FROM clause in the view definition involves multiple (explicit or implicit) range variables, then the view is not updatable.

Finally, of course, a view defined over a nonupdatable view is itself not updatable.

Let us examine the reasonableness of these restrictions. We consider each of the cases (a)–(f) in turn. For each case, we begin by considering an example of a view that illustrates the restriction.

Case (a): View column derived from an expression involving a scalar operator (or a scalar function or a literal)

```
CREATE VIEW P_IN_GRAMS ( P#, GMWT )
     AS SELECT P#, WEIGHT * 454
        FROM   P ;
```

Assuming that table P is as given in Fig. 1.2 (Chapter 1), the set of rows visible through this view is as follows:

P_IN_GRAMS	P#	GMWT
	P1	5448
	P2	7718
	P3	7718
	P4	6356
	P5	5448
	P6	8626

It should be clear that P_IN_GRAMS cannot support INSERT operations, nor UPDATE operations on the column GMWT. (Each of those operations would require the system to be able to convert a gram weight back into pounds, without any knowledge as to how to perform such a conversion.) On the other hand, DELETE operations can be supported (e.g., deleting the row for part P1 from the view can be handled by deleting the row for part P1 from the underlying base table), and so can UPDATE operations on column P# (such UPDATEs simply require a corresponding UPDATE on column P# of that base table).

Similar considerations apply to a view that includes a column that is derived from a scalar function or a literal instead of an operational expression.

Case (b): View column derived from an aggregate function

```
CREATE VIEW TQ ( TOTQTY )
    AS SELECT SUM (QTY)
       FROM    SP ;
```

Sample value:

TQ	TOTQTY
	3100

It should be obvious that none of INSERT, UPDATE, DELETE makes any sense on this view.

Case (c): View defined with GROUP BY (and/or HAVING)

```
CREATE VIEW PQ ( P#, TOTQTY )
    AS SELECT P#, SUM (QTY)
       FROM    SP
       GROUP   BY P# ;
```

Sample values:

PQ	P#	TOTQTY
	P1	600
	P2	1000
	P3	400
	P4	500
	P5	500
	P6	100

It is obvious that view PQ cannot support INSERT operations, nor UPDATE operations against column TOTQTY. DELETE operations, and UPDATE operations against column P#, theoretically *could* be defined to DELETE or UPDATE all corresponding rows in table SP—for example, the operation

```
DELETE
FROM    PQ
WHERE   P# = 'P1' ;
```

could be defined to translate into

```
DELETE
FROM    SP
WHERE   P# = 'P1' ;
```

—but such operations could equally well be expressed directly in terms of table SP anyway. And it is at least arguable that a user who is issuing such operations should have to know exactly which real rows are affected by those operations.

Case (d): View defined with DISTINCT

```
CREATE VIEW CC
    AS SELECT DISTINCT COLOR, CITY
        FROM    P ;
```

Sample values (with corresponding part number(s)):

CC

COLOR	CITY	
Red	London	(from P1,P4,P6)
Green	Paris	(from P2)
Blue	Rome	(from P3)
Blue	Paris	(from P5)

Again, it should be clear that view CC cannot support INSERT operations (INSERTs on the underlying table P require the user to specify a P# value, because part numbers are defined to be NOT NULL). As in case (c), DELETE and UPDATE operations *could* theoretically be defined (to DELETE or UPDATE all corresponding rows in P), but the remarks on this possibility under case (c) apply again here, with perhaps even more force.

Here is another example of case (d):

```
CREATE VIEW PC
    AS SELECT DISTINCT P#, COLOR
        FROM    P ;
```

Sample values:

PC

P#	COLOR
P1	Red
P2	Green
P3	Blue
P4	Red
P5	Blue
P6	Red

This is an example of a view that is obviously updatable in theory—all possible INSERT, UPDATE, and DELETE operations against the view are clearly well-defined. In fact, the view is really a row-and-column-subset view (actually, it is a key-preserving-subset view); but *DB2 is not aware of that fact*. To put it another way, DB2 is not aware of the fact that the DISTINCT specification is actually superfluous here; instead, it simply assumes that the presence of DISTINCT means that any given row of the view *might* be derived from multiple rows of the base table, as in the previous example, and so does not consider the view to be updatable.

Case (e): View involving subquery over same table

```
CREATE VIEW S_UNDER_AVG
    AS SELECT S#, SNAME, STATUS, CITY
       FROM    S
       WHERE   STATUS <
             ( SELECT AVG (STATUS)
               FROM    S ) ;
```

UPDATE and DELETE operations against S_UNDER_AVG are illegal because they would violate the restriction on such operations mentioned at the end of Chapter 7 (Section 7.5). INSERT operations are illegal also, for essentially similar reasons.

Case (f): View involving multiple (explicit or implicit) range variables

```
CREATE VIEW CITY_PAIRS ( SCITY, PCITY )
       AS SELECT DISTINCT S.CITY, P.CITY
          FROM    S, P
          WHERE   S.S# = SP.S#
          AND     SP.P# = P.P# ;
```

This view is not updatable, for reasons that have been adequately discussed already. However, consider this next example:

```
CREATE VIEW P2_SUPPLIERS
    AS SELECT S#, SNAME, STATUS, CITY
       FROM    S, SP
       WHERE   S.S# = SP.S#
       AND     SP.P# = 'P2' ;
```

This view is also not updatable in DB2, even though (once again) it is in fact a key-preserving-subset view; once again, DB2 is not capable of recognizing that fact. What makes this example interesting is that in this case a semantically equivalent view can be defined that *is* updatable, viz:

```
CREATE VIEW P2_SUPPLIERS
    AS SELECT S#, SNAME, STATUS, CITY
       FROM    S
       WHERE   S# IN
             ( SELECT S#
               FROM    SP
               WHERE   P# = 'P2' ) ;
```

This version does not violate the "multiple range variables in the FROM clause" rule.

Finally, we return to the GOOD_SUPPLIERS view once again, in order to discuss a number of remaining issues. The definition of that view (to repeat) is:

```
CREATE VIEW GOOD_SUPPLIERS
    AS SELECT S#, STATUS, CITY
        FROM   S
        WHERE  STATUS > 15 ;
```

This view is a row-and-column-subset view (in fact, it is a key-preserving-subset view), and it is therefore updatable. But note the following:

1. A successful INSERT against GOOD_SUPPLIERS will have to generate an appropriate default value (or null) for the missing column SNAME. Of course, column SNAME must have been defined either with the specification NOT NULL WITH DEFAULT, or with the NOT NULL specification omitted entirely, if the INSERT is to succeed.

2. With our usual data values (see Fig. 1.2), supplier S2 will not be visible through the GOOD_SUPPLIERS view. But that does not mean that the user can INSERT a row into that view with supplier number value S2, or UPDATE one of the other rows so that its supplier number value becomes S2. Such an operation must be rejected, just as if it had been applied directly to table S.

3. Last, consider the following UPDATE:

```
UPDATE GOOD_SUPPLIERS
SET    STATUS = 0
WHERE  S# = 'S1' ;
```

Should this UPDATE be accepted? If it is, it will have the effect of removing supplier S1 from the view, since the S1 row will no longer satisfy the view-defining condition. Likewise, the INSERT operation

```
INSERT
INTO   GOOD_SUPPLIERS ( S#, STATUS, CITY )
VALUES ( 'S8', 7, 'Stockholm' ) ;
```

(if accepted) will create a new supplier row, but that row will instantly vanish from the view. The CHECK option (mentioned in Section 9.2) is designed to deal with such situations. If the clause

```
WITH CHECK OPTION
```

is included in the definition of a view, then all INSERTs and UPDATEs against that view will be checked to ensure that the newly INSERTed or UPDATEd row does indeed satisfy the view-defining condition. If it does not, then the operation will be rejected.

Author's note: It is this writer's opinion that the CHECK option should *always* be specified whenever possible; in fact, it would have been better if WITH CHECK OPTION was assumed by default.

Note, however, that DB2 does not allow the CHECK option to be specified (perhaps reasonably) if the view is not updatable or (less reasonably) if the view definition includes a nested subquery. Note too that if the view is such that UPDATEs are legal on certain columns only (and INSERTs are not allowed at all), then the CHECK option applies only to those UPDATE operations. Note finally that if V is a view for which the CHECK option has been specified, and if W is a view defined on top of V, then the CHECK option for V is automatically inherited by W; that is, updates to V via W will be checked against the defining condition for V. (This rule of inheritance was added to DB2 in Version 1 Release 3; it did not apply to the first two releases.)

9.5 LOGICAL DATA INDEPENDENCE

We have not yet really explained what views are for. One of the things they are for is the provision of what is called *logical data independence*. The notion of *physical* data independence was introduced in Chapter 2: A system like DB2 is said to provide physical data independence because users and user programs are independent of the physical structure of the stored database. A system provides *logical* data independence if users and user programs are also independent of the *logical* structure of the database. There are two aspects to such independence, namely *growth* and *restructuring*.

Growth

As the database grows to incorporate new kinds of information, so the definition of the database must also grow accordingly. (*Note*: We discuss the question of growth in the database here only for completeness; it is important, but it has nothing to do with views as such.) There are two possible types of growth that can occur:

1. The expansion of an existing base table to include a new column (corresponding to the addition of new information concerning some existing type of object—for example, the addition of a COST column to the parts base table);

2. The inclusion of a new base table (corresponding to the addition of a

new type of object—for example, the addition of a projects table to the suppliers-and-parts database).

Neither of these two kinds of change should have any effect on existing users at all (unless those users have been using "SELECT *" or INSERT with the list of column names omitted; as mentioned earlier in this book, the meanings of such statements may change if they happen to be recompiled and the definition of the table concerned has changed in the interim).

Restructuring

Occasionally it might become necessary to restructure the database in such a way that, although the overall information content remains the same, the placement of information within that database changes—i.e., the allocation of columns to tables is altered in some way. Before proceeding further, we make the point that such restructuring is generally undesirable; however, it is sometimes unavoidable. For example, it might be necessary to split a table "vertically," so that commonly required columns can be stored on a faster device and less frequently required columns on a slower device. Let us consider this case in some detail. Suppose for the sake of the example that it becomes necessary (for some reason—the precise reason is not important here) to replace base table S by the following two base tables:

```
SX  ( S#, SNAME, CITY )
SY  ( S#, STATUS )
```

Aside: This replacement operation is not entirely trivial, by the way. One way it might be handled is by means of the following sequence of SQL operations:

```
CREATE TABLE SX
      ( S#      CHAR(5)   NOT NULL,
        SNAME   CHAR(20) NOT NULL WITH DEFAULT,
        CITY    CHAR(15) NOT NULL WITH DEFAULT,
      PRIMARY KEY ( S# ) ) ;

CREATE UNIQUE INDEX XSX ON SX ( S# )  ;

CREATE TABLE SY
      ( S#      CHAR(5)   NOT NULL,
        STATUS  SMALLINT NOT NULL WITH DEFAULT,
      PRIMARY KEY ( S# ) ) ;

CREATE UNIQUE INDEX XSY ON SY ( S# )  ;

INSERT INTO SX ( S#, SNAME, CITY )
      SELECT S#, SNAME, CITY
      FROM   S ;
```

```
INSERT INTO SY ( S#, STATUS )
       SELECT S#, STATUS
       FROM   S ;

DROP TABLE S ;
```

It should also be mentioned in passing that splitting a table "vertically" into two new tables, as in this example, has numerous additional implications—implications, that is, over and above the question of logical data independence that is the principal subject of the present section. For example, DB2 makes it rather difficult to maintain the two tables SX and SY "in synch" with one another once they have been created, for reasons discussed (briefly) in Chapter 11 (Section 11.5, subsection entitled "Delete-Connected"). *End of aside.*

To return to the main topic of discussion: The crucial point to observe in the example is that *the old table S is the (natural) join of the two new tables SX and SY* (over supplier numbers). For example, in table S we had the row (S1,Smith,20,London); in SX we now have the row (S1,Smith,London) and in SY the row (S1,20); join them together and we get the row (S1,Smith,20,London), as before. So we create a *view* that is exactly that join, and we name it S:

```
CREATE VIEW S ( S#, SNAME, STATUS, CITY )
    AS SELECT SX.S#, SX.SNAME, SY.STATUS, SX.CITY
       FROM   SX, SY
       WHERE  SX.S# = SY.S# ;
```

Any program that previously referred to base table S will now refer to view S instead. SELECT operations will continue to work exactly as before (though they will require additional analysis during compilation and will incur additional execution-time overhead). However, update operations will no longer work, because (as explained in Section 9.4) DB2 will not allow updates against a view that is defined as a join. In other words, a user performing update operations is not immune to this type of change, but instead must make some manual alterations to the update statements concerned (and then recompile them).

Thus we have shown that DB2 does *not* provide complete protection against changes in the logical structure of the database (which is why such changes are not a good idea in the first place). But things may not be as bad as they seem, even if manual program alterations are necessary. First, it is easy to discover which programs have to be altered in the light of any such changes; that information can be obtained from the catalog. Second, it is easy to find the statements that need to be changed in those programs; quite apart from anything else, they all start with the prefix EXEC SQL. Third (and most significant), SQL is a very high-level language. The number of statements that have to be changed is therefore usually small, and the meaning of those statements is usually readily apparent; as a result, the necessary changes are usually easy to make. It is *not* like having to change statements in a comparatively low-level language such as COBOL or DL/I (the database language of IMS), where the meaning of a given statement is likely to be highly dependent on the dynamic flow of control through the program to the statement in question. So, even though it is true that manual corrections must be made, the amount of work involved may not be all that great in practice.

To return to the SX-SY example for a moment: Actually, the view S (defined as the join of SX and SY) is a good example of a join view that *is* theoretically updatable. If we assume that the tables SX and SY are kept "in synch" at all times (so that any supplier appearing in SX also appears in SY, and vice versa), then the effect of all possible update operations on view S is clearly defined in terms of SX and SY. (*Exercise*: Do you agree with this statement?) Thus the example illustrates, not only why the ability to update join views would be a useful system feature, but also a case where such updating appears to be a feasible proposition.

9.6 ADVANTAGES OF VIEWS

We conclude this chapter with a brief summary of the advantages of views.

- They provide a certain amount of logical data independence in the face of restructuring in the database, as explained in the previous section.

- They allow the same data to be seen by different users in different ways (possibly even at the same time).

  This consideration is obviously important when there are many different categories of user all interacting with a single integrated database.

- The user's perception is simplified.

  It is obvious that the view mechanism allows users to focus on just the data that is of concern to them and to ignore the rest. What is perhaps not so obvious is that, for retrieval at least, that mechanism can also considerably simplify users' data manipulation operations. In particular, because the user can be provided with a view in which all underlying tables are joined together, the need for explicit operations to step from table to table can be greatly reduced. As an example, consider the view CITY_PAIRS, and contrast (a) the SELECT needed to find cities storing parts that are available from London using that view with (b) the SELECT needed to obtain the same result directly from the underlying base tables. In effect, the complex selection process has been moved out of the realm of data manipulation and into that of data definition (in fact, the distinction between the two realms is far from clearcut in relational languages such as SQL).

▪ Automatic security is provided for hidden data.

"Hidden data" refers to data not visible through some given view. Such data is clearly secure from access through that particular view. Thus, forcing users to access the database via views is a simple but effective mechanism for authorization control. We will discuss this aspect of views in greater detail in the next chapter.

EXERCISES

9.1 Define relation SP of the suppliers-and-parts database as a view of relation SPJ of the suppliers-parts-projects database.

9.2 Create a view from the suppliers-parts-projects database consisting of all projects (project number and city columns only) that are supplied by supplier S1 or use part P1.

9.3 (a) Is your solution to Exercise 9.2 an updatable view?

(b) If it is, can the CHECK option be specified for it?

(c) If it is not, give an updatable version, and repeat part (b) of this exercise.

9.4 Create a view consisting of supplier numbers and part numbers for suppliers and parts that are not "colocated."

9.5 Create a view consisting of supplier rows for suppliers that are located in London (only).

9.6 Given the view definition:

```
CREATE VIEW SUMMARY ( S#, P#, MAXQ, MINQ, AVGQ )
     AS SELECT S#, P#, MAX (QTY), MIN (QTY), AVG (QTY)
        FROM    SPJ
        GROUP   BY S#, P#
        HAVING SUM (QTY) > 50 ;
```

state which of the following retrievals require the view to be materialized.

```
(a)   SELECT *
      FROM    SUMMARY ;

(b)   SELECT *
      FROM    SUMMARY
      ORDER   BY MAXQ ;

(c)   SELECT *
      FROM    SUMMARY
      WHERE   S# ¬= 'S1' ;

(d)   SELECT *
      FROM    SUMMARY
      WHERE   MAXQ > 250 ;
```

```
(e)   SELECT  MAXQ - MINQ, S#, P#
      FROM    SUMMARY
(f)   WHERE   S# = 'S1'
      AND     P# = 'P1' ;
(g)

(h)   SELECT  S#
      FROM    SUMMARY
      GROUP   BY S# ;

      SELECT  S#, MAXQ
      FROM    SUMMARY
      GROUP   BY S#, MAXQ ;

      SELECT  S.S#, SUMMARY.AVGQ
      FROM    S, SUMMARY
      WHERE   S.S# = SUMMARY.S# ;
```

9.7 State the rules concerning the updatability of views in DB2.

9.8 State the rules concerning the CHECK option in DB2.

9.9 Suppose the database is restructured in such a way that tables *A* and *B* are replaced by their natural join *C*. To what extent can the view mechanism conceal that restructuring from existing users?

9.10 Create a view consisting of names of all cities that appear either in the suppliers table or in the parts table.

9.11 Is the following a valid view definition? If so, what does it represent, given the usual suppliers-and-parts data values?

```
CREATE VIEW V4 AS SELECT 2+2 FROM S ;
```

ANSWERS TO SELECTED EXERCISES

9.1 The problem here is: How should the column SP.QTY be defined? The sensible answer seems to be that, for a given (S#,P#) pair, SP.QTY should be the *sum* of all SPJ.QTY values, taken over all J#'s for that (S#,P#) pair:

```
CREATE VIEW SP ( S#, P#, QTY )
    AS SELECT S#, P#, SUM (QTY)
        FROM    SPJ
        GROUP   BY S#, P# ;
```

9.2
```
CREATE VIEW JC ( J#, CITY )
    AS SELECT DISTINCT J.J#, J.CITY
        FROM    J, SPJ
        WHERE   J.J# = SPJ.J#
        AND   ( SPJ.S# = 'S1' OR
                SPJ.P# = 'P1' ) ;
```

9.3 The view defined in the answer to Exercise 9.2 above is not updatable, because it includes multiple range variables in the FROM clause. Here is an updatable version:

```
CREATE VIEW JC ( J#, CITY )
     AS SELECT J.J#, J.CITY
        FROM    J
        WHERE   J.J# IN
              ( SELECT J#
                FROM    SPJ
                WHERE   S# = 'S1' )
                OR      P# = 'P1' ) ;
```

It is not possible to specify the CHECK option for this view, becauses its definition includes a nested subquery.

9.4 CREATE VIEW NON_COLOCATED
AS SELECT S̄#, P#
FROM   S, P
WHERE   S.CITY ¬= P.CITY ;

9.5 CREATE VIEW LONDON_SUPPLIERS
AS SELECT S#, S̄NAME, STATUS
FROM   S
WHERE   CITY = 'London' ;

We have omitted the CITY column from the view, since we know its value must be London for every row visible through the view. Note, however, that this omission means that any row INSERTed through the view will instantly vanish from the view, since its CITY column will be set to blanks (or null). Specifying the CHECK option would avoid this problem (it would of course have the effect of prohibiting all INSERTs through the view).

9.10 Cannot be done; SQL does not permit UNION to appear in a view definition, for reasons—*bad* reasons—that are beyond the scope of this book.

9.11 No, it is not valid, because no column name has been provided for the sole column of the view. The following, by contrast, is valid:

    CREATE VIEW V4 (C4) AS SELECT 2+2 FROM S ;

Given our usual suppliers-and-parts data values, this view looks as follows:

V4	C4
	4
	4
	4
	4
	4

The following definition would have been preferable:

    CREATE VIEW V4 (C4) AS SELECT DISTINCT 2+2 FROM S ;

C H A P T E R

·10·

Security and Authorization

10.1 INTRODUCTION

The term "security" is used in database contexts to mean the protection of the data in the database against unauthorized disclosure, alteration, or destruction. DB2, like most other relational systems, goes far beyond prerelational systems in the degree of security it provides. The unit of data that can be individually protected ranges all the way from an entire table to a specific data value at a specific row-and-column position within such a table. (For certain operations, in fact, the unit can even be greater than one table. For example, the unit for the system operator START and STOP commands is an entire database.) A given user can have different access privileges on different objects (e.g., SELECT privilege only on one table, SELECT and UPDATE privileges on another, and so on). Also, of course, different users can have different privileges on the same object; e.g., user *A* could have the SELECT privilege (only) on a given table, while another user *B* could simultaneously have both SELECT and UPDATE privileges on that same table.

There are two more or less independent features of the system that are involved in the provision of security in DB2:

1. The view mechanism, which (as mentioned at the end of the previous chapter) can be used to hide sensitive data from unauthorized users, and

2. The authorization subsystem, which allows users having specific privileges selectively and dynamically to grant those privileges to other users, and subsequently to revoke those privileges if desired.

We examine the view mechanism in Section 10.3 and the authorization subsystem (specifically, the GRANT and REVOKE statements) in Section 10.4.

Of course, all decisions as to which specific privileges should be granted to which specific users are policy decisions, not technical ones. As such, they are clearly outside the jurisdiction of DB2 per se. All that DB2 can do is *enforce* those decisions once they are made. In order that DB2 should be able to perform this function properly:

(a) The results of those decisions must be made known to the system (this is done by means of the GRANT and REVOKE statements) and must be remembered by the system (this is done by saving them in the catalog, in the form of *authorization constraints*).

(b) There must be a means of checking a given access request against the applicable authorization constraints. (By "access request" here we mean the combination of requested operation plus target object plus requesting user.) Most such checking is done by Bind at the time the original request is compiled (but see the discussion of the BIND command in Chapter 16, Section 16.2).

(c) In order that it may be able to decide which constraints are applicable to a given request, the system must be able to recognize the source of that request—that is, it must be able to recognize which particular user a particular request is coming from. Before getting into a discussion of the view mechanism and the authorization subsystem as such, then, we must first say something about user identification.

10.2 USER IDENTIFICATION

Users are known to DB2 by an "authorization identifier" (authorization ID for short). The authorization ID is what we have been referring to in earlier chapters as the user's "system-known name." If you are a legitimate user of the system, some responsible person in your organization (probably the system administrator—see Section 10.4, later) will have assigned an ID for your particular use. It is your responsibility to identify yourself by supplying that ID when you sign on to the system. Note that you do not sign on directly to DB2 itself; instead, you sign on to (e.g.) the IMS/DC or CICS subsystem (see Chapter 2). That subsystem will then pass your ID on to DB2 when it passes control to DB2. Hence any validation or authentication of your ID (e.g., password checking) is done by the relevant subsystem, not by DB2. DB2 simply assumes that any request that purports to come from authorization ID *xyz* (say) does in fact come from *xyz*.

Note: The foregoing paragraph glosses over one important point, which we now explain. Typically, installations would like to deal with *user functional areas* rather than with individual users per se; for example, they would like to be able to grant some specific authority to "Everyone in the accounting department," say, and to be able to add users to, and remove users from, the accounting department as a separate operation. Typically, therefore, the installation operates as follows:

1. Each individual user is assigned an authorization ID as described above. That ID is used to sign on to the system, and serves as the *primary* ID for the user in question. Tables and other objects that are purely private to that user will typically be created under the control of, and hence be owned by, that primary ID.

2. Each functional area (e.g., each department) in the organization is also assigned an authorization ID. However, that ID is typically *not* given sign-on authority; users sign on to the system under their primary ID, as explained in the previous paragraph. Once signed on, users can operate under their primary ID, or—using the SQL statement SET CURRENT SQLID (see below)—they can switch to a *secondary* ID (i.e., one of the functional area IDs). An external subsystem such as IBM's RACF (Resource Access Control Facility) keeps track of the secondary ID(s) that can legitimately be used by a given primary ID. Observe that a given primary ID can have any number of secondary IDs, also that the same secondary ID can be used by any number of primary IDs. *Note*: "CURRENT SQLID" is a special register, like CURRENT DATE, CURRENT TIME, etc. (see Chapter 3). Its value is an authorization ID.

3. The SET CURRENT SQLID statement has the format:

```
SET CURRENT SQLID = sqlid ;
```

where "sqlid" can be a character string literal, a host variable (if the SET statement is embedded in a host program—see Chapter 12), or

USER. USER has the effect of restoring the primary ID as the current ID. (USER, like CURRENT SQLID, is a special register whose value is an authorization ID.)

Under the foregoing scheme, for example, user Joe can create a table that belongs to the accounting department *and that continues to do so even if Joe leaves that department or is removed from the system*. Any user that can use the accounting department ID as a secondary ID can access that table using that ID. The catalog shows the table as having the accounting department as its owner (confusingly called the CREATOR in the catalog table SYSTABLES) and as having been CREATED BY user Joe (CREATEDBY is another column in SYSTABLES, as explained in Chapter 8).

One final remark: Despite the foregoing, it still seems more intuitive to talk in terms of users rather than authorization IDs, and we will continue to do so for the remainder of this chapter. But the reader should clearly understand that when we say (for example) "User JUDY," we really mean "Any user operating under the (primary or secondary) authorization ID JUDY."

10.3 VIEWS AND SECURITY

To illustrate the use of views for security purposes, we present a series of examples, based once again (for the most part) on the suppliers-and-parts database. *Note*: The creator of a view must have at least the SELECT privilege on every table referenced in the view definition. See the discussion of access privileges in the next section.

1. For a user permitted access to complete supplier rows, but only for suppliers located in Paris:

```
CREATE VIEW PARIS_SUPPLIERS
    AS SELECT S#, SNAME, STATUS, CITY
       FROM   S
       WHERE  CITY = 'Paris' ;
```

Users of this view see a "horizontal subset"—or (better) a row subset or *value-dependent* subset—of base table S.

2. For a user permitted access to all supplier rows, but not to supplier ratings (STATUS values):

```
CREATE VIEW S#_NAME_CITY
    AS SELECT S#, SNAME, CITY
       FROM   S ;
```

Users of this view see a "vertical subset"—or (better) a column subset or *value-independent* subset—of base table S.

3. For a user permitted access to supplier rows for suppliers in Paris (only), but not to supplier ratings:

```
CREATE VIEW PARIS_S#_NAME_CITY
    AS SELECT S#, SNAME, CITY
       FROM   S
       WHERE  CITY = 'Paris' ;
```

Users of this view see a row-and-column subset of base table S.

4. For a user permitted access to catalog rows (i.e., SYSTABLES entries) for tables created by that user only:

```
CREATE VIEW MY_TABLES
    AS SELECT *
       FROM    SYSIBM.SYSTABLES
       WHERE   CREATEDBY = USER ;
```

As explained in Section 10.2, USER is a "special register"—i.e., a zero-argument builtin scalar function (see Chapter 3)—whose value is an authorization ID. It can appear wherever a character string literal can appear. The authorization ID in question is the primary ID for the user issuing the *manipulative* statement that causes the USER reference to be evaluated. In the case at hand, for instance, it does not represent the ID of the user who creates the view, but rather the ID of the user who *uses* the view. For example, if user Joe issues the statement

```
SELECT *
FROM   MY_TABLES ;
```

then DB2 will effectively convert that statement into

```
SELECT *
FROM   SYSIBM.SYSTABLES
WHERE  CREATEDBY = 'JOE' ;
```

Like the view in the first example above, this view represents a "horizontal subset" of the underlying base table. In the present example, however, different users see different subsets (in fact, no two users' subsets overlap). Such views are sometimes described as *context-dependent*, because their precise value depends on the context in which they are used.

5. For a user permitted access to average shipment quantities per supplier, but not to any individual quantities:

```
CREATE VIEW AVQ ( S#, AVGQTY )
     AS SELECT S#, AVG(QTY)
        FROM   SP
        GROUP  BY S# ;
```

Users of this view see a *statistical summary* of the underlying base table SP.

As the foregoing examples illustrate, the view mechanism of DB2 provides a very important measure of security "for free" ("for free" because the view mechanism is included in the system for other purposes anyway, as explained in Chapter 9). What is more, many authorization checks—even value-dependent checks—can be applied at compilation time instead of execution time, a significant performance benefit. However, the view-based approach to security does suffer from some slight awkwardness on occasion—in particular, if some user needs different privileges over different subsets of the same table at the same time. Consider the following example. Suppose a given user is allowed to SELECT ratings (i.e., status values) for all suppliers but is allowed to UPDATE them only for suppliers in Paris. Then two views will be needed:

```
CREATE VIEW ALL_RATINGS
     AS SELECT S#, STATUS
        FROM   S ;

CREATE VIEW PARIS_RATINGS
     AS SELECT S#, STATUS
        FROM   S
        WHERE  CITY = 'Paris' ;
```

SELECT operations can be directed at ALL_RATINGS but UPDATE operations must be directed at PARIS_RATINGS instead. This fact can lead to rather obscure programming. Consider, for example, the structure of a program that scans and prints all supplier ratings and also updates some of them (those for suppliers in Paris) as it goes.

Another drawback has to do with the fact that, when a row is INSERTed or UPDATEd through a view, DB2 does not require that the new or updated row satisfy the view-defining condition. It is possible to impose such a requirement via the CHECK option, but (as explained in Chapter 9) the CHECK option cannot always be used, and in any case it *is* an option—it does not have to be specified. Thus, for example, view PARIS_SUPPLIERS above can prevent the user from seeing suppliers who are not in Paris, but in the absence of the CHECK option it cannot prevent the user from inserting such a supplier or from moving an existing Paris supplier to some other city. Of course, any such operation will cause the new or updated row to vanish from the view, but it will still appear in the underlying base table.

10.4 GRANT AND REVOKE

The view mechanism discussed in Section 10.3 allows the database to be conceptually divided up into subsets (possibly overlapping subsets) in various ways so that sensitive information can be hidden from unauthorized users. However, it does not allow for the specification of the operations that *authorized* users may execute against those subsets. That function is performed by the SQL statements GRANT and REVOKE, which we now discuss.

First, in order to be able to perform any operation at all on any object at all, the user must hold the appropriate *privilege* (or authority) for the operation and object in question; otherwise, the operation will be rejected with an appropriate error message or exception code. For example, even to execute such a simple statement as

```
SELECT *
FROM    S ;
```

successfully, the user must hold the SELECT privilege on table S.

DB2 recognizes a wide range of privileges. Broadly speaking, however, every privilege falls into one of the following classes:

- *Table* privileges, which have to do with operations such as SELECT that apply to tables (both base tables and views);
- *Plan* and *package* privileges, which have to do with such things as the authority to use a given plan, package, or collection of packages;
- *Collection* privileges, which permit the holder to create packages in a given collection;
- *Database* privileges, which apply to operations such as the creation of a table within a particular database;
- *Use* privileges, which have to do with the use of certain "system resources," namely storage groups, table spaces, and buffer pools (all described in Chapter 15);

    and finally

- *System* privileges, which apply to certain system-wide operations such as the creation of a new database.

There are also certain "bundled" privileges, which serve in effect as shorthand for collections of other privileges (not always from just one of the foregoing classes). In particular, the *system administration* privilege (SYSADM) is shorthand for the collection of all other privileges in the system. Thus a user holding the SYSADM privilege can perform any operation in the entire system, providing it is legal. (An example of an operation that would not be "legal" in this sense would be an attempt to drop one of the catalog tables. Even a user with SYSADM authority cannot do that.)

We now present a description (considerably simplified) of how the overall security mechanism works. When DB2 is first installed, part of the installation process involves the designation of a specially privileged user as the *system administrator* for that DB2 system. (The system administrator is identified to DB2 by an authorization ID, of course, just like everyone else.) That user, who is automatically given the SYSADM privilege, will be responsible for overall control of the system throughout the system's lifetime; for example, monitoring DB2 execution and collecting performance statistics are part of the system administrator's job. But here we are concerned only with security considerations. To return to the main thread of the discussion, therefore: Initially, then, there is one user who can do everything—in particular, he or she can grant privileges to other users—and nobody else can do anything at all.

Note, incidentally, that although the system administrator is of course a holder of the SYSADM privilege, not all holders of the SYSADM privilege are the system administrator; other users can subsequently be granted the SYSADM privilege also, *but that privilege can subsequently be revoked again*. The SYSADM privilege can never be revoked from the system administrator.*

Next, a user who creates an object, say a base table, is automatically given full privileges on that object, including in particular the privilege of granting such privileges to another user. Of course, "full privileges" here does not include privileges that do not make sense. For example, if user *U* has the SELECT privilege (only) on base table *T*, and if *U* creates some view *V* that is based on *T*, then *U* certainly does not receive any update privileges on *V*. Likewise, if *U* creates a view *V* that is a join of tables *T1* and *T2*, then *U* does not receive any update privileges on *V*, regardless of whether *U* holds such privileges on *T1* and *T2*, because DB2 does not permit *any* update operations against a join view.

GRANT

Granting privileges is done by means of the GRANT statement. The general format of that statement is:

---

*Of course, this remark should not be construed to mean that there really is a single person who is the system administrator for all time (even if, e.g., that person leaves the company). Rather, there is a single *authorization ID* that is considered by the system to identify the system administrator. Anyone who can sign on to the system under that ID (and can supply the necessary password) will be treated as the system administrator so long as he or she remains signed on. The password *can* of course be changed from time to time, and probably should be.

```
GRANT privileges [ ON [ type ] objects ] TO users ;
```

where "privileges" is a list of one or more privileges, separated by commas, or the phrase ALL PRIVILEGES;* "users" is either a list of one or more authorization IDs separated by commas, or the special keyword PUBLIC (meaning all users); "objects" is a list of names of one or more objects (all of the same type) separated by commas; and "type" indicates the type of that object or those objects (if "type" is omitted, it is assumed to be TABLE—see the last example under "Table privileges" below). The ON clause does not apply when the privileges being granted are system privileges. Here are some examples:

Table privileges:

```
GRANT SELECT ON TABLE S TO CHARLEY ;

GRANT SELECT, UPDATE ( STATUS, CITY ) ON TABLE S
               TO JUDY, JACK, JOHN ;

GRANT ALL PRIVILEGES ON TABLE S, P, SP TO PHIL, FRED ;

GRANT SELECT ON TABLE P TO PUBLIC ;

GRANT DELETE ON S TO PHIL ;
```

Package and plan privileges:

```
GRANT EXECUTE ON PLAN PLANB TO JUDY ;
```

Collection privileges:

```
GRANT CREATE IN COLLQ TO AMANDA ;
```

User AMANDA is permitted to create packages in collection COLLQ[†] (by specifying COLLQ as the relevant collection in the BIND PACKAGE command—see Chapter 16 for further discussion).

Database privileges:

```
GRANT CREATETAB ON DATABASE DBX TO NANCY ;
```

User NANCY is permitted to create tables in database DBX. See Chapter 15 for a discussion of databases.

Use privileges:

```
GRANT USE OF TABLESPACE DBX.TS76 TO TOM ;
```

---

*ALL PRIVILEGES (which can be specified only if "type" is TABLE) does not literally mean all privileges, but rather all privileges for which the user issuing the GRANT has grant authority. See the discussion of the GRANT option, later. The keyword PRIVILEGES in ALL PRIVILEGES is just noise and can be omitted.

[†]If the collection COLLQ does not already exist, the GRANT will effectively create it (note that there is no explicit CREATE COLLECTION operation).

User TOM is permitted to use table space TS76 in database DBX to store any tables he may create. Again, see Chapter 15 for further discussion.

System privileges:

```
GRANT CREATEDBC TO JACQUES, MARYANN ;
```

Users JACQUES and MARYANN are permitted to create new databases. If they do so, they will automatically be given the DBCTRL privilege over those databases (see the subsection on "Bundled Privileges" at the end of this section).

Table Privileges

It is not our purpose in this book to give a complete and exhaustive treatment of all of the numerous privileges that DB2 recognizes. However, we will say a little more about table privileges, since those are probably the ones of widest interest. The privileges that apply to tables (both base tables and views) are as follows:

```
SELECT
UPDATE    (can be column-specific)*
DELETE
INSERT
```

The remaining two apply to base tables only:

```
ALTER    (privilege to execute ALTER TABLE on the table)
INDEX    (privilege to execute CREATE INDEX on the table)
```

To *create* a base table, as already mentioned, requires CREATETAB authority for the database to which the table is to belong. To create a view requires SELECT authority on every table referenced in the definition of that view, as mentioned in Section 10.3.

Note that there are no specific "DROP" privileges; instead, a table (base table or view) can be dropped only by its owner or by a user holding appropriate administrative authority (e.g., SYSADM; again, see the subsection on "Bundled Privileges" at the end of this section).

REVOKE

If user *U1* grants some privilege to some other user *U2*, user *U1* can subsequently *revoke* that privilege from user *U2*. Revoking privileges is done by

---

*Observe that SELECT authority, unlike UPDATE authority, is not column-specific. The reason is that the effect of a column-specific SELECT authority can always be obtained by granting (non-column-specific) SELECT authority on a *view* consisting of just the relevant columns.

means of the REVOKE statement, whose general format is very similar to that of the GRANT statement:

```
REVOKE privileges [ ON [ type ] objects ] FROM users ;
```

Revoking a given privilege from a given user causes all packages dependent on that privilege to be flagged as invalid, and hence causes an automatic rebind on the next invocation of each such package. The process is essentially analogous to what happens when an object such as an index is dropped.*

Here are some examples of the REVOKE statement:

```
REVOKE SELECT ON TABLE S FROM CHARLEY ;

REVOKE UPDATE ON TABLE S FROM JOHN ;

REVOKE CREATETAB ON DATABASE DBX FROM NANCY, JACK ;

REVOKE SYSADM FROM SAM ;
```

It is not possible to be column-specific when revoking an UPDATE privilege.

The GRANT Option

If user *U1* has the authority to grant a privilege *P* to another user *U2*, then user *U1* also has the authority to grant that privilege *P* to user *U2* "with the GRANT option" (by specifying WITH GRANT OPTION in the GRANT statement). Passing the GRANT option along from *U1* to *U2* in this manner means that *U2* in turn now has the authority to grant the privilege *P* to some third user *U3*. And therefore, of course, *U2* also has the authority to pass the GRANT option for *P* along to *U3* as well, etc., etc. For example:

User *U1*:

```
GRANT SELECT ON TABLE S TO U2 WITH GRANT OPTION ;
```

User *U2*:

```
GRANT SELECT ON TABLE S TO U3 WITH GRANT OPTION ;
```

User *U3*:

```
GRANT SELECT ON TABLE S TO U4 WITH GRANT OPTION ;
```

And so on. If user *U1* now issues

---

*Recall from Chapter 2 that sometimes it might be entire plans that are invalidated and subsequently rebound, not just individual packages.

```
REVOKE SELECT ON TABLE S FROM U2 ;
```

then the revocation will *cascade* (that is, *U2*'s GRANT to *U3* and *U3*'s GRANT to *U4* will also be revoked automatically). Note, however, that it does *not* follow that *U2* and *U3* and *U4* no longer have SELECT authority on table S—they may additionally have obtained that authority from some other user *U5*. When *U1* REVOKEs, it is only authorities that are derived from *U1* that are in fact canceled. For example, consider the following sequence of events:

User *U1* at time *t1*:

```
GRANT SELECT ON TABLE S TO U2 WITH GRANT OPTION ;
```

User *U5* at time *t2*:

```
GRANT SELECT ON TABLE S TO U2 WITH GRANT OPTION ;
```

User *U2* at time *t3*:

```
GRANT SELECT ON TABLE S TO U3 ;
```

User *U1* at time *t4*:

```
REVOKE SELECT ON TABLE S FROM U2 ;
```

(*t1* < *t2* < *t3* < *t4*). User *U1*'s REVOKE at time *t4* will not in fact remove the SELECT privilege on table S from user *U2*, because user *U2* has also received that privilege from *U5* at time *t2*. Furthermore, since user *U2*'s GRANT to user *U3* was at time *t3* and *t3* > *t2*, it is possible that that GRANT was of the privilege that was received from user *U5* rather than from *U1*, so user *U3* does not lose the privilege either. And if the REVOKE at time *t4* is from user *U5* instead of user *U1*, users *U2* and *U3* would *still* keep the privilege; *U2* keeps the privilege received from *U1*, and *U2*'s GRANT *could* have been of the privilege received from *U1* instead of *U5*, and so *U3* again does not lose the privilege either.

However, suppose by contrast that the sequence of events had been as follows:

User *U1* at time *t1*:

```
GRANT SELECT ON TABLE S TO U2 WITH GRANT OPTION ;
```

User *U2* at time *t2*:

```
GRANT SELECT ON TABLE S TO U3 WITH GRANT OPTION ;
```

User *U5* at time *t3*:

```
GRANT SELECT ON TABLE S TO U2 WITH GRANT OPTION ;
```

User *U1* at time *t4*:

```
REVOKE SELECT ON TABLE S FROM U2 ;
```

User *U1*'s REVOKE at time *t4* will not remove the SELECT privilege on table S from user *U2*, because user *U2* has also received that privilege from *U5* at time *t3*. In contrast with the previous example, however, it *will* remove the privilege from user *U3* at this time, because user *U2*'s GRANT at time *t2 must* have been of the privilege received from user *U1*.

It is not possible to revoke the GRANT option without at the same time revoking the privilege to which that option applies.

Bundled (Administrative) Privileges

We conclude this section with a brief sketch of the "bundled" privileges SYSADM, SYSCTRL, DBADM, DBCTRL, DBMAINT, SYSOPR, and PACKADM.

- SYSADM

  SYSADM ("system administration") authority allows the holder to execute any operation that the system supports.

- SYSCTRL

  SYSCTRL ("system control") authority allows the holder to execute any operation that the system supports, *except* for operations that access database contents (e.g., operations such as "create storage group" are allowed, but SQL data manipulation operations are not).

- DBADM

  DBADM ("database administration") authority on a specific database allows the holder to execute any operation that the system supports on that database.

- DBCTRL

  DBCTRL ("database control") authority on a specific database allows the holder to execute any operation that the system supports on that database, *except* for operations that access the data content of that database (e.g., utility operations such as "recover database" are allowed, but SQL data manipulation operations are not).

- DBMAINT

  DBMAINT ("database maintenance") authority on a specific database allows the holder to execute read-only maintenance functions (such as the utility operation "image copy") on that database.

- SYSOPR

  SYSOPR ("system operator") authority allows the holder to carry out console operator functions on the system (such as starting and stopping system trace activities).

- PACKADM

  PACKADM ("package administration") authority on a specific collection allows the holder to create packages in that collection and gives the holder all package privileges on all packages in that collection.

For a particular database, DBADM subsumes DBCTRL, and DBCTRL subsumes DBMAINT. SYSCTRL subsumes DBCTRL (for all databases) and SYSOPR. SYSADM, of course, subsumes everything.

10.5 CONCLUSION

By this point the reader may be feeling a little overwhelmed by the extent of the security facilities available with DB2. We therefore summarize below the authorization requirements that are most directly relevant to ordinary *users* (as we have defined that term—i.e., end-users and application programmers).

1. First, no particular privileges at all are needed to precompile a source module to create a database request module or DBRM.

2. Binding a DBRM to produce a new package requires the BINDADD privilege,* plus the CREATE IN privilege for the collection to which the new package is to be assigned. (BINDADD is a system privilege, CREATE IN is a collection privilege.) Binding a DBRM also normally requires the appropriate privileges for all of the SQL statements in the DBRM being bound (but see the discussion of the BIND command in Chapter 16, Section 16.2).

3. Replacement of an existing package by an updated version, which may have to be done several times during the application development process, requires the BIND privilege on that package (plus, again, appropriate privileges for all of the SQL statements involved, except as noted in Chapter 16, Section 16.2).

---

*Or the BINDAGENT privilege. BINDAGENT allows one user (the "agent") to bind packages or plans on behalf of another (the "owner"). This capability allows the clerical task of binding packages and plans (also rebinding and freeing them—see Chapter 16) to be assigned to some user who is not authorized to execute those packages or plans, nor to access the relevant data (the plan or package owner still has to have all of the other relevant privileges, but the agent does not). For simplicity, however, we will generally ignore BINDAGENT throughout the remainder of our discussions in this chapter.

4. Binding a set of packages together to produce a plan requires the EXECUTE privilege on all of the packages (and/or collections of packages) involved.*

5. Execution of a program that invokes an application plan requires the EXECUTE privilege on that plan. Table privileges (etc.) are *not* required.

6. Execution of a SQL statement (or indeed any other kind of operation) through the interactive interface DB2I (or through QMF, etc.) requires the privilege(s) appropriate to that particular statement or operation.

We conclude with a few miscellaneous points.

1. First, the entire DB2 security mechanism is optional. It can be disabled if desired at DB2 start-up time. If it is, then of course anyone can do anything (anything that makes sense, that is; for example, it is still not possible to drop a catalog table). We have ignored this possibility (for obvious reasons) throughout the bulk of this chapter.

2. There is no point in a DBMS providing an extensive set of security controls if it is possible to bypass those controls. DB2's security mechanism would be almost useless if (for example) it were possible to access DB2 data from a conventional MVS program via conventional VSAM calls (remember from Chapter 1 that DB2 data is stored in VSAM linear data sets). For this reason, DB2 works in harmony with all the other software components in its environment—MVS, TSO, VSAM, IMS, CICS, etc.—to guarantee that the total system is secure. In particular, DB2's VSAM data sets can be protected by any or all of the following: MVS passwords, VSAM passwords, RACF (Resource Access Control Facility), and/or third-party security products. In addition, the security facilities of IMS and CICS can be used to provide all of the standard IMS and CICS controls—for example, to restrict the set of terminals from which specific applications or commands can be invoked.

3. A mechanism is provided—the details are beyond the scope of this chapter—by which the environments in which a given package or plan can be used are restricted. For example, a given package might be limited to use in a CICS environment only. See the discussion of the ENABLE and DISABLE options on the BIND command in Chapter 16.

4. A mechanism (the *Data Definition Control Facility*) is also provided by which the use of CREATE, ALTER, and DROP operations on various

---

*If the plan includes any DBRMs as well as or instead of packages, the requirements of paragraph 2 apply also (except for CREATE IN).

objects can be restricted to specific applications—in particular, to frontend tools such as QMF or the Repository Manager.*

5. Finally, DB2 also provides an *Audit Facility* by which an audit trail can be created showing attempted security violations (among other things). The audit information is written (via the DB2 Instrumentation Facility) to SMF or GTF data sets, not to DB2 tables. (SMF—"System Management Facility"—and GTF—"Generalized Trace Facility"—are standard MVS components.) Auditing can be restricted to specific tables and/or specific operations and can be dynamically and selectively started and stopped. The following items can be audited:

- authorization failures
- GRANT and REVOKE operations
- CREATE/ALTER/DROP TABLE operations
- first SELECT (per table per transaction)
- first update (per table per transaction)
- BINDs
- utility operations

Auditing is requested for a given table by means of the AUDIT option on CREATE and ALTER TABLE. AUDIT NONE (default) means no auditing; AUDIT CHANGES means audit INSERT/UPDATE/DELETE operations; AUDIT ALL means audit SELECT operations as well. Changing the AUDIT option (via ALTER TABLE) invalidates all packages (and/or plans) that use the table in question; as usual, such packages (and/or plans) will automatically be rebound the next time they are invoked.

EXERCISES

Exercises 10.1 and 10.2 refer to a base table called STATS, defined as follows:

```
CREATE TABLE STATS
     ( USERID      CHAR(8)   NOT NULL,
       SEX         CHAR(1),
       DEPENDENTS  DECIMAL(2),
       OCCUPATION  CHAR(20),
       SALARY      DECIMAL(7),
       TAX         DECIMAL(7),
       AUDITS      DECIMAL(2),
     PRIMARY KEY ( USERID ) ) ;
```

---

*We note in passing that the Data Definition Control Facility is implemented, not (as might have been expected) by means of GRANT and REVOKE operations, but rather by means of a mechanism similar to that used to implement the Resource Limit Facility RLF (see Chapter 16).

10.1 Write SQL statements to give:

(a) User Ford SELECT privileges over the entire table.

(b) User Smith INSERT and DELETE privileges over the entire table.

(c) Each user SELECT privileges over that user's own row (only).

(d) User Nash SELECT privileges over the entire table and UPDATE privileges over the SALARY and TAX columns (only).

(e) User Todd SELECT privileges over the USERID, SALARY, and TAX columns (only).

(f) User Ward SELECT privileges as for Todd and UPDATE privileges over the SALARY and TAX columns (only).

(g) User Pope full privileges (SELECT, UPDATE, INSERT, DELETE) over rows for preachers (only).

(h) User Jones SELECT privileges as for Todd and UPDATE privileges over the TAX and AUDITS columns (only).

(i) User King SELECT privileges for maximum and minimum salaries per occupation class, but no other privileges.

(j) User Clark DROP privileges on the table.

10.2 For each of parts (a) through (j) under Exercise 10.1, write SQL statements to remove the indicated privilege(s) from the user concerned.

10.3 Let p represent some privilege; let $U1$, $U2$, . . ., $U8$ be a set of authorization IDs; and let $U1$ and $U5$ initially be the only holders of p. Further, assume that $U1$ and $U5$ hold the GRANT option for p. Consider the following sequence of events (note that all GRANTs include the specification WITH GRANT OPTION):

```
User U1 at time t1:    GRANT p TO U2 WITH GRANT OPTION ;
User U1 at time t2:    GRANT p TO U3 WITH GRANT OPTION ;
User U1 at time t3:    GRANT p TO U4 WITH GRANT OPTION ;
User U2 at time t4:    GRANT p TO U6 WITH GRANT OPTION ;
User U5 at time t5:    GRANT p TO U2 WITH GRANT OPTION ;
User U5 at time t6:    GRANT p TO U3 WITH GRANT OPTION ;
User U5 at time t7:    GRANT p TO U6 WITH GRANT OPTION ;
User U4 at time t8:    GRANT p TO U7 WITH GRANT OPTION ;
User U1 at time t9:    REVOKE p FROM U2 ;
User U1 at time t10:   REVOKE p FROM U4 ;
User U3 at time t11:   GRANT p TO U1 WITH GRANT OPTION ;
User U1 at time t12:   REVOKE p FROM U3 ;
User U3 at time t13:   GRANT p TO U7 WITH GRANT OPTION ;
User U5 at time t14:   REVOKE p FROM U6 ;
User U1 at time t15:   GRANT p TO U5 WITH GRANT OPTION ;
User U5 at time t16:   GRANT p TO U8 WITH GRANT OPTION ;
User U8 at time t17:   GRANT p TO U5 WITH GRANT OPTION ;
User U1 at time t18:   GRANT p TO U8 WITH GRANT OPTION ;
User U5 at time t19:   REVOKE p FROM U8 ;
User U1 at time t20:   GRANT p TO U3 WITH GRANT OPTION ;
```

At the end of this sequence, who still holds p?

ANSWERS TO SELECTED EXERCISES

10.1 (a) GRANT SELECT ON TABLE STATS TO FORD ;

(b) GRANT INSERT, DELETE ON TABLE STATS TO SMITH ;

(c) CREATE VIEW MY_REC
      AS SELECT *
         FROM   STATS
         WHERE   USERID = USER ;

    GRANT SELECT ON TABLE MY_REC TO PUBLIC ;

(d) GRANT SELECT, UPDATE (SALARY, TAX)
         ON TABLE STATS TO NASH ;

(e) CREATE VIEW UST
         AS SELECT USERID, SALARY, TAX
         FROM   STATS ;

    GRANT SELECT ON TABLE UST TO TODD ;

(f) CREATE VIEW UST
         AS SELECT USERID, SALARY, TAX
         FROM   STATS ;

    GRANT SELECT, UPDATE (SALARY, TAX)
         ON TABLE UST TO WARD ;

(g) CREATE VIEW PREACHERS
         AS SELECT *
         FROM   STATS
         WHERE   OCCUPATION = 'Preacher' ;

    GRANT ALL PRIVILEGES ON TABLE PREACHERS TO POPE ;

"ALL PRIVILEGES" on a base table includes ALTER and INDEX privileges; on a view (like PREACHERS), it does not, since these operations do not apply to views.

(h) CREATE VIEW UST
         AS SELECT USERID, SALARY, TAX
         FROM   STATS ;

    CREATE VIEW UTA
         AS SELECT USERID, TAX, AUDITS
         FROM   STATS ;

    GRANT SELECT ON TABLE UST TO JONES ;

    GRANT UPDATE (TAX, AUDITS) ON TABLE UTA TO JONES ;

(i) CREATE VIEW SALBOUNDS (OCCUPATION, MAXSAL, MINSAL)
         AS SELECT OCCUPATION, MAX (SALARY), MIN (SALARY)
         FROM   STATS
         GROUP   BY OCCUPATION ;

    GRANT SELECT ON SALBOUNDS TO KING ;

(j) GRANT SYSADM TO CLARK ;

Dropping a table is not an explicitly grantable privilege. A base table can be dropped only by its owner or by someone holding the SYSADM privilege or the DBADM privilege over the database containing the table.

10.2 (a) `REVOKE SELECT ON TABLE STATS FROM FORD ;`

(b) `REVOKE INSERT, DELETE ON TABLE STATS FROM SMITH ;`

(c) `REVOKE SELECT ON TABLE MY_REC FROM PUBLIC ;`

Or perhaps simply:

`DROP VIEW MY_REC ;`

For (d) through (j) below we generally ignore the possibility of simply dropping the view (if applicable).

(d) `REVOKE SELECT, UPDATE ON TABLE STATS FROM NASH ;`

(e) `REVOKE SELECT ON TABLE UST FROM TODD ;`

(f) `REVOKE SELECT, UPDATE ON TABLE UST FROM WARD ;`

(g) `REVOKE ALL PRIVILEGES ON PREACHERS FROM POPE ;`

"ALL PRIVILEGES" in REVOKE does not literally mean all privileges, but rather all privileges that the user issuing the REVOKE has granted.

(h) `REVOKE SELECT ON TABLE UST FROM JONES ;`

   `REVOKE UPDATE ON TABLE UTA FROM JONES ;`

(i) `REVOKE SELECT ON TABLE SALBOUNDS FROM KING ;`

(j) `REVOKE SYSADM FROM CLARK ;`

10.3 All users except $U4$ and $U6$ (i.e., users $U1$, $U2$, $U3$, $U5$, $U7$, and $U8$) still hold p.

C H A P T E R

◆ 11 ◆

Integrity

11.1 INTRODUCTION

The term "integrity" is used in database contexts to refer to the accuracy, validity, or correctness of the data in the database. Maintaining integrity is of paramount importance, for obvious reasons; and it is desirable, again for obvious reasons, that the task of maintaining integrity be handled by the system rather than by the user (to the maximum extent possible). In order that it may carry out this task, the system needs to be aware of any *integrity constraints* or *rules* that apply to the data; it then needs to monitor update operations to ensure that they do not violate any of those constraints or rules. As a trivial example,* the suppliers-and-parts database might be

---

*Trivial it may be, but it cannot readily be handled in the current version of DB2.

subject to the rule that supplier numbers must conform to a certain pattern, consisting of an "S" followed by up to four decimal digits. INSERT and UPDATE operations should therefore be monitored to ensure that they do not introduce a supplier number that fails to conform to this pattern.

The general idea, then, is that integrity constraints should be specified as part of the database definition; they will then be stored in the system catalog, and used by the system to control updates to the database. Now, any given database is likely to be subject to a very large number of constraints. For example, the following might all be constraints that apply to the suppliers-and-parts database:

- Supplier numbers must be of the form S*nnnn* (where *nnnn* stands for up to four decimal digits)
- Part numbers must be of the form P*nnnnn* (where *nnnnn* stands for up to five decimal digits)
- Supplier status values must be in the range 1–100
- Supplier and part cities must be drawn from a certain list
- Part colors must be drawn from a certain list
- Part weights must be greater than zero
- Shipment quantities must be a multiple of 100
- All red parts must be stored in London
- If the supplier city is London, then the status must be 20

and so on. However, most such constraints are *specific*, in the sense that they apply to one specific database. All of the examples above are specific in this sense. The relational model, by contrast, includes two *general* integrity rules—general, in the sense that they apply, not just to some specific database such as suppliers-and-parts, but rather to *every* database (or, at least, every database that claims to conform to the model). These two general rules have to do, respectively, with *primary keys* and with what are called *foreign keys*. They are discussed in detail in Sections 11.2 (primary keys) and 11.3 (foreign keys). It is perhaps worth mentioning that DB2 does a reasonably good job on the two general integrity rules (as of Version 2, when primary and foreign key support was introduced); unfortunately, it is still rather weak on database-specific rules.

Following the discussions in Sections 11.2 and 11.3, Sections 11.4–11.6 go on to examine certain specific aspects of the DB2 support for these concepts in more depth. Specifically, Section 11.4 treats the question of referential cycles, Section 11.5 discusses some DB2 restrictions, and Section 11.6 covers a number of miscellaneous integrity topics.

11.2 PRIMARY KEYS

We have referred informally to the term "primary key" several times already in this book. Informally, the primary key of a table is just a unique identifier for that table. For example, the primary keys for tables S, P, and SP of the suppliers-and-parts database are S.S#, P.P#, and SP.(S#,P#), respectively. Note that, as the last of these examples indicates, the primary key is allowed to be *composite* (i.e., to consist of multiple columns); in fact, it is possible, though perhaps unusual, to have a table where the only unique identifier (i.e., the primary key) is the combination of *all* the columns in the table—i.e., the table is "all key." An example would be the table obtained by eliminating the QTY column from table SP.

It is also possible, though again unusual, for a table to have *more than one* unique identifier. As an example, let us suppose that every supplier always has a unique supplier number *and* a unique supplier name. (This happens to be the case with our sample data values—Fig. 1.2—but here we are supposing that it is true *for all time*; it is not just chance, i.e., it is not just a question of the values that happen to appear in the table at some specific instant.) In such a case we would say that the table has multiple *candidate* keys; we would then choose one of those candidate keys to be the *primary* key, and the remainder would then be said to be *alternate* keys (an alternate key is thus a candidate key that is not the primary key).

Let us now make these ideas a little more precise.

Definition

Let CK be some subset of the columns of table T. Then CK is a *candidate key* for T if and only if it satisfies the following two time-independent properties:

1. *Uniqueness*:
   At any given time, no two rows of T have the same value for CK.

2. *Minimality*:
   No proper subset of CK has the uniqueness property.

Note that the relational model *requires* every table to have at least one candidate key, and hence *requires* every table to have a primary key, as we shall see in a moment. *Note*: This requirement is equivalent to the requirement that, at any given time, no two rows in the table are identical. However, DB2 unfortunately does not enforce this requirement. We shall return to this point also in a moment.

Now we focus on base tables specifically. From the set of candidate keys for a given base table, exactly one is designated as *the primary key* for that table; the remainder, if any, are called *alternate keys*. *Note*: The rationale by which the primary key is chosen, in cases where there is more than one candidate key, is outside the scope of the relational model per se. In practice the choice is usually straightforward. However, it is important to understand that, in practice, it is the *primary* key that is the really significant one, at least for base tables; candidate keys and alternate keys are merely concepts that necessarily arise during the process of defining the (arguably more important) concept "primary key."

So why are primary keys important? One obvious answer to this question is that primary key support is prerequisite to foreign key support, as we shall see in Section 11.3. A more fundamental answer is that primary keys provide the basic *row-level addressing mechanism* in a relational system. That is, the only system-guaranteed way of pinpointing some specific row in some specific base table is *by its primary key value*. For example, the SQL request

```
SELECT *
FROM    P
WHERE   P# = 'P3' ;
```

is guaranteed to retrieve (at most) one row. By contrast, the request

```
SELECT *
FROM    P
WHERE   CITY = 'Paris' ;
```

will retrieve an unpredictable number of rows, in general. It follows that *primary keys are just as fundamental to the successful operation of a relational system as main memory addresses are to the successful operation of the underlying machine*. Tables that do not have a primary key—i.e., tables that permit duplicate rows—are bound to display strange and anomalous behavior in certain circumstances (details beyond the scope of this book). This is why we *strongly* recommend that users always conform to the primary key discipline. (As indicated above, DB2 does in fact permit tables to exist that have no primary key, but we *strongly* recommend that users never exercise this option.)

Primary Key Definition in DB2

Primary keys can be defined when the base table is created via CREATE TABLE, or added to an existing base table via ALTER TABLE. CREATE TABLE is the normal case; ALTER TABLE is intended mainly to assist in migrating tables from an earlier DB2 release that did not support primary keys. A UNIQUE index is required to enforce primary key uniqueness.

Also, every column participating in the primary key must be explicitly declared to be NOT NULL.

Here again is the syntax of CREATE TABLE, Format 1 (repeated from Chapter 4, but ignoring the optional "other parameters"):

```
CREATE TABLE base-table
  ( column-definition [, column-definition ] ...
  [, primary-key-definition ]
  [, alternate-key-definition [, alternate-key-definition ] ... ] )
  [, foreign-key-definition [, foreign-key-definition ] ... ] ) ;
```

where "primary-key-definition" is as follows:

```
PRIMARY KEY ( column [, column ] ... )
```

(for the syntax of "foreign-key-definition," see Section 11.3; "alternate-key-definitions" are discussed at the end of the present section). Here is an example:

```
CREATE TABLE SP
     ( S#      CHAR(5)  NOT NULL,
       P#      CHAR(6)  NOT NULL,
       QTY     INTEGER,
     PRIMARY KEY ( S#, P# ) ... ) ;
```

(The "..." represents some missing foreign key definitions. Again, see Section 11.3.)

After the base table (with its primary key) has been created, it still cannot be accessed via SQL data manipulation operations—in DB2 parlance, its definition is still "incomplete"—until an appropriate UNIQUE index has also been created. That index must be on *exactly* the columns that make up the primary key (no additional columns), in *exactly* the proper left-to-right order (no permutations).* For example:

```
CREATE UNIQUE INDEX XSP ON SP ( S#, P# ) ;
```

The index that enforces primary key uniqueness is referred to as the *primary index* for the table in question. Once the primary index has been created, the table is available for use, and DB2 will reject any attempt to violate the primary key uniqueness constraint. *Note*: If the primary index is subsequently dropped, the table will become "incomplete" again (it cannot even be used for pure retrieval operations), and it will remain so until an appropriate index has been created once again.

Here is the syntax for adding a primary key to an existing base table:

```
ALTER TABLE base-table [ ADD ] primary-key-definition ;
```

---

*ASC/DESC specifications and other index parameters (see Chapter 4) make no difference here, of course.

A suitable UNIQUE index must already exist for this ALTER TABLE to succeed, and all columns involved must have been declared to be NOT NULL. The base table must not already possess a defined primary key. *Note*: Adding a primary key definition to a given base table will invalidate packages and/or plans that refer to that table.

It is also possible to remove the primary key definition from an existing base table:

```
ALTER TABLE base-table DROP PRIMARY KEY ;
```

Any foreign key definitions (see Section 11.3) that previously referred to the now dropped primary key will automatically be dropped also. (The user must hold the ALTER privilege on the tables containing those foreign keys.) The primary index will *not* be dropped, but it will lose its "primary" status.

Entity Integrity

The first of the two general integrity rules of the relational model is called the *entity* integrity rule, and goes as follows:

- No component of the primary key of a base table is allowed to accept nulls.

The justification for this rule is basically that primary key values in base tables serve to identify entities in the real world—for example, supplier number values in table S serve to identify suppliers—and it simply does not make sense to record information in the database about an entity whose identity is unknown. For further discussion, see Appendix A.

Note carefully that, in the case of composite primary keys, the entity integrity rule says that each individual value of the primary key must be *wholly* (not just partially) nonnull. In the case of the shipments table, for example, with composite primary key SP.(S#,P#), S# and P# must *both* have "nulls not allowed"; neither S# nor P# is allowed to accept nulls.

DB2 supports the entity integrity rule, because it requires an explicit declaration of NOT NULL for all primary key components and hence enforces the "nulls not allowed" constraint.

Alternate Key Definition in DB2

Alternate key support was added to DB2 in Version 2.3. An alternate key definition* takes the form

---

*It would be more accurate to call the construct a *candidate* key definition, since DB2 will allow a base table to have one or more UNIQUE clauses without any PRIMARY KEY clause. However, this latter practice is not recommended.

```
UNIQUE ( column [, column ] ... )
```

Unlike primary keys, alternate keys can be defined only when the base table is created via CREATE TABLE; they cannot be added later via ALTER TABLE. As with primary keys, however, a UNIQUE index is required to enforce uniqueness, and every column participating in the alternate key must be explicitly declared to be NOT NULL.

Here is an example. Suppose that supplier *names*, as well as supplier numbers, are required to be unique within the suppliers table. Then we might define that table as follows:

```
CREATE TABLE S
     ( S#       CHAR(5)   NOT NULL,
       SNAME    CHAR(20)  NOT NULL,
       STATUS   SMALLINT  NOT NULL WITH DEFAULT,
       CITY     CHAR(15)  NOT NULL WITH DEFAULT,
     PRIMARY KEY ( S# ),
     UNIQUE ( SNAME ) ) ;
```

Note: If the alternate key involves just a single column, as it does in the example, then it can optionally be defined by means of a UNIQUE specification on the column definition instead of by means of a separate UNIQUE clause. For instance:

```
CREATE TABLE S
     ( S#       CHAR(5)   NOT NULL,
       SNAME    CHAR(20)  NOT NULL UNIQUE,
       STATUS   SMALLINT  NOT NULL WITH DEFAULT,
       CITY     CHAR(15)  NOT NULL WITH DEFAULT,
     PRIMARY KEY ( S# ) ) ;
```

11.3 FOREIGN KEYS

Consider the following (attempted) INSERT operation on the usual suppliers-and-parts database (a repeat of Example 7.2.3):

```
INSERT
INTO    SP ( S#, P#, QTY )
VALUES ( 'S20', 'P20', 1000 ) ;
```

It should be clear that, if this INSERT were to be accepted, there would be a loss of integrity, because the database would now include a shipment for a nonexistent supplier and a nonexistent part. In fact, the example illustrates a very specific kind of loss of integrity, namely a loss of *referential* integrity. In this section we examine the question of referential integrity in some detail. As the example suggests, the basic idea is quite simple:

- It is clear in the case of suppliers-and-parts that every value appearing in column SP.S# at any given time ought simultaneously to appear in column S.S# (the primary key of the S table)—for otherwise the database would include a shipment for a nonexistent supplier. Likewise, every value appearing in column SP.P# at any given time ought simultaneously to appear in column P.P# (the primary key of the P table), for otherwise the database would include a shipment for a nonexistent part.

- Columns such as SP.S# and SP.P# are examples of what are called *foreign keys*. We can define this concept (loosely) as follows: A foreign key is a column (or combination of columns) in one table whose values are required to match values of the primary key in some other table— or possibly in the same table (see later).

    Note, incidentally, that the converse is *not* a requirement—that is, the primary key corresponding to some given foreign key might contain a value that currently does not appear as a value of that foreign key. In the case of the sample data for suppliers-and-parts in Fig. 1.2, for instance, the supplier number S5 appears in table S but not in table SP (supplier S5 does not currently supply any parts).

- A foreign key value represents a *reference* to the row containing the matching primary key value (the *referenced row* or *target row*). The problem of ensuring that the database does not contain any invalid foreign key values is therefore known as the *referential integrity* problem. The constraint that values of a given foreign key must match values of the corresponding primary key is known as a *referential constraint*. The table that contains the foreign key is known as the *referencing* table and the table that contains the corresponding primary key is known as the *referenced table* or *target table*.

- The referential constraints that apply in the case of suppliers and parts can be represented by means of the following *referential diagram*:

$$S \longleftarrow SP \longrightarrow P$$

(each arrow means that there is a foreign key in the table from which the arrow emerges that refers to the primary key of the table to which the arrow points).

Two asides: First, DB2 documentation (perversely) shows the arrows going the other way (i.e., from the target table to the referencing table). Our convention accords better with intuition and is consistent with relational literature. Second, DB2 uses the terms "parent table" and "dependent table" instead of "target table" and "referencing table," respectively. We prefer our own terms, for reasons too numerous to be stated here. *End of asides*.

We now proceed to make these ideas a little more precise. We begin with a formal definition of the term "foreign key"—a definition, however, that is deliberately a trifle more restrictive than that adopted in DB2. We will return to this point in a moment.

Definition

Let FK be some subset of the columns of base table T2. Then FK is a *foreign key* if and only if it satisfies the following two time-independent properties:

1. Each value of FK is either wholly null or wholly nonnull. (By "wholly null or wholly nonnull," we mean that, if FK is composite, then each value of FK either has all components null or all components nonnull, not a mixture.)
2. There exists a base table T1 (the target table) with primary key PK such that each nonnull value of FK is identical to the value of PK in some row of T1.

T1 and T2 are not necessarily distinct; that is, a table might include a foreign key whose (nonnull) values are required to match values of the primary key of that same table. As an example, consider the table

```
EMP  ( EMP#, ..., SALARY, ..., MGR_EMP#, ... )
```

in which column MGR_EMP# represents the employee number of the manager of the employee identified by EMP#. Here EMP# is the primary key and MGR_EMP# is a foreign key that refers to it. A table such as EMP in this example is known in DB2 as a *self-referencing* table. *Exercise*: Invent some sample data for this table.

Notice that foreign keys, unlike primary keys, must sometimes have "nulls allowed." (We remark, however, that nulls in a foreign key column are likely to be of the "value does not exist" variety, rather than the "value unknown" variety.) As an example, consider the self-referencing table EMP shown above. What is the value of MGR_EMP# for the president of the company?

Note: As mentioned earlier, our definition of foreign key is slightly more restrictive than the definition actually used in DB2. The fact is, there is a certain amount of disagreement in the open literature as to the most satisfactory definition of the term. For example, some authorities (and some systems, including DB2, as we shall see) do not require composite foreign key values to be wholly null or wholly nonnull, but instead allow some components to be null and others nonnull simultaneously. Likewise, some authorities and some systems (though *not* DB2) allow foreign keys to reference alternate keys as well as primary keys. And finally, some authorities allow there to be multiple target tables instead of just one. The foreign key definition given above is offered in the belief that:

(a) It is the most satisfactory in most commonly-occurring practical situations; and

(b) It is upward-compatible with a weaker definition (such as one that permits partially null composite foreign keys), should such a weakening ever prove desirable.

Let us consider some of the implications of the foreign key concept. To fix our ideas, let us concentrate on the suppliers table S and the shipments table SP, where we have a referential constraint from SP.S# in the SP table to S.S# in the S table (for simplicity, let us ignore the parts table P). It should be clear that there are basically four potential situations in which the referential constraint might be violated, namely as follows:

- *Case 1*: An INSERT on the SP table might introduce a shipment for which there is no matching supplier. For example:

```
INSERT
INTO    SP ( S#, P#, QTY )
VALUES ( 'S20', ... ) ;
```

- *Case 2*: An UPDATE on column SP.S# of the SP table might introduce a shipment supplier number for which there is no matching supplier. For example:

```
UPDATE SP
SET     S# = 'S20'
WHERE   ... ;
```

- *Case 3*: A DELETE on the S table might remove a supplier for which there exists a matching shipment. For example:

```
DELETE
FROM    S
WHERE   S# = 'S1' ;
```

- *Case 4*: An UPDATE on column S.S# of the S table might remove a supplier number for which there exists a matching shipment. For example:

```
UPDATE S
SET     S# = 'S20'
WHERE   S# = 'S1' ;
```

In order to enforce the referential constraint, therefore, the system must somehow deal with all four of these cases. Let us now turn to the question of foreign key support in DB2 specifically; in particular, let us see how DB2 deals with each of the four potential problems just outlined. We begin by explaining how foreign keys are defined in the first place.

Foreign Key Definition in DB2

Like primary keys, foreign keys can be defined when the base table is created (via CREATE TABLE) or added to an existing base table (via ALTER TABLE). CREATE TABLE is the more usual case; however, ALTER TABLE is needed if there is a constraint cycle (see Section 11.4) or if the table is being migrated from an earlier DB2 release. *Note*: There is no requirement that there be an index on a foreign key, but indexes are usually a good idea for performance reasons. For example, it is very common to perform a primary-to-foreign-key join, and an index on the foreign key may very well improve the performance of such a join. The performance of referential integrity enforcement may also improve in the presence of indexes.

The syntax of a foreign key definition is as follows:

```
FOREIGN KEY [ foreign-key ] ( column [, column ] ... )
          REFERENCES base-table [ ON DELETE effect ]
```

where "effect" is RESTRICT or CASCADE or SET NULL. If the ON DELETE clause is omitted, ON DELETE RESTRICT is assumed. Here is an example:

```
CREATE TABLE SP
     ( S#       CHAR(5)   NOT NULL,
       P#       CHAR(6)   NOT NULL,
       QTY      INTEGER,
     PRIMARY KEY ( S#, P# ) ,
     FOREIGN KEY SFK ( S# ) REFERENCES S
                            ON DELETE CASCADE ,
     FOREIGN KEY PFK ( P# ) REFERENCES P
                            ON DELETE RESTRICT ) ;
```

Explanation:

1. Let T2 be the table containing the foreign key, and let T1 be the target table (i.e., the table named in the REFERENCES specification), thus:

$$T2 \longrightarrow T1$$

Table T1 must have a defined primary key, and must be "complete" in the sense of Section 11.2 (i.e., the index that enforces primary key uniqueness must already exist).

2. The optional "foreign-key" is a name (a *constraint name*) that will be used by DB2 in diagnostic messages relating to this foreign key (it is also used in ALTER . . . DROP statements—see later in this section). We have

introduced the names SFK and PFK in our example. If the user does not supply a name, DB2 will assign one anyway, derived from the name of the first (or only) column participating in the foreign key in question. *Note*: The constraint name is *not* considered as a column name and cannot be used in data manipulation statements such as SELECT.

3. The foreign key and the target primary key must contain the same number of columns, n say, and the ith column of the foreign key and the ith column of the target primary key must have exactly the same data type (i here is in the range 1 to n and refers to the left-to-right order in which the columns are listed in the containing foreign or primary key definition). Note, therefore, that a foreign key will be composite if and only if the primary key it matches is composite also.

4. The ON DELETE clause defines the *delete rule* for the target table with respect to this foreign key—that is, it defines what happens if an attempt is made to delete a row from the target table (i.e., a target row). As explained above, the possible specifications are RESTRICT, CASCADE, and SET NULL (and RESTRICT is assumed if nothing is specified). The meanings are as follows:

- RESTRICT: The delete is "restricted" to the case where there are no matching rows in table T2 (it is rejected if any such rows exist).

- CASCADE: The delete "cascades" to delete all matching rows in table T2 also.

  - Note that table T2 might in turn be referenced by a foreign key in some other table T3. If it is, then if any delete on table T1 cascades to some row r2 in table T2, then the effect is exactly as if an attempt had been made to delete that row r2 directly; i.e., it depends on the delete rule specified for the foreign key from T3 to T2. And so on, recursively, to any number of levels.

- SET NULL: In this case, the foreign key must have "nulls allowed." The target row is deleted and the foreign key is set to null in all matching rows in table T2.

  - If the foreign key is composite, then DB2 actually requires only that *at least one component* of the foreign key have nulls allowed, and SET NULL sets such components (only) to null in matching rows and leaves other components unchanged. (A composite foreign key value that is partly null is ALWAYS regarded as satisfying the referential constraint in DB2, *regardless of the values of the nonnull components*—a state of affairs that can lead to great complexity. For this reason among others, we strongly recommend that composite foreign keys either have nulls allowed for all components or nulls not allowed for all components, not a mixture of the two; and if they have nulls allowed, we strongly recommend that each individual value of the foreign key either has all components null or all components nonnull, not a mixture of the two.)

With the SP definition shown above, therefore, an attempt to delete a specific supplier row will cascade to delete all shipments for that supplier also; an attempt to delete a specific part row will succeed only if there are no shipments for that part.

5. There is no "ON UPDATE" clause to define an "update rule" for (the primary key of) the target table with respect to this foreign key. Instead, any attempt to update the primary key in a row of the target table is "restricted" to the case where there are no matching rows in the referencing table (it is rejected if any such rows exist). In effect, therefore, the only update rule supported is RESTRICT, and that rule can be stated only implicitly, not explicitly.

6. One slight oddity is that, in order to define a foreign key (via either CREATE TABLE or ALTER TABLE—see below) that refers to some target table T1, the user must possess the ALTER privilege on table T1. (Generally, the ALTER privilege is what is needed in order to execute an ALTER TABLE operation on the table in question. However, defining a foreign key referring to T1 does not involve an ALTER TABLE on T1.) By contrast, a user who deletes a row in table T1 and thereby deletes or updates one or more rows in some other table T2 (thanks to a CASCADE or SET NULL delete rule) does *not* require any particular privilege—not even the SELECT privilege—on table T2.

Let us now see how these rules enable DB2 to deal with the four potential problem cases identified earlier. Once again we use the suppliers-and-parts example to fix our ideas.

- *Case 1*: An INSERT on the SP table might introduce a shipment for which there is no matching supplier.

  This situation is prevented by virtue of the fact that SP.S# is a foreign key in table SP matching the primary key S.S# of table S. Such an INSERT will simply be rejected. Of course, an INSERT that introduces a shipment for a supplier that does already exist in table S (and a part that does already exist in table P) will be accepted.

- *Case 2*: An UPDATE on column SP.S# of the SP table might introduce a shipment supplier number for which there is no matching supplier.

  This situation is also prevented by virtue of the fact that SP.S# is a foreign key in table SP matching the primary key S.S# of table S. Such an UPDATE will simply be rejected. Of course, an UPDATE that introduces an SP.S# value that does already exist in table S (and does not introduce an SP.P# value that does not already exist in table P) will be accepted.

- *Case 3*: A DELETE on the S table might remove a supplier for which there exists a matching shipment.

  This situation is handled by the delete rule (CASCADE in the sample definition shown earlier). In general, RESTRICT would mean that the delete will be accepted only if there *are* no such matching shipments; CASCADE would mean that any such matching shipments will be removed anyway; and SET NULL (not possible in the case of suppliers-and-parts, because SP.S# does not have "nulls allowed") would mean that any such matching shipments will not be removed but will be updated so that they are no longer "matching."

- *Case 4*: An UPDATE on column S.S# of the S table might remove a supplier number for which there exists a matching shipment.

  This situation is handled by the (implicit) update rule RESTRICT, which means that the update will be accepted only if no such matching shipments exist.

We now briefly discuss the use of ALTER TABLE to add and remove foreign key definitions. The syntax for adding such a definition is as follows:*

```
ALTER TABLE base-table [ ADD ] foreign-key-definition ;
```

If "base-table" is nonempty (as it might be if it is a table that is being migrated from an earlier release of DB2), adding a foreign key definition causes DB2 to set an internal "check pending" condition on the data. The data now cannot be accessed by SQL at all, not even for retrieval, until the condition has been cleared (i.e., until it has been ascertained that all referential constraints are satisfied). The DB2 CHECK utility can be used to help find and correct any referential constraint violations. *Note*: The CHECK utility and the "check pending" condition are discussed further in Chapter 16 (Section 16.4).

The syntax for removing a foreign key definition is:

```
ALTER TABLE base-table DROP FOREIGN KEY foreign-key ;
```

---

*In certain circumstances, adding a foreign key definition will cause existing plans and/or packages to be invalidated. The details are beyond the scope of this text; refer to the IBM manuals for more information.

Here "foreign-key" is the constraint name assigned when the foreign key was defined.

One final point regarding data definition: If a base table is dropped, any foreign key definitions referring to that table are dropped automatically (perhaps surprisingly, the user does *not* have to hold the ALTER privilege on the tables containing those foreign keys). The delete rules (CASCADE, etc.) for those foreign keys are *not* invoked (thus, e.g., dropping table S does not cause all rows in table SP to be deleted).

Referential Integrity

For completeness, we close this section with a note on the second of the two general integrity rules of the relational model, namely the *referential* integrity rule. The referential integrity rule simply states that the database must not contain any unmatched foreign key values (i.e., nonnull foreign key values for which there does not exist a matching value of the corresponding primary key). DB2 obviously enforces this rule, as the discussions above demonstrate.

11.4 REFERENTIAL CYCLES

Section 11.3 explained the basic foreign key concept and described the relevant DB2 data definition statements. An understanding of the material of that section is probably sufficient to deal with most of the situations that are likely to arise in practice. However, there are a number of additional detailed points that need to be made in any reasonably comprehensive treatment of the subject. The points in question (a slightly mixed bag) are discussed in this section and in Sections 11.5–11.6, later. This section deals with referential cycles.

First we need to introduce the concept of a "referential path" (not an official DB2 term). Let tables Tn, $T(n-1)$, . . ., $T2$, $T1$ be such that there is a referential constraint from table Tn to table $T(n-1)$, a referential constraint from table $T(n-1)$ to table $T(n-2)$, . . ., and a referential constraint from table $T2$ to table $T1$:

```
Tn ──▶ T(n-1) ──▶ T(n-2) ──▶ ... ──▶ T2 ──▶ T1
```

Then the chain of arrows from Tn to $T1$ represents a referential path from Tn to $T1$. We can define this concept (recursively) as follows: There is a *referential path from table Tn to table T1* if and only if (a) table Tn references table $T1$ directly or (b) table Tn references some table $T(n-1)$ such that there is a referential path from table $T(n-1)$ to table $T1$.

Now we can define the term *referential cycle*. Briefly, we say that a referential cycle exists if there is a referential path from some table T to itself. One special case, the self-referencing table, has already been mentioned in Section 11.3; a self-referencing table constitutes a cycle involving just a single table. More generally, however, a cycle might involve any number of tables: If there is a referential constraint from table Tn to table T$(n-1)$, a referential constraint from table T$(n-1)$ to table T$(n-2)$, . . ., a referential constraint from table T2 to table T1, and a referential constraint from table T1 to the original table Tn, then we have a cycle involving n tables (i.e., a cycle of length n):

```
Tn ──▶ T(n-1) ──▶ T(n-2) ──▶ ... ──▶ T2 ──▶ T1 ──▶ Tn
```

Here is an example of a cycle of length two:

```
EMP   ( EMP#, ..., SALARY, ..., DEPT# ... )

DEPT ( DEPT#, ..., MGR_EMP#, ..., BUDGET ... )
```

In table EMP, EMP# is the primary key and DEPT# is a foreign key referring to DEPT; in table DEPT, DEPT# is the primary key and MGR_EMP# (employee number for the department manager) is a foreign key referring to EMP.

In order to specify the referential constraints that form a cycle, it is necessary to use ALTER TABLE for at least one of those specifications, because a FOREIGN KEY clause cannot refer to a table that does not yet exist. Also (as mentioned in Section 1.3), a FOREIGN KEY clause cannot refer to a table that does not yet have an index to enforce uniqueness on its primary key. The general pattern is thus:

```
CREATE TABLE T1 ( ... PRIMARY KEY ... ) ;
CREATE UNIQUE INDEX ON T1 ( primary key ) ;

CREATE TABLE T2 ( ... PRIMARY KEY ... ,
      FOREIGN KEY ... REFERENCES T1 ... ) ;
CREATE UNIQUE INDEX ON T2 ( primary key ) ;

    . . . . . . . . . . . . . . . . . . . . . . . . .

CREATE TABLE Tn ( ... PRIMARY KEY ... ,
      FOREIGN KEY ... REFERENCES T(n-1) ... ) ;
CREATE UNIQUE INDEX ON Tn ( primary key ) ;

ALTER TABLE T1 ADD FOREIGN KEY ... REFERENCES Tn ... ;
```

By way of example, we give the data definition (in outline) for the EMP/DEPT cycle introduced above:

```
CREATE TABLE EMP
      ( EMP#      NOT NULL ,
        ...       ,
        SALARY    ,
        ...       ,
        DEPT#     ,
        ...       ,
      PRIMARY KEY ( EMP# ) ) ;
```

```
CREATE UNIQUE INDEX XEMP ON EMP ( EMP# ) ;

CREATE TABLE DEPT
     ( DEPT#      NOT NULL ,
        ...     ,
       MGR_EMP# ,
        ...     ,
       BUDGET   ,
        ...     ,
       PRIMARY KEY ( DEPT# ) ,
       FOREIGN KEY MFK ( MGR_EMP# ) REFERENCES EMP ) ;

CREATE UNIQUE INDEX XDEPT ON DEPT ( DEPT# ) ;

ALTER TABLE EMP ADD FOREIGN KEY DFK ( DEPT# ) REFERENCES DEPT ;
```

Note that the foregoing pattern applies even in the self-referencing case; that is, the foreign key has to be defined via ALTER TABLE, not as part of the original CREATE TABLE.

Note: In general, it is likely in a cycle that at least one of the foreign keys will have nulls allowed. In the cycle shown above, for example, at least one of the two foreign keys EMP.DEPT# and DEPT.MGR_EMP# will probably have nulls allowed; for otherwise it would be impossible to INSERT the first row (either an EMP row or a DEPT row) into the data-base—*unless* the tables are populated by means of the LOAD utility with referential integrity checking disabled. See Chapter 16 (Section 16.4) for further discussion of this latter possibility.

Referential cycles are subject to certain special restrictions. See Section 11.5 immediately following.

11.5 IMPLEMENTATION RESTRICTIONS

DB2's primary and foreign key support is subject to a number of implementation restrictions, which we discuss in the present section. The general purpose of these restrictions is to enable DB2 to *guarantee predictability*. For example, suppose table T contains just two rows, with primary key values 1 and 2 respectively, and consider the update request "Double every primary key value in T." The correct result is that the rows should now have primary key values 2 and 4, respectively. If DB2 were to update the "2" first (replacing it by "4") and then update the "1" second (replacing it by "2"), the request would succeed. If, on the other hand, it were to update—or, rather, attempt to update—the "1" first (replacing it by "2"), it would run into a primary key uniqueness violation, and the request would fail (the database would remain unchanged). In other words, *the result of the request would be unpredictable.**

In order to avoid such unpredictability, DB2 simply outlaws any situations in which it might occur. As indicated above, this is the purpose of the implementation restrictions. Let us now consider those restrictions in some detail.

1. No UPDATE CURRENT statement is allowed to update a primary key value (see Chapter 12 for an explanation of UPDATE CURRENT).

2. The following three rules apply to self-referencing tables:

- The delete rule must be CASCADE.

- DELETE CURRENT is not allowed (see Chapter 12 for an explanation of DELETE CURRENT).

- INSERT . . . SELECT is allowed only if it inserts at most one row, i.e., the SELECT selects at most one row.

We present an example to illustrate the first of these three rules (only). Fig. 11.1 shows a set of sample rows for a simplified version of the self-referencing table EMP from Section 11.3, in which EMP# is the primary key and MGR_EMP# is a foreign key referencing EMP#.

Suppose the referential constraint from MGR_EMP# to EMP# had a delete rule of RESTRICT, and consider the request:

```
DELETE
FROM    EMP
WHERE   EMP# > 'E0' ;
```

If DB2 accessed the rows in the sequence 3, 2, 1, the DELETE request would succeed and all three rows would be deleted. If it accessed them in any other sequence, the DELETE request would fail and nothing would be deleted. So we would have unpredictability, and so DB2 has a rule to avoid it: The delete rule is not allowed to be RESTRICT.

Now suppose instead that the referential constraint had a delete rule of SET NULL, and consider the request:

```
DELETE
FROM    EMP
WHERE   MGR_EMP# IS NULL ;
```

---

*This example makes the tacit assumption that DB2 is performing "inflight checking" (as it is usually called)—i.e., that it is applying its primary and foreign key checks to each individual row *as it updates that row.* And indeed, for performance reasons, DB2 normally does do its checking "in flight," even though (at least conceptually) it ought really to defer it to the end of the overall statement, or even later in some cases. In situations like the particular example under discussion, however (a multiple-row unique identifier update), inflight checking is not done, and predictability *is* guaranteed.

EMP	EMP#	MGR_EMP#	
	E1	null	(row 1)
	E2	E1	(row 2)
	E3	E2	(row 3)

Fig. 11.1 A self-referencing table

If DB2 accessed the rows in the order 1, 2, 3, all three rows would be deleted; if it accessed them in the order 3, 2, 1, row 1 (only) would be deleted; and consideration of the other possible sequences is left as an exercise for the reader. The point is, however, that again we would have unpredictability, and so again DB2 has a rule to avoid it: The delete rule is not allowed to be SET NULL.

Similar arguments and examples can be constructed to justify the other two aspects of restriction Number 2.

Delete-Connected

In order to explain the remaining restrictions, we need to introduce yet another term, "delete-connected." The basic idea here is that table Tn is considered to be delete-connected to table T1 if and only if a DELETE on table T1 can either *affect* or *be affected by* the content of table Tn. More precisely, table Tn is said to be *delete-connected* to table T1 if and only if (a) table Tn references table T1 directly or (b) table Tn references table T$(n-1)$ directly and there is a referential path from table T$(n-1)$ to table T1 in which every delete rule is CASCADE:

$$\text{T}n \xrightarrow{\ *\ } \text{T}(n-1) \xrightarrow{\ c\ } \text{T}(n-2) \xrightarrow{\ c\ } \ \ldots \ \xrightarrow{\ c\ } \text{T2} \xrightarrow{\ c\ } \text{T1}$$

(the "C"'s here represent a CASCADE delete rule, the asterisk stands for "any" delete rule—i.e., this particular delete rule is immaterial). Observe that—depending on the content of Tn—an attempt to delete rows from T1 can

(a) cause rows to be deleted from Tn, if the "*" delete rule is CASCADE;

(b) cause rows to be updated in Tn, if the "*" rule is SET NULL;

(c) fail, if the "*" rule is RESTRICT.

In other words, a DELETE on T1 can indeed either "affect or be affected by" the content of Tn.

Note: It follows immediately from the definition that every table is delete-connected to every table it references directly. It follows also that every self-referencing table is delete-connected to itself.

Now we can state the remaining DB2 restrictions.

3. If

(a) the user issues a DELETE on table T1, and

(b) table Tn is delete-connected to table T1, and

(c) the WHERE clause in the DELETE statement includes a subquery,

then the FROM clause in that subquery must not refer to table Tn unless the delete rule from Tn to T$(n-1)$—i.e., the last delete rule in the path— is RESTRICT. For example, if the referential constraint from shipments (table SP) to suppliers (table S) has a delete rule of CASCADE, then the following attempt to delete all suppliers who supply no parts is (unfortunately, and perhaps rather surprisingly) ILLEGAL:

```
DELETE                                    -- illegal !!!
FROM    S
WHERE   NOT EXISTS
      ( SELECT *
        FROM    SP
        WHERE   SP.S# = S.S# ) ;
```

Instead, the user should first compile a list of relevant supplier numbers, and then delete all suppliers whose number is given in that list as a separate operation.

We leave it as an exercise for the reader to determine exactly what can go wrong if restriction Number 3 is violated.

4. If table Tn is delete-connected to table T1 via two or more distinct referential paths, then every foreign key in table Tn that is involved in any of those paths must have the same delete rule, and furthermore that rule must not be SET NULL.* For an illustration of this restriction, see Exercise 11.7 at the end of the chapter.

5. In a cycle of length greater than one, no table is allowed to be delete-connected to itself. For example, consider the EMP/DEPT cycle discussed in Section 11.4.

- Suppose first that we try to specify a CASCADE delete rule for both foreign keys:

---

*Interestingly, this restriction is different in kind from the others: It is not due to DB2's inflight checking, but instead reflects a restriction that logically ought to exist in the real world. That is, it can be argued that a database definition that violates restriction Number 4 is *logically* incorrect, in that it cannot correctly represent a real-world situation (unless the "real world" is incorrect too, of course!). For further discussion of this point, the reader is referred to the book *Relational Database Writings 1985–1989*, by C. J. Date (Addison-Wesley, 1990).

```
              C
        ───────►
 EMP            DEPT
        ◄───────
              C
```

Then:

(a) EMP and DEPT are each delete-connected to the other (because each references the other directly);

(b) In addition, EMP is delete-connected to itself, because it references DEPT directly and there is a (rather short!) referential path from DEPT to EMP in which "every" (i.e., the only) delete rule is CASCADE. Likewise, DEPT is also delete-connected to itself.

The structure is thus illegal.

- Suppose, by contrast, that we try to specify a SET NULL or RESTRICT delete rule for the foreign key EMP.DEPT#, but we leave the delete rule for the foreign key DEPT.MGR_EMP# as CASCADE:

```
             N/R
        ───────►
 EMP            DEPT
        ◄───────
              C
```

Then:

(a) EMP and DEPT are again each delete-connected to the other, as before, because each references the other directly;

(b) EMP is still delete-connected to itself, because it references DEPT directly and DEPT references EMP and the delete rule from DEPT to EMP is CASCADE.

The structure is thus still illegal. Note, however, that DEPT is now *not* delete-connected to itself.

- Suppose, therefore, that we specify SET NULL (or RESTRICT) for the foreign key EMP.DEPT# and SET NULL (or RESTRICT) for the foreign key DEPT.MGR_EMP#:

```
             N/R
        ───────►
 EMP            DEPT
        ◄───────
             N/R
```

Now no table is delete-connected to itself, and the structure is legal.

We leave it as an exercise for the reader to invent some sample data for the EMP and DEPT tables and to see exactly what can go wrong if either table is delete-connected to itself.

11.6   MISCELLANEOUS TOPICS

We conclude this chapter with a brief mention of a few miscellaneous integrity topics.

Composite Keys

As explained earlier in the chapter, the relational model does permit primary and foreign keys to be composite. However, there are good reasons, most of them beyond the scope of this book, to be very sparing in the use of composite keys. In fact, every time a composite key arises during the database design process, it is a good idea to ask yourself very carefully whether it might not be better to introduce a new column to act as the key instead. In the case of shipments, for example, it might be worth introducing a new SHIP# column ("shipment number") as the primary key. (The combination SP.(S#,P#) would then be an alternate key.) For further discussion of this point, the reader is referred to the book *Relational Database*: *Selected Writings*, by C. J. Date (Addison-Wesley, 1986).

Even if you do decide to use composite keys, we recommend that you still treat them for the most part as *indivisible entity identifiers* (except perhaps for retrieval purposes); in other words, treat them as if they were simple, even though they are in fact composite. In order to adhere to this guideline:

1. Do not allow key values to be partly null.

2. Do not allow keys to overlap.

This is not the place to examine these recommendations in depth; they are discussed in more detail in the book *Relational Database Writings 1985–1989*, by C. J. Date (Addison-Wesley, 1990).

Other Integrity Constraints

As explained in Section 11.1, every database will be subject to numerous additional integrity constraints, over and above the basic primary and foreign key constraints described in Sections 11.2–11.5. We give below a complete list (not a very long list!) of additional integrity features supported by DB2.

- Data type checking

  DB2 will ensure that every value introduced into a given column is of the appropriate data type. For example, it will reject an attempt to introduce the string 'XYZ' into a column defined as DECIMAL.

- NOT NULL

  See Chapters 3 and 4. Of course, it is not only primary key columns that need to be specified NOT NULL, in general.

- UNIQUE indexes

  See Chapter 4. Of course, it is possible to have a UNIQUE index on a column or column combination that has not been declared to be a primary or alternate key.

- CHECK option in view definitions

  See Chapter 9.

- Validation procedures (VALIDPROCs)

  See Chapter 15.

Utilities

Referential integrity has several implications for DB2 utility functions such as LOAD and RECOVER. See Chapter 16 for further discussion.

EXERCISES

11.1 Define the terms *primary key* and *foreign key*.

11.2 State the entity integrity rule and the referential integrity rule.

11.3 Write a suitable set of data definition statements to specify the necessary primary and foreign key integrity constraints for the suppliers-parts-projects database (Fig. 4.1).

11.4 How would your answer to Exercise 11.3 be different if the database were being migrated from an earlier release of DB2 that did not support primary and foreign keys?

11.5 Using the sample suppliers-parts-projects data values from Fig. 5.1, say what the effect of each of the following operations is:

    (a) UPDATE project J7, setting CITY to New York

    (b) UPDATE part P5, setting P# to P4

    (c) UPDATE supplier S5, setting S# to S8

    (d) DELETE supplier S3, if the relevant delete rule is CASCADE

    (e) DELETE part P2, if the relevant delete rule is RESTRICT

    (f) DELETE project J4, if the relevant delete rule is SET NULL

    (g) UPDATE shipment S1-P1-J1, setting S# to S2

    (h) UPDATE shipment S5-P5-J5, setting J# to J7

(i) UPDATE shipment S5-P5-J5, setting J# to J8

(j) INSERT shipment S5-P6-J7

(k) INSERT shipment S4-P7-J6

(l) INSERT shipment S1-P2-null

11.6 Is there any point in declaring a primary key to be NOT NULL WITH DEFAULT?

11.7 (Based on an example in "An Introduction to the Unified Database Language," in *Relational Database*: *Selected Writings*, by C. J. Date, Addison-Wesley, 1986.) An education database contains information about an in-house company training scheme. For each training course, the database contains details of all prerequisite courses for that course and all offerings for that course; and for each offering it contains details of all teachers and all students for that offering. The database also contains information about employees. The relevant tables are as follows:

```
COURSE   ( COURSE#, TITLE )
PREREQ   ( SUP_COURSE#, SUB_COURSE# )
OFFERING ( COURSE#, OFF#, OFFDATE, LOCATION )
TEACHER  ( COURSE#, OFF#, EMP# )
STUDENT  ( COURSE#, OFF#, EMP#, GRADE )
EMPLOYEE ( EMP#, ENAME, JOB )
```

The meaning of the PREREQ table is that the superior course, represented by SUP_COURSE#, has the subordinate course, represented by SUB_COURSE#, as an immediate prerequisite; the other tables are intended to be self-explanatory. Write a suitable set of SQL data definitions for this database.

11.8 Invent a database of your own that involves a cycle of referential constraints. Invent some sample data for that database. Write an appropriate set of data definitions, with suitable PRIMARY KEY and FOREIGN KEY clauses. Consider the effects of some sample INSERTs, DELETEs, and primary and foreign key UPDATEs on your sample data.

ANSWERS TO SELECTED EXERCISES

We remind the reader that it is usually a good idea to have an index on a foreign key. However, such indexes are not included in the answers below (except in those cases where the foreign key is in fact the leading portion of the primary key of the containing table, where the primary index provides the desired function automatically).

11.3
```
CREATE TABLE S
     ( S#      CHAR(5)  NOT NULL ,
       SNAME   CHAR(20) NOT NULL WITH DEFAULT ,
       STATUS  SMALLINT NOT NULL WITH DEFAULT ,
       CITY    CHAR(15) NOT NULL WITH DEFAULT ,
     PRIMARY KEY ( S# ) ) ;

CREATE UNIQUE INDEX XS ON S ( S# ) ;
```

```
CREATE TABLE P
     ( P#        CHAR(6)   NOT NULL ,
       PNAME     CHAR(20)  NOT NULL WITH DEFAULT ,
       COLOR     CHAR(6)   NOT NULL WITH DEFAULT ,
       WEIGHT    SMALLINT  NOT NULL WITH DEFAULT ,
       CITY      CHAR(15)  NOT NULL WITH DEFAULT ,
     PRIMARY KEY ( P# ) ) ;

CREATE UNIQUE INDEX XP ON P ( P# ) ;

CREATE TABLE J
     ( J#        CHAR(4)   NOT NULL ,
       JNAME     CHAR(10)  NOT NULL WITH DEFAULT ,
       CITY      CHAR(15)  NOT NULL WITH DEFAULT ,
     PRIMARY KEY ( J# ) ) ;

CREATE UNIQUE INDEX XJ ON J ( J# ) ;

CREATE TABLE SPJ
     ( S#        CHAR(5)   NOT NULL ,
       P#        CHAR(6)   NOT NULL ,
       J#        CHAR(4)   NOT NULL ,
       QTY       INTEGER ,
     PRIMARY KEY ( S#, P#, J# ) ,
     FOREIGN KEY SFK ( S# ) REFERENCES S
                            ON DELETE CASCADE ,
     FOREIGN KEY PFK ( P# ) REFERENCES P
                            ON DELETE CASCADE ,
     FOREIGN KEY JFK ( J# ) REFERENCES J
                            ON DELETE CASCADE ) ;

CREATE UNIQUE INDEX XSPJ ON SPJ ( S#, P#, J# ) ;
```

11.4 Remove the PRIMARY KEY and FOREIGN KEY clauses from the CREATE TABLE statements and replace them by the following:

```
ALTER TABLE S   ADD PRIMARY KEY ( S# ) ;
ALTER TABLE P   ADD PRIMARY KEY ( P# ) ;
ALTER TABLE J   ADD PRIMARY KEY ( J# ) ;
ALTER TABLE SPJ ADD PRIMARY KEY ( S#, P#, J# ) ;

ALTER TABLE SPJ ADD FOREIGN KEY SFK ( S# ) REFERENCES S
                                  ON DELETE CASCADE ;
ALTER TABLE SPJ ADD FOREIGN KEY PFK ( P# ) REFERENCES P
                                  ON DELETE CASCADE ;
ALTER TABLE SPJ ADD FOREIGN KEY JFK ( J# ) REFERENCES J
                                  ON DELETE CASCADE ;
```

There will now be a "check pending" condition in effect and the data will not be available (not even for retrieval) until the condition has been cleared.

11.5 (a) Accepted

(b) Rejected (violates primary key constraint on P and implicit "update rule" RESTRICT on P.P#)

(c) Rejected (violates implicit "update rule" RESTRICT on S.S#)

(d) Accepted (supplier S3 and all shipments for supplier S3 deleted)

(e) Rejected (violates delete rule RESTRICT on P)

(f) Impossible (delete rule cannot be SET NULL, because SPJ.J# must be
    NOT NULL—it is part of the primary key of SPJ)

(g) Accepted

(h) Rejected (violates primary key constraint on SPJ)

(i) Rejected (violates foreign key constraint on SPJ.J#)

(j) Accepted

(k) Rejected (violates foreign key constraint on SPJ.P#)

(l) Rejected (violates entity integrity on SPJ)

11.6 Probably not—except possibly if the primary key is of data type DATE or
TIME or (perhaps most likely) TIMESTAMP. See Appendix B, Section B.4.

11.7
```
CREATE TABLE COURSE
       ( COURSE# ... NOT NULL ,
         TITLE   ... NOT NULL WITH DEFAULT ,
       PRIMARY KEY ( COURSE# ) ) ;

CREATE UNIQUE INDEX XC ON COURSE ( COURSE# ) ;

CREATE TABLE PREREQ
       ( SUP_COURSE# ... NOT NULL ,
         SUB_COURSE# ... NOT NULL ,
       PRIMARY KEY ( SUB_COURSE#, SUP_COURSE# ) ,
       FOREIGN KEY SUP ( SUP_COURSE# ) REFERENCES COURSE
                                  ON DELETE RESTRICT ,
       FOREIGN KEY SUB ( SUB_COURSE# ) REFERENCES COURSE
                                  ON DELETE RESTRICT ) ;

CREATE UNIQUE INDEX XPQ
            ON PREREQ ( SUP_COURSE#, SUB_COURSE# ) ;

CREATE TABLE OFFERING
       ( COURSE#  ... NOT NULL ,
         OFF#     ... NOT NULL ,
         OFFDATE  ... NOT NULL WITH DEFAULT ,
         LOCATION ... NOT NULL WITH DEFAULT ,
       PRIMARY KEY ( COURSE#, OFF# ) ,
       FOREIGN KEY OFK ( COURSE# ) REFERENCES COURSE
                                  ON DELETE CASCADE ) ;

CREATE UNIQUE INDEX XO ON OFFERING ( COURSE#, OFF# ) ;

CREATE TABLE EMPLOYEE
       ( EMP#    ... NOT NULL ,
         ENAME   ... NOT NULL WITH DEFAULT ,
         JOB     ... NOT NULL WITH DEFAULT ,
       PRIMARY KEY ( EMP# ) ) ;

CREATE UNIQUE INDEX XE ON EMPLOYEE ( EMP# ) ;
```

```
CREATE TABLE TEACHER
     ( COURSE# ... NOT NULL ,
       OFF#    ... NOT NULL ,
       EMP#    ... NOT NULL ,
     PRIMARY KEY ( COURSE#, OFF#, EMP# )
     FOREIGN KEY TC ( COURSE#, OFF# ) REFERENCES OFFERING
                                      ON DELETE CASCADE ,
     FOREIGN KEY TE ( EMP# )          REFERENCES EMPLOYEE
                                      ON DELETE CASCADE ) ;

CREATE UNIQUE INDEX XT ON TEACHER ( COURSE#, OFF#, EMP# ) ;

CREATE TABLE STUDENT
     ( COURSE# ... NOT NULL ,
       OFF#    ... NOT NULL ,
       EMP#    ... NOT NULL ,
       GRADE   ... NOT NULL WITH DEFAULT ,
     PRIMARY KEY ( COURSE#, OFF#, EMP# )
     FOREIGN KEY SC ( COURSE#, OFF# ) REFERENCES OFFERING
                                      ON DELETE CASCADE ,
     FOREIGN KEY SE ( EMP# )          REFERENCES EMPLOYEE
                                      ON DELETE CASCADE ) ;

CREATE UNIQUE INDEX XS ON STUDENT ( COURSE#, OFF#, EMP# ) ;
```

Note: Columns TEACHER.COURSE# and STUDENT.COURSE# could also be regarded as foreign keys, both of them referring to COURSE. However, if the referential constraints from TEACHER to OFFERING, STUDENT to OFFERING, and OFFERING to COURSE are all properly maintained, the referential constraints from TEACHER to COURSE and STUDENT to COURSE will be maintained automatically. Note, however, that if those latter constraints are explicitly declared, then the delete rules *must* be stated as CASCADE, to be consistent with the existing declarations (see restriction Number 4 in Section 11.5).

11.8 A simple example of a structure that involves a cycle might be a banking system, in which each account has one owner (a bank customer), each bank customer has one personal banker (a bank officer), and each personal banker has one account giving information about that personal banker's customers.

CHAPTER

◆ 12 ◆

Application Programming I: Embedded SQL

12.1 INTRODUCTION

In Chapter 1 we explained that SQL was used in DB2 both as an interactive query language and as a database programming language. Up to this point, however, we have more or less ignored the programming aspects of SQL and have tacitly assumed (where it made any difference) that the language was being used interactively. Now we turn our attention to those programming aspects specifically. In the present chapter we discuss the principal ideas behind "embedded SQL" (as it is usually called); in the next chapter we examine the concept of "transaction processing"; and in Chapter 14 we present an introduction (only) to a somewhat more complex subject, namely "dynamic SQL." But first things first.

The fundamental principle underlying embedded SQL, which we refer to as *the dual-mode principle*, is that *any SQL statement that can be used at the terminal can also be used in an application program*. Of course, as pointed out in Chapter 1, there are various differences of detail between a given interactive SQL statement and its corresponding embedded form, and SELECT statements in particular require significantly extended treatment in the programming environment (see Section 12.4); but the principle is nevertheless broadly true. (Its converse is not, incidentally; that is, there are a number of SQL statements that are programming statements only and cannot be used interactively, as we shall see.)

Note clearly that the dual-mode principle applies to the entire SQL language, not just to the data manipulation operations specifically. It is true that the data manipulation operations are far and away the ones most frequently used in a programming context, but there is nothing wrong in embedding (for example) CREATE TABLE statements in a program, if it makes sense to do so for the application at hand.

The programming languages currently supported by DB2—the so-called "host languages"—are PL/I, COBOL, FORTRAN, C, and System/370 Assembler Language.* In Section 12.2 we consider the mechanics of embedding SQL in these languages. Then in Sections 12.3 and 12.4 we present the major ideas behind the embedding of SQL data manipulation statements specifically. Finally, in Section 12.5, we present a comprehensive programming example.

Note: For reasons of brevity and definiteness, all of our examples are given in terms of PL/I. But of course the ideas are fairly general and translate into the other host languages with only comparatively minor differences.

12.2   PRELIMINARIES

Before we can get into the embedded SQL statements per se, it is necessary to cover a number of preliminary details. Most of those details are illustrated by the program fragment shown in Fig. 12.1.

Points arising:

1. Embedded SQL statements are prefixed by EXEC SQL (so that they can easily be distinguished from statements of the host language), and are terminated by a special termination symbol (a semicolon for PL/I).

2. An *executable* SQL statement (from now on we will usually drop the "embedded") can appear wherever an executable host statement can appear. Note the qualifier "executable" here: Unlike interactive SQL, embed-

---

*As mentioned in Chapter 1, certain IBM language products (e.g., APL2, BASIC) also provide interfaces to DB2 via the "dynamic SQL" facilities discussed in Chapter 14.

```
EXEC SQL BEGIN DECLARE SECTION ;

DCL GIVENS#  CHAR(5) ;
DCL RANK     FIXED BIN(15) ;
DCL CITY     CHAR(15) ;
DCL ALPHA    ... ;
DCL BETA     ... ;

EXEC SQL END DECLARE SECTION ;

EXEC SQL DECLARE S TABLE
                ( S#      CHAR(5)   NOT NULL,
                  SNAME   CHAR(20)  NOT NULL WITH DEFAULT,
                  STATUS  SMALLINT  NOT NULL WITH DEFAULT,
                  CITY    CHAR(15)  NOT NULL WITH DEFAULT ) ;

EXEC SQL INCLUDE SQLCA ;

      . . . . . . . . . .

   IF ALPHA > BETA THEN
GETSTC:
   EXEC SQL SELECT STATUS, CITY
            INTO   :RANK, :CITY
            FROM   S
            WHERE  S# = :GIVENS# ;
      . . . . . . . . . .

   PUT SKIP LIST ( RANK, CITY ) ;
```

Fig. 12.1 Fragment of a PL/I program with embedded SQL

ded SQL includes some statements that are purely declarative in nature, not executable. For instance, BEGIN DECLARE SECTION, END DECLARE SECTION, and DECLARE TABLE (see Fig. 12.1) are all examples of non-executable statements; so too is DECLARE CURSOR (see Section 12.4)

3. SQL statements can include references to host variables; such references are prefixed with a colon to distinguish them from SQL column names. Host variables that will be used within SQL statements must be declared within a "declare section," introduced by the statement BEGIN DECLARE SECTION and terminated by the statement END DECLARE SECTION.* A given program can include any number of declare sections, but they must not be nested. The declaration of a given host variable must physically precede the first use of that variable within a SQL statement.

4. Host variables can appear in SQL data manipulation statements wherever a literal is permitted. They are also used to designate a target for

---

*Declare sections are required for C; they are optional for the other host languages unless the Precompiler option STDSQL(86) is specified (see Appendix E), but should be specified anyway for reasons of compatibility with the SQL standard.

retrieval. In other words, such variables can appear in the following positions:

- INTO clause in SELECT or FETCH (target for retrieval)
- SELECT clause (value to be retrieved)
- WHERE or HAVING clause (value to be compared)
- SET clause in UPDATE (value to be assigned)
- VALUES clause in INSERT (value to be inserted)
- element of a scalar expression in SELECT, WHERE, HAVING, or SET (not VALUES), where that expression in turn evaluates to the value to be retrieved, compared, or assigned

They can also appear in SET CURRENT PACKAGESET (see Chapter 2), SET CURRENT SQLID (see Chapter 10), CONNECT (see Chapter 17), and in certain embedded-only statements (details to follow). They cannot appear in any other SQL contexts.

5. Any tables (base tables or views) used in the program can optionally be declared by means of an EXEC SQL DECLARE TABLE statement, in order to make the program more self-documenting and to enable the Precompiler to perform certain diagnostic checks on the manipulative statements. See the discussion of DCLGEN in Section 12.5.

6. After any SQL statement has been executed, certain feedback information (reflecting the outcome of that execution) is returned to the program in two special host variables called SQLCODE (a 31-bit signed binary integer) and SQLSTATE (a character string of length 5), respectively. *Note*: Earlier releases of DB2 supported SQLCODE only; SQLSTATE was added in Version 2.3 for reasons of compatibility with the SQL standard.

- *SQLCODE*: A SQLCODE value of zero means that the statement executed successfully; a positive value means that the statement did execute, but some exceptional condition occurred (for example, a value of +100 indicates that no data was found to satisfy the request); and a negative value means that an error occurred and the statement did not complete successfully.*

- *SQLSTATE*: SQLSTATE values consist of a two-character "class code" followed by a three-character "subclass code." Each of the five characters is the character string representation of a decimal digit. Class code 00 means that the statement executed successfully (the subclass code will be 000 in this case). Class code 01 means that the statement

---

*This description is slightly oversimplified. See Section 12.5 (description of the WHENEVER statement) for further discussion.

did execute, but some warning condition exists (e.g., class code 00 with subclass code 502 means that nulls were ignored in the evaluation of an aggregate function). Class code 02 means that no data was found (again, the subclass code will be 000 in this case). For details of other possible class and subclass codes, the reader is referred to the IBM manuals.

In principle, therefore, every SQL statement in the program should be followed by a test on either SQLCODE or SQLSTATE (and appropriate action taken if the value is not what was expected), but we do not show any such tests in Fig. 12.1. (In practice such explicit testing may *not* be necessary, as we show in Section 12.5.)

Every program that includes one or more executable SQL statements, then, must include a SQLCODE variable and (optionally) a SQLSTATE variable also. Such variables can of course be explicitly declared, just like other host language variables. Alternatively, the program can contain a statement of the form

```
EXEC SQL INCLUDE SQLCA ;
```

(as shown in Fig. 12.1). This statement causes the Precompiler to insert a declaration into the program for a structure called the SQL Communication Area or SQLCA.* That declaration in turn contains declarations for both SQLCODE and SQLSTATE, together with a number of other feedback variables that will also be set after the execution of each SQL statement (again, for details the reader is referred to the IBM manuals).

Note: "INCLUDE SQLCA" is the normal case; the option of declaring SQLCODE and SQLSTATE explicitly is provided for compatibility with the SQL standard. A program must not do both (i.e., it must not specify "INCLUDE SQLCA" *and* declare SQLCODE and SQLSTATE explicitly). Which of the two techniques is used by a given program is specified by means of the Precompiler option STDSQL—STDSQL(NO) means the SQLCA is included, STDSQL(86) means explicit declarations. See Appendix E for more discussion.

For simplicity, we will ignore SQLSTATE for the remainder of this chapter (and for the next two chapters), and do all of our exception testing in terms of SQLCODE alone. We will also assume that the program does indeed specify "INCLUDE SQLCA."

7. As indicated in paragraph 3 above, the embedded SQL SELECT statement requires an INTO clause, specifying the host variables to which values

---

*The EXEC SQL INCLUDE statement can also be used to include program source text from a partitioned data set.

retrieved from the database are to be assigned. The variables in that INTO clause can be scalar variables or structures; a structure is considered simply as a shorthand for the list of scalars that make up that structure. Structures can also be used in the VALUES clause in INSERT.

8. Host variables must have a data type compatible with the SQL data type of columns they are to be compared with or assigned to or from. Data type compatibility is defined in Chapter 3 (Section 3.5). If significant digits or characters are lost on assignment (either to or from the database) because the target is too small, a warning or error indication is returned to the program in the SQLCA.

9. Host variables and database columns can have the same name. A host variable can be an element of a structure. For example:

```
DCL 1 STRUC,
    2 S#  CHAR(5),
    2 ... ;

EXEC SQL SELECT ...
         FROM    S
         WHERE   S# = :STRUC.S# ;
```

Note that PL/I-style name qualification is used for host variable references, not COBOL-style (:STRUC.S#, not :S# OF STRUC), even when the host language is in fact COBOL.

So much for the preliminaries. In the rest of this chapter we concentrate on the SQL data manipulation operations SELECT, UPDATE, DELETE, and INSERT specifically. As already indicated, most of those operations can be handled in a fairly straightforward fashion (i.e., with only minor changes to their syntax). SELECT statements require special treatment, however. The problem is that executing a SELECT statement causes a *table* to be retrieved—a table that, in general, contains multiple rows—and languages such as PL/I, COBOL, etc., are simply not well equipped to handle more than one row at a time. It is therefore necessary to provide some kind of bridge between the set-at-a-time level of the SQL SELECT statement and the row-at-a-time level of the host; and *cursors* provide such a bridge. A cursor is a new kind of SQL object, one that applies to embedded SQL only (because of course interactive SQL has no need of it). It consists essentially of a kind of *pointer* that can be used to run through a set of rows, pointing to each of the rows in the set in turn and thus providing addressability to those rows one at a time. However, we defer detailed discussion of cursors to Section 12.4, and consider first (in Section 12.3) those statements that have no need of them.

12.3 OPERATIONS NOT INVOLVING CURSORS

The data manipulation statements that do not need cursors are as follows:

- "Singleton SELECT"
- UPDATE (except the CURRENT form—see Section 12.4)
- DELETE (again, except the CURRENT form—see Section 12.4)
- INSERT

We give examples of each of these statements in turn.

12.3.1 Singleton SELECT. Get status and city for the supplier whose supplier number is given by the host variable GIVENS#.

```
EXEC SQL SELECT STATUS, CITY
         INTO   :RANK, :CITY
         FROM   S
         WHERE  S# = :GIVENS# ;
```

We use the term "singleton SELECT" to mean a SELECT statement for which the retrieved table contains at most one row. A singleton SELECT cannot include a GROUP BY or HAVING clause. We explain the operation of such a SELECT in terms of the example:

- If there exists exactly one row in table S satisfying the WHERE condition, then the STATUS and CITY values from that row will be delivered to the host variables RANK and CITY as requested, and SQLCODE will be set to zero.
- If no S row satisfies the WHERE condition, the host variables RANK and CITY will remain unchanged, and SQLCODE will be set to +100.
- Finally, if more than one S row satisfies the WHERE condition, the program is in error: SQLCODE will be set to a negative value, and the values of the host variables RANK and CITY will be unpredictable. *Note*: This last case cannot actually occur in the example (why not?).

The foregoing explanation raises another point. What if the SELECT statement does indeed select exactly one row, but the STATUS value in that row happens to be null? (Assume for the sake of the example that column S.STATUS has "nulls allowed," so that nulls are possible.) With the SELECT statement as shown above, an error will occur (SQLCODE will be set to a negative value). In general, if there is a chance that the source of a retrieval operation might be null, the user should include an *indicator variable* in the INTO clause in addition to the normal target variable, as illustrated here:

```
EXEC SQL SELECT STATUS, CITY
         INTO   :RANK INDICATOR :RANKIND, :CITY
         FROM   S
         WHERE  S# = :GIVENS# ;
IF RANKIND = -1 THEN /* STATUS was null */ ... ;
```

If the value to be retrieved is null and an indicator variable has been specified, then that indicator variable will be set to the value − 1* and the ordinary target variable will remain unchanged. Indicator variables are specified as shown—i.e., as another host variable (with the usual colon prefix) following the corresponding target variable, optionally separated from that target variable by the explicit keyword INDICATOR. Indicator variables should be declared as 15-bit signed binary integers.

Note: Indicator variables are permitted but probably should not be used in a WHERE or HAVING clause. For example, the statement

```
RANKIND = -1 ;
EXEC SQL SELECT CITY
         INTO   :CITY
         FROM   S
         WHERE  STATUS =
                :RANK INDICATOR :RANKIND ;
```

does not do what the user presumably wants (why not?). The straightforward way to select cities where the status is null is:

```
EXEC SQL SELECT CITY
         INTO   :CITY
         FROM   S
         WHERE  STATUS IS NULL ;
```

12.3.2 INSERT.   Insert a new part (part number, name, and weight given by host variables PNO, PNAME, PWT, respectively; color and city unknown) into table P.

```
EXEC SQL INSERT
         INTO   P ( P#, PNAME, WEIGHT )
         VALUES ( :PNO, :PNAME, :PWT ) ;
```

We are assuming here that either nulls or default values are allowed for columns P.COLOR and P.CITY.

Indicator variables can be used in the VALUES clause. For example, if PCOLOR and PCITY are two further host variables, and if COLORIND and CITYIND are corresponding indicator variables, then the sequence

---

*It will be set to − 2 if the null is not directly derived from a database column but is instead generated by DB2. DB2 will generate a null if the value to be retrieved is denoted by an operational expression (such as X + Y) and an error—e.g., division by zero or a data type conversion error—occurs in evaluating that expression.

```
COLORIND = -1 ;
CITYIND  = -1 ;
EXEC SQL INSERT
         INTO   P ( P#, PNAME, COLOR, WEIGHT, CITY )
         VALUES ( :PNO, :PNAME, :PCOLOR INDICATOR :COLORIND,
                  :PWT,    :PCITY  INDICATOR :CITYIND ) ;
```

has the same effect as the INSERT shown previously (assuming now specifically that nulls, not defaults, are allowed for columns P.COLOR and P.CITY).

12.3.3 UPDATE. Increase the status of all London suppliers by the amount given by the host variable RAISE.

```
EXEC SQL UPDATE S
         SET    STATUS = STATUS + :RAISE
         WHERE  CITY = 'London' ;
```

If no S rows satisfy the WHERE condition, SQLCODE will be set to +100. Indicator variables can appear on the right-hand side of an assignment in the SET clause; for example, the sequence

```
RANKIND = -1 ;
EXEC SQL UPDATE S
         SET    STATUS = :RANK INDICATOR :RANKIND
         WHERE  CITY = 'London' ;
```

will set the status for all London suppliers to null. So also of course will the statement

```
EXEC SQL UPDATE S
         SET    STATUS = NULL
         WHERE  CITY = 'London' ;
```

12.3.4 DELETE. Delete all shipments for suppliers whose city is given by the host variable CITY.

```
EXEC SQL DELETE
         FROM   SP
         WHERE  :CITY =
                ( SELECT CITY
                  FROM   S
                  WHERE  S.S# = SP.S# ) ;
```

Again SQLCODE will be set to +100 if no rows satisfy the WHERE condition.

For simplicity, we will ignore indicator variables and the possibility of nulls in most of what follows (both in this chapter and in the next two chapters).

Assignment to Host Variables

We conclude this section on noncursor operations with a brief discussion of a special embedded-SQL-only statement, "SET host variable." Here is an example:

```
SET :UNAME = USER ;
```

The general syntax is:

```
SET host-variable = special-register ;
```

(see Chapter 3 for a list of the special registers). The current value of the designated special register is assigned to the designated host variable. The host variable must not have an associated indicator variable.*

12.4 OPERATIONS INVOLVING CURSORS

Now we turn to the case of a SELECT that selects a whole set of rows, not necessarily just a single row. As explained in Section 12.2, what is needed here is a mechanism for accessing the rows in the set one by one; and *cursors* provide such a mechanism. The process is illustrated in outline in the example of Fig. 12.2, which is intended to retrieve supplier details (S#, SNAME, and STATUS) for all suppliers in the city given by the host variable Y.

Explanation:

1. The DECLARE X CURSOR . . . statement defines a cursor called X, with an associated query as specified by the SELECT that forms part of that DECLARE. The SELECT is not executed at this point; DECLARE CURSOR is a purely declarative statement.

2. The SELECT *is* (effectively) executed when the cursor is opened (in the procedural part of the program), using the current value of the host variable Y.

3. The FETCH . . . INTO . . . statement is then used to retrieve rows of the result table one at a time. The INTO clause in that statement must specify a list of *n* host variables, where *n* is the number of expressions in the SELECT clause in the cursor declaration. (Note that the SELECT in the cursor declaration does not have an INTO clause of its own.) Each time the FETCH is executed, the current value of the *i*th

---

*As mentioned, "SET host variable" can be used in embedded SQL only, not in interactive SQL. The same is true of SET CURRENT PACKAGESET, but not of SET CURRENT SQLID.

```
EXEC SQL DECLARE X CURSOR FOR          -- define cursor X
          SELECT S#, SNAME, STATUS
          FROM   S
          WHERE  CITY = :Y ;

EXEC SQL OPEN X ;                       -- execute the query
          DO for all S rows accessible via X ;
              EXEC SQL FETCH X INTO :S#, :SNAME, :STATUS ;
                                       -- fetch next supplier
              .........
          END ;
EXEC SQL CLOSE X ;                      -- deactivate cursor X
```

Fig. 12.2 Retrieving multiple rows

expression in the SELECT clause in the cursor declaration is assigned to the *i*th variable in the INTO clause ($i = 1$ to n). In the example, therefore, the supplier number is assigned to the host variable S#, the supplier name to the host variable SNAME, and the status to the host variable STATUS. (For simplicity we have given each host variable the same name as the corresponding database column.)

4. Since there will be multiple rows in the result table (in general), the FETCH will normally appear within a loop (DO . . . END in PL/I); the loop will be repeated so long as there are more rows still to come in that result table. An attempt to FETCH the next row when no rows remain will set SQLCODE to +100; that condition can then be used to cause exit from the loop on the next attempt at iteration.

5. On exit from the loop cursor X is closed (deactivated) via an appropriate CLOSE statement.

Now let us consider cursors and cursor operations in more detail. First, a cursor is declared by means of a DECLARE CURSOR statement, which takes the general form

```
EXEC SQL DECLARE cursor CURSOR [ WITH HOLD ]
          FOR union-expression
          [ ORDER BY column(s) ]
          [ FOR [ FETCH ONLY | UPDATE OF column(s) ] ]
          [ OPTIMIZE FOR integer ROW[S] ] ;
```

where "union-expression" is defined as follows—

```
union-term  |  union-expression UNION [ ALL ] union-term
```

—and "union-term" in turn is either a SELECT-FROM-WHERE-GROUP BY–HAVING expression or a union-expression in parentheses. *Note*: The union-expression represents the most general form of a SQL query, as discussed in Chapter 6.

Explanation:

1. As already stated, the DECLARE CURSOR statement is declarative, not executable; it declares a cursor with the specified name and having the specified union-expression permanently associated with it. Notice that that union-expression can include (and typically will include) host variable references. A program can include any number of DECLARE CURSOR statements, each of which must (of course) be for a different cursor.

2. We defer explanation of the optional specification WITH HOLD to Chapter 13.

3. If and only if no UPDATE CURRENT and no DELETE CURRENT operations will be performed via this cursor (see later in this section), then the cursor declaration may optionally include an ORDER BY clause (possibly with ASC/DESC specifications), exactly as in a conventional SELECT statement. That ORDER BY clause will control the order in which result rows are retrieved via FETCH (if no ORDER BY clause is specified, result rows will be retrieved in a system-determined order). An attempt to perform an UPDATE CURRENT or DELETE operation via this cursor will fail at run time if ORDER BY is specified. Note, therefore, that it is not possible to retrieve a set of rows via a cursor in some specified order *and* UPDATE or DELETE some of those rows via that same cursor at the same time. See Exercise 12.4 at the end of this chapter.

4. If and only if no UPDATE CURRENT and no DELETE CURRENT operations will be performed via this cursor (again, see below), then the cursor declaration may optionally include the specification FOR FETCH ONLY. In certain circumstances, such a specification can have the effect of improving performance (especially in a distributed database context—see Part III of this book). Note, however, that DB2 will assume a FOR FETCH ONLY specification by default if it can determine for itself that UPDATE CURRENT and DELETE CURRENT are not permitted (see the end of the present section). An attempt to perform an UPDATE CURRENT or DELETE CURRENT operation via this cursor will fail at run time if FOR FETCH ONLY is specified.

5. If UPDATE CURRENT operations will be performed via this cursor (in which case neither ORDER BY nor FOR FETCH ONLY can be specified), then the cursor declaration may optionally include a FOR UPDATE clause, specifying all columns that will be targets in such an UPDATE. Whether or not such a clause is required depends on whether

or not the Precompiler NOFOR option is specified.* If NOFOR is specified, the FOR UPDATE clause is not required, and columns can be UPDATEd (via the cursor) freely. If NOFOR is not specified, the FOR UPDATE clause is required, and an attempt to UPDATE (via the cursor) any column not mentioned in that clause will fail at run time.

6. The optional specification OPTIMIZE FOR n ROWS (where n is an unsigned integer literal) is provided purely for performance reasons. If the user expects to retrieve n rows via this cursor (i.e., to execute FETCH against this cursor n times), then informing DB2 of that fact can sometimes cause the optimizer to choose a more efficient access path—especially if n is significantly less than the total number of rows in the result table.

Three executable statements are provided specifically for operating on cursors: OPEN, FETCH, and CLOSE.

1. The statement

```
EXEC SQL OPEN cursor ;
```

opens or *activates* the specified cursor (which must not currently be open). In effect, the union-expression associated with that cursor is executed (using the current values for any host variables referenced within that expression); a set of rows is thus identified and becomes the *active set* for the cursor. The cursor also identifies a *position* within that set, namely the position just before the first row in the set. (Active sets are always considered to have an ordering, so that the concept of position has meaning; the ordering is either that defined by ORDER BY, if specified, or a system-determined ordering otherwise.)

2. The statement

```
EXEC SQL FETCH cursor INTO target [, target ] ... ;
```

where each "target" is of the form

```
: host-variable [ [ INDICATOR ] : host-variable ]
```

(as in singleton SELECT), and where the identified cursor must be open, advances that cursor to the next row in the active set and then assigns values from that row to host variables as explained earlier. If

---

*The Precompiler option STDSQL(86) implies the Precompiler option NOFOR. See Appendix E.

there is no next row when FETCH is executed, then SQLCODE will be set to $+100$ and no data will be retrieved.

Note, incidentally, that FETCH (i.e., "fetch next") is the *only* cursor movement operation. It is not possible to move a cursor (e.g.) "forward three positions" or "backward two positions" or "directly to the *i*th row," etc.

3. The statement

```
EXEC SQL CLOSE cursor ;
```

closes or *deactivates* the specified cursor (which must currently be open). The cursor now has no corresponding active set. However, it can subsequently be opened again, in which case it will acquire another active set—probably not exactly the same set as before, especially if the values of host variables referenced in the cursor declaration have changed in the meantime. Note that changing the values of those host variables while the cursor is open has no effect on the active set.

Two further statements can include references to cursors. These are the CURRENT forms of UPDATE and DELETE. If a cursor, X say, is currently positioned on a particular row in the database, then it is possible to UPDATE or DELETE the "current of X," i.e., the row on which X is positioned. Syntax:

```
EXEC SQL UPDATE table
         SET    column = scalar-expression
              [, column = scalar-expression ] ...
         WHERE  CURRENT OF cursor ;

EXEC SQL DELETE
         FROM   table
         WHERE  CURRENT OF cursor ;
```

For example:

```
EXEC SQL UPDATE S
         SET    STATUS = STATUS + :RAISE
         WHERE  CURRENT OF X ;
```

UPDATE CURRENT and DELETE CURRENT are not permitted if the cursor declaration involves UNION (with or without ALL) or ORDER BY or FOR FETCH ONLY, or if the union-expression in that declaration would define a nonupdatable view if it were part of a CREATE VIEW statement (see Section 9.4 in Chapter 9). In the case of UPDATE CURRENT, as explained earlier, the cursor declaration must include a FOR UPDATE clause identifying all the columns that appear as targets of a SET clause in an UPDATE CURRENT statement for that cursor (unless the Precompiler NOFOR option is specified).

12.5 A COMPREHENSIVE EXAMPLE

We conclude this chapter with a somewhat contrived, but nevertheless comprehensive, example (Fig. 12.3) to illustrate a number of additional points. The program accepts four input values: a part number (GIVENP#), a city name (GIVENCIT), a status increment (GIVENINC), and a status level (GIVENLVL). The program scans all suppliers of the part identified by GIVENP#. For each such supplier, if the supplier city is GIVENCIT, then the status is increased by GIVENINC; otherwise, if the status is less than GIVENLVL, the supplier is deleted. (We assume that corresponding shipments are automatically deleted also by virtue of a CASCADE delete rule, as discussed in Chapter 11.) In all cases supplier information is listed on the printer, with an indication of how that particular supplier was handled by the program.

For definiteness, we assume in this example that the Precompiler option NOFOR will not be specified, and hence that appropriate FOR UPDATE clauses are required.

Points arising:

1. Note the two DECLAREs for tables S and SP. It is obvious that those declarations are nothing but slight textual variations on the corresponding CREATE TABLE statements of SQL. A special utility program, the declarations generator (DCLGEN), is provided to construct such declarations on the user's behalf. (*Note*: The name DCLGEN is usually pronounced "deckle gen," with a soft g.) Basically, DCLGEN uses the information in the DB2 catalog to build both

(a) a DECLARE TABLE statement for the table, and

(b) a corresponding PL/I, C, or COBOL declaration for a structure the same shape as the table (to be used as a target for retrieval and/or a source for update).

DCLGEN stores its output as a member of a partitioned data set under a user-specified name. That output can then be included into a host program by means of the statement

```
EXEC SQL INCLUDE member ;
```

where "member" is the name of the member concerned.

It can be seen from the foregoing that DCLGEN (like the catalog) provides some of the functions that have traditionally been considered the responsibility of a separate dictionary product in older systems.

2. As explained in Section 12.2, every SQL statement should in principle be followed by a test of the returned SQLCODE value (or returned

```
SQLEX: PROC OPTIONS (MAIN) ;

       EXEC SQL BEGIN DECLARE SECTION ;

       DCL GIVENP#        CHAR(6) ;
       DCL GIVENCIT       CHAR(15) ;
       DCL GIVENINC       FIXED BINARY(15) ;
       DCL GIVENLVL       FIXED BINARY(15) ;
       DCL S#             CHAR(5) ;
       DCL SNAME          CHAR(20) ;
       DCL STATUS         FIXED BINARY(15) ;
       DCL CITY           CHAR(15) ;

       EXEC SQL END DECLARE SECTION ;

       DCL DISP           CHAR(7) ;
       DCL MORE_SUPPLIERS BIT(1) ;

       EXEC SQL INCLUDE SQLCA ;

       EXEC SQL DECLARE S TABLE
                     ( S#        CHAR(5)   NOT NULL,
                       SNAME     CHAR(20)  NOT NULL WITH DEFAULT,
                       STATUS    SMALLINT  NOT NULL WITH DEFAULT,
                       CITY      CHAR(20)  NOT NULL WITH DEFAULT ) ;

       EXEC SQL DECLARE SP TABLE
                     ( S#        CHAR(5)   NOT NULL,
                       P#        CHAR(6)   NOT NULL,
                       QTY       INTEGER   NOT NULL WITH DEFAULT ) ;

       EXEC SQL DECLARE Z CURSOR FOR
                SELECT S#, SNAME, STATUS, CITY
                FROM   S
                WHERE  EXISTS
                     ( SELECT *
                       FROM   SP
                       WHERE  SP.S# = S.S#
                       AND    SP.P# = :GIVENP# )
                FOR UPDATE OF STATUS ;

       EXEC SQL WHENEVER NOT FOUND CONTINUE ;
       EXEC SQL WHENEVER SQLERROR CONTINUE ;
       EXEC SQL WHENEVER SQLWARNING CONTINUE ;

       ON CONDITION ( DBEXCEPTION )
       BEGIN ;
          PUT SKIP LIST ( SQLCA ) ;
          EXEC SQL ROLLBACK WORK ;
          GO TO QUIT ;
       END ;
```

Fig. 12.3 A comprehensive example (part 1 of 2)

```
GET LIST ( GIVENP#, GIVENCIT, GIVENINC, GIVENLVL ) ;
EXEC SQL OPEN Z ;
IF SQLCODE ¬= 0
THEN SIGNAL CONDITION ( DBEXCEPTION ) ;
MORE_SUPPLIERS = '1'B ;
DO WHILE ( MORE_SUPPLIERS ) ;
    EXEC SQL FETCH Z INTO :S#, :SNAME, :STATUS, :CITY ;
    SELECT ;               /* a PL/I SELECT, not a SQL SELECT */
    WHEN ( SQLCODE = 100 )
        MORE_SUPPLIERS = '0'B ;
    WHEN ( SQLCODE ¬= 100 & SQLCODE ¬= 0 )
        SIGNAL CONDITION ( DBEXCEPTION ) ;
    WHEN ( SQLCODE = 0 )
        DO ;
            DISP = 'bbbbbbb' ;
            IF CITY = GIVENCIT
            THEN
                DO ;
                    EXEC SQL UPDATE S
                            SET    STATUS = STATUS + :GIVENINC
                            WHERE  CURRENT OF Z ;
                    IF SQLCODE ¬= 0
                    THEN SIGNAL CONDITION ( DBEXCEPTION ) ;
                    DISP = 'UPDATED' ;
                END ;
            ELSE
                IF STATUS < GIVENLVL
                THEN
                    DO ;
                        EXEC SQL DELETE
                                FROM   S
                                WHERE  CURRENT OF Z ;
                        IF SQLCODE ¬= 0
                        THEN SIGNAL CONDITION ( DBEXCEPTION ) ;
                        DISP = 'DELETED' ;
                    END ;
            PUT SKIP LIST ( S#, SNAME, STATUS, CITY, DISP ) ;
        END ;    /* WHEN ( SQLCODE = 0 ) ... */
    END ;    /* PL/I SELECT */
END ;    /* DO WHILE */
EXEC SQL CLOSE Z ;
EXEC SQL COMMIT WORK ;
QUIT:
RETURN ;
END ;    /* SQLEX */
```

Fig. 12.3 A comprehensive example (part 2 of 2)

SQLSTATE value). The WHENEVER statement is provided to simplify this process. The WHENEVER statement has the syntax:

```
EXEC SQL WHENEVER condition action ;
```

where "condition" is one of the following:

```
NOT FOUND
SQLWARNING
SQLERROR
```

and "action" is either CONTINUE or a GO TO statement. WHENEVER is not an executable statement; rather, it is a directive to the Precompiler. "WHENEVER condition GO TO label" causes the Precompiler to insert an "IF condition GO TO label" statement after each executable SQL statement it encounters. "WHENEVER condition CONTINUE" causes the Precompiler not to insert any such statements (the implication being that the programmer will insert such statements by hand). The three "conditions" are defined as follows:

```
NOT FOUND       means      SQLCODE = 100
SQLWARNING      means      SQLCODE > 0 and SQLCODE ¬= 100
                           or SQLWARN0 is 'W'
SQLERROR        means      SQLCODE < 0
```

Note: SQLWARN0 is another field in the SQLCA. It is set to W if certain nondisastrous exceptions occur—for example, if a string value from the database has to be truncated during FETCH because the target host variable is too small. For details, see the IBM manuals. We have ignored SQLWARN0 entirely in the code of Fig. 12.3.

Each WHENEVER statement the Precompiler encounters on its sequential scan through the program text (for a particular condition) overrides the previous one it found (for that condition). At the start of the program text there is an implicit WHENEVER statement for each of the three possible conditions, specifying CONTINUE in each case.

In the sample program, all exception-testing is done explicitly, for tutorial reasons. If any exception occurs, control is passed to a procedure that prints diagnostic information (the SQL Communication Area, in the example), issues a ROLLBACK (see the next paragraph below), and then branches to the final RETURN.

3. When a program updates the database in some way, that update should initially be regarded as *tentative only*—tentative in the sense that, if something subsequently goes wrong, *the update may be undone* (either by the program itself or by the system). For example, if the program encounters an unexpected error, say an overflow condition, and terminates abnormally, then the system will automatically undo all such tentative updates

on the program's behalf. Updates remain tentative until one of two things happens:

(a) A COMMIT WORK statement (abbrev. COMMIT) is executed, which makes all tentative updates firm ("committed"); or

(b) A ROLLBACK WORK statement (abbrev. ROLLBACK) is executed, which undoes all tentative updates.

Once committed, an update is guaranteed never to be undone (this is the definition of "committed").

In the example, the program issues COMMIT when it reaches its normal termination, but issues ROLLBACK if any SQL exception is encountered. Actually, that explicit COMMIT is not necessary; DB2 will automatically issue a COMMIT on the program's behalf for any program that reaches normal termination. It will also automatically issue a ROLLBACK on the program's behalf for any program that does not reach normal termination; in the example, however, an explicit ROLLBACK *is* necessary, because the program is designed to reach its normal termination even if a SQL exception occurs.

Note: The foregoing discussion assumes either a TSO or a "pure batch" environment. COMMIT and ROLLBACK are legal only in those environments. Under IMS (either IMS/DC or IMS batch) and CICS, the effects of COMMIT and ROLLBACK are obtained via corresponding IMS and CICS operations. The entire question of "committed updates" and the related notion of *transaction processing* are considered in much greater depth in the next chapter.

EXERCISES

12.1 Using the suppliers-parts-projects database, write a program with embedded SQL statements to list all supplier rows, in supplier number order. Each supplier row should be immediately followed in the listing by all project rows for projects supplied by that supplier, in project number order.

12.2 What purpose do you think is served by the FOR UPDATE clause?

12.3 Revise your solution to Exercise 12.1 to do the following in addition:

(a) Increase the status by 50 percent for any supplier who supplies more than two projects;

(b) Delete any supplier who does not supply any projects at all.

12.4 Write a program to read and print all part rows in part number order, deleting every tenth one as you go.

12.5 CREATE VIEW includes an optional WITH CHECK OPTION specification. Why do you think there is no corresponding option on DECLARE CURSOR?

12.6 (Harder.) Given the tables

```
CREATE TABLE PARTS
     ( P# ... NOT NULL,
       DESCRIPTION ... ,
     PRIMARY KEY ( P# ) ) ;

CREATE TABLE PART_STRUCTURE
     ( MAJOR_P# ... NOT NULL,
       MINOR_P# ... NOT NULL,
       QTY        ... ,
     PRIMARY KEY ( MAJOR_P#, MINOR_P# ) ,
     FOREIGN KEY ( MAJOR_P# ) REFERENCES PARTS ... ,
     FOREIGN KEY ( MINOR_P# ) REFERENCES PARTS ... ) ;
```

where PART_STRUCTURE shows which parts (MAJOR_P#) contain which other parts (MINOR_P#) as first-level components, write a SQL program to list all component parts of a given part, to all levels (the "parts explosion" problem). *Note*: The following sample values may help you visualize this problem:

PART_STRUCTURE	MAJOR_P#	MINOR_P#	QTY
	P1	P2	2
	P1	P4	4
	P5	P3	1
	P3	P6	3
	P6	P1	9
	P5	P6	8
	P2	P4	3

ANSWERS TO SELECTED EXERCISES

12.1 There are basically two ways to write such a program. The first involves two cursors, CS and CJ say, defined along the following lines:

```
EXEC SQL DECLARE CS CURSOR FOR
         SELECT S#, SNAME, STATUS, CITY
         FROM   S
         ORDER  BY S# ;

EXEC SQL DECLARE CJ CURSOR FOR
         SELECT J#, JNAME, CITY
         FROM   J
         WHERE  J# IN
              ( SELECT J#
                FROM   SPJ
                WHERE  S# = :CS_S# )
         ORDER BY J# ;
```

When cursor CJ is opened, host variable CS_S# will contain a supplier number value, fetched via cursor CS. The procedural logic is essentially as follows:

```
EXEC SQL OPEN CS ;
DO for all S rows accessible via CS ;
   EXEC SQL FETCH CS INTO :CS_S#, :CS_SN, :CS_ST, :CS_SC ;
   print CS_S#, CS_SN, CS_ST, CS_SC ;
   EXEC SQL OPEN CJ ;
   DO for all J rows accessible via CJ ;
      EXEC SQL FETCH CJ INTO :CJ_J#, :CJ_JN, :CJ_JC ;
      print CJ_J#, CJ_JN, CJ_JC ;
   END ;
   EXEC SQL CLOSE CJ ;
END ;
EXEC SQL CLOSE CS ;
```

The trouble with this solution is that it does not exploit the set-level processing capabilities of SQL to the full. In effect, the programmer is hand-coding a join. The second approach uses a single cursor, and so does take advantage of SQL's set-level capabilities; unfortunately, however, the join required is an *outer* join, so the program must first construct that outer join, as follows. (This second solution may therefore be less efficient than the first, because it effectively requires the same data to be scanned multiple times. Direct SQL support for an outer join operator, which is desirable anyway for usability reasons, might alleviate this problem.)

```
EXEC SQL DECLARE CSJ CURSOR FOR
        SELECT S#, SNAME, STATUS, S.CITY, J#, JNAME, J.CITY
        FROM   S, SPJ, J
        WHERE  S.S# = SPJ.S# AND SPJ.J# = J.J#
        UNION  ALL
        SELECT S#, SNAME, STATUS, S.CITY, 'bb', 'bb', 'bb'
        FROM   S
        WHERE  NOT EXISTS
              ( SELECT * FROM SPJ WHERE SPJ.S# = S.S# ) ;
        ORDER  BY 1, 5 ;

EXEC SQL OPEN CSJ ;
DO for all rows accessible via CSJ ;
   EXEC SQL FETCH CSJ INTO :CS_S#, :CS_SN, :CS_ST, :CS_SC,
                          :CJ_J#, :CJ_JN, :CJ_JC ;
   IF CS_S# different from previous iteration
   THEN print CS_S#, CS_SN, CS_ST, CS_SC ;
   print CJ_J#, CJ_JN, CJ_JC ;
END ;
EXEC SQL CLOSE CSJ ;
```

12.2 Suppose the program includes a DECLARE CURSOR statement of the form

```
EXEC SQL DECLARE X CURSOR FOR
        SELECT ...
        FROM   T
        ...... ;
```

The DB2 optimizer is responsible for choosing an access path corresponding to the cursor X. Suppose it chooses an index based on column C of table T. The "active set" of rows accessible via X when X is opened will then be ordered according to values of C. If the program were allowed to UPDATE a value of C via the cursor X—i.e., via an UPDATE statement of the form

```
EXEC SQL UPDATE T
         SET    C = ...
         WHERE  CURRENT OF X ;
```

—then the updated row would probably have to be "moved" (logically speaking), because it would now belong in a different position with respect to the ordering of the active set. In other words, cursor X would effectively jump to a new position, with unpredictable results. To avoid such a situation, the optimizer must be informed of any columns to be updated, so that it will not choose access paths based on those columns. The FOR UPDATE clause is one way (not the only way) of providing the necessary information.

12.3 First, note that cursor CSJ in the second of our two approaches to Exercise 12.1 does not permit updates, because its declaration involves a UNION; we are therefore forced to use the first approach. Second, note that cursor CS in that first approach does not permit updates either, because its declaration involves an ORDER BY; we are therefore forced to use "out of the blue" updating (i.e., we cannot use the CURRENT forms of UPDATE and DELETE). Apart from these considerations, the solution is basically straightforward. The relevant embedded statements are

```
EXEC SQL UPDATE S
         SET    STATUS = STATUS * 1.5
         WHERE  S# = :CS_S# ;

EXEC SQL DELETE
         FROM   S
         WHERE  S# = :CS_S# ;
```

Note: We are tacitly assuming here that RR isolation level is in effect (see Chapter 13). If such is not the case, the problem becomes much more complex, and a fully correct solution is beyond the scope of this chapter.

12.4 Outline procedure:

```
EXEC SQL DECLARE CP CURSOR FOR
         SELECT P#, PNAME, COLOR, WEIGHT, CITY
         FROM   P
         ORDER  BY P# ;

count = 0 ;
EXEC SQL OPEN CP ;
DO for all P rows accessible via CP ;
   EXEC SQL FETCH CP INTO :P#, :PNAME, :COLOR, :WEIGHT :CITY ;
   print P#, PNAME, COLOR, WEIGHT, CITY ;
   count = count + 1 ;
   IF count is a multiple of 10 THEN
   EXEC SQL DELETE FROM P WHERE P# = :P# ;
END ;
EXEC SQL CLOSE CP ;
```

Note that the "DELETE FROM P" cannot be of the DELETE CURRENT variety, because the declaration of cursor CP involves an ORDER BY clause.

12.5 A good question.

12.6 This is a good example of a problem that SQL in its current form does not handle well. The basic difficulty is as follows: We need to "explode" the given part to *n* levels, where the value of *n* is unknown at the time of writing the program. If it were possible, the most straightforward way of performing such an *n*-level "explosion" would be by means of a recursive program, in which each recursive invocation creates a new cursor, as follows (pseudocode):

```
GET LIST ( GIVENP# ) ;
CALL RECURSION ( GIVENP# ) ;
RETURN ;

RECURSION: PROC ( UPPER_P# ) RECURSIVE ;
   DCL UPPER_P# ... ;
   DCL LOWER_P# ... ;
   EXEC SQL DECLARE C "reopenable" CURSOR FOR
            SELECT MINOR_P#
            FROM   PART_STRUCTURE
            WHERE  MAJOR_P# = :UPPER_P# ;

   print UPPER_P# ;
   EXEC SQL OPEN C ;
   DO for all PART_STRUCTURE rows accessible via C ;
       EXEC SQL FETCH C INTO :LOWER_P# ;
       CALL RECURSION ( LOWER_P# ) ;
   END ;
   EXEC SQL CLOSE C ;
END ; /* of RECURSION */
```

We have assumed that the (fictitious) specification "reopenable" means that it is legal to issue "OPEN C" for a cursor C that is already open, and that the effect of such an OPEN is to create a new *instance* of the cursor for the specified query (using the current values of any host variables referenced in that query). We have further assumed that references to C in FETCH (etc.) are references to the "current" instance of C, and that CLOSE destroys that instance and reinstates the previous instance as "current." In other words, we have assumed that a reopenable cursor forms a *stack*, with OPEN and CLOSE serving as the "push" and "pop" operators for that stack.

Unfortunately, those assumptions are purely hypothetical today. There is no such thing as a reopenable cursor in SQL today (indeed, an attempt to issue "OPEN C" for a cursor C that is already open will fail). The foregoing code is illegal. But the example makes it clear that "reopenable cursors" would be a very desirable extension to current SQL.

Since the foregoing procedure does not work, we give a sketch of one possible (but very inefficient) procedure that does.

```
GET LIST ( GIVENP# ) ;
CALL RECURSION ( GIVENP# ) ;
RETURN ;
RECURSION: PROC ( UPPER_P# ) RECURSIVE ;
   DCL UPPER_P# ... ;
   DCL LOWER_P# ... INITIAL ( 'bbbbbb' ) ;
```

```
EXEC SQL DECLARE C CURSOR FOR
          SELECT MINOR_P#
          FROM    PART_STRUCTURE
          WHERE   MAJOR_P# = :UPPER_P#
          AND     MINOR_P# > :LOWER_P#
          ORDER   BY MINOR_P# ;

     DO forever ;
        print UPPER_P# ;
        EXEC SQL OPEN C ;
        EXEC SQL FETCH C INTO :LOWER_P# ;
        IF not found THEN RETURN ;
        IF found THEN
        DO ;
            EXEC SQL CLOSE C ;
            CALL RECURSION ( LOWER_P# ) ;
        END ;
     END ;
END ; /* of RECURSION */
```

Note in this solution that the same cursor is used on every invocation of RECURSION. (By contrast, new instances of UPPER_P# and LOWER_P# are created dynamically each time RECURSION is invoked; those instances are destroyed at completion of that invocation.) Because of this fact, we have to use a trick—

```
... AND MINOR_P# > :LOWER_P# ORDER BY MINOR_P#
```

—so that, on each invocation of RECURSION, we ignore all immediate components (LOWER_P#s) of the current UPPER_P# that have already been processed.

·13·

Application Programming II: Transaction Processing

13.1 INTRODUCTION

The notion of transaction processing was touched on briefly at the end of the previous chapter. In this chapter, we explain in more detail what exactly a transaction is and what is meant by the term "transaction management." In particular, we discuss the problems of recovery and concurrency control that the transaction concept is intended to solve. Also, of course, we examine the relevant aspects of DB2 and SQL in some detail. Note, however, that much of the chapter is very general and could apply with little change to many other systems. The reader who is already familiar with the basic ideas of transaction processing might like to skip the background explanations and go directly to the SQL-specific material in Sections 13.3 and 13.5–13.7.

13.2 WHAT IS A TRANSACTION?

A transaction (as we use the term) is a *logical unit of work*. Consider the following example. Suppose for the sake of the example that table P, the parts table, includes an additional column TOTQTY representing the total shipment quantity for the part in question. In other words, the value of TOTQTY for any given part is supposed to be equal to the sum of all SP.QTY values, taken over all SP rows for that part. Now consider the following sequence of operations, the intent of which is to add a new shipment (S5,P1,1000) to the database:

```
EXEC SQL WHENEVER SQLERROR GO TO UNDO ;
EXEC SQL INSERT
         INTO    SP ( S#, P#, QTY )
         VALUES ('S5','P1',1000) ;
EXEC SQL UPDATE P
         SET     TOTQTY = TOTQTY + 1000
         WHERE   P# = 'P1' ;
EXEC SQL COMMIT WORK ;
         GO TO FINISH ;
UNDO :
     EXEC SQL ROLLBACK WORK ;
FINISH :    RETURN ;
```

The INSERT adds the new shipment to the SP table, the UPDATE updates the TOTQTY column for part P1 appropriately.

The point of the example is that what is presumably intended to be a single, atomic operation—"Create a new shipment"—in fact involves *two* updates to the database. What is more, the database is not even consistent between those two updates; it temporarily violates the requirement that the value of TOTQTY for part P1 is supposed to be equal to the sum of all SP.QTY values for part P1. Thus a logical unit of work (i.e., a transaction) is not necessarily just one SQL operation; rather, it is a *sequence* of several such operations, in general, that transforms a consistent state of the database into another consistent state, without necessarily preserving consistency at all intermediate points.

Now, it is clear that what must *not* be allowed to happen in the example is for one of the two updates to be executed and the other not (because then the database would be left in an inconsistent state). Ideally, of course, we would like a cast-iron guarantee that both updates will be executed. Unfortunately, it is impossible to provide any such guarantee: There is always a chance that things will go wrong, and go wrong moreover at the worst possible moment. For example, a system crash might occur between the two updates, or an I/O error might occur on the second of them, etc. But a system that supports *transaction processing* does provide the next best thing to such a guarantee. Specifically, it guarantees that if the transaction executes some updates and then a failure occurs (for whatever reason) before the transaction reaches its normal termination, *then those updates will be undone*. Thus the transaction *either* executes in its entirety *or* is totally canceled (i.e., made as if it never executed at all). In this way a sequence of operations that is fundamentally not atomic can be made to look as if it really were atomic from an external point of view.

The system component that provides this atomicity (or semblance of atomicity) is known as the *transaction manager*, and the COMMIT WORK and ROLLBACK WORK operations (usually referred to as just COMMIT and ROLLBACK, respectively) are the key to the way it works:

- The COMMIT operation signals *successful* end-of-transaction: It tells the transaction manager that a logical unit of work has been successfully completed, the database* is (or should be) in a consistent state again, and all of the updates made by that unit of work can now be "committed" or made permanent.

- The ROLLBACK operation, by contrast, signals *unsuccessful* end-of-transaction: It tells the transaction manager that something has gone wrong, the database might be in an inconsistent state, and all of the updates made by the logical unit of work so far must be "rolled back" or undone.

In the example, therefore, we issue a COMMIT if we get through the two updates successfully, which will commit the changes in the database and make them permanent. If anything goes wrong, however—i.e., if either update returns a negative SQLCODE value—then we issue a ROLLBACK instead, to undo any changes made so far.

Note: For the sake of the example (and as a matter of good practice), we show the COMMIT and ROLLBACK operations explicitly. However, as mentioned at the end of Chapter 12, under DB2 the system will automatically issue a COMMIT for any program that reaches its normal termination, and will automatically issue a ROLLBACK for any program that does not (regardless of the reason; in particular, if a program terminates abnormally because of a *system* failure, a ROLLBACK will be issued on its behalf when the system is restarted). In the example, therefore, we could have omitted the explicit COMMIT, but not the explicit ROLLBACK.

At this juncture the reader may be wondering how it is possible to undo an update. The answer is that (as mentioned in Chapter 2) the system in-

---

*For simplicity we assume throughout this chapter that the application interacts with just one database—or, equivalently, that in this context the term "database" refers to the collection of *all* data used by the application, no matter how many distinct DB2 databases that data actually spans. See Chapter 15 for an explanation of what the term "database" really means in the DB2 context.

cludes a *log*, in which details of all update operations—in particular, before and after values—are recorded. (In fact, the log entry for any given update is written to the log *before* that update is applied to the database. See the next section for an explanation of this point.) Thus, if it becomes necessary to undo some particular update, the system can use the corresponding log entry to restore the updated item to its previous value.

One final point: As explained in Chapter 1, the data manipulation statements of SQL are *set-level* and typically operate on multiple rows at a time. What then if something goes wrong in the middle of such a statement? For example, is it possible that a multiple-row UPDATE could update some of its target rows and then fail before updating the rest? The answer is no, it is not; DB2 guarantees that all SQL statements are individually atomic, at least so far as their effect on the database is concerned. If an error does occur in the middle of such a statement, then the database will remain totally unchanged—even if multiple tables are affected by the statement in question, as might be the case with a CASCADE delete rule, for example.

13.3 COMMIT AND ROLLBACK

From the previous section, it should be clear that COMMIT and ROLL-BACK are not really database operations at all, in the sense that SELECT, UPDATE, etc., are database operations. The COMMIT and ROLLBACK statements are not instructions to the database management system. Instead, they are instructions to the *transaction manager*; and the transaction manager is certainly not part of the DBMS—on the contrary, the DBMS is subordinate to the transaction manager, in the sense that the DBMS is just one of possibly several "resource managers" that provide services to transactions running under that transaction manager. In the case of DB2 in particular, there are several such transaction managers, corresponding to the several different environments in which DB2 transactions can operate. As explained (in different terms) in Chapter 2:

- A transaction running under IMS (online or batch) can use the services of three resource managers—IMS/DB, IMS/DC (online only), and DB2. IMS acts as the transaction manager in this case.*

- A transaction running under CICS can also use the services of three resource managers—IMS/DB, CICS, and DB2. Here CICS acts as the transaction manager.

---

*A slight oversimplification. It is true that IMS is the transaction manager in the online case, but actually DB2 itself is the transaction manager in the batch case. Nevertheless, "commit" and "rollback" functions must be requested in IMS style, not DB2 style, even in the batch case (see later).

- A transaction running under TSO (online or batch) or the Call Attach Facility can use the services of just one resource manager, namely DB2. Here DB2 itself acts as the transaction manager.

Consider a transaction that updates both an IMS database and a DB2 database. If that transaction completes successfully, then *all* of its updates, to both IMS data and DB2 data, must be committed; conversely, if it fails, then *all* of its updates must be rolled back. It must not be possible for the IMS updates to be committed and the DB2 updates rolled back (or conversely); for then the transaction would no longer be atomic (all or nothing). Thus, it obviously does not make sense for the transaction to issue, say, a COMMIT to IMS and a ROLLBACK to DB2; and even if it issued the same instruction to both, the system could still fail in between the two, with unfortunate results. Instead, therefore, the transaction issues a single *system-wide* COMMIT (or ROLLBACK) to the appropriate transaction manager, and the transaction manager in turn guarantees that all resource managers will commit or will roll back the updates they are responsible for *in unison*. (What is more, it provides that guarantee even if the system fails in the middle of the process, thanks to a protocol known as *two-phase commit*. But the details of that protocol are beyond the scope of this book.) That is why the DBMS(s) is (are) subordinate to the transaction manager; COMMIT and ROLLBACK must be global (system-wide) operations, and the transaction manager acts as the necessary central control point to ensure that this is so.

The foregoing also explains why "commit" and "rollback" functions are requested differently in different environments. Since they are not really database operations at all, but rather transaction manager operations, they must be requested in the style prescribed for the transaction manager in question. In the TSO and "pure batch" environments, where DB2 itself serves as the transaction manager, they are requested via the explicit SQL operators COMMIT and ROLLBACK (details below). In the IMS and CICS environments, they are requested via the corresponding IMS and CICS calls, details of which can be found in the IBM manuals for those systems. In the remainder of this section, we concentrate on the TSO and batch environments specifically.*

Before getting into details of the COMMIT and ROLLBACK statements as such, we first define the important notion of "synchronization point" (abbreviated synchpoint). A synchpoint represents a boundary point

---

*We also concentrate on the *application programming* environment. It is possible to enter COMMIT and ROLLBACK statements interactively, but the practice is not recommended because (as will become clear later in this chapter) it might mean that locks will be held for an undesirably long time.

between two consecutive transactions; loosely speaking, it corresponds to the end of a logical unit of work, and thus to a point at which the database is in a state of consistency. Program initiation, COMMIT, and ROLLBACK each establish a synchpoint, and no other operation does. (Remember, however, that COMMIT and ROLLBACK may sometimes be implicit.)

COMMIT

The SQL COMMIT statement takes the form

```
COMMIT [ WORK ] ;
```

A successful end-of-transaction is signaled and a synchpoint is established. All updates made by the program since the previous synchpoint are committed. All open cursors are closed, except for cursors whose declaration includes the optional specification WITH HOLD (explained following the description of ROLLBACK below). Likewise, all row locks are released, except for locks needed to hold position for cursors not closed.* Locks acquired via LOCK TABLE may or may not be released (see Sections 13.5 and 13.6).

The optional operand WORK is purely a noiseword and has no effect on the execution of the statement. It is required by the SQL standard, however.

ROLLBACK

The SQL ROLLBACK statement takes the form

```
ROLLBACK [ WORK ] ;
```

An unsuccessful end-of-transaction is signaled and a synchpoint is established. All updates made by the program since the previous synchpoint are undone. All open cursors are closed. All row locks are released;[†] locks acquired via LOCK TABLE may or may not be released (see Sections 13.5 and 13.6).

The optional operand WORK is purely a noiseword and has no effect on the execution of the statement. It is required by the SQL standard, however.

---

*"Row locks" here really means *page* locks. See Section 13.5.
[†]Again, "row locks" here really means *page* locks.

The WITH HOLD Option

Recall from Chapter 12 that WITH HOLD is an optional specification on a cursor declaration.* In order to explain the purpose of that option, it is convenient to begin by considering what happens in its absence. Suppose we need to process some large table one row at a time by means of a cursor, and suppose too that we need to update some of the rows as we go. It is often desirable (for performance and other reasons) to divide the work up into batches and to make the processing of each batch into a separate transaction (by issuing a COMMIT at the end of each one); thus, e.g., a table of one million rows might be processed by a sequence of 10,000 transactions, each one dealing with just 100 rows. This way, for example, if it becomes necessary to roll a given transaction back, then at most 100 updates will have to be undone, instead of potentially as many as a million.

The problem with this approach, however, is that every time we issue a COMMIT, we implicitly close the cursor, thereby losing our position within the table. The first thing each transaction has to do, therefore, is to execute some repositioning code in order to get back to the row that is due to be processed next. And that repositioning code can often be quite complex, especially if the processing sequence for the table is determined by a combination of several columns (consider, e.g., a program that is processing line items within purchase orders within customers within regions).

If the cursor declaration specifies WITH HOLD, however, COMMIT does *not* close the cursor; instead, it leaves it open, positioned such that the next FETCH will move it to the next row in sequence. The possibly complex repositioning code is thus no longer required.† Note, however, that the first operation on the cursor following the COMMIT *must* be FETCH (or possibly CLOSE); UPDATE and DELETE CURRENT are illegal.

A number of points arise from the foregoing definitions and explanations that are worth spelling out explicitly.

1. First, note that *every* SQL operation in DB2 is executed within the context of some transaction.‡ This includes data definition operations such as CREATE TABLE and data control operations such as GRANT. It also includes SQL operations that are entered interactively (e.g.,

---

*WITH HOLD is ignored for message-driven IMS transactions and CICS pseudoconversations.

†Unless any of the transactions fails and terminates with a ROLLBACK instead of a COMMIT. ROLLBACK does close all cursors, even those with the WITH HOLD option.

‡This statement is not quite accurate for CONNECT and "local SET" operations, but it is true for all practical purposes. See Chapter 17.

through DB2I). The synchpoints for operations entered through DB2I are established in a manner to be explained in Chapter 16 (Section 16.2).

2. It follows from the definitions that transactions cannot be nested inside one another, because each COMMIT or ROLLBACK terminates one transaction and (effectively) starts another.

3. As a consequence of the previous point (and as already indicated by our discussion of WITH HOLD), we can see that a single program execution consists of a *sequence* of one or more transactions (frequently but not necessarily just one). If it is just one, it will often be possible to code the program without any explicit COMMIT or ROLLBACK statements at all; however, this practice (of omitting the explicit statements) is not recommended, even if they do happen to be strictly unnecessary.

Finally, it follows from all of the above that transactions are not only the unit of work but also the unit of *recovery*. For if a transaction successfully COMMITs, then the transaction manager must guarantee that its updates will be permanently established in the database, even if the system crashes the very next moment. It is quite possible, for instance, that the system will crash after the COMMIT has been honored but before the updates have been physically written to the database (they may still be waiting in the main storage buffer and so be lost at the time of the crash). Even if that happens, the system's restart procedure will still install those updates in the database; it is able to discover the values to be written by examining the relevant entries in the log. (It follows that the log must be physically written before COMMIT processing can complete. This rule is known as the *Write-Ahead Log Protocol*.) Thus the restart procedure will recover any units of work (transactions) that completed successfully but did not manage to get their updates physically written prior to the crash; hence, as stated earlier, the transaction can reasonably be defined as the unit of recovery.

13.4 THREE CONCURRENCY PROBLEMS

DB2 is a *shared system*; that is, it is a system that allows any number of transactions to access the same database at the same time. Any such system requires some kind of *concurrency control mechanism* to ensure that concurrent transactions do not interfere with each other's operation, and of course DB2 includes such a mechanism, namely *locking*. For the benefit of readers who may not be familiar with the problems that can occur in the absence of such a mechanism—in other words, with the problems that such a mechanism must be able to solve—this section is devoted to an outline explanation of those problems. We defer specific discussion of the DB2 facilities to Sections 13.5–13.7. Readers who are already familiar with the basic ideas of concurrency control may wish to turn straight to those sections.

There are essentially three ways in which things can go wrong—three ways, that is, in which a transaction, though correct in itself, can nevertheless produce the wrong answer because of interference on the part of some other transaction* (in the absence of suitable controls, of course). The three problems are:

1. The *lost update* problem,
2. The *uncommitted dependency* problem, and
3. The *inconsistent analysis* problem.

We consider each in turn.

The Lost Update Problem

Consider the situation illustrated in Fig. 13.1. That figure is intended to be read as follows: Transaction *A* retrieves some row *R* at time *t1*; transaction *B* retrieves that same row *R* at time *t2*; transaction *A* updates the row (on the basis of the values seen at time *t1*) at time *t3*; and transaction *B* updates the same row (on the basis of the values seen at time *t2*, which are the same as those seen at time *t1*) at time *t4*. Transaction *A*'s update is lost at time *t4*, because transaction *B* overwrites it without even looking at it.

Transaction A	time	Transaction B
–		–
–		–
FETCH R	t1	–
–		–
–	t2	FETCH R
–		–
UPDATE R	t3	–
–		–
–	t4	UPDATE R
–		–

Fig. 13.1 Transaction *A* loses an update at time *t4*

---

*Note that the interfering transaction may also be correct in itself. It is the *interleaving* of operations from the two individually correct transactions that produces the overall incorrect result.

The Uncommitted Dependency Problem

The uncommitted dependency problem arises if one transaction is allowed to retrieve (or, worse, update) a row that has been updated by another transaction and has not yet been committed by that other transaction. For if it has not yet been committed, there is always a possibility that it never will be committed but will be rolled back instead—in which case the first transaction will have seen some data that now no longer exists (and in a sense "never" existed). Consider Figs. 13.2 and 13.3.

In the first example (Fig. 13.2), transaction *A* sees an uncommitted update (also called an uncommitted change) at time *t2*. That update is then undone at time *t3*. Transaction *A* is therefore operating on a false assumption—namely, the assumption that row *R* has the value seen at time *t2*, whereas in fact it has whatever value it had prior to time *t1*. As a result, transaction *A* may well produce incorrect output. Note, incidentally, that the ROLLBACK of transaction *B* may be due to no fault of *B*'s—it could, for example, be the result of a system crash. (And transaction *A* may already have terminated by that time, in which case the crash would not cause a ROLLBACK to be issued for *A* also.)

Transaction A	time	Transaction B
-		-
-		-
-	t1	UPDATE R
-		-
FETCH R	t2	-
-		-
-	t3	ROLLBACK
-		

Fig. 13.2   Transaction *A* becomes dependent on an uncommitted change at time *t2*

Transaction A	time	Transaction B
-		-
-		-
-	t1	UPDATE R
-		-
UPDATE R	t2	-
-		-
-	t3	ROLLBACK
-		

Fig. 13.3   Transaction *A* updates an uncommitted change at time *t2*, and loses that update at time *t3*

The second example (Fig. 13.3) is even worse. Not only does transaction *A* become dependent on an uncommitted change at time *t2*, but it actually loses an update at time *t3*—because the ROLLBACK at time *t3* causes row *R* to be restored to its value prior to time *t1*. This is another version of the lost update problem.

The Inconsistent Analysis Problem

Consider Fig. 13.4, which shows two transactions *A* and *B* operating on account (ACC) rows: Transaction *A* is summing account balances, transaction *B* is transferring an amount 10 from account 3 to account 1. The result produced by *A* (110) is clearly incorrect; if *A* were to go on to write that result back into the database, it would actually leave the database in an inconsistent state. We say that *A* has seen an inconsistent state of the database and has therefore performed an inconsistent analysis. Note the differ-

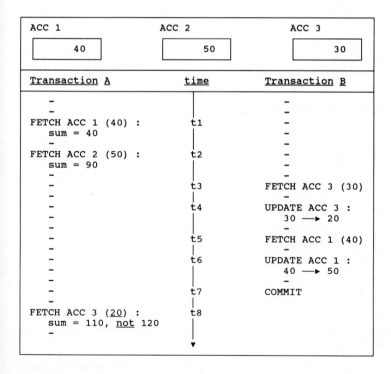

Fig. 13.4 Transaction *A* performs an inconsistent analysis

ence between this example and the previous one: There is no question here of *A* being dependent on an uncommitted change, since *B* COMMITs all its updates before *A* sees ACC 3.

13.5 HOW DB2 SOLVES THE THREE CONCURRENCY PROBLEMS

As mentioned at the beginning of the previous section, the DB2 concurrency control mechanism—like that of most other systems commercially available—is based on a technique known as *locking*. The basic idea of locking is simple: When a transaction needs an assurance that some object that it is interested in—typically a database row—will not change in some unpredictable manner while its back is turned (as it were), it *acquires a lock* on that object. The effect of the lock is to lock other transactions out of the object, and thereby to prevent them from changing it. The first transaction is thus able to carry out its processing in the certain knowledge that the object in question will remain in a stable state for as long as that transaction wishes it to.

We now give a more detailed explanation of the way locking works in DB2 specifically. We start by making some simplifying assumptions:

1. We assume for the most part that the only kind of object that is subject to the locking mechanism is the database row, i.e., a row of a base table. However, perhaps we should point out right away that:

(a) Index entries are also subject to locking, just as database rows are, and for exactly the same reasons;

(b) DB2 does not *physically* lock database rows, it locks entire "pages," or entire tables, or even larger units. (A page is a unit of physical storage. See Chapter 15.)

More details are given in Section 13.6.

2. We discuss only two kinds of lock, namely shared locks (S locks) and exclusive locks (X locks). Other types of lock exist in some systems (in fact, DB2 itself supports additional types, as we will see), but S and X are the most important ones for present purposes. *Note*: S and X locks are sometimes referred to as read and write locks, respectively.

3. We consider row-level operations only (FETCH, UPDATE CURRENT, etc.). For locking purposes, set-level operations (SELECT–FROM–WHERE, etc.) can be thought of just as shorthand for an appropriate series of row-level operations.

4. We assume that if a transaction requests a lock that is not currently available, the transaction simply waits until it is. In practice, the installation

can specify a maximum wait time; then, if any transaction ever reaches this threshold in waiting for a lock, it "times out" and the lock request fails (a negative SQLCODE is returned).

5. We assume that RR ("repeatable read") isolation level is in effect. See Section 13.6 for an explanation of this assumption, also for an explanation of the effects of relaxing it.

We now proceed with our detailed explanations.

1. First, if transaction A holds an exclusive (X) lock on row R, then a request from transaction B for a lock of either type on R will cause B to go into a wait state. B will wait until A's lock is released.

2. Next, if transaction A holds a shared (S) lock on row R, then:

(a) A request from transaction B for an X lock on R will cause B to go into a wait state (and B will wait until A's lock is released);

(b) A request from transaction B for an S lock on R will be granted (that is, B will now also hold an S lock on R).

These first two points can conveniently be summarized by means of a *compatibility matrix* (Fig. 13.5). The matrix is interpreted as follows: Consider some row R; suppose transaction A currently holds a lock on R as indicated by the entries in the column headings (dash = no lock); and suppose some distinct transaction B requests a lock on R as indicated by the entries down the left-hand side (for completeness we again include the "no lock" case). An N indicates a *conflict* (B's request cannot be satisfied and B goes into a wait state), a Y indicates compatibility (B's request is satisfied). The matrix is obviously symmetric.

To continue with our explanations:

3. Transaction requests for row locks are always implicit. When a transaction successfully FETCHes a row, it automatically acquires an S lock on that row. When a transaction successfully updates a row, it automatically acquires an X lock on that row (if it already holds an S lock on the row,

	X	S	–
X	N	N	Y
S	N	Y	Y
–	Y	Y	Y

Fig. 13.5 Lock type compatibility matrix (X, S)

as it will in a FETCH/UPDATE or FETCH/DELETE sequence, then the UPDATE or DELETE "promotes" the S lock to X level).

4. All locks are held until the next synchpoint—or, in the case of locks acquired on behalf of a cursor declared WITH HOLD, until the next synchpoint after the cursor is closed.*

Now we are in a position to see how DB2 solves the three problems described in the previous section. Again we consider them one at a time.

The Lost Update Problem Revisited

Fig. 13.6 is a modified version of Fig. 13.1, showing what would happen to the interleaved execution of that figure under the locking mechanism of DB2. As you can see, transaction A's UPDATE at time $t3$ is not accepted, because it is an implicit request for an X lock on R, and such a request conflicts with the S lock already held by transaction B; so A goes into a wait state. For analogous reasons, B goes into a wait state at time $t4$. Now both transactions are unable to proceed, so there is no question of any update being lost. DB2 thus solves the lost update problem by reducing it

Transaction A	time	Transaction B
-		-
-		-
FETCH R	t1	-
(acquire S lock on R)		-
-		-
-	t2	FETCH R
-		(acquire S lock on R)
-		-
UPDATE R	t3	-
(request X lock on R)		-
wait		-
wait	t4	UPDATE R
wait		(request X lock on R)
wait		wait
wait		wait
wait		wait

Fig. 13.6 No update is lost, but deadlock occurs at time $t4$

---

*This sentence is accurate for X locks (though, in the case of a cursor declared WITH HOLD, such locks are downgraded to S level at each synchpoint). It is also accurate for S locks, provided that (as we assume) RR isolation level is in effect. See Section 13.6 for further discussion.

to another problem!—but at least it does solve the original problem. The new problem is called *deadlock*; it is discussed in Section 13.7.

The Uncommitted Dependency Problem Revisited

Figs. 13.7 and 13.8 are, respectively, modified versions of Figs. 13.2 and 13.3, showing what would happen to the interleaved executions of those figures under the locking mechanism of DB2. As you can see, transaction *A*'s operation at time *t2* (FETCH in Fig. 13.7, UPDATE in Fig. 13.8) is not accepted in either case, because it is an implicit request for a lock on *R*, and such a request conflicts with the X lock already held by *B*; so *A* goes

```
Transaction A              time    Transaction B

     -                       |          -
     -                       |          -
     -                      t1       UPDATE R
     -                       |       (acquire X lock on R)
     -                       |          -
FETCH R                     t2          -
(request S lock on R)        |          -
   wait                      |          -
   wait                     t3       synchpoint
   wait                      |       (release X lock on R)
resume : FETCH R            t4
(acquire S lock on R)        |
     -                       ▼
```

Fig. 13.7 Transaction *A* is prevented from seeing an uncommitted change at time *t2*

```
Transaction A              time    Transaction B

     -                       |          -
     -                       |          -
     -                      t1       UPDATE R
     -                       |       (acquire X lock on R)
     -                       |          -
UPDATE R                    t2          -
(request X lock on R)        |          -
   wait                      |          -
   wait                     t3       synchpoint
   wait                      |       (release X lock on R)
resume : UPDATE R          t4
(acquire X lock on R)        |
     -                       ▼
```

Fig. 13.8 Transaction *A* is prevented from updating an uncommitted change at time *t2*

into a wait state. It remains in that wait state until *B* reaches a synchpoint (either COMMIT or ROLLBACK), when *B*'s lock is released and *A* is able to proceed; and at that point *A* sees a *committed* value (either the pre-*B* value, if *B* terminates with a ROLLBACK, or the post-*B* value otherwise). Either way, *A* is no longer dependent on an uncommitted update.

The Inconsistent Analysis Problem Revisited

Fig. 13.9 is a modified version of Fig. 13.4, showing what would happen to the interleaved execution of that figure under the locking mechanism of DB2. As you can see, transaction *B*'s UPDATE at time *t6* is not accepted, because it is an implicit request for an X lock on ACC 1, and such a request conflicts with the S lock already held by *A*; so *B* goes into a wait state. Likewise, transaction *A*'s FETCH at time *t7* is also not accepted, because

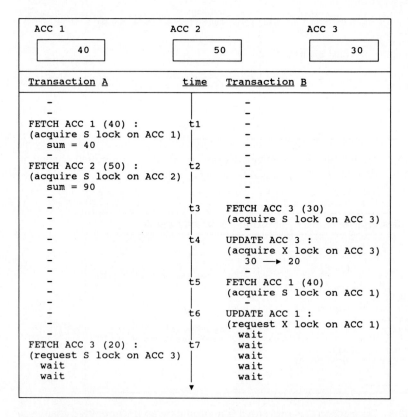

Fig. 13.9 Inconsistent analysis is prevented, but deadlock occurs at time *t7*

it is an implicit request for an S lock on ACC 3, and such a request conflicts with the X lock already held by *B*; so *A* goes into a wait state also. Thus (again) DB2 solves the original problem (the inconsistent analysis problem, in this case) by forcing a deadlock. As already mentioned, deadlock is discussed in Section 13.7.

13.6 EXPLICIT LOCKING FACILITIES

In addition to the implicit locking mechanism described in the previous section, DB2 provides certain explicit facilities which the programmer should at least be aware of (though the implicit facilities will be adequate in many situations). The explicit facilities—a somewhat mixed bag—consist of (1) the SQL statement LOCK TABLE, (2) the ISOLATION parameter on the BIND PACKAGE command, (3) the table space LOCKSIZE parameter, and (4) the ACQUIRE/RELEASE parameters on the BIND PLAN command. *Note*: BIND PACKAGE and BIND PLAN are the commands that invoke the DB2 Bind component to produce a package from a Database Request Module and to produce an application plan from a set of packages, respectively; see Chapter 16 for further discussion.*

LOCK TABLE

The SQL LOCK TABLE statement takes the form

```
LOCK TABLE table IN mode MODE ;
```

where "mode" is SHARE or EXCLUSIVE, and where "table" must designate a base table, not a view. For example:

```
LOCK TABLE SP IN EXCLUSIVE MODE ;
```

This LOCK TABLE acquires an X lock on the *entire SP base table* on behalf of the transaction issuing the statement. Of course, the transaction may have to wait for a while before it can acquire the lock, if some other transaction already holds a conflicting lock, either on the table itself or on some row within that table. Once the lock is acquired, no other transaction will be able to acquire any lock on the table or on any part of it—in other words, no other transaction will be able to access any part of the table in any way—until the original lock is released. (When that original lock is

---

*In the interests of accuracy, we should mention that (a) the ISOLATION parameter can also be specified on the BIND PLAN command, and (b) the RELEASE parameter (but not the ACQUIRE parameter) can also be specified on the BIND PACKAGE command. We omit detailed discussion of these possibilities for reasons of simplicity.

released depends on the applicable RELEASE parameter. See later in this section.)

If SHARE is specified instead of EXCLUSIVE, then the transaction will of course acquire an S lock instead of an X lock. Again, of course, it may have to wait before it can acquire the lock. Once the lock is acquired, other transactions will not be able to acquire an X lock on the table or on any part of it until the original lock is released, but they *will* be able to acquire an S lock on the table or on some part of it before that time.

The purpose of the LOCK TABLE statement is as follows. If a transaction accesses a large number of individual rows and locks them one at a time as described in the previous section, then the locking overhead for that transaction may be quite high, in terms of both space and time (space for holding the locks in main storage and time for acquiring them). Consider, for example, a program that scans and prints some large percentage of the entire SP table. For such a program, it may well be better to acquire a single table-level lock as in the example above, and thus to dispense with the need for row-level locks (for that table) entirely. Of course, concurrency will suffer, but the performance of the individual transaction will improve, possibly to such an extent that overall system throughput will improve also.

Acquiring a table-level X lock will indeed (as just suggested) dispense with the need for row-level locks entirely for the table concerned. Acquiring a table-level S lock will dispense with the need for row-level S locks, but not for row-level X locks (again, for the table concerned); that is, if the program updates any row in the table, it will still need to acquire an X lock on that particular row, in order to prevent concurrent transactions from seeing an uncommitted change.

Note: If the table in question resides in a "segmented table space" (see Chapter 15), LOCK TABLE does indeed lock the table per se. If the table resides in some other kind of table space, however, LOCK TABLE actually locks the *entire table space* that contains that table. In some cases, therefore, DB2 may physically lock more than the user has asked for, because some table spaces will contain more than one table. Again, see Chapter 15 for further information regarding table spaces.

The ISOLATION Parameter

The ISOLATION parameter on the BIND PACKAGE command specifies the *isolation level* for the package being created. There are two possible values, RR ("repeatable read") and CS ("cursor stability"). RR is the default.

- "Cursor stability" means that if at execution time the package:

(a) obtains addressability to some particular row by setting a cursor to point to it, and thus

(b) acquires a lock on that row, and then

(c) relinquishes its addressability to the row without updating it, and so

(d) does not promote its existing lock to X level, then

(e) that existing lock can be released without having to wait for the next synchpoint.

- "Repeatable read" means that row-level S locks are held until the next synchpoint, like X locks.

Isolation level CS may provide more concurrency than isolation level RR, but from a theoretical standpoint, at least, it is generally not a good idea (that is why RR is the default). The problem with CS is that a transaction operating at that level on some part of the database may have a row changed "behind its back," as in Fig. 13.4, and so may produce a wrong answer. In fact, if a transaction operates on any part of the database under isolation level CS, then it is *always* theoretically possible to define a second transaction that can run interleaved with the first in such a way as to produce an overall incorrect result. By contrast, a transaction that uses isolation level RR for everything can behave completely as if it were executing in a single-user system; i.e., RR guarantees *safety*.*

The explanations of Section 13.5 ("How DB2 Solves the Three Concurrency Problems") require some slight modification if isolation level CS is in effect, as follows:

- If a transaction obtains addressability to a row under CS, and if the cursor permits updates (i.e., if there is a possibility that the transaction might update the row), then DB2 gives the transaction an "update lock" (U lock) instead of an S lock.

- U locks are compatible with S locks but not with other U locks (and of course not with X locks); that is, if transaction *A* holds a U lock on row *R*, then a request from transaction *B* for a U (or X) lock on *R* will cause *B* to go into a wait state. If transaction *A* now updates *R*, its U

---

*On the other hand, RR can lead to unacceptable overhead in some situations (especially as it applies to entire packages, not just to individual tables). In such cases, it might be better to specify CS for the package, and then use explicit LOCK TABLE operations on individual tables to achieve the effect of RR for just those tables.

lock will be promoted to X level; otherwise the U lock will be released (like an S lock) when *A* relinquishes addressability to *R*.

The advantage of U locks (intuitively speaking) is that they may reduce the number of deadlocks. See Exercises 13.2 and 13.3 at the end of the chapter.

Note finally that although it is specified as part of the BIND PACKAGE command rather than as part of the program, the programmer does need to be aware of the isolation level, because the logic of the program may depend on it (i.e., it may affect the way the program has to be coded).

The LOCKSIZE Parameter

(We mention this topic here only for completeness. The following description might not make much sense until the reader has studied Chapter 15.)

The implicit locking mechanism of DB2 is defined in terms of row-level locks, as explained in Section 13.5. However, that definition is a *logical* definition only. Physically, DB2 locks data in terms of *pages* or *tables* or *table spaces*. That is, when a given transaction logically locks some individual row, DB2 physically locks the page or the table or the table space that contains that row, depending on what was specified as the LOCKSIZE for the relevant table space in the CREATE or ALTER TABLESPACE operation. For a given table space, the LOCKSIZE can be specified as PAGE, TABLE, TABLESPACE, or ANY:

- TABLESPACE means that all locks acquired on data in the table space will be at the table space level.

- TABLE means that locks acquired on data in the table space will be at the table level. TABLE applies only to segmented table spaces.

- PAGE means that locks acquired on data in the table space will be at the page level whenever possible. Our discussions in Section 13.5 tacitly assumed page-level locking. Sometimes, however, DB2 may still acquire locks at the table or table space level, even if page-level locking is specified (details beyond the scope of this text).

- ANY (which is the default) means that DB2 itself will decide the appropriate physical unit of locking for the table space *for each plan*—e.g., one plan may acquire locks at the page level, while another acquires them at the table space level, both on the same table space. Also, in some cases DB2 may acquire page locks initially (for some given plan and some given table space), but then trade all those locks in for a single table lock or single table space lock, if the number of page locks reaches some installation- specified threshold (a process known as *lock escalation*).

The ACQUIRE/RELEASE Parameters

(Again we mention this topic here primarily for completeness. For further discussion, see the IBM manuals.)

Despite the discussion of page- and table-level locking above, the fact is that DB2 *always* implicitly acquires locks of some kind—sometimes shared or exclusive locks, sometimes less restrictive "intent" locks—at the table space level. The ACQUIRE and RELEASE parameters on the BIND PLAN command specify when such table space locks (and table locks also, in the case of segmented table spaces) are to be acquired and released.* For ACQUIRE, the possible specifications are USE and ALLOCATE; for RELEASE, they are COMMIT and DEALLOCATE.

- ACQUIRE (USE) means that such implicit locks are acquired on first use (i.e., when the table space or table in question is first "touched"). ACQUIRE (ALLOCATE) means that such locks are acquired when the plan is "allocated" (loosely, when the program begins execution).
- RELEASE (COMMIT) means that table and table space locks are released at each synchpoint—both implicitly acquired locks and locks acquired explicitly via LOCK TABLE. RELEASE (DEALLOCATE) means that such locks are held until the plan is "deallocated" (loosely, when the program terminates). If ACQUIRE (ALLOCATE) is specified, RELEASE (DEALLOCATE) must be specified also.

Note: There are a number of exceptions to the foregoing. First, locks obtained via dynamic SQL (see Chapter 14) are always acquired on first use and released at the next synchpoint, regardless of what has been specified for the ACQUIRE and RELEASE parameters. Second, ACQUIRE (USE) is always assumed for all locks acquired by packages, even if ACQUIRE (ALLOCATE) is specified on the BIND PLAN command. Third, RELEASE (COMMIT) is ignored for locks that are required to keep position for cursors defined with the WITH HOLD option.

---

*In the interests of accuracy once again, we should point out that ACQUIRE and RELEASE apply to other resources as well as locks. For details, see the IBM manuals.

13.7 DEADLOCK

We have seen how locking can be used to solve the three basic problems of concurrency. Unfortunately, however, we have also seen that locking introduces problems of its own, principally the problem of deadlock. Section 13.5 gave two examples of deadlock. Fig. 13.10 shows a slightly more generalized version of the problem. *Note*: The LOCK operations shown in that figure are intended to represent any operations that acquire locks, not necessarily SQL LOCK TABLE statements specifically.

Deadlock is a situation in which two or more transactions are in a simultaneous wait state, each one waiting for one of the others to release a lock before it can proceed. Fig. 13.10 shows a deadlock involving two transactions, but deadlocks involving three, four, . . . transactions are also possible, at least in theory. In practice, however, deadlocks almost never involve more than two transactions.

If a deadlock occurs, the system will detect it and break it. Breaking a deadlock involves choosing one of the deadlocked transactions as the *victim* and—depending on the transaction manager concerned—either rolling it back automatically or requesting it to roll itself back (a request that cannot be refused, incidentally). Either way, the transaction will release its locks and thus allow some other transaction to proceed. In general, therefore, *any operation that requests a lock*—which means *any executable SQL operation*—may be rejected with a negative SQLCODE indicating that the transaction has just been selected as the victim in a deadlock situation and has either been rolled back or is requested to do so. The problem of deadlock is thus a significant one so far as the application programmer is concerned, because application programs may need to include explicit code to deal with it if it arises. For example:

```
Transaction A              time      Transaction B

    -                        |            -
    -                        |            -
LOCK R1 IN X MODE           t1           -
    -                        |            -
    -                       t2        LOCK R2 IN X MODE
    -                        |            -
LOCK R2 IN X MODE           t3           -
  wait                       |            -
  wait                      t4        LOCK R1 IN X MODE
  wait                       |          wait
  wait                       ▼          wait
```

Fig. 13.10 An example of deadlock

```
EXEC SQL ... ;
IF SQLCODE = value indicating "deadlock victim"
THEN DO ;
        EXEC SQL ROLLBACK WORK ;
        reinitialize variables from initial input data ;
        GO TO beginning of processing cycle ;
    END ;
```

Here we are assuming that the program has saved its initial input data somewhere (not in the database!—why not?) in preparation for just such an eventuality. Note too that the possibility of deadlock* means that programs will probably have to include repositioning logic, in general, even for cursors declared WITH HOLD.

13.8 SUMMARY

In this rather lengthy chapter we have discussed the question of transaction management, both in general terms and as it is addressed in DB2 specifically. A transaction is a logical unit of work—also a unit of recovery and (as can be seen from the last few sections) a unit of concurrency. Transaction management is the task of supervising the execution of transactions in such a way that each transaction can be considered as an all-or-nothing proposition, even given the possibility of arbitrary failures on the part of either individual transactions or the system itself, and given also the fact that multiple independent transactions may be executing concurrently and accessing the same data. In fact, the overall function of the system might well be defined as *the reliable execution of transactions*.

In DB2 specifically, transactions are delimited by *synchpoints*, which are established by program initiation, COMMIT (successful termination), and ROLLBACK (unsuccessful termination). (*Note*: COMMIT and ROLLBACK are the operations used in the TSO and batch environments; other, analogous operations are used in other environments.) DB2 guarantees the atomicity of such transactions, as explained in Sections 13.2 and 13.3.

Concurrency control in DB2 is based on locking. Basically, every row a transaction accesses is locked; if the transaction goes on to update the row, then that lock will be promoted to exclusive level. Exclusive locks are held until the next synchpoint. This simple protocol solves the three basic problems of concurrency, but also introduces the possibility of deadlock; hence application programs must be prepared to deal with that eventuality. Deadlock is signaled by a negative SQLCODE value that may potentially be returned after any SQL operation that requests a lock.

---

*Or any other kind of transaction failure, come to that.

EXERCISES

13.1 The following list represents the sequence of events in an interleaved execution of a set of DB2 transactions *T1*, *T2*, . . ., *T12*, all using isolation level RR for all data. *A*, *B*, . . ., *H* are intended to be rows, not cursors.

```
time t0    . . . . . . . . . .
time t1    (T1)   :   FETCH A
time t2    (T2)   :   FETCH B
   —       (T1)   :   FETCH C
   —       (T4)   :   FETCH D
   —       (T5)   :   FETCH A
   —       (T2)   :   FETCH E
   —       (T2)   :   UPDATE E
   —       (T3)   :   FETCH F
   —       (T2)   :   FETCH F
   —       (T5)   :   UPDATE A
   —       (T1)   :   COMMIT
   —       (T6)   :   FETCH A
   —       (T5)   :   ROLLBACK
   —       (T6)   :   FETCH C
   —       (T6)   :   UPDATE C
   —       (T7)   :   FETCH G
   —       (T8)   :   FETCH H
   —       (T9)   :   FETCH G
   —       (T9)   :   UPDATE G
   —       (T8)   :   FETCH E
   —       (T7)   :   COMMIT
   —       (T9)   :   FETCH H
   —       (T3)   :   FETCH G
   —       (T10)  :   FETCH A
   —       (T9)   :   UPDATE H
   —       (T6)   :   COMMIT
   —       (T11)  :   FETCH C
   —       (T12)  :   FETCH D
   —       (T12)  :   FETCH C
   —       (T2)   :   UPDATE F
   —       (T11)  :   UPDATE C
   —       (T12)  :   FETCH A
   —       (T10)  :   UPDATE A
   —       (T12)  :   UPDATE D
   —       (T4)   :   FETCH G
time tn    . . . . . . . . .
```

Are there any deadlocks at time *tn*?

13.2 Draw a compatibility matrix showing the interactions among lock types X, U, and S.

13.3 Consider the concurrency problems illustrated in Figs. 13.1–13.4 once again. What would happen in each case if all transactions were executing under isolation level CS instead of RR?

13.4 The following list represents the sequence of events in an interleaved execution of a set of DB2 transactions *T1*, *T2*, . . ., *T12*, all using isolation level CS for all data. All cursors permit updates. (As in Exercise 13.1, however, *A*, *B*, . . ., *H* are rows, not cursors.)

```
time t0      . . . . . . . . . .
time t1      (T1)   :  FETCH A
time t2      (T2)   :  FETCH B
  —          (T1)   :  FETCH C
  —          (T4)   :  FETCH D
  —          (T5)   :  FETCH A
  —          (T2)   :  FETCH E
  —          (T2)   :  UPDATE E
  —          (T3)   :  FETCH F
  —          (T2)   :  FETCH F
  —          (T1)   :  COMMIT
  —          (T5)   :  UPDATE A
  —          (T6)   :  FETCH A
  —          (T5)   :  ROLLBACK
  —          (T6)   :  FETCH C
  —          (T6)   :  UPDATE C
  —          (T7)   :  FETCH G
  —          (T8)   :  FETCH H
  —          (T9)   :  FETCH G
  —          (T8)   :  FETCH E
  —          (T7)   :  COMMIT
  —          (T9)   :  UPDATE G
  —          (T9)   :  FETCH H
  —          (T3)   :  FETCH G
  —          (T10)  :  FETCH A
  —          (T6)   :  COMMIT
  —          (T11)  :  FETCH C
  —          (T12)  :  FETCH D
  —          (T2)   :  UPDATE B
  —          (T10)  :  UPDATE A
  —          (T4)   :  FETCH G
time tn      . . . . . . . . .
```

Are there any deadlocks at time *tn*?

13.5 (Modified version of Exercise 12.4) Write a program to read and print all part rows in part number order, deleting every tenth one as you go, and beginning a new transaction after every tenth row. Give two solutions to this exercise, one using WITH HOLD and one not. *Recommendation*: Try solving the problem without using WITH HOLD first.

ANSWERS TO SELECTED EXERCISES

13.1 At time *tn* *no* transactions are doing any useful work at all! There is one deadlock, involving transactions *T2*, *T3*, *T9*, and *T8*; in addition, *T4* is waiting for *T9*, *T12* is waiting for *T4*, and *T10* and *T11* are both waiting for *T12*. We can represent the situation by means of a graph (the *Wait-For Graph*), in which the nodes represent transactions and a directed edge from node *Ti* to node *Tj* indicates that *Ti* is waiting for *Tj* (see Fig. 13.11). Edges are labeled with the name of the row and level of lock they are waiting for. Note that *T1*, *T6*, and *T7* have all completed successfully and *T5* has completed unsuccessfully.

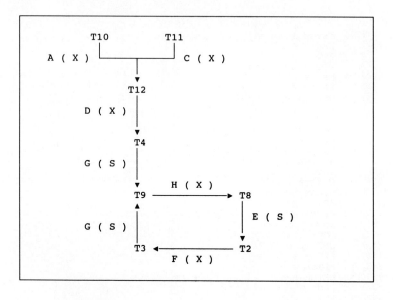

Fig. 13.11 The Wait-For Graph for Exercise 13.1

13.2 See Fig. 13.12.

13.3 Effects of isolation level CS:

- The lost update problem (Fig. 13.1): *B*'s FETCH at time *t2* is not accepted, because it is an implicit request for a U lock on *R*, and such a request conflicts with the U lock already held by *A*. *B* waits until *A* has updated *R* (thereby promoting its U lock to X level) and then reached a synchpoint (at which time *A*'s lock is released, and *B* is able to resume). *B* is thus forced to see the effect of *A*'s update.

- The uncommitted dependency problem (Figs. 13.2, 13.3): *A*'s operation at time *t2* is not accepted, because it is an implicit request for an S lock (at least) on *R*, and such a request conflicts with the X lock already held by *B*. *A* waits until *B* reaches a synchpoint, when *B*'s lock is released and *A* is able to proceed; and

	X	U	S	–
X	N	N	N	Y
U	N	N	Y	Y
S	N	Y	Y	Y
–	Y	Y	Y	Y

Fig. 13.12 Lock type compatibility matrix (X, U, S)

at that point *A* sees a committed value of *R* (either the pre-*B* value, if *B* terminates with ROLLBACK, or the post-*B* value otherwise). Either way, *A* is no longer dependent on an uncommitted change.

- The inconsistent analysis problem (Fig. 13.4): Isolation level CS does not solve this problem; *A* must execute under RR in order to retain its locks until the next synchpoint, for otherwise it will still produce the wrong answer. (Alternatively, of course, *A* could use LOCK TABLE to lock the entire accounts table. This solution would work under both CS and RR isolation levels.)

13.4 At time *tn* only transactions *T10* and *T11* are doing any useful work. There is one deadlock, involving transactions *T2*, *T3*, *T9*, and *T8*; in addition, *T4* is waiting for *T9*, and *T12* is waiting for *T4* (refer to Fig. 13.13). Note that *T1*, *T6*, and *T7* have all completed successfully and *T5* has completed unsuccessfully.

13.5 This exercise is typical of a wide class of applications, and the following solutions are typical too. The first does not use the WITH HOLD option on the cursor declaration:

```
EXEC SQL DECLARE CP CURSOR FOR
         SELECT P#, PNAME, COLOR, WEIGHT, CITY
         FROM   P
         WHERE  P# > previous_P#
         ORDER  BY P# ;

previous_P# = 'bbbbbb' ;
eof = false ;
DO WHILE (eof = false) ;
   EXEC SQL OPEN CP ;
   DO count = 1 TO 10 ;
      EXEC SQL FETCH CP INTO :P#, ... ;
      IF SQLCODE = +100 THEN
```

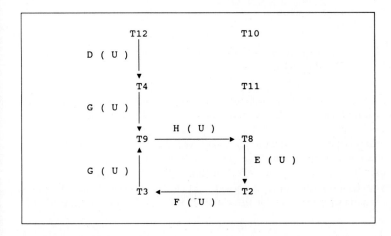

Fig. 13.13 The Wait-For Graph for Exercise 13.4

```
        DO ;
            EXEC SQL CLOSE CP ;
            EXEC SQL COMMIT WORK ;
            eof = true ;
        END ;
      ELSE print P#, ... ;
    END ;
    EXEC SQL DELETE FROM P WHERE P# = :P# ;
    EXEC SQL CLOSE CP ;
    EXEC SQL COMMIT WORK ;
    previous_P# = P# ;
END ;
```

Observe that we lose position within the parts table at the end of each transaction (even if we did not close cursor CP explicitly, the COMMIT would close it automatically anyway). The foregoing code will therefore not be particularly efficient, because each new transaction requires a search on the parts table in order to reestablish position. Matters might be improved somewhat if there happens to be an index on column P.P#—as in fact there will be, since P.P# is the primary key for table P—and the optimizer chooses that index as the access path for the table.

Here now is a second solution to the problem, using WITH HOLD:

```
EXEC SQL DECLARE CP CURSOR WITH HOLD FOR
              SELECT P#, PNAME, COLOR, WEIGHT, CITY
              FROM    P
              ORDER   BY P# ;

eof = false ;
EXEC SQL OPEN CP ;
DO WHILE (eof = false) ;
    DO count = 1 TO 10 ;
        EXEC SQL FETCH CP INTO :P#, ... ;
        IF SQLCODE = +100 THEN
            DO ;
                EXEC SQL CLOSE CP ;
                EXEC SQL COMMIT WORK ;
                eof = true ;
            END ;
        ELSE print P#, ... ;
    END ;
    EXEC SQL DELETE FROM P WHERE P# = :P# ;
    EXEC SQL COMMIT WORK ;
END ;
```

This solution is more efficient than the previous one, and apparently a little simpler too, because it no longer includes any repositioning code. The increase in simplicity is somewhat spurious, however, because we have tacitly ignored the possibility that one of the transactions might fail (in particular, we have ignored the possibility that one of the transactions might be chosen as a victim in a deadlock situation). If we take these possibilities into account, we find that we have to include repositioning code in the application after all (even though that code will presumably not be executed very often). Consideration of the details is left as a further exercise for the reader.

·14·

Application Programming III: Dynamic SQL

14.1 INTRODUCTION

"Dynamic SQL" consists of a set of embedded SQL facilities that are provided specifically to allow the construction of generalized applications—for example, an application that is intended to support online, possibly interactive, access to the database from an end-user at an online terminal. (The statements of dynamic SQL cannot themselves be entered interactively—they are available only in the embedded environment.) The topic of this chapter is therefore somewhat specialized; basically, the only people who need to know the material are people directly concerned with the writing of generalized applications. Other readers may wish to ignore the chapter altogether, at least on a first reading.

Let us consider the case of an application that supports interactive access in some detail. Consider what such an application has to do. In outline, the steps it must go through are as follows.

1. Accept a command from the terminal.
2. Analyze that command.
3. Issue appropriate SQL statements to the database.
4. Return a message and/or results to the terminal.

If the set of commands the program can accept is fairly small, as in the case of (perhaps) a program handling airline reservations, then the set of possible SQL statements to be issued may also be small and can be "hardwired" into the program. In this case, Steps 2 and 3 above will consist simply of logic to examine the input command and then branch to the part of the program that issues the predefined SQL statement(s). If, on the other hand, there can be great variability in the input—in other words, if the application is reasonably generalized—then it may not be practicable to predefine and "hardwire" SQL statements for every possible command. Instead, it will probably be necessary to construct the required SQL statements dynamically, and then to compile and execute those constructed statements dynamically. The facilities of dynamic SQL are provided to assist in this process.

Incidentally, the process just described is exactly what happens when SQL statements themselves are entered interactively—for example, through DB2I. DB2I itself is a generalized online application; it is ready to accept an extremely wide variety of input, namely any valid (or invalid!) SQL statement. It uses the facilities of dynamic SQL to construct suitable SQL statements corresponding to its input, to compile and execute those constructed statements, and to return messages and results back to the terminal.

If the statement to be dynamically compiled and executed is a SELECT statement, special considerations apply. (As in ordinary embedded SQL, retrieval is more complicated and involves more work on the part of the user.) Section 14.2 therefore considers the other statements first, then Section 14.3 addresses the problem of SELECT statements specifically.

14.2 HANDLING STATEMENTS OTHER THAN SELECT

The two principal statements of dynamic SQL are PREPARE and EXECUTE.* Their use is illustrated by the following (accurate but unrealistically simple) PL/I example.

---

*There is also an EXECUTE IMMEDIATE statement, which effectively combines the functions of PREPARE and EXECUTE into a single operation.

```
         DCL      SQLSOURCE CHAR(256) VARYING ;
  EXEC SQL DECLARE SQLOBJ STATEMENT ;

         SQLSOURCE = 'DELETE FROM SP WHERE QTY < 100' ;
  EXEC SQL PREPARE SQLOBJ FROM :SQLSOURCE ;
  EXEC SQL EXECUTE SQLOBJ ;
```

Explanation:

1. SQLSOURCE is a PL/I varying length character string variable in which the program will construct the source form (i.e., character string representation) of some SQL statement (a DELETE statement, in our particular example).

2. SQLOBJ, by contrast, is a *SQL* variable, not a PL/I variable, that will be used (conceptually) to hold the compiled form of the SQL statement whose source form is given in SQLSOURCE. (The names SQLSOURCE and SQLOBJ are arbitrary, of course.) The name SQLOBJ is said to be a *statement name.*

3. The assignment statement "SQLSOURCE = ... ;" assigns to SQLSOURCE the source form of a SQL DELETE statement. (As suggested in Section 14.1, the process of constructing such a source statement is likely to be somewhat more complicated in practice, involving, e.g., the input and analysis of some command from the terminal.)

4. The PREPARE statement then takes that source statement and compiles it to produce an executable version, which it stores in SQLOBJ.

5. Finally, the EXECUTE statement executes that SQLOBJ version and thus (in the example) causes the actual DELETE to occur. Feedback information from the DELETE will be returned in the SQLCA as usual.

Note, incidentally, that since it denotes a SQL variable, not a PL/I variable, the statement name SQLOBJ does *not* have a colon prefix in the PREPARE and EXECUTE statements.

PREPARE

The syntax of the PREPARE statement is as follows.

```
  EXEC SQL PREPARE statement FROM string ;
```

Here "string" is an expression of the host language that yields the character string representation of a SQL statement, and "statement" is the name of a SQL variable that will be used to contain the PREPAREd (i.e., compiled) version of that SQL statement. The statement to be PREPAREd must be one of the following (only):

```
UPDATE (including CURRENT form)
DELETE (including CURRENT form)
INSERT
SELECT (excluding INTO form)

CREATE
DROP
ALTER
COMMENT
LABEL

GRANT
REVOKE

COMMIT
ROLLBACK
LOCK

SET CURRENT SQLID

EXPLAIN
```

In other words, the following statements cannot be PREPAREd: BEGIN/END DECLARE SECTION, CLOSE, DECLARE CURSOR, DECLARE STATEMENT, DECLARE TABLE, DESCRIBE, EXECUTE, FETCH, INCLUDE, OPEN, PREPARE, SELECT (INTO form), SET (except CURRENT SQLID form), and WHENEVER. Also, the source form of a statement to be PREPAREd must not include either EXEC SQL or a statement terminator. Nor can it include any host variable references.

EXECUTE

The syntax of the EXECUTE statement is as follows.

```
EXEC SQL EXECUTE statement [ USING argument(s) ] ;
```

The PREPAREd SQL statement in the SQL variable identified by "statement" is executed. The USING clause is explained in the subsection "Arguments and Parameters" immediately following.

Arguments and Parameters

As already indicated, SQL statements that are to be PREPAREd cannot include any references to host variables. However, they can include *parameters*, denoted in the source form of the statement by question marks. Basically, parameters can appear wherever host variables can appear (with certain exceptions—details beyond the scope of this book). For example:

```
SQLSOURCE = 'DELETE
             FROM    SP
             WHERE   QTY > ?
             AND     QTY < ?' ;

EXEC SQL PREPARE SQLOBJ FROM :SQLSOURCE ;
```

Arguments to replace the parameters are specified when the statement is EXECUTEd, via the USING clause. For example:

```
EXEC SQL EXECUTE SQLOBJ USING :LOW, :HIGH ;
```

In the example, the statement actually executed is equivalent to the ordinary embedded SQL statement

```
EXEC SQL DELETE FROM SP WHERE QTY > :LOW AND QTY < :HIGH ;
```

In general, the USING clause in the EXECUTE statement takes the form

```
USING argument [, argument ] ...
```

where each "argument" in turn takes the form

```
: host-variable [ [ INDICATOR ] : host-variable ]
```

just like a target reference in an INTO clause (note that null indicator variables are permitted). The ith argument in the list of arguments corresponds to the ith parameter—i.e., ith question mark—in the source form of the PREPAREd statement.

14.3   HANDLING SELECT STATEMENTS

As indicated earlier, the procedure outlined in Section 14.2 is adequate for the dynamic preparation and execution of all SQL operations (all SQL operations that may legally be PREPAREd, that is), except SELECT. The reason that SELECT is different is that it returns data to the program; all the other statements return feedback information (in the SQLCA) only.

A program using SELECT needs to know something about the data values to be retrieved, since it has to specify a set of target variables to receive those values. In other words, it needs to know at least how many values there will be in each result row, and also what the data types and lengths of those values will be. If the SELECT is generated dynamically, it will usually not be possible for the program to know this information in advance; therefore, it must obtain the information dynamically, using another dynamic SQL statement called DESCRIBE. In outline, the procedure such a program must go through is as follows.

1. It builds and PREPAREs the SELECT statement *without* an INTO clause. (As indicated in Section 14.2, a SELECT statement that is to be PREPAREd must not include an INTO clause.)

2. It uses DESCRIBE to interrogate the system about the results it can expect when the SELECT is executed. The description of those results is returned in an area called the SQL Descriptor Area (SQLDA).

3. Next, it allocates storage for a set of target variables to receive those results in accordance with what it has just learned from DESCRIBE, and places the addresses of those target variables back into the SQLDA.

4. Finally, it retrieves the result rows one at a time by means of a cursor, using the cursor statements OPEN, FETCH, and CLOSE. It can also use UPDATE CURRENT and DELETE CURRENT statements on those rows, if appropriate (however, those statements will probably have to be PREPAREd and EXECUTEd versions).

In order to make these ideas a little more concrete, we present a simple example to show what such a program might look like (in outline). The example is written in PL/I. Note that it *must* be written in a language like PL/I that provides explicit support for dynamic storage allocation. IBM OS/VS COBOL, for example, does not provide any such support; hence a generalized application that is to perform data retrieval cannot be written in OS/VS COBOL. (An application that is to use only the facilities described in Section 14.2 can be written in OS/VS COBOL if desired, however. The same is true for an application that needs to do data retrieval, in the simple special case in which the SELECT-list is known at the time of writing the program.)

```
              DCL SQLSOURCE CHAR(256) VARYING ;
      EXEC SQL DECLARE SQLOBJ STATEMENT ;
      EXEC SQL DECLARE X CURSOR FOR SQLOBJ ;

      EXEC SQL INCLUDE SQLDA ;
      /* Let the maximum number of expected values to be     */
      /* retrieved be N.                                     */
              SQLSIZE = N ;
              ALLOCATE SQLDA ;

              SQLSOURCE = 'SELECT * FROM SP WHERE QTY > 100' ;
      EXEC SQL PREPARE SQLOBJ FROM :SQLSOURCE ;

      EXEC SQL DESCRIBE SQLOBJ INTO SQLDA ;

      /* Now SQLDA contains the following information (among  */
      /* other things):                                       */
      /*  - actual number of values to be retrieved in SQLN   */
      /*  - name (or label), data type, and length of ith     */
      /*                               value in SQLVAR(i)      */
```

```
/* Using the information returned by DESCRIBE, the    */
/* program can now allocate a storage area for each   */
/* value to be retrieved, and place the address of the */
/* ith such area in SQLVAR(i). Then:                   */

EXEC SQL OPEN X ;
        DO WHILE ( more-rows-to-come ) ;
           EXEC SQL FETCH X
                    USING DESCRIPTOR SQLDA ;
              .....
        END ;
EXEC SQL CLOSE X ;
```

Explanation:

1. SQLSOURCE and SQLOBJ are basically as in Section 14.2; SQLSOURCE will contain the source form of a SQL statement (a SELECT statement, of course, in this example), and SQLOBJ will contain the corresponding object form. X is a cursor for that SELECT; note that it is declared by a new form of the DECLARE CURSOR statement, as follows:

```
EXEC SQL DECLARE cursor CURSOR FOR statement ;
```

2. The declaration of the SQL Descriptor Area (SQLDA) is brought into the program by the statement

```
EXEC SQL INCLUDE SQLDA ;
```

This statement generates a declaration for a PL/I BASED structure called SQLDA, also a declaration for a numeric variable called SQLSIZE. The program must set SQLSIZE to the value N (where N is an upper bound on the number of values to be retrieved per row by the SELECT statement), then allocate storage for SQLDA (the amount of storage allocated will be a function of the value of SQLSIZE).

3. Next, the desired SELECT statement is constructed in source form in SQLSOURCE, and is then PREPAREd to yield the corresponding object form in SQLOBJ. Then the program issues a DESCRIBE against SQLOBJ to obtain a description of the values expected per row from the SELECT. That description consists of two parts:

(a) The actual number of values to be retrieved (in a field of SQLDA called SQLN);

(b) The name or label,* the data type, and the length for each of those values (in an array of entries within SQLDA called SQLVAR).

---

*See the discussion of the LABEL statement in Chapter 8.

Using this description, the program can now allocate storage for each of the values described. It then places the addresses of the storage areas it allocates back into the SQLDA—actually into the SQLVAR array.

4. Finally, the program uses OPEN, FETCH, and CLOSE statements on cursor X to retrieve the actual data. Note, however, that a new form of the FETCH statement is used; instead of an INTO clause, it has a USING DESCRIPTOR clause, and the structure named in that clause (usually SQLDA) in turn identifies the target variables for the values to be retrieved.

It is also possible to PREPARE a SELECT statement that includes parameters (identified by question marks). For example:

```
SQLSOURCE = 'SELECT *
             FROM    SP
             WHERE   QTY > ?
             AND     QTY < ?' ;

EXEC SQL PREPARE SQLOBJ FROM :SQLSOURCE ;
```

Arguments are specified in the corresponding OPEN statement. For example:

```
EXEC SQL OPEN X USING :LOW, :HIGH ;
```

(EXECUTE does not apply to SELECT. The function of EXECUTE is performed by OPEN when the statement to be executed is a SELECT.)

We conclude this section with a brief mention of DESCRIBE TABLE, which was added to DB2 in Version 2.3. The statement

```
DESCRIBE TABLE :TNV INTO SQLDA ;
```

(where TNV is not the name of a table but the name of a host variable whose *value* is the name of a table) will return information in SQLDA concerning the table in question. (The table in question can be either a base table or a view, and it can be identified by its name or by an alias or synonym.) Thus, DESCRIBE TABLE provides a means of obtaining a table description without first having to PREPARE a SELECT statement against that table.

14.4 CONCLUSION

This brings us to the end of our discussion of the facilities of dynamic SQL, and indeed to the end of our three chapters on SQL application programming. Of those three chapters:

- Chapter 12 describes all the major principles of the embedded SQL approach. The material of that chapter is thus relevant to all SQL programming, and should be of interest to anyone who is concerned in any way with application programming in DB2.

- Chapter 13 is also concerned with principles that are relevant to all users—to be specific, it discusses the concepts of transaction management (concurrency and recovery), and it shows how those concepts are exposed in the SQL language. However, the nature of SQL is such that users need to worry explicitly about such matters only very rarely; most of the time, DB2's implicit mechanisms are entirely adequate.

- The present chapter, by contrast, has been concerned with a very specialized topic, namely that of how to write a generalized application in SQL. Such an application requires the facilities of dynamic SQL— principally the PREPARE and EXECUTE statements, and (if it is a SELECT statement that is to be PREPAREd) also the DESCRIBE statement. *Note*: The other portions of the language are sometimes referred to as *static* SQL, to distinguish them from the dynamic facilities that we have been discussing in this chapter.

  It should be pointed out that it is of course possible to use the facilities of dynamic SQL whenever greater variability is required than is provided by the conventional static SQL statements. For example, the following statement:

```
EXEC SQL SELECT * FROM :TNV ;
```

(where, as in the discussion of DESCRIBE TABLE above, TNV is a host variable whose value is a table name) is not a valid SELECT statement in conventional static SQL, but dynamic SQL can be used to achieve the desired effect.

To conclude the entire set of three chapters, we offer the following comment. The fact that DB2 uses essentially the same language (SQL) for both interactive and programmed access to the database has one very significant consequence: It means that the database portions of an application program can be tested and debugged interactively. Using the interactive interface, it is very easy for a programmer to create some test tables, load data into them, execute (interactive versions of) the programmed SQL statements against them, query the tables and/or the catalog to see the effect of those statements, and so on. In other words, the interactive interface provides a very convenient *programmer debugging facility*. Of course, it is attractive for other reasons too; for example, the data definition process is normally carried out through this interface, and so too is the process of granting and revoking authorization. Also, of course, the interface provides a rudimentary but serviceable ad hoc query facility.

CHAPTER
·15·

Storage Structure

15.1 INTRODUCTION

As explained in Chapter 4, the data definition statements of SQL can conveniently be divided into two classes, namely logical and physical—the logical statements having to do with objects that are genuinely of interest to users, such as base tables and views, and the physical statements having to do with objects that are more of interest to administrators (i.e., system administrators and database administrators). In this chapter we take a brief look at the latter class of objects. The data definition statements corresponding to those objects are somewhat complicated, however, involving (as they necessarily must) a great deal of low-level detail. For that reason, we will not describe those statements in detail here; we content ourselves with the observation that they fall into the same broad pattern as the logical statements, in the sense that, for each kind of object, there is a CREATE statement, an ALTER statement, and a DROP statement. (Even this simple remark is not 100 percent true, as a matter of fact—not all kinds of object permit all three kinds of operation. But we leave all discussion of the details to the IBM manuals.)

Fig. 15.1 is a schematic representation of the major storage objects and their interrelationships. The figure is meant to be interpreted as follows.

- The total collection of stored data is divided up into a number of disjoint *databases*—several user databases and several system databases, in general. One system database, the catalog database, is shown in the figure.

- Each database is divided up into a number of disjoint "spaces"—several *table* spaces and several *index* spaces, in general. A "space" is a dynamically extendable collection of *pages*, where a page is a block of physical storage (it is the unit of I/O, i.e., the unit transferred between primary and secondary storage in a physical I/O operation). The pages in a given "space" are all the same size—4K bytes for index spaces, and either 4K bytes or 32K bytes for table spaces (K = 1024).

- Each table space contains one or more *stored tables*. A stored table is the physical representation of a base table; it consists of a set of *stored records*, one for each row of the corresponding base table.* A given stored table must be wholly contained within a single table space.

- Each index space contains exactly one *index*. A given index must be wholly contained within a single index space. A given stored table and all of its associated indexes must be wholly contained within a single database.

- As explained in Chapter 9, *views* are not stored objects at all. They are included in the figure just to illustrate the point that a given view can span multiple databases—that is, it can include data from multiple stored tables, and those stored tables do not necessarily all have to be from the same database.

- Each "space" (table space or index space) has an associated *storage group*.† A storage group is a collection of direct access volumes, all of the same device type. When a given space needs to be extended, storage is acquired from the appropriate storage group. The spaces in a given database do not all have to have the same storage group, nor do all the spaces that share a given storage group have to come from the same

---

*Recall from Chapter 1 that base tables in DB2 "physically exist," in the sense that they have a direct storage representation—despite the fact that, strictly speaking, physical existence is *not* the distinguishing characteristic of base tables in the relational model.

†A *partitioned* space (table space or index space) can have a distinct storage group for each partition. See Section 15.3.

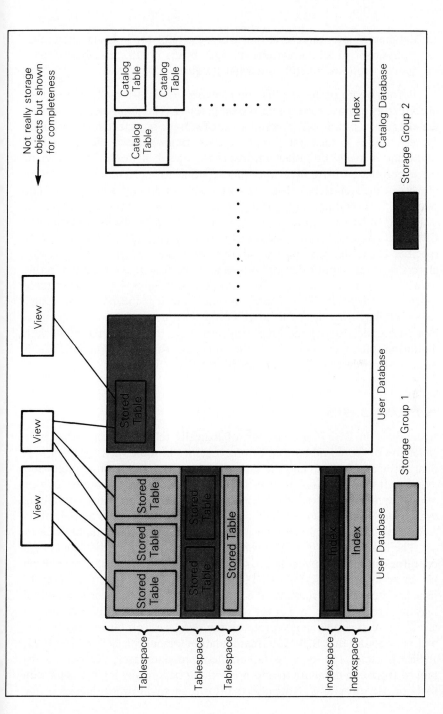

Fig. 15.1 The major storage objects of DB2

database. Note, therefore, that storage groups are in a sense the most "physical" of all the various storage objects in DB2; databases, table spaces, etc., are all still somewhat "logical."

Before we go on to amplify the foregoing ideas, we make one further introductory remark concerning *system defaults*. The basic idea behind system defaults is as follows: The full array of storage objects (databases, table spaces, storage groups, etc.) might appear somewhat complicated at first sight, and it would be rather unfortunate—indeed, it would be counter to the overall ease-of-use objective—if users had to understand all of those objects in their entirety before they were able to do any useful work. For example, it should not be necessary to have to know about table spaces in order just to be able to create and use a new base table. Now, the complete CREATE TABLE statement does include an option ("IN table space") that specifies the table space into which the new table is to go. However, it is always possible to omit that option (as we have done in all examples in this book so far), in which case DB2 will automatically create a *default* table space and will place the new table in that. Thus it is indeed not necessary to be familiar with the table space notion in order to be able to create a new base table. Analogous simplifications apply to most of the other data definition statements and most of the other storage objects. The full default mechanism is described in more detail in Section 15.8.

15.2   DATABASES

A database in DB2 is a collection of logically related objects—that is, a collection of stored tables that belong together in some way, together with their associated indexes and the various spaces that contain those tables and indexes. It thus consists of a set of table spaces (each containing one or more stored tables), together with a set of index spaces (each containing exactly one index). As explained earlier, a given stored table and all of its associated indexes must be wholly contained within a single database.

The database is *the unit of start and stop*, in the sense that the system operator can make a given database available or unavailable for processing via an appropriate START or STOP command. Note, therefore, that objects are grouped together into the same database primarily for operational reasons; users (in our sense of the term) need have no concern for databases at all, but can simply concentrate on the *data*, i.e., on tables (base tables and views; note that SQL data manipulation statements such as SELECT, INSERT, etc., refer only to tables, never to databases). Tables can be moved from one database to another without having any logical impact on users or user programs. Note also that (as suggested toward the end of the previous section a database is not even a particularly "physical" kind of object; in particular, it is typically *not* contained within a single disk, or single set of disks, but rather occupies portions of many disks, other portions of which might well be allocated to other databases.

15.3 TABLE SPACES

A table space can be thought of as a *logical address space* on secondary storage that is used to hold one or more stored tables ("logical" because it is typically not just a set of physically adjacent areas). As the amount of data in those tables grows (or as their number increases), so storage will be acquired from the appropriate storage group and added to the table space accordingly. One table space can be up to approximately 64 billion bytes in size, and there is effectively no limit to the number of table spaces in a database, nor to the number of databases. As mentioned in Section 15.1, the pages in a given table space are either all 4K bytes or all 32K bytes in size.

Fundamentally, the table space is the storage unit for recovery and reorganization purposes; that is, it is the unit that can be recovered via the RECOVER utility or reorganized via the REORG utility (see Chapter 16). If the table space is very large, however, recovery and reorganization could take a very long time. DB2 therefore provides the option to *partition* a large table space into smaller pieces; for a partitioned table space, the unit of recovery and reorganization is the individual partition, rather than the entire table space.

Table spaces come in three varieties, *simple*, *partitioned*, and *segmented*. We discuss each in turn. *Note*: Version 1 of DB2 supported simple and partitioned table spaces only, and "simple" at that time just meant "not partitioned." Segmented table spaces were added in Version 2.

Simple Table Spaces

A simple table space can contain more than one stored table, though one is usually the best option. One reason for having more than one is that stored records for different stored tables can be clustered together in such a way as to improve access times to logically related data. For example, if tables S and SP were assigned to the same table space, then it would be possible (by loading the data in an appropriately interleaved manner) to store all the shipments for supplier S1 close to—i.e., on the same page as—the stored record for supplier S1, all the shipments for supplier S2 close to the stored record for supplier S2, and so on. Queries such as "Get details of supplier S1 and all corresponding shipments"—in particular, certain join queries—would then be handled more efficiently, since the number of I/O operations would be reduced. A similar remark applies to referential integrity enforcement; for example, deleting a supplier and cascading that delete to all corresponding shipments would also be more efficient if the data were appropriately clustered.

Note, however, that such cross-table clustering will not be maintained (in general) in the face of arbitrary updates; moreover, neither the optimizer nor the REORG utility has any understanding of such clustering. Furthermore, sequential access ("table space scan") may well be slowed down, inasmuch as the system will now have to scan not only stored records for the table of interest, but also stored records for other tables that happen to be mixed in with that first table. On the whole, one stored table per table space is almost always the most satisfactory arrangement in the case of simple table spaces.

Partitioned Table Spaces

As indicated earlier, partitioned table spaces are intended for stored tables that are sufficiently large—hundreds of thousands or even millions of rows—that it is operationally difficult (e.g., for recovery purposes) to deal with the entire table as a unit. A partitioned table space thus contains exactly one stored table (probably large), partitioned in accordance with value ranges of a partitioning column or column combination. For example, if the shipments table SP were assigned to a partitioned table space, then it could be partitioned by values of the P# column, such that all shipments for part P1 were stored in partition one, all shipments for part P2 were stored in partition two, and so on. A clustering index (see Section 15.6) is required for the partitioning column or column combination; furthermore, UPDATE operations on that column or column combination are not allowed.

As already stated, individual partitions of a partitioned table space are independent of one another, in the sense that they can be independently recovered and reorganized. They can also be associated with different storage groups; thus, for example, it is possible to store different partitions on different devices and thereby spread the table space I/O load.

Segmented Table Spaces

Segmented table spaces were added to DB2 in Version 2. Like simple table spaces, they can contain any number of stored tables; unlike simple table spaces, however, segmented table spaces do not support any kind of cross-table clustering—that is, they do not allow records for different stored ta-

bles to be interleaved on a single page. Instead, they keep the tables physically separated, as follows.

- First, the space within the table space is divided up into *segments*,
  where a segment consists of a logically contiguous set of *n* pages (*n*
  must be a multiple of 4 in the range 4 to 64 and is the same for all
  segments in the table space).

- Second, no segment (and therefore certainly no page) is allowed to contain records for more than one stored table. If a particular table grows
  in size to fill all segments currently allocated to it, a new segment will
  be obtained for that table (by acquiring more space from the associated
  storage group, if necessary, as explained at the beginning of this section).

Thus, for example, table S might currently be stored in segments 1 and
3 and table SP in segments 2, 4, 5, and 6, all within the same segmented
table space. If table S subsequently outgrows the capacity of its existing
segments (1 and 3), a new segment (7) will be obtained for it.

The advantages of such an arrangement (compared with having multiple stored tables in a simple table space) include the following.

- Sequential access ("table space scan") to a particular stored table is
  more efficient, since there is no need to scan segments or pages that
  contain records for other tables.

- Segmented table spaces are much more efficient than simple (and partitioned) table spaces in the way they handle variable-length records.

- Reorganizing the table space via the REORG utility will restore every
  stored table in the table space to its clustered order. ("Clustered order"
  here does not refer to cross-table clustering, it refers to physical ordering within one stored table. See Section 15.6 for further discussion.)
  Reorganizing a simple table space that contains multiple stored tables
  does not restore clustered order.

- LOCK TABLE on a table in a segmented table space genuinely does
  lock the table, not the entire table space (and likewise for all other
  operations in the system that would acquire locks at the table space
  level in the case of a simple or partitioned table space).

- If a table in a segmented table space is dropped, the space for that table
  can be reclaimed without the need to perform a reorganization of the
  table space.

- "Mass DELETE" (i.e., deleting all rows from a table—DELETE without a WHERE clause) is much more efficient on a segmented table
  space than on other kinds of table space.

- All tables in the table space can be recovered as a unit (i.e., via a single invocation of the RECOVER utility). This capability is particularly useful in connection with "referential structures" (i.e., sets of tables that are logically related by referential constraints). See Chapter 16 for further discussion. *Note*: Actually, this advantage applies to the simple table space case also.

15.4 STORED TABLES

A stored table is the stored representation of a base table. It consists of a set of stored records, one for each data row in the base table in question. Each stored record will be wholly contained within a single page; however, one stored table can be spread over multiple pages, and (in a simple table space) one page can contain stored records from multiple stored tables.

A stored record is *not* identical to the corresponding row of the base table. Instead, it consists of a byte string, made up as follows:

- A stored record prefix, containing control information such as the internal system identifier for the stored table of which this stored record is a part; followed by

- Up to N stored fields, where N is the number of columns in the base table. There might be fewer than N if, e.g., the stored record is varying length and one or more fields at the right-hand end are set to null or the nonnull default value for the field in question (nulls and default values at the right-hand end of a varying length record need not be physically stored).

Each stored field, in turn, consists of:

- A length prefix (if the field is varying length), giving the length of the actual data, including the null indicator prefix if there is one (see below);

- A null indicator prefix (if nulls are allowed), indicating whether the value in the data part of the field is to be (a) taken as a genuine data value or (b) ignored (i.e., interpreted as null);

- An encoded form of the actual data value. Stored data is encoded in such a manner that the System/370 "compare logical" instruction (CLC) will always yield the appropriate response when applied to two values of the same SQL data type. For example, INTEGER values are stored with their sign bit reversed. Thus all stored data fields are considered simply as byte strings by the Data Manager; any interpretation of such a string as, e.g., an INTEGER value is performed above the Data

Manager interface. The advantage of such a scheme is that new data types can be introduced without any impact on the low-level components of the system. As an exercise, the reader may like to try working out suitable encodings for the other DB2 data types.

All stored fields are byte-aligned. There are no gaps between fields. Varying length data occupies only as many bytes as are needed to store the actual value.

Note: The foregoing describes the standard representation of a stored record. For any given base table, however, the installation has the option of providing either or both of the following:

1. An "edit procedure" (EDITPROC), which will be given control every time a record is stored or fetched. On "store," the edit procedure can convert the standard representation for the record to any other form desired, and the record will be stored in that form. On "fetch," of course, the edit procedure must perform the opposite conversion.

2. One or more "field procedures" (FIELDPROCs). A field procedure is basically an edit procedure in the sense just described, but applies to an individual field rather than to an entire record. Field procedures were introduced into DB2 in conjunction with the GRAPHIC and VARGRAPHIC data types in order to facilitate (e.g.) the definition of installation-specific collating sequences for such data. However, they can be used with any string column of length less than 255 bytes (except columns to which dates, times, or timestamps are to be assigned and columns defined as NOT NULL WITH DEFAULT), and they can be used for any kind of data editing desired. There is a maximum of one FIELDPROC per field.

Thus, for example, the installation can decide to store data in a compressed or encrypted form; furthermore, it can make that decision on a table-by-table basis, or even on a field-by-field (column-by-column) basis. Note, however, that there are many restrictions on edit and field procedures, including the following among others:

- They must be written in Assembler Language.
- They cannot invoke any operating system services involving supervisor calls; in particular, they cannot perform any I/O operations.
- They cannot perform any DB2 operations.

To return to the main thread of the discussion: Internally, stored records are addressed by "record ID" or RID. For example, all pointers within indexes are RIDs. RIDs are unique within the containing table space. Fig.

15.2 shows how RIDs are implemented. The RID for a stored record *R* consists of two parts, namely the page number of the page *P* containing *R*, and a byte offset from the bottom of *P* identifying a slot that contains, in turn, the byte offset of *R* from the top of *P*. This scheme represents a good compromise between the speed of direct addressing and the flexibility of indirect addressing: Records can be rearranged within their containing page—e.g., to close up the gap when a record is deleted or to make room when a record is inserted—without having to change RIDs (only the local offsets at the foot of the page have to change); yet access to a record given the RID is fast, involving only a single page access.*

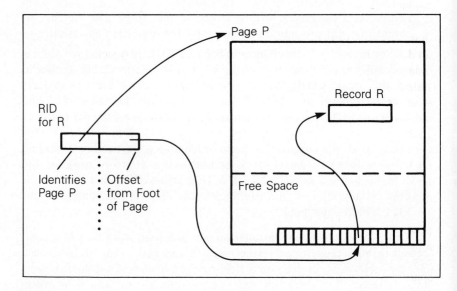

Fig. 15.2   Implementation of RIDs

---

*In rare cases it might involve two page accesses (but never more than two). This can happen if a varying length record is updated in such a way that it is now longer than it was before (i.e., the value in some varying length field has expanded), and there is not enough free space on the page to accommodate the increase. In such a situation, the updated record is placed on another ("overflow") page, and the original record is replaced by a pointer (another RID) to the new location. If the same thing happens again, so that the updated record has to be moved to still a third page, then the pointer in the original page is changed to point to this newest location.

We conclude our discussion of stored tables with a note on "validation procedures" (VALIDPROCs). A validation procedure resembles an edit procedure in that it is a procedure that can be specified by the installation for a given base table (maximum of one VALIDPROC per table). The validation procedure for a given table is given control each time a row of that table is INSERTed, UPDATEd, or DELETEd. The purpose of the procedure is to perform validation checks to ensure that the operation being performed is valid (and to reject it if not). Note, however, that validation procedures are subject to the same major restrictions as edit and field procedures; for example, they must be coded in Assembler Language.

15.5 INDEX SPACES

An index space is to an index what a table space is to a stored table. However, since the correspondence between indexes and index spaces (unlike that between stored tables and table spaces) is always one-to-one, there are no data definition statements for index spaces per se; instead, the necessary index space parameters are specified on the corresponding index definition statements. Thus, for example, there is no CREATE INDEXSPACE; instead, the index space is created automatically when the corresponding index is created, via CREATE INDEX, and that CREATE INDEX can include such parameters as the name of the associated storage group, etc.

As mentioned in Section 15.1, the pages in an index space are always 4K bytes in size. The unit for locking purposes can be less than one page, however (another difference from table spaces); it can, for example, be a quarter-page (1024 bytes).

Like table spaces, index spaces can be reorganized and recovered independently. An index space that contains the (required) clustering index for a partitioned table space is itself considered to be partitioned; all other index spaces are simple (nonpartitioned). A partition of a partitioned index space can be reorganized independently. Individual partitions can be associated with different storage groups.

15.6 INDEXES

Indexes in DB2 are based on a structure known as the *B-tree*. A B-tree is a multilevel, tree-structured index with the property that the tree is always *balanced*; that is, all leaf entries in the structure are equidistant from the root of the tree, and this property is maintained as new entries are inserted into the tree and existing entries are deleted. As a result, the index provides uniform and predictable performance for retrieval operations. Details of how this effect is achieved are beyond the scope of this book; however, Fig. 15.3 shows a simple example of what such an index might look like.*

As you can see, the index consists of a root page, zero or more intermediate pages (at zero or more intermediate levels—there is one such intermediate level in the example), and a set of leaf pages. The leaf level contains an entry for each distinct value of the indexed field (column), giving the indexed value and pointers (RIDs) to all records that contain that value for the indexed field; the leaf pages are chained together, so that they can be used for fast *sequential* access to the indexed data (in index sequence). Each level above the leaf level, in turn, contains an entry (highest field value plus pointer) for every page of entries in the level below; thus the root page and intermediate pages together provide fast *direct* access to the leaf pages, and hence fast direct access to the indexed data also.

A given stored table can have any number of associated indexes, and thus any number of logical orderings imposed on it. (It always has exactly one physical ordering, of course. Also, if the installation follows our recommendation that every base table have a primary key, then every stored table will necessarily have at least one index, namely the primary index, as explained in Chapter 11.)

To perform an exhaustive search on a given stored table according to a given index, the Data Manager will access all records in that stored table in the sequence defined by that index ("index scan"); and since that sequence may be quite different from the stored table's physical sequence, a given data page may be accessed many times. (On the other hand, data pages not containing any records of the stored table in question will not be accessed at all.) It follows that exhaustive search via an index could potentially be much slower than exhaustive search via physical sequence ("table space scan")—unless the index concerned is a *clustering index*:

- A clustering index is one for which the sequence defined by the index *is* the same as, or close to, the physical sequence. (Note that "clustering" here refers to clustering within a single stored table, not cross-table clustering as described in Section 15.3.) The index is used to control physical placement of the indexed records—i.e., newly inserted records are physically stored such that the physical sequence of those records in storage closely approximates the logical sequence as defined by the index.

---

*We assume for simplicity that the index is on a single column, not a combination of columns. The necessary extensions to our explanations and discussions to deal with the multiple-column case are straightforward but tedious.

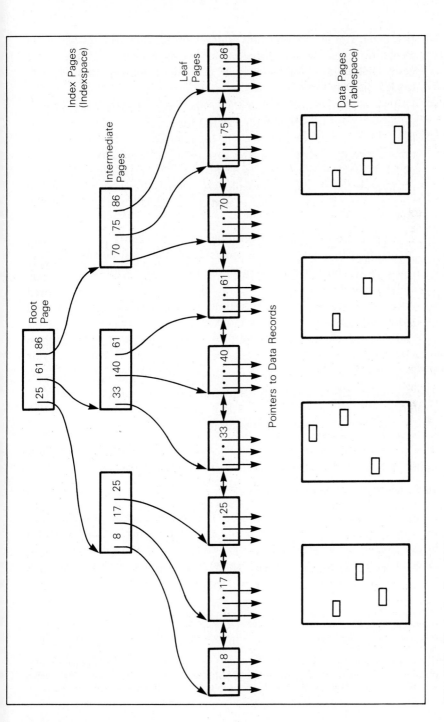

Fig. 15.3   Example of an index

- If a given stored table has any indexes at all, then *exactly one* is the clustering index for that stored table.* As the previous paragraph suggests, that index should ideally be created before any data has been loaded into the table in question.

- If a given stored table has a clustering index, then records must be initially loaded into that table via the load utility in clustering order (i.e., they must be sorted first). The loaded records will be stored in the table space (or partition, in the case of a partitioned table space) in order of arrival from left to right—i.e., in increasing address sequence—with periodic gaps to allow for future insertions. Gap size and frequency are determined by installation-specified "free space" parameters.

- If a given stored table has no indexes, then records can be initially loaded into that table in any order; again they will be stored left to right, with gaps as determined by the installation-specified "free space" parameters.

- After loading, subsequent insertions to a given stored table will be stored in a gap (if a clustering index exists and the record can be physically stored close to its logical position), otherwise at the right-hand end.

Clustering indexes are extremely important for optimization purposes: The optimizer will always try to choose an access path that is based on a clustering index, if one is available, and if clustering sequence is appropriate for the SQL request under consideration.

15.7 STORAGE GROUPS

A storage group is a named collection of direct access volumes, all of the same device type. Each table space and each index space (or each partition in the case of a partitioned table space or index space) normally has an associated storage group.† When storage is needed for the space or parti-

---

*Once again, if the installation follows our recommendation that every base table have a primary key, then every stored table will have at least one index, and hence a fortiori will have a clustering index. Note, however, that the clustering index and the primary index are not necessarily the same.

†For a given space or partition, the installation always has the option of not using a storage group at all. If it does not, then it must use VSAM's Access Method Services utilities to define and delete data sets as necessary. The details of this option are beyond the scope of this book.

tion, it is taken from the specified storage group. Storage groups thus provide a means for the installation to control data separation and data affinity—for example, they can force two stored tables to be assigned to different volumes—while at the same time they allow most of the details of allocating data sets, extents, etc., to be handled automatically by the system.

Within each storage group, spaces and partitions are stored using VSAM linear data sets (many data sets per space or partition, in general). DB2 uses VSAM for such things as direct access space management, data set cataloging, and physical transfer of pages into and out of main memory. However, space management within pages (i.e., VSAM control intervals) is handled by DB2, not by VSAM, and VSAM indexing is not used at all. Note that it is not possible to use the facilities of DB2 (e.g., the SQL language) to access nonDB2 VSAM data sets.

15.8 CONCLUDING REMARKS

In this chapter we have presented a brief overview of the storage objects supported by DB2. As explained in Section 15.1, it is not our intent in this book to give all the details of the corresponding data definition statements; however, we mention the following points.

- The table space for a given base table is specified in the CREATE TABLE statement for that table.

- The database for a given table space is specified in the CREATE TABLESPACE statement for that table space; the database for a given index space is implied by the table over which the index is defined (an index space must be included within the same database as the table space that contains the indexed table).

- Details of the partitioning (value ranges, etc.) for a partitioned table space are specified in the CREATE INDEX statement for the (required) clustering index. Details of the partitioning for the corresponding index space are also specified in that CREATE INDEX statement.

- The storage group for a given space or partition is specified in the statement (CREATE TABLESPACE or CREATE INDEX) that defines that space or partition.

- The volumes that make up a given storage group are specified in the CREATE STOGROUP statement that creates that storage group.

In addition to all of the above (and as mentioned in Section 15.1), DB2 provides a comprehensive system of defaults that are designed to make it easy to "get on the air." The full default mechanism is as follows:

- CREATE TABLE can specify a database instead of a table space. If it does, then DB2 will automatically create a table space within that database for the new base table; that table space will automatically be dropped when the base table is dropped. It is not even necessary to specify a database; if neither a database nor a table space is specified, DB2 will create a table space for the new base table within the *default database*, which is a system database that is created for such purposes when the system is installed.

- If CREATE TABLESPACE does not specify a database, the new table space will be assigned to the default database.

- A storage group can be specified at any or all of the following levels:
  - the database level (in CREATE DATABASE)
  - the space level (in CREATE TABLESPACE and CREATE INDEX)
  - the partition level (in the partition specification within CREATE TABLESPACE and CREATE INDEX)

  If no storage group is specified at the partition level for a given partition, the storage group that applies to that partition is the storage group that applies to the containing space. If no storage group is specified at the space level for a given space, the storage group that applies to that space is the storage group that applies to the containing database. If no storage group is specified at the database level for a given database, the storage group that applies to that database is the *default storage group*, which is a storage group that is created for such purposes when the system is installed.

From all of the above, it follows that the data definition statements discussed in Chapter 4 are indeed adequate for "getting on the air." In most realistic situations, however, the installation will probably wish to exercise the tighter control that is possible without the use of defaults. The purpose of the defaults is primarily to allow users to learn to use the system quickly, rather than to serve as an appropriate set of specifications for a full production environment.

We conclude this section (and this chapter) with a brief mention of a couple of miscellaneous points, namely *buffer pools* and *catalog storage structures*.

1. First, buffer pools. The buffers in main storage are grouped together into a number of pools. A given space can use only one such pool; the

buffer pool for a given space is specified via yet another parameter in the appropriate CREATE statement (as usual, of course, a default is assumed if the parameter is omitted). In this way, the installation can control to some degree the separation and affinity of data in main memory. For example, a given index space and its corresponding table space might be assigned to different buffer pools, thus increasing the likelihood that index entries and data records might be present in main memory simultaneously.

2. Second, catalog storage structures. It is obvious that the catalog is a critical component in the overall DB2 system. In particular, it needs very careful management on the part of DB2 to ensure that it does not become a performance bottleneck (because it is on the critical path for so many operations). For this reason, the catalog makes use of certain storage structures that are currently not available for ordinary user data. Those structures include hashing (DB2 Version 1 Release 1 only— but hashing is still used in Version 2 in the *directory*), parent/child links (i.e., pointer chains), and various additional kinds of physical cluster- ing. It seems reasonable to expect that some or all of these structures will eventually be made available for ordinary user data also.

CHAPTER
·16·

Administration Facilities

16.1 INTRODUCTION

In this chapter we take a brief look at DB2's administration facilities. The facilities in question fall into two broad categories, facilities for database administration and facilities for system administration. We consider each in turn.

Database administration involves the design, implementation, and maintenance of individual DB2 databases and associated applications. (Note, therefore, that we are using the term "database administration" here to include the full range of development activities.) Two DB2 features that can assist with these tasks are the "DB2 Interactive" component (DB2I) and the EXPLAIN facility; they are discussed in Sections 16.2 and 16.3, respectively (Section 16.2 in particular includes an extensive discussion of the commands for binding packages and plans). Section 16.4 then goes on to discuss the various utilities provided for such functions as database recovery, database reorganization, etc.

System administration covers the installation, monitoring, tuning, control, and maintenance of the overall DB2 system itself. Section 16.5 discusses the system utilities that are used to assist in maintaining the Boot Strap Data Set (BSDS), and Section 16.6 covers the service aids that can be used to diagnose errors that might arise during DB2 operation. Last, Section 16.7 describes DB2's facilities for monitoring and controlling system operation.

16.2 THE DB2 INTERACTIVE INTERFACE

Almost all of the function of DB2 is available online through the DB2 Interactive interface, DB2I. That interface provides, not only the ability to execute ad hoc SQL statements and to invoke prewritten application programs,* but also, e.g., the ability to issue operator commands, the ability to invoke database utilities, and the ability to prepare application programs for execution (i.e., precompile and compile them, bind the corresponding packages and plans, and so on). With regard to this last point, in fact, preparing programs interactively via DB2I is the normal mode of operation (although of course it is always possible to use batch if you prefer—see the end of this section).

Fig. 16.1 illustrates the TSO environment. In particular, it shows how DB2I relates to TSO. As explained in Chapter 2, TSO supports both batch and online DB2 applications: TSO batch applications execute under the TSO monitor program directly, TSO online applications execute under the control of the Interactive System Productivity Facility (ISPF), which is a screen/dialog manager for TSO. DB2I itself is a TSO online application. It provides (among other things) the ability to execute SQL statements online by means of a component called SPUFI ("SQL Processor Using File Input"; the name SPUFI is usually pronounced "spoofy"). SPUFI is discussed in a separate subsection below.

The following is the sequence of events for invoking DB2I:

- Log on to TSO in the normal way and enter ISPF.

- From the ISPF primary option menu, select the "DB2I" option.

- The DB2I main menu will appear, offering the following options (see Fig. 16.2):
  - SPUFI
  - DCLGEN

---

*Note, however, that programs invoked for execution via DB2I are TSO applications (DB2I runs under TSO); such programs must therefore not contain any IMS or CICS calls (see Chapter 2).

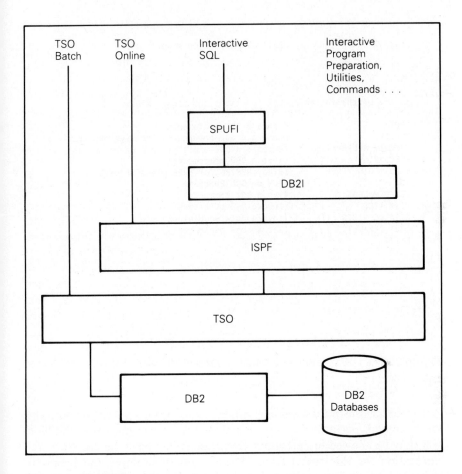

Fig. 16.1 The TSO environment

- program preparation
- precompile
- bind/rebind/free
- run
- DB2 commands
- utilities
- catalog visibility
- DB2I defaults
- exit

```
                        DB2I PRIMARY OPTION MENU

===>_


Select one of the following DB2 functions and press ENTER.

   1   SPUFI                  (Process SQL statements)
   2   DCLGEN                 (Generate SQL and source language declarations)
   3   PROGRAM PREPARATION    (Prepare a DB2 application program to run)
   4   PRECOMPILE             (Invoke DB2 precompiler)
   5   BIND/REBIND/FREE       (BIND, REBIND, or FREE plans or packages)
   6   RUN                    (RUN an SQL Program)
   7   DB2 COMMANDS           (Issue DB2 commands)
   8   UTILITIES              (Invoke DB2 utilities)
   9   CATALOG VISIBILITY     (Invoke catalog dialogs)
   D   DB2I DEFAULTS          (Set global parameters)
   X   EXIT                   (Leave DB2I)




   PRESS:    END to exit       HELP for more information
```

Fig. 16.2 The DB2I main menu (slightly simplified)

Selecting one of these options will lead you through a series of prompts and menus to perform the corresponding task. (As usual, of course, you will only be allowed to perform a given task if you have the necessary authorization for that task.) Each of those sets of prompts and menus is backed by a set of help and tutorial panels, so that in most cases you should have no need of the printed manuals; most of the reference material you will require is available online.

We now proceed to discuss the DB2I options in more detail.

SPUFI

As explained above, SPUFI supports the online execution of SQL statements from a TSO terminal. The basic idea is that you can create a text file containing one or more SQL statements (using the ISPF editor), then execute that file of statements via SPUFI, and then use "ISPF Browse" to browse through the results of those statements (which will have been written to another text file). Note, therefore, that SPUFI is really a DP professional's tool, not an end-user's tool; *QMF* is the corresponding end-user facility (see Part IV of this book). SPUFI is intended primarily for application programmers who wish to test the SQL portions of their programs, or administrators who wish to perform SQL definitional operations (though in fact QMF can also be used to perform both of those functions).

Among other things, the SPUFI menus allow (or in some cases require) the user to specify the following parameters:

- The file that is to contain the SQL statements; this file must already exist, though it may currently be empty.

- Whether that file is to be edited via the ISPF editor before it is ready to be executed (normally YES).

- The file that is to receive the results from executing the SQL statements; this file need not already exist (if it does not, then SPUFI will create it).

- Whether "autocommit" is YES or NO (normally YES). YES means that SPUFI will automatically issue a COMMIT after execution of the statements in the input file if no errors have occurred, or a ROLLBACK otherwise. NO means either that the input file itself includes COMMIT statements or (if it does not) that the user is to be asked interactively after execution which of COMMIT and ROLLBACK is to be issued.

- The name of a remote "server" site (if the SQL statements are to be executed at a remote site). See Chapter 17 for further discussion of this latter possibility.

- The isolation level (RR or CS). See Chapter 13 for an explanation of this option.

If the input file contains multiple SQL statements, SPUFI will stop execution of those statements as soon as it encounters an error in any one of them. The output file will contain a sequence of results, one for each statement (including the relevant SQLCODE and SQLSTATE values), followed by a summary of the overall execution (including, in particular, an indication as to which of COMMIT and ROLLBACK occurred). Fig. 16.3 shows an example of a SPUFI output file.

DCLGEN

The DCLGEN menu allows the user to invoke the declarations generator program. As noted in Chapter 12, DCLGEN is a program that creates embedded SQL DECLARE TABLE statements and corresponding PL/I, C, or COBOL structure declarations from table descriptions in the catalog. The output from DCLGEN is stored as a member of a partitioned data set,

```
BROWSE-- CJDATE.RESULT  ------------------------------------ COLUMNS 001 072
COMMAND INPUT ===>                                           SCROLL ===> PAGE
--------+---------+---------+---------+---------+---------+---------+-------
SELECT *                                                               00010000
FROM    P                                                              00020000
WHERE   WEIGHT IN ( 12, 16, 17 )                                       00030000
ORDER   BY P# ;                                                        00040000
--------+---------+---------+---------+---------+---------+---------+-------
P#      PNAME                    COLOR   WEIGHT  CITY
--------+---------+---------+---------+---------+---------+---------+-------
P1      Nut                      Red       12    London
P2      Bolt                     Green     17    Paris
P3      Screw                    Blue      17    Rome
P5      Cam                      Blue      12    Paris
--------+---------+---------+---------+---------+---------+---------+-------
DSNE610I NUMBER OF ROWS DISPLAYED IS 4.
DSNE616I STATEMENT EXECUTION WAS SUCCESSFUL, SQLCODE IS 100.
--------+---------+---------+---------+---------+---------+---------+-------
--------+---------+---------+---------+---------+---------+---------+-------
DSNE617I COMMIT PERFORMED, SQLCODE IS 0.
--------+---------+---------+---------+---------+---------+---------+-------
```

Fig. 16.3 SPUFI output file example (slightly simplified)

from which it can be copied into an application program by means of an embedded SQL INCLUDE statement.

Program Preparation

The program preparation menus allow the user to perform any or all of the following:

- Precompilation
- Compilation or assembly
- Linkage editor processing
- Bind processing
- Program execution (TSO applications only)

All of the necessary parameters to the Precompiler, Bind, etc., can be supplied via the menus. Note that the source program itself must already have been created via an appropriate text editor, such as the ISPF editor.

Precompile

The PRECOMPILE menu is effectively just the "precompile" portion of the program preparation menu set. It allows the user to precompile an application program source module.

Bind/Rebind/Free

This menu allows the user to create, replace, and drop packages and plans, using the BIND, REBIND, and FREE commands. The full details of these commands are quite complex; we therefore defer detailed discussion until later (see the subsection "The BIND, REBIND, and FREE Commands" at the end of this section).

Run

The RUN menu is effectively just the "program execution" portion of the program preparation menu set. It allows the user to execute a previously prepared application program—provided that, as mentioned earlier, the program in question is a TSO application.

Operator Commands

This menu allows the user to enter system operator commands such as START DATABASE, STOP DATABASE, etc.

Utilities

This menu allows the user to invoke various database utilities. The utilities in question are discussed in Section 16.4.

Catalog Visibility

As mentioned in Chapter 10, the Catalog Visibility menu effectively allows certain queries to be formulated against the DB2 catalog without the direct use of SQL, displaying the results of those queries in a more readable (more "user-friendly") form than SQL does. Examples of information that can be displayed in this way include:

- The privileges granted on a given table
- The indexes defined on a given base table

- The packages dependent on a given table
- The referential constraints involving a given base table
- The storage groups used by a given index

and so on. The menu also provides a "revoke impact" function that allows the administrator to determine the overall effect of executing a proposed REVOKE operation.

DB2I Defaults

This menu allows the user to set certain defaults for the DB2I session (e.g., the specific DB2 instance to be accessed).

Exit

Selecting this option causes termination of the DB2I session.

Bypassing DB2I

As mentioned in the introduction to this section, the use of DB2I is not mandatory. It is possible to invoke a DB2 application interactively without using DB2I by issuing the TSO command "DSN" (which invokes DB2), followed by the command

```
RUN PROGRAM ( program ) PLAN ( plan )
```

It is also possible to invoke a DB2 application in "TSO batch" mode through JCL statements that (a) specify the TSO Terminal Monitor Program (TMP) as the program to be run, and (b) pass the DSN and RUN commands as input to that program. Refer to Chapter 2 for a brief explanation of "TSO batch."

The BIND, REBIND, and FREE Commands

As explained in Chapter 2, the BIND command comes in two versions, BIND PACKAGE and BIND PLAN. "BIND PACKAGE" refers to the process of binding a DBRM to produce a package; "BIND PLAN" refers to the process of binding a list of packages and/or DBRMs together to produce a plan. Analogous remarks apply to the REBIND and FREE commands. In the discussion that follows, we treat the PACKAGE commands first, then the PLAN commands.

1. BIND PACKAGE is used to create a package from a Database Request
Module (DBRM). *Note*: Packages have a four-part name, viz.:

```
location . collection . dbrm . version
```

The four components have the following meanings:

- *location* is the name of the site at which the package is to be created
  (see Chapter 17). The local site is the default.

- *collection* is the name of the collection (unique within "location") to
  which the created package is to belong. Note that every package does
  indeed belong to exactly one collection; however, as discussed in Chapter 2, the same DBRM can be bound any number of times to produce
  any number of essentially identical packages, each in a different collection, and this capability is sometimes loosely described as "allowing
  the same package to belong to multiple collections."

- *dbrm* is the name of the source DBRM. It is used to identify the package within "location.collection" (in fact, the IBM manuals refer to it,
  somewhat confusingly, as the "package ID").

- *version* is a version number and is taken from the source DBRM (it is
  specified originally as a parameter to the precompilation process that
  produced that DBRM). *Note*: The version number is intended to assist
  with such matters as fallback to a previous version of some application;
  however, it is optional, and furthermore should be omitted for SAA
  compatibility (see Part IV of this book). We will omit it in our examples.

Of these four components, the first three are specified as parameters to the
BIND PACKAGE command (see below); the fourth ("version") is specified
at precompile time, as just mentioned.

The following parameters (among others) can be specified on BIND
PACKAGE:

- *PACKAGE*: The "location" and "collection" components of the package name.

- *MEMBER*: The "dbrm" component of the package name.

- *OWNER*: The authorization ID that is to "own" the package, if that
  ID is different from the ID of the user issuing the BIND PACKAGE
  command. This feature enables an individual user to bind a package
  on behalf of some functional area (e.g., "the accounting department"),
  and thus make that package available to all users within that area. See
  the discussion of the BINDAGENT privilege in Chapter 10 (Section
  10.5).

- *QUALIFIER*: The authorization ID to be assumed as the high-level qualifier for unqualified references within the DBRM being bound to (e.g.) base tables, if that ID is different from the ID of the package owner.

- *ISOLATION*: The isolation level (RR or CS) for the package (again, see Chapter 13 for an explanation of this option).

- *VALIDATE*: Defines whether the package is to be "validated" at bind time or at run time. Validation is the process of checking that references to tables, columns, etc., are syntactically correct, that the tables, columns, etc. do exist, and that the would-be package owner is authorized to execute the SQL operations in the DBRM being bound. Validation is normally performed at bind time. In some cases, however, it may not be possible to perform such checks at bind time; for example, the DBRM might include references to a table that does not yet exist (maybe the DBRM itself creates that table), or it may include operations for which the user does not yet have the required authority. In such cases runtime validation must be requested. *Note*: Actually, validation checking is *always* performed at bind time; the point is, however, that if runtime validation is requested, then checks that fail at bind time will be repeated at run time.

- *RELEASE*: Specifies when locks (and other resources) acquired during execution of the package are to be released. The possibilities are COMMIT and DEALLOCATE (see Chapter 13).

- *EXPLAIN*: Requests "EXPLAIN output" for SQL statements in the package (see Section 16.3).

- *ACTION*: Indicates whether the package to be created is brand new ("bind add") or is a replacement for an existing one ("bind replace").

- *ENABLE/DISABLE*: These parameters are mutually exclusive. ENABLE specifies the DB2 "connection types" (e.g., BATCH, CICS, IMSMPP) and connection names (e.g., CICS (CICSSYSA)) that are allowed to use the package. DISABLE specifies the connection types and names that are not allowed to use the package.*

---

*These parameters are not well named. If neither is specified, all connections are effectively enabled. Thus, "ENABLE(*x*)" effectively means "*dis*able everything except *x*"!—i.e., explicitly enabling some connection actually *restricts* the range of possibilities, instead of (as might have been expected) expanding it. By the same token, "DISABLE(*x*)" effectively means "*en*able everything except *x*." The parameters might better have been named "ALLOW ONLY" and "ALLOW ALL EXCEPT," respectively.

2. The REBIND PACKAGE command is used to rebind an existing package. It differs from the "replace" version of BIND PACKAGE (see 1. above) in that its input is the SQL statements that were saved in the catalog when the package was originally bound, not a DBRM (though it does involve many of the same parameters—OWNER, QUALIFIER, VALIDATE, etc.—as BIND PACKAGE does). The "replace" version of BIND PACKAGE would be used if the original SQL statements have been changed; by contrast, REBIND PACKAGE would be used after the physical structure of the database has changed sufficiently—for example, new indexes have been created—that a reevaluation of access strategy is warranted for the package in question. REBIND should also be used after RUNSTATS has been executed (see Section 16.4).

3. The FREE PACKAGE command is used to drop an existing package.

Now we turn to the PLAN commands.

4. BIND PLAN is used to create an application plan from one or more packages and/or DBRMs. The following parameters (among others) can be specified:

- *PLAN*: The plan name.

- *MEMBER*: Specifies a list of DBRMs to be explicitly bound into the plan. For such DBRMs, the BIND PLAN parameters OWNER, QUALIFIER, ISOLATION, VALIDATE, RELEASE, EXPLAIN, and ENABLE/DISABLE parameters perform the same functions as the corresponding BIND PACKAGE parameters do when binding a DBRM into a package (see 1. above).

  Let D be a DBRM, and let d be the compiled version of D. If D is explicitly bound into the plan, then invoking d at run time will cause control to be passed to the copy of d explicitly included in the plan. If D is not explicitly bound into the plan, however, then invoking d at run time will cause control to be passed to the first copy of d found by searching the "package list" instead (see PKLIST below).

- *PKLIST*: Specifies a list of packages and/or package collections to be associated with the plan.

- *ACQUIRE*: Specifies when locks and other resources are to be acquired during execution of the plan. The possibilities are USE and ALLOCATE (see Chapter 13). *Note*: There is no ACQUIRE parameter on BIND PACKAGE because ACQUIRE(USE) always applies to packages.

- *ACTION*: Indicates whether the plan to be created is brand new ("bind add") or is a replacement for an existing one ("bind replace").

- *CURRENTSERVER*: Specifies a remote site ("location"), to which a connection will automatically be established at execution time. This option eliminates the need for the application to issue an explicit CONNECT statement to establish such a connection. See Chapter 17 for further discussion.

5. The REBIND PLAN command is used to rebind an existing plan. The differences between this command and the "replace" version of BIND PLAN (see 4. above) are exactly analogous to those between REBIND PACKAGE and the "replace" version of BIND PACKAGE. See 2. above for further discussion.

6. The FREE PLAN command is used to drop an existing plan.

16.3 EXPLAIN

Officially, EXPLAIN is regarded as a statement of the SQL language; however, the function performed is much more in the nature of a utility, which is why we include it in this chapter. EXPLAIN allows the user to obtain information regarding the optimizer's choice of access strategy for a specified SQL statement. The information provided includes indexes used, details of any sorts that will be needed, and (if the specified statement involves any joins) the order in which tables will be joined and the methods by which the individual joins will be performed. Such information can be useful for tuning existing applications, also for determining how projected applications will perform. The syntax of EXPLAIN (somewhat simplified) is as follows:

```
EXPLAIN type FOR statement
```

Here "type" is PLAN or ALL (ALL has the same meaning as PLAN and is supported only for compatibility with SQL/DS), and "statement" is the SQL statement to be EXPLAINed (SELECT, INSERT, UPDATE, or DELETE—in practice, usually SELECT). The output from the execution of the EXPLAIN statement is placed into a table called *xyz*.PLAN_TABLE, which must already exist (*xyz* here is the authorization ID of the user issuing the EXPLAIN). Here is an example:

```
EXPLAIN PLAN FOR
        SELECT S.S#, P.P#
        FROM   S, P
        WHERE  S.CITY = P.CITY ;
```

When this EXPLAIN is executed, DB2 will place information regarding its implementation of the specified SELECT statement into the PLAN_TABLE of the user issuing the EXPLAIN. The user can then interrogate that table by means of ordinary SELECT statements in order to discover, for example, whether a particular index is being used or whether creating a new index might obviate the need for a sort.

Some additional points:

- The EXPLAIN statement includes a "query number" option by which the user can give a unique numeric identifier to each statement being EXPLAINed. The query number is needed to distinguish between the results of distinct EXPLAINs in the PLAN_TABLE.

- The EXPLAIN output does *not* include the source form of the statement being EXPLAINed. Instead, users are recommended to save that source form (together with the appropriate query number) in a table of their own, for purposes of subsequent reference.

- EXPLAIN does not produce any output regarding additional operations that might be performed for referential integrity reasons. For example, if the statement to be EXPLAINed is a DELETE, there is nothing in the output regarding, e.g., any additional DELETEs caused by a CASCADE delete rule.

EXPLAIN output can also be produced when binding a package or application plan (see Section 16.2 above). If the option EXPLAIN (YES) is specified on the relevant BIND command, then EXPLAIN output will be produced for every SQL statement in the package or plan being bound.

For more details of EXPLAIN—in particular, for details of the format of the PLAN_TABLE and guidance as to how to interpret its contents— the reader is referred to the IBM manuals.

16.4 DATABASE UTILITIES

The DB2 database utilities are all *online* utilities; that is, they can be invoked online (via DB2I), without having to stop execution of the DB2 system. They execute as regular MVS batch applications, using their own private interface to communicate with DB2 (i.e., they do not require the services of IMS/DC, CICS, or TSO). The necessary utility control statements to direct the operation of the specific utility in question must be created using a standard MVS editor and stored in a card image file before the utility is invoked. The necessary MVS job control (JCL) statements for the utility job can be created either via DB2I or by means of a DB2-provided CLIST called DSNU.

The main database utilities are as follows.

- *CHECK DATA*: The CHECK DATA utility can be used to check a table space to see if there are any referential integrity violations. Any rows it finds that contain an unmatched foreign key value can optionally be copied to an exception table, and optionally deleted as well. If any such rows are found (and remain undeleted), the table space will now be in the "check pending" state. See the end of this section for an explanation of "check pending."

- *CHECK INDEX*: The CHECK INDEX utility can be used to test whether indexes are consistent with the data they index. A warning message is issued if an inconsistency is found.

- *COPY*: The COPY utility creates full or incremental backup copies ("image copies") of a table space or partition. An incremental copy is a copy of just the data pages that have changed since the previous copy—full or incremental—was taken. Up to four copies can be made, two for use on the local system, and two for use at a disaster recovery site. Information about the copies created is recorded in a DB2 catalog table called SYSCOPY. Information in SYSCOPY about copies that are no longer required for recovery can be deleted using the MODIFY utility. *Note*: Certain operations, such as loading data (via the LOAD utility) into a table space with logging disabled, will place the table space in question into the "copy pending" state, meaning that a backup copy *must* be made before the data can be used.

- *DIAGNOSE*: The DIAGNOSE utility is used to aid in determining and correcting certain system problems. For example, it can be used to take a dump of the system when certain error conditions occur.

- *LOAD*: The LOAD utility loads data from a sequential data set into one or more tables within one or more partitions of a specified table space. The tables in question can be initially empty or can contain existing data. Input rows that violate a uniqueness constraint (primary key or otherwise) will not be loaded.

  As indicated under the discussion of COPY above, LOAD can be run with logging enabled or disabled. Also, LOAD on a table that contains a foreign key can be run with referential integrity checking enabled or disabled. If checking is enabled, input rows that violate the referential constraint will not be loaded. If checking is disabled, a "check pending" condition will be set on the applicable table space (again, see below for a discussion of "check pending").

  Note: Input rows that fail a uniqueness check or violate a referential constraint can optionally be copied to a rejects file.

  The input data set for LOAD can consist of data unloaded from a VSAM data set, or from an IMS database, or from a DB2 or SQL/DS table. See the discussion of DXT in Part IV of this book.

- *MERGECOPY*: The MERGECOPY utility merges a full copy and one or more incremental copies to produce an up-to-date full copy, or a set of incremental copies to produce an up-to-date composite incremental copy (for a given table space or partition).

- *MODIFY*: The MODIFY utility is used to perform maintenance operations on recovery information in the DB2 catalog. It can, for example, be used to delete information from the SYSCOPY catalog table concerning image copies that are no longer required for recovery.

- *QUIESCE*: The QUIESCE utility is used to quiesce operations (temporarily) on a specified collection of table spaces. The quiesced state corresponds to a single point in the log, so that the collection of table spaces can subsequently be recovered as a unit (the quiesce point is recorded in the catalog in SYSCOPY). In particular, QUIESCE can be useful in establishing a "point of consistency" for a collection of table spaces that are related via referential constraints, thus ensuring that subsequent recovery to that point will restore the data to a consistent state (see the discussion of RECOVER, below).

- *RECOVER*: The RECOVER utility uses the most recent full copy, any subsequent incremental copies, and any subsequent log data to recover one or more table spaces, partitions, or pages after a media failure has occurred. RECOVER can also be used:

1. To perform "point-in-time" recovery by recovering from a specific image copy or recovering to a specific point in the log. Point-in-time recovery will set "check pending" on the applicable table space(s) unless recovery is to a point of consistency (established via QUIESCE—see above).

2. To rebuild one or more indexes or index partitions for a specific table space. Multiple indexes can be rebuilt on a single RECOVER invocation.

   The backup data sets (image copies, etc.) needed for a specific RECOVER invocation are automatically determined from the catalog (SYSCOPY table) and the Boot Strap Data Set (see Chapter 2).

- *REORG*: The REORG utility reorganizes a table space or index space (or table space or index partition) to reclaim wasted space and to reestablish clustering sequence (if applicable). The fact that a reorganization has been done is recorded in SYSCOPY.

- *REPAIR*: The REPAIR utility is used to "repair" stored data—for example, to set the byte string at some specific relative byte adress within some specific page to some specific value. REPAIR can also be used to reset conditions such as "check pending."

- *REPORT*: The REPORT utility produces certain reports that are useful in connection with managing the database recovery process. Specifically, it can be used to determine the image copies and archive log data sets required for a given table space recovery, or the collection of table spaces that need to be recovered as a unit during point-in-time recovery in order to avoid a "check pending" condition.

- *RUNSTATS*: The RUNSTATS utility computes statistics on specified stored data (e.g., a specified table space or a specified index or a specified table and column(s)) and writes them to the system catalog. For details of the actual statistics computed, see the IBM manuals. Bind uses those statistics in its process of optimization. They can also be useful for determining when to reorganize a table space or index. RUNSTATS should be executed whenever a table has been loaded, an index has been created, a table space has been reorganized, or generally whenever there has been a significant amount of update activity on some table. It should then be followed by an appropriate set of REBINDs.

   Note: As mentioned in Chapter 10, it is also possible to update certain statistics "manually" (i.e., via direct UPDATE on the relevant catalog columns); the only authority needed—rather surprisingly—is UPDATE authority on the column(s) to which the statistics apply. One reason for permitting such manual updating is to allow the database administrator to make the statistics on a test database match those on the corresponding production database, so that Bind will generate test packages and plans that genuinely resemble the ultimate production versions. However, this "manual statistics updating" facility should obviously be used sparingly and with extreme caution.

- *STOSPACE*: The STOSPACE utility gathers information regarding the amount of space allocated to a given set of table spaces and indexes and stores that information in the DB2 catalog. Such information is useful for tracking disk space usage.

As indicated at the beginning of this section, all of the foregoing utilities execute while DB2 is active, and most are restartable in the event of a failure. Each invocation of a utility is associated with a *utility identifier*, which is used by DB2 to track the status of execution of the utility concerned. This status information is kept in a DB2 directory table called SYSUTIL and can be displayed using the DB2 DISPLAY UTILTY command. This command can, for example, be used to determine if a utility has abnormally terminated. The DB2 operator can also force the termination of a utility using the DB2 TERM UTILTY command. If as a result of a TERM UTILTY command DB2 determines that a table space or index may contain invalid data, it sets a "recover pending" condition, meaning that the table space or index must be recovered before it can be used.

Check Pending

Let T be a table space. As indicated above, certain operations will cause T to be placed in the "check pending" state. "Check pending" means that T either actually or potentially contains one or more unmatched foreign key values—i.e., foreign key values for which no target primary key value exists. The operations that set "check pending" are as follows:

- Actual detection of such a foreign key value via the CHECK DATA utility

- Defining a new foreign key for an existing nonempty table in T, via ALTER TABLE

- LOAD or RECOVER utility operations, either on some referencing table in T or on some target table that is referenced by some table in T, if such operations might possibly violate some referential constraint

While T is in "check pending," data manipulation operations (SELECT, UPDATE, etc.) and COPY, REORG, and QUIESCE utility operations will not be accepted on T. Data definition operations will be accepted, however. The "check pending" condition can be reset either by the CHECK DATA utility (presumably the normal case) or by the REPAIR utility.

16.5 SYSTEM UTILITIES

DB2 provides two system utilities for managing the Boot Strap Data Set (BSDS). The Boot Strap Data Set contains certain essential system control information—in particular, information having to do with the DB2 log; among other things, it includes a list of all log data sets (both active and archive). It also contains system-wide checkpoint information and "conditional restart" control records (see below).

The BSDS utilities are as follows.

- *CHANGE LOG INVENTORY*: This utility allows the contents of the BSDS to be modified. It can be used to add data sets to, or delete data sets from, the lists of active and archive log data sets. It can also be used to define data set passwords for the archive logs and the DB2 system catalog and directory, and to maintain "conditional restart" control records. "Conditional restart" refers to the process of restarting DB2 when a normal restart is not possible because part of the DB2 log has been damaged. BSDS conditional restart control records tell DB2 about the damaged log data so that it can avoid that part of the log during the conditional restart.

> *Aside*: Of course, conditional restart might lead to a loss of data integrity. This is where the DB2 service aids come into play (see Section 16.6); for example, the DSN1LOGP service aid could be used to determine the extent of the loss. *End of aside.*

The Change Log Inventory utility can be run only when DB2 is not active—i.e., it is an *offline* utility.

- *PRINT LOG MAP*: This utility is used to format and print the contents of the BSDS. It executes as a batch job and can be run when DB2 is active or inactive.

16.6 SERVICE AIDS

The DB2 service aids are batch utilities that can be run only when DB2 is not active. They are intended primarily for use in diagnosing certain error conditions, most details of which are beyond the scope of this book. We will limit our discussion to a brief overview of each aid. The main ones are as follows.

- *DSN1CHKR*: DSN1CHKR is a diagnostic aid used to check the correctness of the DB2 catalog and directory—in particular, to check that all internal pointers are valid. If it finds any errors, a formatted listing of the damaged pages can be produced. *Note*: Errors can be corrected using the REPAIR utility.

- *DSN1COPY*: DSN1COPY is used to copy DB2 data (table space or index) to a sequential data set, or vice versa. It can thus serve as a primitive export/import facility (i.e., to move data between DB2 systems). It can also be used to perform internal validity checking on the consistency of DB2 data.

- *DSN1LOGP*: DSN1LOGP is used to format and print DB2 system log information. It is intended to help in the diagnosis of particularly complex error situations—for example, to assist in determining the extent of the loss on a conditional restart, as suggested in Section 16.5. (Other, more complex examples could be given, but they are mostly beyond the scope of this text.)

- *DSN1PRNT*: DSN1PRNT is used to format and print the contents of table spaces, indexes, image copies, and sequential data sets created by DSN1COPY.

- *DSN1SDMP*: DSN1SDMP is used under guidance from IBM service staff to force dumps of the system and to produce trace records when certain DB2 events occur. This aid can be run only while the DB2 system is active.

16.7 MONITORING AND TUNING FACILITIES

DB2 provides several facilities for monitoring, tuning, and controlling DB2 system operation. In this section, we list some of the main ones and present a brief overview of their capabilities.

Instrumentation Facility

The DB2 Instrumentation Facility is responsible for gathering system diagnostic information, system-wide statistics, performance information, and accounting and audit data. This information can be written to an MVS System Management Facility (SMF) and/or Generalized Trace Facility (GTF) data set. The type and amount of data gathered is controlled by the DB2 START TRACE and STOP TRACE commands. Data produced by the Instrumentation Facility can be analyzed offline by a separate IBM product, the DB2 Performance Monitor (DB2PM). Reports produced by DB2PM include:

- Graphical summaries of accounting and system statistics data
- Processing time information ("transit time") for SQL, Bind, utility, and command execution
- I/O summaries
- Information on locking efficiency (number of deadlocks, number of waits, number of timeouts, etc.)
- A detailed trace of SQL statement execution

DB2PM also provides an online monitor that can be used to display information about an active DB2 subsystem. Features of the online monitor include:

- Detail and summary statistical reports on various aspects of DB2 processing (e.g., buffer pool activity, distributed database processing)
- Exception processing that flags statistics having values that exceed specified limits
- Accounting and locking information for active "threads" (i.e., transactions, in our terminology, also known as *logical units of work*)

- A display of the DB2 system initialization parameters (DSNZPARM—see the subsection "Initialization Parameters" below)

DB2 also provides an application program interface to the Instrumentation Facility that allows authorized applications (e.g., third-party online performance monitors) to access DB2 trace data, create user trace records, and issue DB2 operator commands. *Note*: This facility is not intended to be used as an automated operator interface, since it provides no means for dealing with unsolicited messages from DB2 (e.g., I/O error messages).

Resource Limit Facility

The DB2 Resource Limit Facility (RLF) is a "DB2 governor": It allows the installation to limit the amount of CPU time that can be consumed during the execution of dynamically compiled SQL data manipulation statements—i.e., SELECT, INSERT, UPDATE, and DELETE statements that are compiled at execution time, instead of at some earlier time.* The statements in question may originate at the local site or at a remote site. *Note*: RLF was extended in DB2 Version 2.3 to permit the installation additionally to prohibit specified users from performing BIND and REBIND operations.

The RLF limits are defined by means of a special table (created and populated by means of SQL in the usual way) called a Resource Limit Specification Table (RLST). Any number of RLSTs can exist in the system simultaneously, but only one can be active at any given time. Operator commands are provided for starting and stopping the Resource Limit Facility and for specifying the RLST to be used. The CREATE TABLE for an RLST looks like this:

```
CREATE TABLE DSNRLSTxx
       ( AUTHID   CHAR(8)   NOT NULL WITH DEFAULT,
         PLANNAME CHAR(8)   NOT NULL WITH DEFAULT,
         ASUTIME  INTEGER,
         LUNAME   CHAR(8)   NOT NULL WITH DEFAULT,
         RLFFUNC  CHAR(1)   NOT NULL WITH DEFAULT,
         RLFBIND  CHAR(1)   NOT NULL WITH DEFAULT,
         RLFCOLLN CHAR(18)  NOT NULL WITH DEFAULT,
         RLFPKG   CHAR(8)   NOT NULL WITH DEFAULT ) ;
```

---

*RLF applies to dynamically compiled statements only, since the intent is basically to control ad hoc query usage rather than planned applications; the assumption is that planned applications are subject to (external) controls of their own anyway. It is a little strange, however, that CPU time is the *only* resource that RLF pays any attention to; it would seem desirable to take numerous other factors into account, such as I/O's, tables being accessed, time of day, etc.

Explanation:

- *xx* is any two alphanumeric characters.
- A UNIQUE index is required on the combination of AUTHID and PLANNAME.
- AUTHID is the authorization ID to which this RLST entry applies (blank means it applies to all IDs).
- PLANNAME is the name of the plan to which this RLST entry applies (blank means it applies to all plans).
- ASUTIME is the CPU time limit—i.e., the maximum number of MVS "CPU service units" permitted for the compilation and execution of any single dynamically compiled SQL statement (null means no limit, zero or a negative value means such SQL statements are not permitted at all). If the limit is exceeded, processing of the SQL statement is terminated (in the case of a noncursor operation, the effects on the database, if any, are undone), and a negative SQLCODE value is returned together with a corresponding SQLSTATE value.

The remaining five columns are optional:

- LUNAME is the name of the site to which this RLST entry applies (PUBLIC means all sites in the network, blank or omitted means the local site).
- RLFFUNC specifies the type of control represented by this RLST entry: "1" means it applies to bind operations (see RLFBIND below), "2" means it applies to dynamically compiled SQL statements for specific packages (see RLFCOLLN and RLFPKG below), and blank or omitted means it applies to dynamically compiled SQL statements for specific plans (see PLANNAME above).
- RLFBIND indicates whether bind operations are allowed ("N" means they are not, "Y" or omitted means they are).
- RLFCOLLN is the name of the collection to which this RLST entry applies (blank or omitted means all collections at the specified site).
- RLFPKG is the name of the package to which this RLST entry applies (blank or omitted means all packages at the specified site).

Here is an example of an RLST:

AUTHID	PLANNAME	ASUTIME
CJDATE	QMF220	3000
CJWHITE	QMF220	3000
bbb	QMF220	1000
bbb	bbb	200

In this example, authorization IDs CJDATE and CJWHITE are limited to 3000 CPU units when entering a SQL statement through QMF (QMF220 is the name of the QMF plan). All other QMF users have a limit of 1000 CPU units. When entering dynamic SQL through any program other than QMF, all users (including CJDATE and CJWHITE) are subject to a limit of 200 units.

Note: Users holding SYSADM authority are not subject to any RLF constraints at all, regardless of what RLST happens to be in effect.

Initialization Parameters

During system startup DB2 loads a module known as DSNZPARM which contains parameters that control the operation of DB2. These parameters define such things as whether dual logging is in effect, the size of the database buffer pools, the size of log buffers, locking thresholds, and so forth. DB2 provides a set of macros which allow DB2 administrators to modify the contents of DSNZPARM to tailor and tune it to optimize DB2 operation.

Operator Monitoring Commands

Several DB2, CICS, and IMS operator commands are provided for monitoring an active DB2 subsystem. We limit our discussion to a brief overview of some of the most important of these commands, as follows:

- *-DISPLAY*: The DB2 DISPLAY command permits the operator to display information regarding DB2 "threads" (i.e., transactions), databases, connected subsystems, connections to remote DB2 subsystems, active traces, utility status, applications waiting for or holding locks, and so forth.

- */DISPLAY*: The IMS /DISPLAY command displays the names of the DB2 subsystems connected to IMS and their status.

- *DSNC DISPLAY*: The DSNC DISPLAY command is provided with the CICS Attachment Facility of DB2, which defines and controls the connection between DB2 and CICS subsystems. The command displays information on CICS applications accessing DB2, and statistical counters about the DB2 threads used by these applications.

- *-START RLIMIT and -STOP RLIMIT*: The DB2 RLIMIT commands are used to start and stop the DB2 Resource Limit Facility.

- *-START TRACE and -STOP TRACE*: The DB2 TRACE commands are used to stop and start the DB2 Instrumentation Facility.

PART

III

DISTRIBUTED DATABASE MANAGEMENT

C H A P T E R

·**17**·

Distributed DB2: Concepts and Facilities

17.1 INTRODUCTION

In this chapter we provide a detailed introduction to DB2's distributed database capabilities. Support for distributed database was a major feature of IBM's announcement of both Version 2.2 and Version 2.3 of the DB2 product. Unfortunately, however, the Version 2.3 support is not just a simple extension of the Version 2.2 support, as we shall see. The rationale for this somewhat confusing state of affairs is explained by the following summary of relevant events:

1. DB2 Version 2.2 was announced in October 1988. In a simultaneous announcement, IBM also added certain distributed database capabili-

ties to its Systems Application Architecture, SAA. DB2 Version 2.2 was the first release of DB2, and indeed the first IBM product, to support any of those new SAA capabilities. *Note*: SAA was mentioned briefly in Chapter 1 of this book and is described in more detail in Part IV (see Chapter 18).

2. In June 1990, IBM published a further extension to SAA called *Distributed Relational Data Architecture* (DRDA). DRDA is a set of rules and protocols that are intended to serve as a basis for distributed database support across possibly disparate DBMSs (for example, DB2 and SQL/ DS). DRDA thus constitutes a specification for how to build a DBMS that can provide the SAA distributed database capabilities mentioned in the previous paragraph (or some of them, at any rate; DRDA itself is still evolving and is certain to be extended at some future time). *Note*: DRDA also is described in a little more detail in Chapter 18.

3. The important thing to understand about DRDA is that it is *publicly documented*. In principle, therefore, anyone (not just IBM) can build a DRDA-compliant DBMS that can participate with other such DBMSs in an SAA distributed system.

4. DB2 Version 2.3 (announced in September 1990) was the first version of DB2 to use DRDA protocols, and it does indeed provide a level of support for distributed database across different DBMSs (see Section 17.4). DB2 Version 2.2, by contrast, uses an IBM-proprietary set of protocols, and it provides DB2-to-DB2 support only.

5. Of course, DB2 Version 2.3 does still provide all of the capabilities of DB2 Version 2.2, but the new DRDA capabilities are clearly "the wave of the future," and—other things being equal—they are clearly the implementation of choice. The trouble is, other things are *not* equal. The DRDA capabilities of Version 2.3 in certain respects provide *strictly less functionality* than the proprietary capabilities of Version 2.2. Then again, they also provide *more* functionality in certain other respects. Thus, choosing which set of capabilities to use in any given situation might not be an entirely straightforward matter.

Because of the foregoing, it is necessary (or at least desirable) to discuss the two versions somewhat independently, and we shall do as much in this chapter. The plan of the chapter is thus as follows. Following this introductory section, Section 17.2 discusses the basic concepts of distributed database, with special reference to the corresponding features of SAA and DRDA. Section 17.3 then describes the relevant facilities of Version 2.2. Finally, Section 17.4 does the same for Version 2.3 and (by way of conclusion) offers a brief comparison of the two versions.

17.2 DISTRIBUTED DATABASE IN SAA

In this section we explain some of the basic ideas behind distributed database in general, and then discuss what distributed database means in SAA terms specifically. Of course, distributed database is a big topic in its own right, and the discussions that follow are necessarily somewhat superficial; more detailed treatments can be found in the books *Relational Database Writings 1985–1989*, by C. J. Date (Addison-Wesley, 1990), and *Relational Database Writings 1989–1991*, by C. J. Date and Hugh Darwen (Addison-Wesley, 1992).

We begin with a (very loose) working definition: A *distributed database system* is a system involving multiple computer sites connected together in some kind of communications network, in which:

1. Each site is a database system site in its own right, with its own local stored data, its own local DBMS, its own local lock manager, its own local recovery log, and so forth;

2. Users (both end-users and application programmers) can access data anywhere around the network exactly as if the data were all stored at the user's own site.

Thus, a *distributed database* is a kind of virtual object, consisting of data that is physically stored at multiple distinct sites, and a *distributed DBMS* is a kind of partnership among multiple distinct single-site DBMSs operating at multiple distinct sites. Again, of course, these definitions are still very loose. The key point, however, is that from the user's perspective a distributed database behaves—at least for data manipulation purposes— exactly as if it were *not* distributed, i.e., as if it were a local database stored in its entirety at the user's own local site. Users are isolated (logically speaking) from all details of the physical distribution.

The advantages of a distributed database system include the following (in general—but note that most of these do *not* fully apply to DB2 or DRDA in their present form):

1. *Location independence* (also known as location transparency): As just explained, users and user programs do not have to know where data is stored. As a result, data can be moved from one site to another in response to changing patterns of usage, without necessitating any re-writing of application programs.

2. *Capacity and performance*: Transaction volumes and database size are essentially unlimited because the network can grow to any size, again without necessitating the rewriting of application programs. Throughput is increased because of the parallelism inherent in the system struc-

ture. Response times can be reduced by placing data at the site at which it is most frequently used.

3. *Incremental growth*: Individual sites can be added, upgraded, and replaced in a transparent and nondisruptive fashion. Existing applications will continue to work after a nondistributed system has evolved into a distributed one; they will also continue to work as the distributed system itself evolves and new sites are added and/or data is redistributed across existing sites.

4. *Application portability*: Applications can be developed on one machine and can then run unchanged on another. Applications can easily be moved from one site to another around the network.

5. *Improved productivity*: As a consequence of the previous points, users have universal and uniform access to data throughout the network. Data manipulation operations (SELECT, INSERT, UPDATE, DELETE, plus cursor-based operations and COMMIT and ROLLBACK) work against the distributed database exactly as if it were an ordinary local database. Application programs (both user-written applications and IBM-provided frontend subsystems such as QMF) therefore also operate exactly as if the database were purely local.

6. *Local autonomy*: Despite the fact that data is universally accessible as explained in the previous paragraph, local sites can still maintain control (for security and integrity and performance purposes) of data that logically belongs to them—they do not have to relinquish such control to some remote "master" site. Also, local applications (i.e., applications that do not need access to remote data) remain truly local; they are not penalized in any way by the fact that their local data is now accessible to remote sites. In particular, applications that ran before the system became distributed will continue to run afterwards.

7. *System independence*: In general, users and user programs should be independent of the underlying machines, operating systems, and network protocols. Such independence is certainly not fully available today, but it is presumably IBM's ultimate intent to provide full distributed database support across the complete range of SAA environments—i.e., to allow DB2 sites, SQL/DS sites, OS/400 Database Manager sites, and OS/2 Database Manager sites all to participate as partners in a distributed system and together to present a "single-system image" to the user.

Let us turn now to SAA specifically. As mentioned in Section 17.1, SAA was extended in 1988 to include certain distributed database capabilities ("Distributed Relational Data in SAA"), and extended again in 1990 to include an architecture ("Distributed Relational Data Architecture,"

DRDA) for implementing certain of those capabilities. In a document entitled *Introduction to Distributed Relational Data*, dated September 1988, IBM defined four levels of distributed database functionality, as follows:

1. Remote request
2. Remote unit of work
3. Distributed unit of work
4. Distributed request

We should make it clear immediately, however, that of these four levels, only numbers 2 and 3 are currently included in SAA and supported (partially) by DB2, and only number 2 is currently included in DRDA. We explain the four levels as follows.

1. *Remote request* means that an application at one site X can send an individual database request (i.e., SQL statement) to some remote site Y for execution. That request is executed *and committed* (or rolled back) entirely at site Y. The original application at site X can subsequently send another request to site Y (or possibly to another site Z), regardless of whether the first request was successful or unsuccessful.

   IBM's ECF product ("Enhanced Connectivity Facilities") is an example of a product that supports remote requests. For example, under ECF, a user on a PC can perform a SQL operation (possibly even an update) on data that is stored on a mainframe. However, remote request support is not part of SAA and cannot be invoked from DB2.

2. *Remote unit of work* (abbrev. RUW) means that an application at one site X can send all of the database requests in a given "unit of work" (i.e., a transaction, in our terms—in other words, a logically related set of SQL statements) to some remote site Y for execution. The database processing for the transaction is thus executed in its entirety at the remote site Y; however, the local site X decides whether the transaction is to be committed or rolled back.* (Of course, it *must* decide to roll it back if a failure has occurred at site Y.)

   Support for remote unit of work is included in SAA and DRDA and is provided (partially) by DB2. More details are given in the next two sections.

3. *Distributed unit of work* (abbrev. DUW) means that an application at one site X can send some or all of the database requests in a given unit of work (transaction) to one or more remote sites Y, Z, . . ., for

---

*Throughout this section and the remainder of this chapter, we use the term "local site" to mean the site where the application originates—i.e., the site executing the nonSQL portions of the code.

execution. The database processing for the transaction is thus spread across multiple sites, in general; each individual request is still executed in its entirety at a single site, but different requests can be executed at different sites. However, site X is still the cooordinating site, i.e., the site that decides whether the transaction is to be committed or rolled back. (Again, of course, it must decide to roll it back if a failure has occurred at any of the other sites.)

As with the previous level (remote unit of work), support for distributed unit of work is included in SAA (although not in DRDA as yet) and is partially provided by DB2. *Note*: In fact, of course, any DBMS that provides DUW support will a fortiori provide RUW support also. However, RUW support is not just a special case of DUW support, for reasons that will be explained in Section 17.4.

4. *Distributed request* is really the only one of the four levels that approaches what is commonly accepted (in the research world, at least) as true distributed database support. Distributed request means everything that distributed unit of work means, *plus* it permits individual database requests (SQL statements) to span multiple sites—for example, a request originating from site X might ask for a join or union to be performed between a table at site Y and a table at site Z. Note that it is only at this level that the system can be said to be providing genuine location independence; in all three previous cases, users do have to have *some* knowledge regarding the physical location of data.

This level is not part of SAA at this time and is not supported by DB2.

Note: It is worth pointing out that IBM's "remote unit of work" (RUW) support is an example of what many vendors call *client/server* computing, in which an application (the client) running at one site performs database operations on a DBMS (the server) at another site. The client site could be a workstation (e.g., an OS/2 site) and the server site could be a mainframe (e.g., an MVS/DB2 site). Client/server support is becoming increasingly important in customer organizations, because it allows applications to run on local (and cheap) workstations, and yet access a common shared database in a properly controlled manner.

17.3 DISTRIBUTED DATABASE IN VERSION 2.2

Overview

The distributed database support in Version 2.2 provides DB2-to-DB2 access only; it is not possible, for example, to have a single distributed transaction that accesses a mixture of DB2 and SQL/DS data. Within a given transaction, each SQL statement must be wholly executed at one DB2 site; however, different SQL statements can be executed at different sites. (By "SQL statements" here, we mean SQL *data manipulation* statements specifically; data definition and other SQL statements can be executed only at the local site.) Version 2.2 thus supports the SAA "distributed unit of work" capability (and hence the SAA "remote unit of work" capability also)—with the following major restrictions:

- All update operations in the transaction (INSERTs and/or UPDATEs and/or DELETEs), if any, must be performed at the same site.

- Furthermore, if the transaction is executing under IMS or CICS, then the single site at which all updates are performed must be the *local* site. Note, however, that the update site can optionally be remote under TSO or the Call Attach Facility (and, of course, different transactions can have different remote update sites in this case).

Some Technical Details

We now address certain technical aspects of Version 2.2's support in a little more detail.

1. *General*: As mentioned in Chapter 2, DB2's distributed database support is provided by the Distributed Data Facility component (DDF), which operates in its own MVS address space. Intersite communication is performed using the Advanced Program-to-Program Communication (APPC) facilities of VTAM; each DB2 site acts as a VTAM "logical unit." Each site has a unique *location name* of 16 characters.

2. *Data naming*: If a system is truly to provide location independence, then users must continue to refer to data (i.e., tables) exactly as if the data were local, regardless of where the data is physically stored. The following is a sketch of how table naming works in a distributed DB2 environment (more accurately, in a distributed *SAA* environment):

- First, each named table in the entire distributed system has a globally unique three-part name, as follows—

```
location . user . name
```

—where "location" is the name of the site to which the table really belongs, "user" is an authorization ID at that site, and "name" is the table's regular unqualified name (the second and third of these components constitute an ordinary two-part name as in DB2 prior to Version 2.2—see Chapter 4). *Note*: The "user" component is referred to in DRDA by the more generic (and undefined) term "collection," implying that in a nonDB2 DRDA DBMS this component might not be an authorization ID per se. (Note that "collection" here does *not* necessarily have the specialized meaning discussed in Chapter 2.) Of course, this consideration is irrelevant for the purposes of the present section.

- Second, users *can* refer to named tables directly by their three-part name. However, to do so would clearly compromise the objective of location independence. Instead, users will normally use an *alias*. Recall from Chapter 8 that an alias is an alternative name for a table, introduced by means of the SQL statement CREATE ALIAS. For example:

```
CREATE ALIAS SUPPLIERS FOR SFO.CJDATE.S ;
```

Users at the site at which the alias was created can refer to the name SUPPLIERS in SQL data manipulation statements exactly as if it identified a local table. For example:

```
SELECT S#, CITY
FROM    SUPPLIERS
WHERE   STATUS > 5 ;
```

Recall also from Chapter 8 that aliases are *public*, in the sense that they are available to every user at the site at which they are defined (though users other than the alias creator will have to use the creator's authorization ID as a high-level qualifier, as explained in Chapter 8). They are registered in the SYSTABLES table in the catalog—that is, SYSTABLES includes a row for each alias known at the site, showing the alias as a recognized table name and giving (among other things) the corresponding three-part name for that alias.

3. *Authorization*: Authorization is another area that requires extended consideration in the distributed environment. If user U*x* operating at site X is to be allowed to operate on data belonging to some user at site Y, then user U*x* must somehow be known at site Y so that the owner of the data in question can grant the appropriate access privileges to that user U*x*. DB2 therefore supports the concept of "authorization ID translation," which works as follows (in outline.

- First, user U*x* at site X is allocated another authorization ID, U*y* say, at site Y. The owner of the data at site Y can now issue an appropriate GRANT operation:

```
GRANT .... ON ... TO Uy ;
```

- Second, a special system table at site X called SYSUSERNAMES maps authorization IDs known at that site to authorization IDs at other sites. In the example, SYSUSERNAMES at site X would include a row indicating that authorization ID U*x* at that site corresponds to authorization ID U*y* at site Y. The SYSUSERNAMES table is kept, not in the catalog, but in a special database at site X, the *Communications Database* (CDB), and is maintained using ordinary SQL statements. *Note*: The CDB serves a variety of other purposes as well, purposes that are however beyond the scope of the present discussion.

- When a SQL request is submitted to site Y from site X on behalf of user U*x*, the system will send the authorization ID U*y* along with that request. Authorization checking will then be done at site Y.* Note, therefore, that—unlike the situation prior to Version 2.2, in which, by definition, all requests were purely local—authorization checking for remote requests is always done at run time, not ahead of time as part of some separate bind step. In fact, as we shall see in a moment, there *is* no separate bind step for remote requests in Version 2.2.

- An extended form of GRANT TO PUBLIC is supported:

    GRANT ... TO PUBLIC AT ALL LOCATIONS ;

- An analogous form of REVOKE is also supported.

4. *Data definition*: The SQL data definition statements are basically unaffected by DB2's distributed database support (but remember that such statements can be executed at the local site only). There are a couple of limitations, however, namely as follows:

- It is not possible to define a view that spans sites (because, of course, no SQL data manipulation statement is allowed to span sites).

- It is not possible to define a foreign key at one site that references a primary key at another site, for essentially the same reason.

5. *Data manipulation*: The SQL data manipulation statements are unaffected by DB2's distributed database support (indeed, that is the whole object of the exercise). There is one point to be made, however, regarding implementation: Requests for access to remote data are always processed by dynamic bind—that is, the optimization and compilation functions (etc.) are always performed at run time, not ahead of time in a separate bind step. (*Local* requests, by contrast, are still bound ahead of time as in DB2 prior to Version 2.2.)

---

*We are describing the case where authorization ID translation is done at the sending site. It is also possible to do it at the receiving site instead. For details, the reader is referred to the IBM manuals.

6. *Application programming*: Consider an application at site X that is using a cursor to run through a set of rows that are physically stored at site Y. If each individual FETCH causes just one row of data to be transmitted across the communications network, the total overhead for retrieving all of the data is likely to be extremely high (it is well known that row-at-a-time access across a communications network is generally a bad idea).

Because of this problem, Version 2.2 uses *block FETCH* wherever possible; that is, it batches up the data to be retrieved into blocks of up to 32K bytes each, and physically transmits the data a block at a time instead of a row at a time. Block FETCH is used whenever it can be guaranteed that no UPDATE CURRENT or DELETE CURRENT operations will be applied to the cursor (if such updates will be done, it unfortunately becomes necessary to keep the two sites X and Y "in synch," and block FETCH cannot be used). Regardless of whether block FETCH is used or not, of course, the effect from the programmer's point of view is still as if each FETCH retrieves a single row; the block transmission is only from the system buffer at site Y to the system buffer at site X, and is generally "transparent to the user."

How then does DB2 know whether to use block FETCH or not? One way is for the programmer to state explicitly that no UPDATEs or DELETEs will be applied to the cursor, by specifying FOR FETCH ONLY in the cursor declaration (as explained in Chapter 12). For example:

```
EXEC SQL DECLARE W CURSOR FOR
                SELECT S#, CITY
                FROM   SUPPLIERS
                WHERE  STATUS > 5
                ORDER  BY S#
           FOR FETCH ONLY ;
```

If FOR FETCH ONLY is not specified but FOR UPDATE OF . . . is specified instead, DB2 obviously will not use block FETCH. But what if neither is specified? It might still be the case that UPDATE CURRENT or DELETE CURRENT operations will be applied to the cursor (recall in particular that there is no such thing as a "FOR DELETE" clause). In this case, DB2 can still tell whether the cursor can possibly *permit* such operations, by examining the form of the cursor declaration itself; for example, the presence of an ORDER BY clause means that such operations cannot be permitted* (refer to the discussion at the end of Section 12.4 for details). If such operations are not permitted, DB2 will still use block FETCH. Otherwise, it will not.

---

*Which implies, incidentally, that the FOR FETCH ONLY in our example is actually redundant.

7. *Deadlock*: It should be pointed out that distributed database support opens the door to the possibility of *multisite deadlock* (sometimes called "global" deadlock). A multisite deadlock is a deadlock involving multiple sites. For example, suppose we have two sites X and Y and two transactions T1 and T2. Suppose further that transaction T1 holds a lock on object *x* at site X and requests a lock on object *y* at site Y; and suppose finally that transaction T2 holds a lock on object *y* at site Y and requests a lock on object *x* at site X. Deadlock! Refer to Chapter 13 for a detailed discussion of deadlocks.

8. *Administration*: Certain DB2 administration facilities are extended in the distributed environment. For example, the Resource Limit Facility is extended to cover time spent on remote requests as well as local ones (see Chapter 16), and the Instrumentation Facility is extended to support accounting operations at multiple sites. For more details, see the IBM manuals.

17.4 DISTRIBUTED DATABASE IN VERSION 2.3

Overview

First, a general remark: All of the statements made in Section 17.3 above apply to DB2 Version 2.3 also unless explicitly overridden by something in the present section. In particular, of course, all of the distributed database functionality introduced in Version 2.2 is still supported in Version 2.3. Thus, DUW support (and therefore RUW support also) is still provided across DB2 sites, and furthermore different sites can now be running different DB2 versions (Version 2.2 at some sites and Version 2.3 at others).

In addition, Version 2.3 introduced an alternative implementation of remote unit of work, based on DRDA. Recall from Section 17.2 that RUW represents a *lower* level of functionality than DUW: All SQL operations in the transaction have to be performed at *the same site*. Because it is based on DRDA, however, this new capability includes support for *heterogeneous* distributed systems—i.e., systems in which different sites can be running different DBMSs.

In order to amplify the foregoing remark, we first remind the reader that remote unit of work is a specific example of what is more usually referred to as *client/server computing*. Intersite communication under DRDA involves a *requester* program at the client site and a *server* program—i.e., a DBMS—at the server site. The purpose of the requester is to accept SQL statements from the client application, format them into DRDA messages, and send them to the server. IBM's DB2, SQL/DS, and SQL/400 DBMSs all provide both requester and server capabilities. However, the OS/2 Database Manager does not; instead, requester capabilities are provided in the PC environment by a separate product, DDCS/2 ("Distributed Database Connection Services/2"), and server capabilities are currently not available at all.* To be specific, therefore, the client site and the server site can each be any of the following under DRDA:

- An MVS site running DB2 Version 2.3
- A VM site running SQL/DS Version 3.3
- An OS/400 site running the OS/400 Database Manager Version 2.1 Modification Level 1
- An OS/2 site running DDCS/2 (client only)

Thus, e.g., an OS/2 transaction can retrieve and/or update DB2 data at a remote site, and a DB2 transaction can retrieve and/or update SQL/DS data at a remote site. In the case of a DB2 transaction, however, the single site at which all SQL operations are performed must be the *local* site if the transaction is executing under IMS or CICS and any updating is done.

Some Technical Details

1. *Packages and plans*: Version 2.3's new DRDA support for remote unit of work relies on the use of packages.† Basically, an application must have a compiled package (at least one) at every site at which it intends to perform any database operations. The plan for the application must involve all of those packages, and is thus conceptually spread out across all of the relevant sites; however, it is physically created (i.e., bound) at the local site.

Here is an example. Suppose the network includes sites SFO, LAX, and JFK, and suppose we are at site SFO (i.e., SFO is the local site). First we issue the command (not intended to be valid BIND syntax):

```
1. BIND PACKAGE ( SFO.CJDCOLL.PKGX ) FROM ( DBRMX ) ;
```

This command compiles a DBRM called DBRMX and creates a package called PKGX in the collection CJDCOLL at site SFO. Note that (as explained in Chapter 16) packages have a three-part name of the form shown ("location.collection.package"); the "location" component can be omit-

---

DRDA server capabilities, that is. A version of the OS/2 Database Manager does exist that can act as a server on a local area network (LAN) to DOS, DOS Windows, and OS/2 clients.
†Packages are called *access modules* in SQL/DS. They are also, very confusingly, often referred to as *programs*, both in DB2 and SQL/DS.

ted, in which case it defaults to the local site, but the other two components must always be specified in any reference to the package.*

Note: We deliberately do not use actual DB2 syntax for the BIND command here because it is unnecessarily confusing. Note too that (again as explained in Chapter 16) DB2 actually uses the name of the DBRM as the third ("package") component of the package name, but we choose not to do this in our examples, for clarity once again.

Next, we issue the command:

2. `BIND PACKAGE ( LAX.CJDCOLL.PKGY ) FROM ( DBRMY ) ;`

This command, although issued at SFO, actually creates a package at LAX. That package is assigned to a collection at LAX called CJDCOLL. (Note that this collection has the same unqualified name as the one in SFO; nevertheless, it is a different collection.) *Note*: We could have specified DBRMX in place of DBRMY, in which case the compiled package would have been essentially identical to the SFO package created above. Of course, LAX and SFO would have to have essentially identical database definitions for this to be sensible—at least for those portions of the database referenced in DBRMX.

Finally we issue the command:

3. `BIND PACKAGE ( JFK.CJDCOLL.PKGZ ) FROM ( DBRMZ ) ;`

Now we have three packages, one at each of the three sites. We bind them together as follows:

4. `BIND PLAN ( PLANXYZ ) FROM ( SFO.CJDCOLL.PKGX,`
   `                            LAX.CJDCOLL.PKGY,`
   `                            JFK.CJDCOLL.PKGZ ) ;`

Now we have a plan at site SFO called PLANXYZ. An application at SFO that uses this plan can access data at each of the three sites SFO, LAX, and JFK (though any *transaction* within the application can access only one of the three, of course, because we are talking about RUW support only).

A number of points arise as a consequence of the foregoing:

- First, SQL statements are compiled ahead of time in Version 2.3, even for remote access. This is a significant area of difference between Version 2.2 and Version 2.3.

---

*We remind the reader that (as stated in Chapter 16) we choose to ignore the optional "version number" component of a package name.

- Note that a DBRM that is to be compiled into a package at a remote location might have to use a nonDB2 SQL dialect (i.e., if the remote DBMS is not DB2 but, say, SQL/DS). The DB2 Precompiler option SQL(*xxx*), where *xxx* is either DB2 or ALL, indicates whether DB2 should expect DB2 syntax only or other dialects; SQL(DB2) means that the Precompiler should treat nonDB2 syntax as an error, SQL(ALL) means that nonDB2 syntax is to be accepted (with a warning) and that a final syntax check is to be done at "bind package" time.

- In Chapter 2, we said that BIND PLAN checks that the user who is to be the owner of the plan is authorized to execute all of the applicable packages. However, such bind-time checking is not performed for remote packages; instead, the necessary checking is done when the package in question is executed.

2. *Connecting to a remote site*: In order to access data at a remote site, a transaction must first *connect* to that site. The SQL CONNECT statement is provided for this purpose. The syntax is:

```
CONNECT { TO server | RESET } ;
```

Here "server" is either the name of a site or a reference to a host variable (of type character string) that contains such a site name; that site becomes the "current server" (its name is placed in the CURRENT SERVER special register). CONNECT RESET reestablishes the local site as the current server. *Note*: Prior to the first CONNECT executed by an application, the current server is as specified by the CURRENTSERVER option on the BIND PLAN command (see Chapter 16). If no such option is specified, the initial current server is the local site.

CONNECT is legal only in embedded SQL, not in interactive SQL. Also, the SQL statement (if any) most recently executed prior to the CONNECT must be COMMIT, ROLLBACK, another CONNECT, or a "local SET"—i.e., SET CURRENT PACKAGESET, or SET host-variable = CURRENT PACKAGESET, or SET host-variable = CURRENT SERVER. What this means, loosely speaking, is that each transaction should execute at most one explicit CONNECT operation, and that CONNECT should be the first SQL statement executed in that transaction.

Note, incidentally, that the need for an (explicit or implicit) CONNECT represents a minor (?) violation of location independence. It is also the justification for the remark in Section 17.2 to the effect that RUW support is not just a special case of DUW support.

3. *Data definition*: Another difference from Version 2.2 is that Version 2.3's DRDA remote unit of work support allows data definition operations, as well as data manipulation operations, to be executed at a remote site.

Thus, for example, a user at SFO can execute a package at LAX that creates a base table at LAX. Of course, it is still the case (as with Version 2.2) that views and referential constraints cannot span sites.

4. *Character string data*: Another difference between Versions 2.2 and 2.3 arises in connection with character string data. Different sites might very well use different character string representations; for example, one might use EBCDIC and another ASCII. In Version 2.3, however, the system will be aware of such differences, and will automatically and transparently perform any necessary conversions when transferring data between sites.

5. *Block FETCH*: Version 2.3 does support block FETCH, but to a more limited extent than Version 2.2. Details of the differences are beyond the scope of this text.

6. *Administration*: Like Version 2.2, Version 2.3 introduced some enhancements to certain of the DB2 administration facilities, in particular in the area of distributed database support. Again we leave the details to the IBM manuals.

To conclude this section (and this chapter), we give in Fig. 17.1 (overleaf) a brief summary of the major points of difference between Version 2.2's DUW support and Version 2.3's RUW support. A "Y" ("yes") in the table means that the feature in question is supported, an "N" ("no") means it is not.

	Version 2.2 DUW	Version 2.3 RUW	Version 2.3 DUW
access multiple sites in one SQL statement	N	N	N
access multiple sites in one transaction	Y	N	Y
update multiple sites in one transaction	N	N	N
access multiple sites in one application	Y	Y	Y
no need for CONNECT	Y	N	Y
data definition at remote site	N	Y	N
compiled SQL at remote site	N	Y	N
implements DRDA	N	Y	N
heterogeneous system support	N	Y	N
update remote site (TSO, batch)	Y	Y	Y
update remote site (IMS, CICS)	N	N	N
automatic character set conversion	N	Y	Y

Fig. 17.1 A comparison between the distributed database support of Version 2.2 and Version 2.3

PART

◆ IV ◆

THE DB2
PRODUCT FAMILY

·18·

Related Products: An Overview

18.1 INTRODUCTION

Up to this point in the book we have concentrated (for the most part) purely on the base DB2 product itself. Like most DBMSs, however, DB2 is accompanied by numerous auxiliary products—application generators, report writers, database design tools, and so on. Such products are available both from IBM and from independent third-party vendors. In this part of the book we examine this area in some detail. The present chapter provides a general overview of the subject; the next two chapters then go on to discuss some of the more important products in more detail. *Note*: It is obviously not possible in a book of this size to cover every product from every vendor in detail. We therefore limit most of our detailed discussions to IBM's own products specifically—although we do at least mention some of the best-known nonIBM products in passing, where appropriate.

IBM regards DB2 and its associated tools as key members of its "Systems Application Architecture" (SAA) product set. SAA is intended as a basis for achieving consistency, compatibility, and interoperability across IBM's diverse range of hardware and software offerings: It defines a set of common software interfaces, conventions, and protocols to be used by IBM's program product offerings running under the various SAA operating systems, viz., MVS (TSO, batch, CICS, IMS), VM, OS/400, and OS/2. *Note*: IBM also provides some limited support for SAA in its other operating systems VSE, DOS, and AIX.

With SAA as a foundation, IBM has defined a variety of so-called "solution frameworks." Each such framework includes a set of products (both IBM and nonIBM) that conform to SAA and together address one particular aspect of computer usage in the customer environment. These frameworks allow customers to integrate applications and tools from IBM and independent third-party vendors. Four such frameworks are currently defined, viz., *AD/Cycle*, *OfficeVision*, *Information Warehouse*, and *SystemView*.

- *AD/Cycle*: The "AD" here stands for "Application Development." This framework includes process and data modeling tools, language products, application generators, knowledge-based systems, and test tools. It also provides a repository and a set of services and specifications for integrating these various application development tools.

- *Information Warehouse*: The Information Warehouse framework provides a set of facilities and products (e.g., ad hoc query subsystems, report writers, etc.) for managing and delivering business information to end-users in an SAA environment.

- *OfficeVision*: This framework provides for the management of documents and messages and their transfer between SAA systems. It includes electronic mail, address book, calendar, and library services, as well as document processing and decision support tools.

- *SystemView*: This framework provides tools and services for managing the operational aspects of the overall system. It includes support for change management, system configuration, performance monitoring and tuning, and problem determination across heterogeneous (interconnected) SAA systems.

Of these four frameworks, only the first two, AD/Cycle and the Information Warehouse, are directly relevant to database management per se, and we ignore the other two from this point forward. Following further discussion of SAA in the next section, therefore, the next two sections of this chapter (Sections 18.3 and 18.4) discuss AD/Cycle and the Information

Warehouse respectively, surveying the range of products available in each case. Sections 18.5 and 18.6 then go on to describe certain aspects of the Information Warehouse in more detail. (Also, certain specific AD/Cycle and Information Warehouse products are discussed further in Chapters 19 and 20 immediately following.)

18.2 SYSTEMS APPLICATION ARCHITECTURE

In this section we briefly sketch the facilities of SAA—mainly by way of background, but also to provide some indication as to IBM's SAA direction with regard to database management specifically. SAA consists of three major components:

- *Common User Access*: Defines a set of rules and guidelines for designing the screen interface to applications that interact with terminals and workstations. The purpose of this component is to ensure that applications have a uniform "look and feel" and generally behave in a consistent fashion from the user's point of view.

- *Common Programming Interface*: Consists of a set of "DP professional" languages and services. These facilities are intended for use by application programmers, either directly or indirectly via some higher-level application development tool such as an application generator.

- *Common Communications Support*: Provides a set of protocols and standards to support communication between different applications, operating systems, and networks. The protocols and standards in question include both IBM-defined and OSI (Open Systems Interconnection) standards, and thus support IBM-to-nonIBM connections as well as IBM-to-IBM. *Note*: The Distributed Relational Database Architecture (DRDA) protocols discussed in Chapter 17 are part of this SAA component.

From a database standpoint, the most important piece of SAA is the Common Programming Interface. The Common Programming Interface, in turn, divides into components in two areas, namely *languages* and *services*. At the time of writing, the SAA languages are:

- C, COBOL, FORTRAN, PL/I, RPG
- A *procedures language* based on the REXX language
- An *application generation language* based on Cross System Product, CSP (see Chapter 19)

The services components include:

- A *Communications Interface* supporting interprogram communication using Advanced Program-to-Program Communication (APPC LU6.2)
- A *Database Interface* using SQL
- A *Dialog Interface* based on the OS/2 Dialog Manager
- A *Language Environment Interface* (a common library of run-time services—storage management services, message handling services, date/time services, etc.) based on the Language Environment/370 product and intended for use by applications written in any of the SAA languages C, COBOL, FORTRAN, PL/I, or RPG
- A *Presentation Interface* similar to that provided by the OS/2 Presentation Manager
- A *Query Interface* based on Query Management Facility, QMF (see Chapter 20)
- A *Repository Interface* (part of the AD/Cycle framework—see Section 18.3)
- A *Resource Recovery Interface*, which supports two-phase commit (see Chapter 13) and thereby allows applications to issue COMMITs and ROLLBACKs that span multiple resource managers (spanning multiple sites also, in principal)

Note in particular that SQL is defined as the SAA database interface. IBM provides four SAA relational DBMSs that support SQL:

- IBM DATABASE 2 (DB2) for the MVS environment
- Structured Query Language/Data System (SQL/DS) for the VM (and VSE) environments
- Operating System/400 (OS/400) Database Manager (supporting SQL/400) for the AS/400 environment
- Operating System/2 (OS/2) Database Manager for the OS/2 environment*

DB2 is designed for both operational processing and end-user computing against large—possibly very large—centralized databases; SQL/DS, OS/400 Database Manager, and OS/2 Database Manager are intended for

---

*The OS/2 Database Manager was originally an integral component of OS/2 Extended Edition. With the release of OS/2 Version 2.0, however, the Database Manager and the OS/2 Communications Manager were removed from the operating system per se and packaged together as a separate product called *Extended Services*. Extended Services runs on both OS/2 Version 2.0 and OS/2 Version 1.3.

lower-volume operational processing and end-user computing against smaller databases, perhaps departmental or even personal databases.

Caveat: Although these products are all regarded as SAA relational DBMSs, it is only fair to point out that:

- None of the four supports everything in SAA SQL exactly as SAA prescribes—each has its own sanctioned deviations.

- With the possible exception of SQL/400, each of the four supports SQL features that are not in SAA and SQL features that are not supported by any of the other three.

- As a result, no two of the four support exactly the same SQL dialect.

The consequences of the foregoing for the objectives of compatibility, interoperability, etc., are (needless to say) a trifle unfortunate. The implication is that users need to be somewhat circumspect in their use of SQL if they wish to exploit the promise of SAA in this area.

18.3 AD/CYCLE

AD/Cycle provides a framework for managing the development and maintenance of applications throughout the entire development process. It consists of two major components (refer to Fig. 18.1):

- An *application development platform* containing a repository and associated interfaces and services

- *Application development tools* to support the complete range of application development activities, from modeling to maintenance

Application Development Platform

The application development platform consists of:

- A common *User Interface*, which allows development tools all to present the same style of interface to the application developer. This interface follows the Common User Access standards of SAA.

- *Workstation Services*, which allow OS/2 development workstations to work in a cooperative manner with host systems such as MVS. These services are provided by the OS/2 operating system.

- *Tool Services*, which support the installation, registration, and execution of AD/Cycle application development tools. These capabilities are included in Workstation Platform/2, which runs under OS/2.

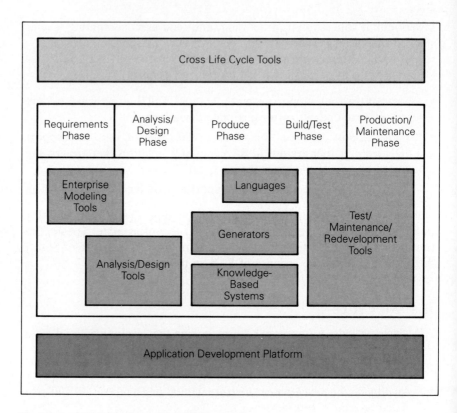

Fig. 18.1   AD/Cycle framework (after IBM)

- *Library Services*, which support library management, application regeneration, and so forth. These services are provided by the MVS-based ISPF/PDF Software Configuration and Library Manager working in conjunction with Workstation Platform/2.

- *Repository Services*, in the form of a repository manager to provide a single point of control for storing, accessing, and manipulating application specifications (known as "metadata"). IBM's Repository Manager/MVS provides these services in the MVS environment, with remote access from the OS/2 workstation environment. See below for further discussion.

- An *Application Development Information Model*, which defines the structure and format of repository metadata (again, see below for further discussion).

The main objective of the AD/Cycle repository is to act as a central database for the storing and maintenance of metadata by application development tools. These storage and maintenance functions are performed using supplied interfaces (e.g., the Repository Interface component of the SAA Common Programming Interface), which provide a consistent way for tools to manipulate information stored in the repository; the interfaces in question include interactive and batch interfaces on the host system* and an interactive OS/2 interface. Note that the metadata *cannot* be directly manipulated via SQL statements.

A key aspect of the repository is the *Application Development Information Model*, which defines standard formats for repository metadata (such as COBOL data structures, DB2 object definitions, data flow diagrams, etc.) and thus facilitates the sharing of that metadata among application development tools. That sharing in turn allows the tools to work together, and thus enables IBM and third-party vendors to build an integrated application development environment. The Application Development Information Model consists of an *enterprise modeling* portion, a *global submodel*, and a *technology* portion:

- The *enterprise modeling* portion provides constructs for modeling the activities and information of a business enterprise. It contains technology-independent process and data models, and supports the planning and analysis steps of the application life cycle.

- The *global submodel* provides common utility functions for use by other components of the information model.

- The *technology* portion contains the IMS DL/I, High Level Languages, Common Relational Database, and MVS Relational Database submodels. The Common Relational Database submodel supports information common to IBM's relational DBMSs, such as tables and columns. By contrast, the MVS Relational Database submodel supports objects that are specific to DB2, such as table spaces and storage groups.

Caveat: Of course, metadata can be shared only if the tools that use the repository do indeed adhere to the information model. It will take time for that model to develop to a level that can completely subsume the existing models used by the various application development tools already in existence; moreover, it will also take time for vendors to modify their products to support the repository and information model fully.

---

*I.e., the system where the repository manager executes. As already mentioned, that system must currently be MVS (the metadata is stored using DB2). Future versions of the repository manager will run in the VM and OS/400 environments.

Application Development Tools

The AD/Cycle application development tools are intended for use by DP professionals rather than end-users. The tools are grouped into categories according to the type of development activity they support; some are supplied directly by IBM, others are supplied by one or other of IBM's "International Alliance Partners" working in collaboration with IBM. These partners also assist IBM in the overall development of the AD/Cycle framework—for example, by helping to define the information model. At the time of writing the partners are:

- Bachman Information Systems, Inc.
- Digitalk, Inc.
- Easel Corporation
- INTERSOLV, Inc.
- KnowledgeWare, Inc.
- Micro Focus Limited
- Synon Corporation
- Systematica Limited

We give below a brief summary of the AD/Cycle tool categories, together with a few examples of IBM and International Alliance Partner products within each one:

- *Cross life cycle tools*, such as project management and documentation tools, that span the multiple phases of application development. *Example*: IBM Application Development Project Support (ADSP).
- *Enterprise modeling tools* for defining an enterprise business model of data and processes. *Examples*: IBM DevelopMate, BACHMAN/ Analyst, KnowledgeWare ADW/Planning Workstation and ADW/ Rapid Application Development Workstation, INTERSOLV Excelerator II.
- *Analysis and design tools* for supporting requirements analysis and database and application design. *Examples*: BACHMAN/DBA, BACHMAN/Designer for CSP, EASEL Workbench, KnowledgeWare ADW/Analysis Workstation and ADW/Design Workstation, INTERSOLV Excelerator II.
- *Languages* for developing and debugging third-generation language (3GL) programs. *Examples*: IBM Language Environment/370, IBM Cooperative Development Environment/370, Micro Focus COBOL/2 Workbench.

- *Generators* for developing and generating applications using higher-level languages. *Examples*: IBM Cross System Product (CSP), Digitalk Smalltalk/V, EASEL Workbench, KnowledgeWare ADW/CSP Enablement Facility, SYNON CSP Enablement Facility, SYNON/2E for OS/400, SYNON/2G for OS/2. *Note*: CSP (IBM's main generator product) is an application development system for building MVS (TSO, CICS, IMS, batch) and OS/2 applications. It provides an integrated environment for screen development, application coding, application testing and debugging, etc. CSP applications can process data stored in DB2, OS/2 Database Manager, and IMS databases, also in VSAM files. CSP is discussed in detail in Chapter 19.*

- *Knowledge-based systems* for developing applications using expert systems technology. *Example*: The Integrated Reasoning Shell (TIRS) from IBM.

- *Test, maintenance, and redevelopment tools* for building, testing, and maintaining applications. *Examples*: IBM ISPF/PDF Software Configuration and Library Manager, IBM Workstation Interactive Test Tool, IBM Software Analysis Test Tool, INTERSOLV Design Recovery Series and PVCS Series.

18.4 INFORMATION WAREHOUSE

The Information Warehouse provides a framework for delivering enterprise-wide (i.e., corporate) data to so-called "knowledge" or "information" workers, i.e., end-users who need such data to manage the day-to-day operation of the business. The framework involves three major components (refer to Fig. 18.2):

- *Enterprise Data*: Database products (e.g., DB2, SQL/DS, IMS) for managing the data stored in the warehouse

- *Data Delivery*: SQL interfaces to relational and nonrelational data, and tools for copying and moving data between warehouse files and databases

- *Decision Support Systems*: End-user tools for accessing, manipulating, and analyzing warehouse data

---

*The CSP environments mentioned in this paragraph are those that apply to the most recent version of CSP. Earlier versions supported additional environments, such as VM and VSE. Presumably the new version will be extended to support additional environments in the future.

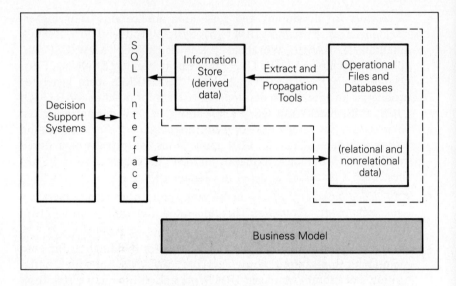

Fig. 18.2   Information Warehouse framework

Enterprise Data

Warehouse data may consist of operational data stored in existing data-bases and files, or data that has been copied from such operational data-bases and files into an enterprise-level "information store," or a mixture of the two. Whichever it may be—i.e., regardless of where the data may actually reside—the objective of the Information Warehouse is to provide uniform and transparent SQL-style access to that data (where by "transpar-ent" we mean that the user should not have to know where and how the data is physically stored).

Giving information workers direct access to operational data raises sev-eral issues. The main one is that a significant percentage of operational data today still resides in nonrelational databases and files. Providing a compatible and well-performing SQL interface to such data is no mean feat, even if the databases and files are well designed, which often they are not. Furthermore, nonrelational data is often not in a suitable form for access by end-users—it tends to involve such things as encoded values, un-concealed system control information, overlapping fields, anonymous fields, mixed record types, etc., etc. If we consider this issue together with the operational problems posed by direct end-user access to operational data (e.g., performance impact on operational systems, the need for end-users to access consistent data that is not being constantly updated), we see that the idea of copying the data over to a separate information store does have a number of attractions:

- The data can be "cleaned up" before it is placed in the store.

- Likewise, it can be summarized and otherwise refined during the copying process.

- It can represent a consistent snapshot of the operational data.

- It can be stored in relational form for easier SQL access.

The disadvantages of the separate information store are the additional processing power and disk storage required, and the problem of keeping the store up to date.

Data Delivery

There are two aspects to data delivery:

- A common SQL *Application Program Interface* (API) to enterprise data

- *Tools* for moving and copying data between files and databases in the warehouse

We discuss each of these in turn. First, the SQL API. The objective of this API is to provide developers of decision support tools with a common SQL interface to warehouse data. One very important aspect of this interface—given the fact that warehouse data can reside "anywhere"—is the ability to access remote data; e.g., the tool might typically run on an OS/2 workstation and access data managed by DB2 running on MVS. IBM's direction for providing such remote access to relational data is based on the use of SQL in conjunction with DRDA, IBM's Distributed Relational Data Architecture, introduced in Chapter 17 and further discussed in Section 18.5 below. *Note*: That further discussion logically belongs in the present section, but is lengthy enough to deserve a section of its own (it would unduly interfere with the overall flow of the presentation if we included it at this juncture).

In addition to the foregoing—i.e., the IBM direction, based on DRDA—the Information Warehouse framework already includes a product from Information Builders Inc. (IBI) called Enterprise Data Access/SQL (EDA/SQL), which provides SQL access, possibly remote, to both relational and nonrelational data. We defer detailed discussion of EDA/SQL (for reasons of length once again), this time to Section 18.6.

Turning now to the tools: The purpose of the tools, to repeat, is to support the moving and copying of data between files and databases in the warehouse. IBM provides two products for performing these functions:

- *Data Extract* (DXT): DXT allows data to be extracted from relational and nonrelational databases and files and copied into DB2 and SQL/DS tables. It has two separate features, the *Relational Data Extract Feature* for extracting data from DB2 and SQL/DS databases, and the *General Data Extract Feature* for extracting data from IMS databases, VSAM and sequential files, and other data sources. DXT also works in conjunction with another product, DXT/D1, to copy data from DEC systems to IBM systems. DXT is covered in more detail in Chapter 20.

- *Data Propagator* (DPROP): DPROP supports *data propagation* between IMS and DB2 databases. The objective of propagation is to maintain consistency between the two databases, so that as changes are made to one they are reflected in the other. DPROP supports *synchronous* and *asynchronous* propagation. With synchronous propagation, IMS update transactions cannot complete until both the IMS and DB2 copies of the updated data have been committed. With asynchronous propagation, changes made to IMS data are passed to user-written programs to allow them to be saved for later application to the corresponding DB2 data by DPROP. DPROP is also covered in more detail in Chapter 20.

Decision Support Systems

Decision support systems are end-user tools for performing ad hoc query, report writing, spreadsheet analysis, graphical display, and other similar functions against warehouse data. IBM provides several tools in this area—for example:

- *Data Interpretation System* (DIS): DIS (developed by Metaphor Computer Systems, which is now owned by IBM) lets end-users develop and run OS/2 applications that access, analyze, and display data stored in DB2, SQL/DS, OS/400 Database Manager, and OS/2 Database Manager databases. The product employs graphics and icon-based interfaces and requires few computer skills on the part of the user.

- *Query Management Facility* (QMF): QMF is an MVS- and VM-based query tool for both DB2 and SQL/DS. It allows end-users to enter SQL queries to produce a variety of reports and graphs from the results of those queries. QMF is discussed in more detail in Chapter 20.

- *Personal Application System* (PAS) and *Application System* (AS): PAS allows OS/2 workstation users to query, report, and display data stored in PAS files and OS/2 Database Manager databases. Data can be imported into PAS from dBASE and other common PC file formats and (via the host-based AS product) from DB2 and SQL/DS databases. Optional statistics and application development features are also available. AS is a host-based version of PAS, providing analogous capabilities for VM and MVS users; it supports AS files and DB2 and SQL/DS databases.

- *SAA LanguageAccess*: This product is an MVS- and VM-based natural language query processor for querying and reporting on data stored in DB2 and SQL/DS databases. It consists of three components:

1. *Natural Language Engine* (NLE), which accepts natural language queries and translates them into SQL statements for execution. At the time of writing NLE supports the English and German languages.

2. *Query Interface*, which allows QMF and AS users to employ LanguageAccess to retrieve data from DB2 and SQL/DS tables and use the report writing and display capabilities of QMF and AS for data presentation.

3. *Customization Tool*, which is used to create a conceptual model of the database and to add application-specific terms to the LanguageAccess vocabulary. This product runs under OS/2 and uses cooperative processing to communicate with MVS and VM systems.

Summary

In addition to the IBM products discussed above, many third-party vendors tools have also been announced that will support the Information Warehouse framework. But then again, any end-user tool that can access an IBM database or file system could claim to fit into this framework, and the reader might justifiably feel that, apart from DRDA and EDA/SQL (see the next two sections), there is nothing really new here; after all, we have been querying and copying data for many years.

The important message is, perhaps, that vendors are now beginning to realize the need customers have for information, and to understand that they must therefore provide tools and services to make that information available in forms suitable for use as a basis for managing the business. Indeed, the original idea for the Information Warehouse arose from exactly such a need within IBM Ireland (see B. A. Devlin and P. T. Murphy, "An Architecture for a Business and Information System," *IBM Systems Journal 27*, No. 1, 1988).

One key aspect of the Information Warehouse is that IBM is encouraging customers to document the data they already have, and to determine the information that knowledge workers need to be effective in their jobs. To this end, IBM has established an International Alliance Partnership with Bachman Information Systems, Inc. to provide technology and tools to allow users to develop a model of available data and the processes the business is interested in. This model can be built top down using tools such as BACHMAN/Analyst, or bottom up using tools that capture information about existing data such as the BACHMAN/DA Capture products.

It is important for users to establish rules and procedures (sometimes called an "information architecture") for controlling the flow of business data within the organization, and to put in place tools that can turn that data into information for managing the business. The Information Warehouse provides a basis for implementing such an "architecture."

18.5   DISTRIBUTED RELATIONAL DATA ARCHITECTURE

We saw in Section 18.4 that the vehicle by which IBM intends to provide access to remote data within the Information Warehouse framework is DRDA ("Distributed Relational Data Architecture"). DRDA can be characterized as a set of Formats and Protocols (FAPs) that a tool vendor (or anyone else, for that matter) can use to issue SQL statements against a remote database server—provided, of course, that the remote server in question understands those FAPs, i.e., is a "DRDA server." As we saw in Chapter 17, IBM's DB2, SQL/DS, and SQL/400 products can all act as DRDA servers.

Recall from Chapter 17 that access to a DRDA server involves communication between two programs, the DRDA server itself, referred to in this context as the *application server*, and the requesting program, referred to as the *application requester*. The application requester accepts SQL statements through an API, formats them into DRDA messages, and sends them to the DRDA server. Now, writing an application requester is a complex task, in general; as explained in Chapter 17, however, a prebuilt application requester for the OS/2 environment is provided in IBM's Distributed Database Connection Services/2 (DDCS/2) product, which allows DOS, DOS Windows, and OS/2 applications to issue SQL statements against DRDA servers such as DB2.

Many third-party tool and DBMS vendors already supply their own SQL interface and proprietary FAPs for accessing DB2 from remote applications. Examples include:

- Apple Data Access Language (DAL)
- ASK/Ingres DB2 Gateway
- DEC RdbAccess
- Gupta SQLNetwork
- Microsoft/Micro Decisionware Database Gateway
- Oracle SQL*CONNECT for DB2
- Sybase Open Server for CICS and Open Gateway for DB2

It is likely that these products will be extended over the next few years to include DRDA support. There are, however, several distinct ways in which such support might be provided:

1. The vendor's tools could support the SQL API to the DDCS/2 application requester. This option would allow the tools to access DRDA-supported servers such as DB2. This option represents the simplest and easiest level of support.
2. The vendor could develop an application requester that talks directly to IBM DRDA servers.
3. The vendor DBMS could add DRDA support to its DBMS product to allow it to act as a DRDA application server.

We are likely to see various combinations of these possibilities supported by third-party vendors over the next few years.

18.6 ENTERPRISE DATA ACCESS/SQL

As explained in Section 18.4, IBI's Enterprise Data Access/SQL product (or product set, rather), EDA/SQL, provides local or remote access to any combination of relational and nonrelational data. (Access to nonrelational data is currently read-only, however.) At the time of writing, several vendors, including Easel Corporation, ParcPlace Systems, and Software Publishing Corporation, have announced EDA/SQL support—i.e., products (end-user and application development tools) that will run on top of EDA/SQL.

EDA/SQL consists of the following components (refer to Fig. 18.3):

- *EDA/SQL Servers*: An EDA/SQL Server receives SQL requests from applications and passes them to an EDA/Data Driver (described below) for execution against the target relational database. If the target is not relational, the SQL request is passed through the *Universal SQL Trans-*

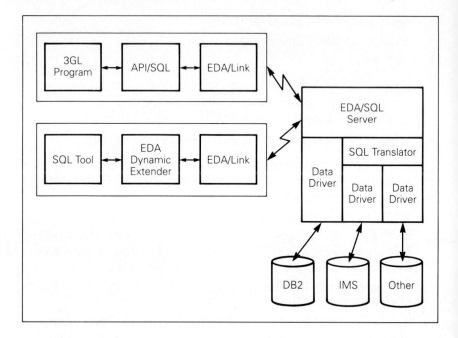

Fig. 18.3 EDA/SQL

lator, which maps the request into the data manipulation language of the target file or database. If the original request involves data from different databases (if, for example, it joins a DB2 table to an IMS "table"), the necessary merging of result data is done by the Server. IBI provides Servers for several environments, including (at the time of writing) IBM MVS, VM, OS/2, and AIX.

- *EDA/Data Drivers*: Each EDA/Data Driver runs under the control of an EDA/SQL Server. EDA/Data Drivers are used to access data from underlying files and databases. IBI provides Drivers for over 40 file and database types, including ADABAS, DB2, IDMS/R, IMS, ORACLE, SQL/DS, SYBASE, and VSAM.

- *API/SQL*: Provides a call-level API that allows 3GL programs to issue SQL statements for execution by an EDA/SQL Server. If the target data is not relational, the SQL statements in question must be "ANSI Level 1 compliant" and read-only;* otherwise, they can be any SQL

---

*"ANSI Level 1 compliant" means that the statements must conform to the "lowest common denominator" level of the official (ANSI) SQL standard. For more information, see C. J. Date, *A Guide to the SQL Standard* (2nd edition, Addison-Wesley, 1989).

statement supported by the target DBMS. IBI provides API/SQL support for several environments, including MVS, VM, OS/400, OS/2, AIX, and Apple Macintosh.

- *Dynamic Extenders*: These components allow existing tools and applications to use EDA/SQL Servers and Data Drivers. An Extender intercepts data requests from a tool or application, converts them to API/SQL, and passes them to an EDA/Server for execution. IBI provides Extenders for DB2, OS/2 Database Manager, Lotus 1-2-3, Apple Hypercard XCMDS, etc. For example, the DB2 Extender allows products such as IBM's Query Management Facility (QMF) to access nonIBM files and databases. (Note, however, that the DB2 Extender is a DB2 application and thus requires DB2 to run. Note too that it supports dynamic SQL only; that is, an existing DB2 tool and application will be able to access nonDB2 data via the DB2 Extender only if it uses dynamic SQL for such access, not static SQL.)

- *EDA/Link*: Provides the Formats and Protocols (FAPs) that allow API/SQL clients to communicate with EDA/SQL Servers. The FAPs are proprietary and (at the time of writing) do not support DRDA. Protocols supported include LU0, LU2, LU6.2, TCP/IP, and DECnet.

In summary, EDA/SQL's key advantage lies in its ability to provide SQL access to nonrelational data (which DRDA does not, of course). The issue here is that providing such access is not a simple matter.* Also, as we said earlier, it is at least debatable whether users should access operational data directly anyway. Our view is that a separate information store may frequently be a better approach.

---

*In fact, at the 100 percent level it is impossible. See the paper "Why Is It So Difficult to Provide a Relational Interface to IMS?" in C. J. Date, *Relational Database: Selected Writings* (Addison-Wesley, 1986).

· **19** ·

AD/Cycle Tools

19.1 INTRODUCTION

We discussed in Section 18.3 how AD/Cycle provides a framework for developing and maintaining applications throughout the entire development process. In this chapter we concentrate on AD/Cycle tools (principally IBM's own product CSP) that can be used to build DB2 applications. Such applications generally fall into two broad categories:

- Centralized MVS/DB2 applications that run completely on the mainframe under the control of CICS, IMS, or TSO.

- Distributed processing applications that run partly on the mainframe under MVS and partly on a desktop computer under DOS or OS/2.

Most high-volume operational applications will fall into the first category—i.e., they will be DB2-only applications, running on the mainframe. However, less performance-critical applications can take advantage of distributed (or "cooperative") processing technology and desktop computers.

For example, the mainframe component of a distributed processing application could be used to access corporate data stored in DB2 databases, and the desktop component could be used to provide a graphical user interface (GUI) to the end-user. GUIs are more user-friendly than the interfaces typically provided by centralized terminal-driven applications. Interaction between the desktop and mainframe components of a distributed processing application is supported by products such as CICS OS/2, which allows a DOS or OS/2 application written in C or COBOL to communicate with a CICS mainframe application. The desktop end-user interface in this case could use DOS Windows or OS/2 Presentation Manager and could be developed by third-party tools, such as the EASEL Workbench or Digitalk Smalltalk/V, that work in conjunction with CICS OS/2.

There are numerous tools that support the development of DB2 applications, and a detailed discussion of all of those tools is clearly beyond the scope of this book. We will instead restrict ourselves to a look at one of IBM's main development tools in this area, Cross System Product (CSP). Section 19.2 provides a brief overview of CSP, and subsequent sections look at the process of application development under CSP.

19.2 CSP OVERVIEW

CSP consists of a set of DP professional tools for application development and execution. It is called *Cross System* Product because it permits applications to be developed in one environment for execution in another; for example, a CSP DB2 application can be developed on the desktop under OS/2, and executed under CICS MVS.

CSP is really several products, not just one:

- Cross System Product/370 Application Development (CSP/370AD), which runs under MVS (CICS or TSO)

- Cross System Product/2 Application Development (CSP/2AD), which runs under OS/2

- Cross System Product/370 Runtime Services (CSP/370RS), which runs under MVS (CICS, IMS, TSO, or batch)

- Cross System Product/2 Runtime Services (CSP/2RS), which runs under OS/2 (CICS)

CSP applications are developed and tested interactively using CSP/370AD or CSP/2AD (see Fig. 19.1). During development, the applications—more accurately, the application *specifications*—are stored as members of a VSAM data set called the *Member Specification Library* (MSL), which can be thought of as a data dictionary for CSP. When the application

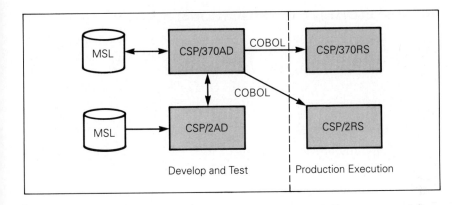

Fig. 19.1 CSP structure

has been fully developed, tested, and debugged, it is *generated* as a COBOL program using CSP/370AD. It can then be executed under CSP/370RS or CSP/2RS. *Note*: Cooperative processing applications, where part of the application runs under CICS OS/2 and part under CICS MVS, can also be developed and executed using CSP.

Application specifications can also be created outside the CSP environment using third-party development tools and then imported into the MSL using a special IBM file format known as *External Source Format* (ESF). Several third-party application development products generate ESF files. CSP will also generate ESF files for export to other products.

CSP applications can access a variety of different databases and files—DB2 and OS/2 Database Manager databases, IMS databases, VSAM files, and so forth. In this chapter, of course, we concentrate on the use of CSP/370AD to build applications that access DB2 data.

Note: The foregoing sketch of the way CSP works is based on the most recent version of CSP/370AD (viz., Version 4). IBM still markets an earlier version (CSP/AD Version 3) that generates applications for use under *CSP/Application Execution* (CSP/AE Version 3). CSP/AE applications run as CSP interpretive applications (i.e., not as COBOL applications) under MVS (CICS, TSO, or batch), VSE (CICS or batch) VM, OS/400, OS/2, and DOS. Thus, applications developed using CSP/AD Version 3 can be executed in any SAA environment. IBM's intention is to replace CSP/AE by runtime service products like CSP/370RS that execute COBOL programs. In the VM environment this will be achieved using CSP/370RS, and in the OS/400 environment it will be done by Synon Corporation products that accept ESF files generated by CSP.

19.3   DEVELOPING CSP APPLICATIONS

CSP applications are built and tested using CSP/370AD (under MVS) or CSP/2AD (under OS/2). In this chapter we concentrate on the MVS case, but most of the discussion applies equally well to OS/2 (except of course that the OS/2 product CSP/2AD uses GUI screen formats rather than the 3270 screen formats used with CSP/370AD). For simplicity, we will abbreviate "CSP/370AD" to just "CSP/AD" for the remainder of the chapter.

Fig. 19.2 illustrates the main components of a CSP application, namely record, map, and process definitions. *Note*: Each component has its own name and is stored as a separate member in the Member Specification Library.

- *Record definitions* specify the data to be retrieved and manipulated by the application. A record definition for processing DB2 data consists of fields (columns) from one or more DB2 tables and is defined using CSP/AD's Record Definition screens. Existing DB2 definitions (for

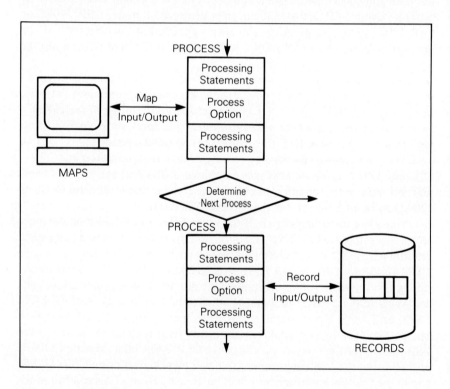

Fig. 19.2 CSP application components

both base tables and views) can be retrieved from the DB2 catalog to help with the record definition process.

- *Map definitions* specify the screen and printer formats to be used by the application. The CSP/AD *screen painter* provides a set of Map Definition screens for defining such formats and for defining data "edit rules." Edit rules are used to validate data entered by the application user or to format data displayed to the application user (such data will be entered or displayed at execution time via the maps). For example, we might define a rule to verify that any value entered for a shipment quantity is greater than 99 (say).

- *Process definitions* specify the application processing logic. Among other things, they control the display of maps and the reading and writing of records. Processes are defined by means of the CSP/AD Application Definition and Application Process Definition screens. A process definition consists of:

  - A *process option*, which specifies the major task (data access or map display) to be performed by the process, and

  - A set of *processing statements*, which perform computations, control the execution flow from one process to the next, etc.

  CSP/AD provides several process options for operating on DB2 data (most of which correspond to SQL operations in a fairly obvious manner). It also provides a wide range of processing statements.

Once the application definition is complete, testing can begin. When the application has been fully tested and debugged, it can be generated as a COBOL application for execution under CSP Runtime Services.

We have now summarized all of the major tasks involved in developing CSP applications. We now proceed to give some indication as to what is involved in using CSP to build a SHIPMENT application that will use the suppliers-and-parts database to display information about shipments for a given supplier. The input to the application is a supplier number; the output consists of the supplier number and city, plus part number, part city, and shipment quantity for all parts supplied by that supplier. We begin by examining the record definition for this application (Section 19.4 immediately following).

19.4 CSP RECORD DEFINITION

CSP application specifications are created using a series of interactive screens that allow the developer to define the various components—records, maps, and processes—that go to make up a CSP application. The

normal procedure is to define the records first, then the maps, and finally
the processes.

The process of creating a CSP application starts with the CSP/AD Definition screen (not illustrated), which permits us to invoke specific screens
to define records, maps, processes, and so forth. Selecting the "Record"
option, and entering a name, say SHIPREC, on this screen leads us to the
CSP Record Definition screen shown in Fig. 19.3.

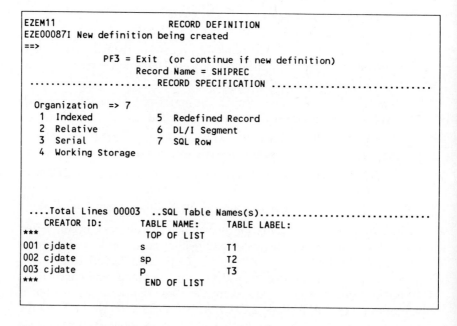

```
EZEM11                    RECORD DEFINITION
EZE00087I New definition being created
==>
              PF3 = Exit  (or continue if new definition)
                   Record Name = SHIPREC
 .................... RECORD SPECIFICATION ............................

  Organization  => 7
   1  Indexed          5  Redefined Record
   2  Relative         6  DL/I Segment
   3  Serial           7  SQL Row
   4  Working Storage




  ....Total Lines 00003  ..SQL Table Names(s)...........................
     CREATOR ID:      TABLE NAME:    TABLE LABEL:
 ***                  TOP OF LIST
 001 cjdate           s              T1
 002 cjdate           sp             T2
 003 cjdate           p              T3
 ***                  END OF LIST
```

Fig. 19.3 Sample CSP/AD Record Definition screen

Note: CSP/AD screens are usually divided into a *fixed area* and a
scrollable area (though not all screens have both). Generally speaking, the
fixed area is used to respond to CSP/AD prompts, and the scrollable area
(from "TOP OF LIST" to "END OF LIST") is used for entering record,
map, and process definitions (etc.). The CSP/AD editor supports standard
line-oriented editing commands for editing text within this latter area. The

editor is context-sensitive, in that it recognizes invalid processing statements, unclosed IF statements, etc.

As indicated at the end of the previous section, the SHIPMENT application needs data from all three of the database tables S, SP, and P (S#, P#, and QTY from SP, S.CITY from S, and P.CITY from P). On the Record Definition screen, therefore, we specify the "SQL Row" option, and enter the qualified names of these three tables (owner name plus table name) in the scrollable area created by selecting that option. The *labels* T1, T2, and T3 are generated automatically by CSP/AD; references to the tables on subsequent screens (e.g., in generated SQL statements) will use these unique labels instead of the qualified names. From the record definition, CSP/AD builds a set of default SQL statements for accessing the required data.

Once the required tables have been specified via the Record Definition screen, CSP/AD displays the SQL Row Definition screen (Fig. 19.4). This screen allows the developer to indicate which specific columns of those tables are needed. Most of the information displayed on this screen is ob-

```
EZEM15                    SQL ROW DEFINITION

==>
 PF3 = Exit     PF4 = SQL Compare
 Record Name = SHIPREC                Default Scope = GLOBAL
Total lines 0012 ........ DATA ITEM DEFINITION ...........................

    NAME       TYPE  LENGTH DEC BYTES  READ KEY SCOPE   SQL COLUMN NAME
                                       ONLY
***                       TOP OF LIST
-> S#          CHA   00005      00005  YES  NO  GLOBAL  T1.S#
d> SNAME       CHA   00020      00020  YES  NO  GLOBAL  T1.SNAME
d> STATUS      BIN   00004      00002  YES  NO  GLOBAL  T1.STATUS
-> scity       CHA   00015      00015  YES  NO  GLOBAL  T1.CITY
d> S#          CHA   00005      00005  YES  NO  GLOBAL  T2.S#
d> P#          CHA   00005      00005  YES  NO  GLOBAL  T2.P#
-> QTY         BIN   00009      00004  YES  NO  GLOBAL  T2.QTY
-> P#          CHA   00006      00006  YES  NO  GLOBAL  T3.P#
d> PNAME       CHA   00020      00020  YES  NO  GLOBAL  T3.PNAME
d> COLOR       CHA   00006      00006  YES  NO  GLOBAL  T3.COLOR
d> WEIGHT      BIN   00004      00002  YES  NO  GLOBAL  T3.WEIGHT
-> pcity       CHA   00015      00015  YES  NO  GLOBAL  T3.CITY
***                       END OF LIST
```

Fig. 19.4 CSP/AD SQL Row Definition screen

tained by CSP from the DB2 catalog. The READ ONLY specification is set to YES for every column, because multiple tables are involved—SHIPREC involves a join—and DB2 does not permit joins to be updated. *Note*: CSP/AD automatically creates a set of host variables with the same names as the DB2 columns (S#, SNAME, etc.). These variables are used in (e.g.) INTO clauses in generated SQL SELECT statements.

The following editing has been performed in Fig. 19.4:

- The line editor command "d" ("delete") has been used to remove the columns not required for SHIPREC.

- The column names for S.CITY and P.CITY have been changed to SCITY and PCITY, respectively, to avoid ambiguity.

The developer is free to make other changes on the Row Definition screen—columns can be added or deleted, column definitions can be modified, and so forth. To ensure that everything matches the appropriate DB2 definitions, PF key 4 can be pressed to request a comparison with the DB2 catalog entries. Any discrepancies found will be displayed on a separate screen.

Finally, CSP/AD needs to know the SQL SELECT statement to be used to retrieve SHIPREC data from the database. This information is specified by means of the *SQL Row Record Definition* screen (see Fig. 19.5). CSP/AD generates a candidate SQL statement automatically, with appropriate SELECT and FROM clauses; if SHIPREC had been drawn from a single underlying table, CSP/AD would also generate an appropriate WHERE clause. As it is, however, SHIPREC involves a join, and therefore we must enter the WHERE condition (the *selection condition*) explicitly. In the example, we have specified the "obvious" join of tables S, SP, and P over supplier numbers and part numbers.

19.5 CSP MAP DEFINITION

Note: Maps in CSP have little to do with DB2 per se—they are concerned with operations on the terminal, not operations on the database. We therefore present only a very brief overview of the map definition process.

Maps provide the medium of communication between the CSP application and the user of that application (i.e., the end-user). They permit:

- The application to display information to the end-user (typically information retrieved from the database), and

- The end-user to submit information to the application (typically information to be used for updating the database or for controlling retrieval from the database).

```
EZEM16                   SQL ROW RECORD DEFINITION
EZE006421 SQL syntax check has completed successfully
==>
 PF3 = File and exit PF4 = Reset to default statement PF5 = SQL syntax check
 Record  = SHIPREC
                                              Modified clause = YES
Total lines 0011 .... DEFAULT SELECTION CONDITIONS DEFINITION ..............

***                      TOP OF LIST
*** SELECT
***    T1.S#, T1.CITY,
***    T2.QTY,
***    T3.P#, T3.CITY
*** FROM
***    cjdate.s T1,
***    cjdate.sp T2,
***    cjdate.p T3
*** WHERE
010    t1.s# = t2.s# and
011    t2.p# = t3.p#
***                      END OF LIST
```

Fig. 19.5 CSP/AD SQL Row Record Definition screen

All the maps used in a given application are considered to belong to the same *mapgroup*. We will assume that the maps in our SHIPMENT example are called SHIP001, SHIP002, etc., and that together they constitute a mapgroup called SHIP. SHIP001 will be used to request a supplier number from the user; SHIP002 will be used to display corresponding output information back to the user. Let us consider what is involved in defining one of these maps, say SHIP002. We go through the following steps:

- Starting with the CSP/AD Definition screen, we select the "MAP" option, specifying mapgroup SHIP and map SHIP002.

- We define the device or devices to be used to display the map on the *Map Definition-Device Selection* screen (not illustrated).

- We define the size of the map and its position on the display using the *Map Definition-Map Specification* screen (not illustrated).

- We use a series of *Map Definition* screens to define the map appearance, map variables, and associated edit rules (if any). The rest of this section describes the use of these Map Definition screens in more detail. For the sake of the example, we assume that the map we are defining (SHIP002) is to appear as shown in Fig. 19.6.

```
                      Shipment Information


       Supplier:                      Supplier City:

       Part:                          Part City:

       Quantity:
```

Fig. 19.6 Map SHIP002

To define the SHIP002 layout, we use the CSP/AD screen painter and
the Map Definition screen shown in Fig. 19.7. *Note*: The fields that make
up a map are divided into constant fields and variable fields. Constant
fields contain fixed text data; variable fields contain data that can be modified by the user or by the application. Fields are delimited in the map definition by special code or attribute bytes, which indicate properties of the field
such as color, brightness, whether constant or variable, etc.
    We explain Fig. 19.7 as follows.

- The application developer has entered the values for constant fields (the
  "Shipment Information" heading, etc.) and has used the "#" code to
  mark the position of those fields.

- The developer has also used the "¬" code (represented in the figure
  by a tilde, "~") to mark the position of variable fields (to be used for
  data entry and display).

    A code of "/" can also be used to left- or right-justify or center text
on the map. Various screen painter commands can be entered on the sub-

```
EZEM22                      MAP DEFINITION

==>
                  PF3 = Exit (or continue if new definition)
Total positions 079      Map Name = SHIP SHIP002      Positions 001 to 079
Total lines    024 ...       C(#) V(~) S(/)      ... Lines    001 to 014



                  #Shipment Information


     #Supplier:~      #              #Supplier City:~            #

     #Part:    ~      #                #Part City:~              #

     #Quantity: ~     #

   ~
                                                                    #



```

Fig. 19.7 CSP/AD Map Definition: using the screen painter

command line (Line 3 on the screen) to specify field attributes (color, protection, brightness, etc.), field positioning, text copying and modification, and so forth. For example, the screen painter command TEST displays the current version of the map as it would appear during execution.

Having defined the map layout, the developer must now specify names for the variable fields so that they can be referenced from within the application (see Fig. 19.8). CSP/AD automatically numbers each variable field and displays an area for the developer to assign names corresponding to those numbers. In our example, we have specified field names MSNO, MSCITY, . . ., and MQTY (respectively) for the five variable fields labeled Supplier, Supplier City, . . ., and Quantity on the map. The sixth field, EZEMSG, allows the application to display messages to the application user.

Finally, the developer can specify edit rules for variable fields, using other CSP Map Definition screens. Such rules are used to constrain the set of values that can legally be entered by the end-user and to control the format of values that are displayed to the end-user. A discussion of the edit rule options is beyond the scope of this chapter.

```
EZEM24                       MAP DEFINITION

==>
                 PF3 = Exit (or continue if new definition)
0001 <= Number of first field to name          Map Name = SHIP SHIP002
...................... VARIABLE FIELD NAMING ..........................
        NAME                      NAME                      NAME
    1  MSNO                   2  MSCITY                 3  MPNO
    4  MPCITY                 5  MQTY                   6  EZEMSG

Total positions 079                            Positions 001 to 079
Total lines     024 ........................... Lines     007 to 014
    Supplier: 1                    Supplier City: 2

    Part:    3                     Part City: 4

    Quantity: 5


6
```

Fig. 19.8   CSP/AD Map Definition: variable field naming

19.6 CSP PROCESS DEFINITION

As explained in Section 19.2, a CSP application contains one or more named processes (refer to Fig. 19.9). The processes define the processing logic for the application. Processing logic involves displaying maps, reading and writing database data, performing computational operations, etc. A process consists of:

- A single *process option*, which performs some specific task, typically involving a CSP record (database access) or a CSP map (terminal I/O), together with

- Zero or more *processing statements*, which perform various computational or flow-of-control functions.

   Processing statements can appear *before* or *after* a process option (or both) and/or in a *flow section*. Statements appearing before the process option are typically used to clear fields on a map, or to specify data to be read from the database. Statements appearing after the process option are typically used to check data entered by the user, or to check return codes after performing database access. Statements appearing in a flow section

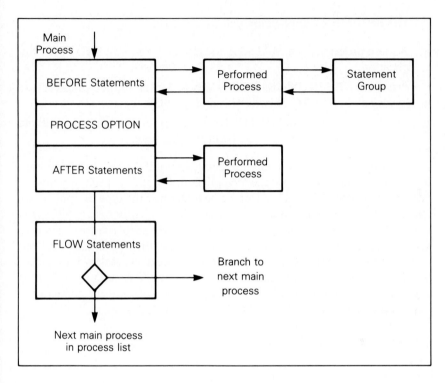

Fig. 19.9 Application process structure

are used to control the execution flow between the main processes of an application. *Note*: A main process can also invoke other processes by means of the PERFORM statement (see Fig. 19.9); a PERFORMed process can include BEFORE and AFTER statements, but no FLOW statements.

Processing statements can also be used to build common subroutines called *statement groups*. A statement group is invoked simply by specifying its name. Statement groups do not contain a process option.

In order to give some idea as to what is involved in process definition, let us first assume that the logical structure of our SHIPMENT application is as indicated by the following pseudocode:

```
do initialization ;
get supplier number from user using map SHIP001 ;
set up for database read loop ;
do until no more SHIPREC records for this supplier ;
   retrieve next SHIPREC record from database ;
   display SHIPREC record using map SHIP002;
end ;
```

The SHIPMENT application will use:

- A main process called MAIN001 to control the overall logic of the application;
- Processes GETSNUM and DISPDATA to get the supplier number and to display SHIPREC records at the terminal;
- Processes READIT and GETNEXT to set up for the database read and to read the SHIPREC records from the database.

As usual, the starting point for definition is the CSP/AD Definition screen. This time, we choose the "Application" option, specifying the application name SHIPMENT. After we have defined the type of application we are building (batch or online, for example), the *Application Definition* screen shown in Fig. 19.10 will be displayed. We then use this screen to define the main processes (known as the *process list*) for the application. The process list contains the name of each process, its processing option, the CSP map or record ("object") to be used by the processing option (if any), and a description of what the process does. We enter the name of the single main process, MAIN001, which will be invoked using the EXECUTE

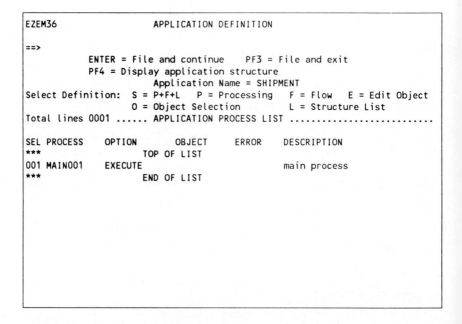

```
EZEM36                    APPLICATION DEFINITION

==>
             ENTER = File and continue     PF3 = File and exit
             PF4 = Display application structure
                    Application Name = SHIPMENT
Select Definition:  S = P+F+L    P = Processing    F = Flow   E = Edit Object
                    O = Object Selection          L = Structure List
Total lines 0001 ...... APPLICATION PROCESS LIST .........................

SEL PROCESS     OPTION      OBJECT     ERROR     DESCRIPTION
***                     TOP OF LIST
001 MAIN001     EXECUTE                          main process
***                     END OF LIST
```

Fig. 19.10 CSP/AD Application Definition screen

processing option. No object name is entered because MAIN001 does not use any CSP maps or records.

We can now enter the "s" Select Definition option on line 001 under the SEL column to display screens for entering the BEFORE, AFTER, and FLOW processing statements for MAIN001. After we have defined these statements (see the subsection "Processing Statements" below for the details), we use the "l" option to display the *Structure List* screen shown in Fig. 19.11. This screen shows the structure of SHIPMENT as defined so far. It shows that MAIN001 invokes the lower level ("LVL 002") processes GETSNUM, READIT, GETNEXT, and DISPDATA. The processing options, object names, and process descriptions for these lower level processes can now be entered on the screen as shown. Once this has been done, the "p" Select Definition option can be entered alongside each process name in turn to define the processing statements for the selected process. *Note*: Option "p" is used instead of option "s" because lower level processes do not have a flow section.

We are returned to the Structure List screen after defining the statements for each process. Pressing the PF 4 key on this screen will cause the screen to be refreshed with the latest process structure for the application.

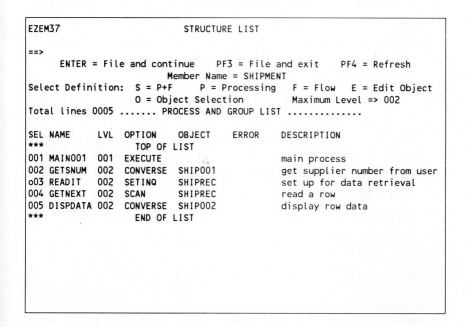

Fig. 19.11 SHIPMENT application Structure List

To explain the process options and statements in more detail we will consider the process called READIT.

Process Options

The process option for READIT, namely SETINQ, corresponds in SQL terms to declaring a cursor for some specified query. This query will access the object of the process option, which we have specified as SHIPREC (see Fig. 19.11). In general, the process option can be any of the following (by way of explanation, we give an approximate SQL equivalent in each case):

- INQUIRY — retrieve a single table row (singleton SELECT)
- UPDATE — retrieve a single row for update (DECLARE CURSOR FOR UPDATE-OPEN-FETCH)
- SETINQ — define a set of rows to be retrieved (DECLARE CURSOR-OPEN)
- SETUPD — define a set of rows to be retrieved and updated (DECLARE CURSOR FOR UPDATE-OPEN)
- SCAN — retrieve a row from a defined set (FETCH)
- REPLACE — update a retrieved row (UPDATE CURRENT)
- DELETE — delete a retrieved row (DELETE CURRENT)
- CLOSE — terminate processing of defined set (CLOSE)
- ADD — insert a single row (INSERT)
- SQLEXEC — execute the specified SQL statement (used to execute SQL statements not supported by the process options above)

In addition there are three process options that have no SQL equivalents (i.e., that have nothing to do with database access at all):

- EXECUTE — execute the specified process
- CONVERSE — display a map and edit the response from the user
- DISPLAY — display a map (no response from user)

As already stated, the object of the SETINQ process option in our example is SHIPREC. The SQL statement generated by CSP/AD for this combination of process option and object can be displayed and subsequently edited by means of the CSP/AD Application Definition screen shown in Fig. 19.12. This screen is displayed by entering the option "o" alongside the READIT process name on the Structure List screen for the SHIPMENT application (refer back to Fig. 19.11).

```
EZEM3M                     APPLICATION DEFINITION
EZE005901 You may edit lines preceded by line numbers
==>
 PF3 = File and exit PF4 = Reset to default statement PF5 = SQL syntax check
 Process = READIT    Description = set up for data retrieval
 Option  = SETINQ    Object      = SHIPREC    Modified statements = YES
Total lines 0012 ... OBJECT SELECTION: SQL STATEMENT DEFINITION ............
***                      TOP OF LIST
*** SELECT
002   T1.S#, T1.CITY,
003   T2.QTY,
004   T3.P#, T3.CITY
*** INTO
006   :S#, :SCITY, :QTY,
007   :P#, :PCITY
*** FROM
***    cjdate.s T1,
***    cjdate.sp T2,
***    cjdate.p T3
*** WHERE
010   t1.s# = t2.s# and
011   t2.p# = t3.p# and t1.s# = :s#
012 order by t3.p#
***                      END OF LIST
```

Fig. 19.12 SELECT statement for the READIT process

The SQL statement is initially generated by CSP/AD using the SHIPREC record defined earlier; we have tailored it for the READIT process by adding an extra search condition and an ORDER BY clause. The purpose of the extra search condition is to ensure that SHIPREC records are retrieved for the required supplier only.

Processing Statements

The CSP/AD *Application Process Definition* screen shown in Fig. 19.13 is displayed as a result of selecting the "p" option on the Structure List screen (refer back to Fig. 19.11 once again). The Application Process Definition screen allows us to specify the processing statements for the process under consideration. In the simple example shown, the BEFORE processing consists of a single MOVE statement to copy the supplier number entered by the user (via the map SHIP001) into the S# field of the SHIPREC record. The process option SETINQ will use the S# field to retrieve shipment information using the SHIPREC record. There are no AFTER processing statements.

```
EZEM39                  APPLICATION PROCESS DEFINITION

==>
  PF3 = File and exit  (or file and continue if more selected )
Process = READIT    Description = set up for data retrieval
 Option = SETINQ         Object = SHIPREC
Total lines 0001 ...    STATEMENT DEFINITION ...........................
***                     TOP OF LIST
001 MOVE SHIP001.SNUM TO SHIPREC.S#;
***  ------------------ PROCESS OPTION -----------------------
***                     END OF LIST
```

Fig. 19.13 READIT process definition

A more complex example appears in Fig. 19.14. That figure shows the processing statements for the MAIN001 process of the SHIPMENT application. This process has a processing option of EXECUTE, which simply causes the statements in the process to be executed (no map or record processing is performed). There are no BEFORE processing statements. The AFTER processing statements control the flow of the lower level processes. *Note*: The example of Fig. 19.14 is intended to illustrate process definition in general terms, not to represent a totally realistic application. The statements shown are intended to be more or less self-explanatory.

CSP processing statements fall into the following general categories:

- *Computational* statements to do arithmetic operations, to move data between CSP objects, to set fields to specific values, etc.

- *Conditional* statements to perform flow-of-control operations (IF/ ELSE/END, WHILE/END) or to check status after map and record processing, etc.

- *Application linkage* statements to invoke, or transfer control to, another CSP or user-written application

```
EZEM39                    APPLICATION PROCESS DEFINITION

==>
       PF3 = File and exit  (or file and continue if more selected )
    Process = MAIN001   Description = set up for data retrieval
     Option = EXECUTE          Object =
Total lines 0010 ...     STATEMENT DEFINITION ............................
***                      TOP OF LIST
*** ------------------ PROCESS OPTION ----------------------
001 PERFORM GETSNUM ;    GET SUPPLIER NUMBER
002 SET SHIP002 ;        CLEAR DISPLAY
003 PERFORM READIT ;     SET UP FOR DATABASE READ
004 PERFORM GETNEXT ;    READ FIRST ROW
005 IF SHIPREC IS NRF ;  SUPPLIER NOT FOUND TELL USER
006   MOVE "INVALID SUPPLIER" TO EZEMSG;
007 ELSE
008   WHILE SHIPREC NOT NRF ;
008    PERFORM DISPDATA ; DISPLAY ROW
009    PERFORM GETNEXT ;  READ NEXT ROW
009   END ;
010 END ;
***                      END OF LIST
```

Fig. 19.14   MAIN001 process definition

- *Unconditional* statements to invoke the next lower level process, to invoke a named statement group, or to invoke a specified CSP function, etc.

19.7 GENERATING THE CSP APPLICATION

During application testing all database processing is done using dynamic SQL. After the application has been tested and debugged, a production version can be generated for execution under CSP/370RS or CSP/2RS; that production version will use COBOL with embedded (i.e., static) SQL. The COBOL program is prepared for execution on DB2 by means of the standard DB2 program preparation procedures (see Chapter 17); the CSP generation process will create the necessary JCL automatically, if requested.

◆20◆

Information Warehouse Tools

20.1 INTRODUCTION

As explained in Chapter 18, the objective of the IBM Information Warehouse is to provide an integrated framework for delivering enterprise-wide data to end-users who need corporate information to manage day-to-day business operations. In this chapter we describe some of the main IBM products for use within this framework. Section 20.2 discusses the Query Management Facility (QMF), which is an end-user query and report-writing tool for the Decision Support System component of the framework. Sections 20.3 and 20.4 look at Data Extract (DXT) and Data Propagator (DPROP), which are Data Delivery component tools for copying data between files and databases of the warehouse.

20.2 QUERY MANAGEMENT FACILITY

Overview

As indicated above, Query Management Facility (QMF) is an ad hoc query and report-writing tool supporting end-user processing of data stored in either DB2 under MVS (TSO or CICS) or SQL/DS under VM. We focus here on the DB2 case, but most of the discussion is equally applicable to SQL/DS.

A report in QMF is the displayed (or printed) output from a QMF query. QMF queries can be formulated in several different ways:

- By means of direct SQL statements.

- By means of a *relational prompted query* interface, which allows users unfamiliar with SQL language details to construct certain SQL queries in a simple manner.

- By means of a language called *Query-By-Example* (QBE). QBE is another relational language, comparable in some ways to SQL but more user-friendly in certain respects. However, it is clear that IBM regards SQL as far more important than QBE; we therefore do not discuss QBE in this book.

- By means of an *entity/relationship* prompted query interface, which allows users to access data from the IBM Repository Manager using the SAA Repository Interface (see Section 18.3). However, our main focus in this section is on access to business data, not "metadata," and we will therefore not discuss this interface.

QMF reports are formatted in accordance with a set of report specifications called a *form*. When a given query is executed, the user has the option of specifying the corresponding form explicitly or of letting QMF create an appropriate *default* form. After viewing the report at the terminal, the user can revise the form and display the query output again in accordance with the revised version (without having to go back to the database to repeat the query). This cycle can be repeated as many times as necessary, until the user is satisfied. Thus a typical QMF session might go as follows (refer to Fig. 20.1):

1. The user constructs the query—i.e., any single SQL (or QBE) statement—in a QMF work area called QUERY.

2. The user issues RUN QUERY to execute the query in QUERY. The result is stored in another work area, called DATA (unless it is too large to be kept entirely in main memory, in which case it will be kept partly in an external "spill file").

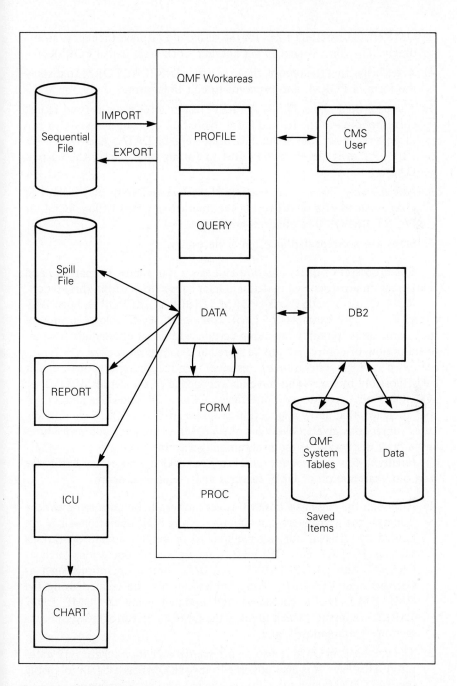

Fig. 20.1   QMF structure

3. QMF creates a default form for the result and displays the report accordingly. The form is kept in yet another work area, called FORM.

4. After inspecting the report, the user issues DISPLAY FORM to display the form in FORM, and proceeds to edit that form.

5. The user then issues DISPLAY REPORT to produce a revised report corresponding to the revised form. Note that it is not necessary to run the query again; the result has been kept in DATA, and DISPLAY REPORT uses the current FORM to format and display the current DATA.

6. Alternatively, the user can use DISPLAY CHART to display a chart or graph instead of a report (using the Interactive Chart Utility, ICU), or PRINT REPORT to obtain a hard copy.

7. Steps 4–6 are repeated as often as necessary.

The processes of query creation and execution, report formatting, and chart creation are discussed in detail in later subsections within this section.

RUN QUERY, DISPLAY FORM, DISPLAY REPORT, DISPLAY CHART, etc., are examples of QMF *commands*. QMF allows groups of such commands, possibly including certain additional commands for performing flow-of-control etc., to be stored as a named *procedure*. QMF procedures permit the generation of "canned" production reports on a regular basis, possibly by users who have no knowledge of the details of QMF or SQL. QMF also provides two interfaces, a *Command* interface and a *Callable* interface, that allow application programs to invoke QMF commands. Later subsections give an overview of the QMF commands and procedures and a brief discussion of the programming interfaces.

Finally, a few additional preliminary remarks are necessary before we start our examination of QMF features and facilities in depth:

1. Although the emphasis in QMF is very naturally on data *retrieval*, the "query" the user enters can actually be any SQL operation—it is not limited to retrieval but can include, for example, update operations such as INSERT and DELETE, data definition operations such as CREATE and DROP TABLE, and data control operations such as GRANT and REVOKE. *Note*: Tables can also be created using the QMF SAVE DATA command and updated using the QMF EDIT TABLE command (which invokes the QMF table editor). See the subsection "Commands," later.

2. The emphasis in QMF is also on *interactive execution* (again very naturally). However, it is also possible to invoke QMF as a batch job using the BATCH command (again, see the subsection "Commands").

3. As usual we will base our examples on the familiar suppliers-and-parts database.

Creating a New Query

After starting QMF, the user is presented with the QMF *home panel* (Fig. 20.2). Like most QMF panels, this panel offers the user three possible actions:

- Press PF key 1 to get help, or
- Type a QMF command on the command line, or
- Press a PF key to execute a preassigned QMF command.

We now consider what is involved in creating a new query. Until further notice, we will assume that the query is to be constructed directly in SQL; we will discuss the relational prompted query case later in this section. *Note*: It is possible to switch dynamically among the various interfaces (SQL, QBE, prompted relational, prompted entity/relationship) using the

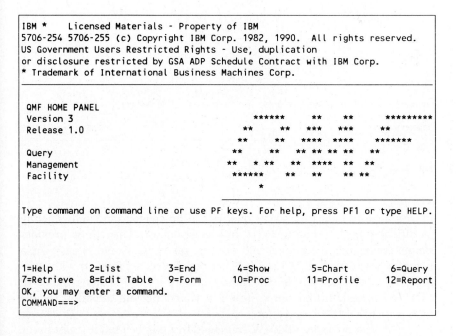

Fig. 20.2 The QMF home panel

RESET QUERY command. The default interface for any given user is defined in that user's "QMF profile," which is (typically) created by the *QMF administrator*, but can be modified by the user at any time by means of appropriate QMF commands.

To enter a query, the user first types DISPLAY QUERY or presses PF key 6. QMF responds by displaying a panel for entering the query. The user can then enter the required SQL statement using the QMF full-screen editor. An example is shown in Fig. 20.3.

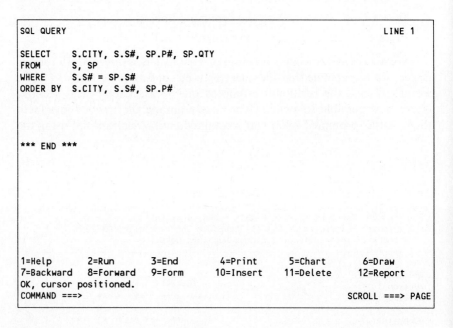

```
SQL QUERY                                                    LINE 1

SELECT     S.CITY, S.S#, SP.P#, SP.QTY
FROM       S, SP
WHERE      S.S# = SP.S#
ORDER BY   S.CITY, S.S#, SP.P#




*** END ***








1=Help       2=Run        3=End        4=Print      5=Chart      6=Draw
7=Backward   8=Forward    9=Form       10=Insert    11=Delete    12=Report
OK, cursor positioned.
COMMAND ===>                                          SCROLL ===> PAGE
```

Fig. 20.3 Sample QMF query (SQL)

As already indicated, QMF queries can be created (and subsequently modified) using the builtin QMF full-screen editor. This editor provides simple commands for adding and deleting query lines, and is easy for a novice to learn and use. More experienced users who are familiar with more powerful editors can use one of those editors instead by issuing the QMF EDIT command. In this book, however, we restrict our attention for the most part to QMF's own editor.

QMF also provides a DRAW command that can be used to assist in the process of constructing queries. DRAW "draws" a skeleton query on the screen for the table named in the DRAW command. For example, the command

```
DRAW S ( TYPE = SELECT )
```

will produce the following SELECT statement skeleton for the suppliers table (table S):

```
SELECT S#, SNAME, STATUS, CITY   -- S
FROM    S                        -- S
```

This skeleton query can now be edited to produce the query actually desired. *Note*: The "-- S" at the right-hand side of each of the two lines of the skeleton query is a comment.

Once the query has been created, the user can execute it by issuing RUN QUERY or by pressing PF key 2. The result is displayed at the user's terminal using the default form constructed automatically by QMF. That form can be displayed by issuing DISPLAY FORM or by pressing PF key 9. Figs. 20.4 and 20.5 show the report and the default form, respectively, for the query of Fig. 20.3.

```
REPORT                                        LINE 1      POS 1    79

   CITY              S#     P#            QTY
 ----------------   -----  ------   -----------
   London            S1     P1            300
   London            S1     P2            200
   London            S1     P3            400
   London            S1     P4            200
   London            S1     P5            100
   London            S1     P6            100
   London            S4     P2            200
   London            S4     P4            300
   London            S4     P5            400
   Paris             S2     P1            300
   Paris             S2     P2            400
   Paris             S3     P2            200




1=Help      2=          3=End        4=Print     5=Chart      6=Query
7=Backward  8=Forward   9=Form      10=Left     11=Right      12=
OK, this is the REPORT from your RUN command.
COMMAND ===>                                      SCROLL ===> PAGE
```

Fig. 20.4 Report for the query of Fig. 20.3

```
FORM.MAIN

COLUMNS:                      Total Width of Report Columns: 45
 NUM  COLUMN HEADING                     USAGE   INDENT  WIDTH  EDIT   SEQ
 ---  ------------------------------     -------  ------  -----  -----  ---
   1  CITY                                  2       15      C     1
   2  S#                                    2        5      C     2
   3  P#                                    2        6      C     3
   4  QTY                                   2       11      L     4
      *** END ***

PAGE:    HEADING ===>
         FOOTING ===>
FINAL:   TEXT ===>
BREAK1:  NEW PAGE FOR BREAK? ===> NO
         FOOTING ===>
BREAK2:  NEW PAGE FOR BREAK? ===> NO
         FOOTING ===>
OPTIONS: OUTLINE? ===> YES              DEFAULT BREAK TEXT? ===> YES

1=Help     2=Check    3=End      4=Show        5=Chart       6=Query
7=Backward 8=Forward  9=         10=Insert      11=Delete     12=Report
OK, FORM is displayed.
COMMAND ===>                                    SCROLL ===> PAGE
```

Fig. 20.5 Default form for the query of Fig. 20.3

The user can now edit the form, if desired, and then display a revised report corresponding to that edited form by issuing DISPLAY REPORT or by pressing PF key 12. (See later in this section for a detailed discussion of form editing.) These two steps can be repeated as many times as necessary, until the user is satisfied with the result; the final report can then be printed by issuing PRINT REPORT, or by pressing PF key 4.

Saving and Reexecuting a Query

At any given time, the QMF working area includes at most five current "QMF items": one query, one result (DATA), one form, one procedure, and one profile (refer to Fig. 20.1). Thus, e.g., executing a new query will cause the current contents of DATA to be overwritten. However, any current item can be saved for later use by means of an appropriate SAVE command. For instance, the command

```
SAVE QUERY AS CITYQUERY
```

will save the current query as CITYQUERY. Saved queries can subsequently be executed by means of the RUN QUERY command. For instance, the command

```
RUN CITYQUERY ( FORM = CITYFORM )
```

will execute the saved query CITYQUERY, formatting the result in accordance with a form named CITYFORM.

The command LIST QUERIES can be used to display a list of saved queries. Options exist to limit the output to just those queries saved by a particular user and/or those having a particular generic name. For example, the command

```
LIST QUERIES ( OWNER = ALL  NAME = CITY% )
```

will list all saved queries having "CITY" as the first four characters of their name. The user can then enter various QMF commands on the screen alongside any given query in the list. For example, if the user types the command DISPLAY against the query name CITYQUERY, QMF will bring that query into the QUERY working area, thereby making it the current query again.

Variables (i.e., parameters) are permitted in saved queries. For example, if the query

```
SELECT S#, SNAME
FROM   S
WHERE  CITY = &CITYNAME
```

is saved under the name CITYQUERY, it can be executed later via the command

```
RUN CITYQUERY ( &CITYNAME = 'London' )
```

If the user forgets to supply a value for the &CITY variable, QMF will prompt for one.

Creating a Prompted Query

So far we have seen how QMF queries can be created using SQL statements directly. However, many users are either not able or not inclined to learn all the complexities of SQL, and for such users some simpler kind of interface is desirable. The QMF *prompted query* facility provides such an interface: It allows queries to be constructed by means of a series of "pop-up" windows, which eliminate the need to know the syntax of SQL in detail and provide assistance in identifying the tables and columns to be accessed. The user's QMF profile indicates whether the prompted query facility is to be used.

Figs. 20.6, 20.7, and 20.8 show how the prompted query facility could be used to construct the SQL query already shown in Fig. 20.3:

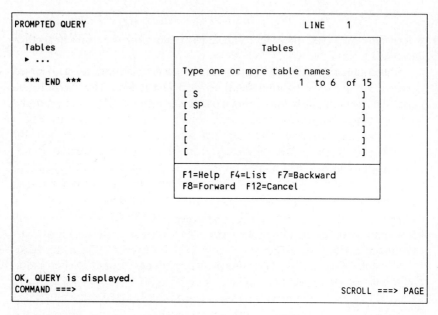

Fig. 20.6 Specifying the tables in a prompted query

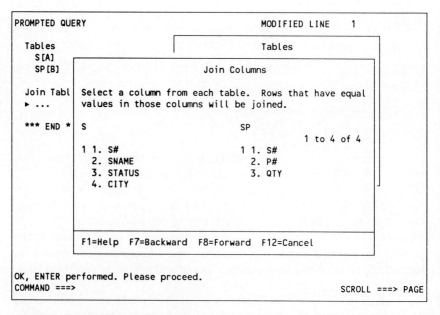

Fig. 20.7 Specifying the join columns in a prompted query

- First, the required tables are specified, using the "Tables" window (Fig. 20.6). A list of known tables can be displayed if desired to help with this step.

- Once the tables (S and SP in the example) have been identified, the next step is to indicate how those tables are to be joined. This information is provided via the "Join Columns" window (Fig. 20.7), which displays the column names for each table, together with an associated column number in each case. The user indicates the columns over which the join is to be performed by means of those column numbers; in the example, we have specified that the join is to be taken over column 1 (S#) of table S and column 1 (S#) of table SP. *Note*: The "Join Columns" window assumes that the join is an equijoin. See Section 5.3 if you need to refresh your memory concerning the different types of join.

- Further windows (not shown) are used to specify the columns to be retrieved from the result of the join and the desired row sequence for the final output. Fig. 20.8 shows the completed query. *Note*: It also shows the generated SQL. The command CONVERT QUERY can be used to convert the original query into executable SQL form. The converted query can then be edited, run, or saved.

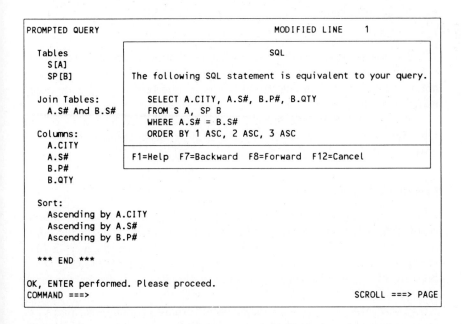

```
PROMPTED QUERY                          MODIFIED LINE    1

   Tables                              SQL
    S[A]
    SP[B]           The following SQL statement is equivalent to your query.

   Join Tables:        SELECT A.CITY, A.S#, B.P#, B.QTY
    A.S# And B.S#      FROM S A, SP B
                       WHERE A.S# = B.S#
   Columns:            ORDER BY 1 ASC, 2 ASC, 3 ASC
    A.CITY
    A.S#            F1=Help  F7=Backward  F8=Forward  F12=Cancel
    B.P#
    B.QTY

   Sort:
    Ascending by A.CITY
    Ascending by A.S#
    Ascending by B.P#

   *** END ***

OK, ENTER performed. Please proceed.
COMMAND ===>                                    SCROLL ===> PAGE
```

Fig. 20.8 The completed query and its SQL equivalent

The example does not illustrate the point, but the prompted query facility also allows scalar expressions to be specified as well as simple column names (for both the SELECT clause and the WHERE clause, in SQL terms). It also supports aggregate functions (SUM, AVG, etc.), arbitrarily complex "WHERE clause" conditions (involving AND, OR, etc.), and duplicate row elimination (DISTINCT).

Controlling Query Execution

QMF provides two mechanisms by which it is possible for the installation to exercise some control over the use of the product (and hence over the use of certain system resources). The first consists of a simple time estimating facility; if the QMF administrator requests this facility, QMF will inform users of its estimated execution time for each query, and queries for which the estimate exceeds some threshold can simply be canceled. The second, more sophisticated mechanism is the QMF *governor* facility, by which the QMF administrator can provide an exit routine to control, by individual user or user class, such matters as:

- the number of rows fetched from DB2
- the amount of CPU time used to execute a QMF command
- the QMF commands that can or cannot be used
- the time periods during which QMF can be used

The governor facility thus allows the installation to prevent users from entering queries, inadvertently or otherwise, that would use an excessive amount of some system resource or would interfere unduly with other activities in the system.

Note: QMF query execution can also be controlled by means of the DB2 Resource Limit Facility (RLF), either as well as or instead of the QMF governor. Refer to Chapter 16 for details of RLF.

Creating a Report

After composing and executing a query, the user can produce a tailored report from the result by means of a set of *form panels*. The starting point in this process is the default form produced by QMF when the query is first executed. That form can be displayed by issuing DISPLAY FORM, or by pressing PF key 9, after running the query; the effect is to display the form on a panel called FORM.MAIN (refer back to Fig. 20.5).

FORM.MAIN supports a set of basic formatting functions; more extensive formatting can be performed using additional form panels. We will first discuss the use of FORM.MAIN and then move on to describe the other panels. As already indicated, the default form we will be using as a basis for discussion is the one shown in Fig. 20.5 (the default form for the sample query of Fig. 20.3).

Basic Formatting

To demonstrate basic formatting, we will make some updates to the default form of Fig. 20.5. The modified form is shown in Fig. 20.9, and the resulting report (displayed by issuing DISPLAY REPORT or by pressing PF key 12) is shown in Fig. 20.10. By comparing Fig. 20.9 with the original default form (Fig. 20.5), we can see the effect of each of the major components of FORM.MAIN.

- COLUMN HEADING

  The column headings on the default form are the same as the column names in the table, unless column labels are being used (see the discussion of the SQL LABEL statement in Section 8.3). Those headings can be changed to any name of up to 40 characters. In the example, the

```
FORM.MAIN

COLUMNS:               Total Width of Report Columns: 40
  NUM   COLUMN HEADING                    USAGE    INDENT  WIDTH  EDIT   SEQ
  ---   -------------------------------   -------  ------  -----  -----  ---
    1   City                              BREAK1   3       8      C      1
    2   Supplier                                   3       8      C      2
    3   Part                                       3       4      C      3
    4   Quantity                          SUM      3       8      L      4
        *** END ***

PAGE:      HEADING ===> Shipments by Supplier City - Date: &DATE
           FOOTING ===> Page: &PAGE
FINAL:     TEXT ===> *** Grand Total
BREAK1:    NEW PAGE FOR BREAK? ===> NO
           FOOTING ===> * Total for &1
BREAK2:    NEW PAGE FOR BREAK? ===> NO
           FOOTING ===>
OPTIONS:   OUTLINE? ===> YES              DEFAULT BREAK TEXT? ===> YES

1=Help      2=Check    3=End      4=Show       5=Chart       6=Query
7=Backward  8=Forward  9=         10=Insert    11=Delete     12=Report
OK, cursor positioned.
COMMAND ===>                                   SCROLL ===> PAGE
```

Fig. 20.9 Modified form for the query of Fig. 20.3

```
Shipments by Supplier City - Date: 87/06/23

City        Supplier   Part   Quantity
--------    --------   ----   --------
London      S1         P1        300
            S1         P2        200
            S1         P3        400
            S1         P4        200
            S1         P5        100
            S1         P6        100
            S4         P2        200
            S4         P4        300
            S4         P5        400
                                --------
        * Total for London       2200

Paris       S2         P1        300
            S2         P2        400
            S3         P2        200
                                --------
        * Total for Paris         900
                                ========
        ***  Grand Total         3100
                                        Page: 1
```

Fig. 20.10 Tailored report using the form of Fig. 20.9

name CITY has been changed to City, and the names S#, P#, and QTY have been changed to the more meaningful names Supplier, Part, and Quantity, respectively.

▪ USAGE

USAGE codes determine how data columns are to be processed in producing the report. If no USAGE code is specified for a given column, values in that column are simply displayed without any special processing. The meanings of some of the main USAGE codes are as follows.

· OMIT means that the column is to be omitted from the report.

· BREAK*n* (*n* = 1 to 6) specifies that a *control break* is to occur each time a value change occurs in the indicated column; BREAK1 signifies the most significant (major) control break column, BREAK2 the next most significant, and so on. The main purpose of specifying control breaks is to let QMF compute and display subtotals (or similar partial results—see below) when the report is produced. In our example, a control break will occur each time the City value changes. Because USAGE for the Quantity column has been specified as SUM, QMF will sum the Quantity values at each control break (observe that a request for subtotals will automatically cause QMF to compute a grand total also). *Note*: The SQL query must include an appropriate ORDER BY specification for control breaks to make sense.

- BREAKnX is the same as BREAKn, except that the column is to be omitted from the report.

- In addition to SUM, other available "aggregate function" USAGE codes include AVERAGE, COUNT, FIRST, LAST, MAXIMUM, MINIMUM, and STDEV (standard deviation).

- The USAGE code GROUP causes one line of summary data to be displayed for each distinct value in the indicated column. (As with BREAKn, the data must be appropriately sorted for GROUP to make sense.) In our example, if we were to specify GROUP for the Supplier column (in addition to the BREAK1 and SUM codes already specified for the City and Quantity columns), the effect would be to group all rows for a particular supplier within a particular city together and to display a single line for that combination, giving the corresponding total quantity. The final result would thus look somewhat as follows (ignoring page headings and footings):

```
City        Supplier    Quantity
_____    _____    _____

London      S1              1300
            S4               900
                         _____
  * Total for London        2200

Paris       S2               700
            S3               200
                         _____
  * Total for Paris          900
                         _____
    *** Grand Total         3100
```

The Part column is automatically omitted from the report because no aggregate USAGE is specified for it.

- The USAGE code CALCn specifies that this is a "CALC column"— i.e., the results of "calculation$n$" are to be used as values for this column in the report. Calculations are defined using the FORM.CALC panel (see "Advanced Formatting" below). CALC columns can be added to a form by means of the QMF INSERT command. *Note*: Columns—any columns, not just CALC columns— can also be removed from a form by means of the QMF DELETE command.

- Finally, the USAGE code ACROSS can be used in conjunction with GROUP to produce a report in which each line of summary data for the GROUP column has an entry for each corresponding value of the ACROSS column. For example, suppose we wanted to display quantity totals by city across all suppliers, as well as quantity totals for each individual supplier. By specifying ACROSS for Supplier and GROUP for City, the required result is produced:

			Supplier		
City	← S1 → Quantity	← S2 → Quantity	← S3 → Quantity	← S4 → Quantity	←TOTAL→ Quantity
London	1300	0	0	900	2200
Paris	0	700	200	0	900
	1300	700	200	900	3100

Note: The suppliers-and-parts database does not permit the same supplier to appear in more than one city. The foregoing report is thus unrealistically simple. Nevertheless, the example does serve to illustrate the basic idea of "cross-summary" reporting.

- INDENT

  INDENT specifies the number of blanks to appear between the indicated column and the one to its immediate left. All INDENT values in the example have been changed from 2 to 3.

- WIDTH

  WIDTH specifies the width of the indicated column as it is to appear in the report (in terms of characters). In the example, the City, Supplier, Part, and Quantity widths have been changed from 15 to 8, 5 to 8, 6 to 4, and 11 to 8, respectively.

- EDIT

  EDIT codes determine how column values are to be formatted. Codes C and L, for example, mean character and decimal, respectively. Various options exist for formatting numbers, dates and times, and so forth. It is also possible to supply installation-defined exit routines to perform customized column value formatting. The reader is referred to the QMF manuals for details of all these possibilities. No changes were made to the EDIT codes in our example.

- SEQ

  SEQ defines the order in which the columns are to appear in the displayed report. For example, if we changed the SEQ values to read 1, 3, 2, 4 (vertically), the columns would be displayed in the sequence

City, Part, Supplier, Quantity (left to right). By default, the columns will appear in the left-to-right order specified in the SQL SELECT clause.

- PAGE HEADING, PAGE FOOTING, FINAL

  PAGE HEADING and FOOTING define one line of heading and footing text to be produced on each page of the report. FINAL defines one line of text to be displayed on the final summary line (if any) of the report. Our example uses the variable &DATE to display the current date (in the format *yy/mm/dd*) in the heading text, and &PAGE to display the current page number in the footing text. The variable &TIME can also be used to display the current time in the format *hh:mm*.

- BREAK1

  Two options are possible here, each specifying what is to be done when a control break occurs in the BREAK1 column. The first specifies whether a new page is to be started; the second specifies the text to be displayed on the corresponding summary line. Such text can include references to variables of the form &*n*. If it does, QMF will substitute the current value of column *n* before displaying the summary line. (The column number is shown under NUM on FORM.MAIN.) In the example, the variable &1 refers to column 1 on the form, and the current value of City will be displayed each time a control break on City occurs. *Note*: Variables can also be used in heading and footing text.

- BREAK2

  BREAK2 is the same as BREAK1, mutatis mutandis. *Note*: There are no BREAK3, BREAK4, etc., options on FORM.MAIN; for information on how to code the text for control breaks 3 through 6, see "Advanced Formatting" below.

- OPTIONS

  FORM.MAIN includes two further options, OUTLINE and DEFAULT BREAK TEXT. The example specifies an OUTLINE option of YES, which causes values to be displayed in a control break column only when the value changes; NO causes a value to be displayed on every line. The DEFAULT BREAK TEXT option specifies what is to happen when control breaks are used, but the user has not indicated any break footing text; YES causes a line of asterisks to be displayed, NO suppresses this default.

Advanced Formatting

The example discussed under "Basic Formatting" above gives some idea of how easy it is to use FORM.MAIN to produce a customized report. Sometimes, however, more sophisticated tailoring will be required. The form panels described below provide the necessary additional tailoring facilities:

- FORM.COLUMNS: Contains the same column information as FORM.MAIN, except that more column entries can be displayed on a single screen.

- FORM.PAGE: Allows multiple lines of heading and footing text (compared with just one on FORM.MAIN). Other options control text alignment and position, and the number of blank lines before and after the heading and footing.

- FORM.FINAL: Allows multiple lines of final report text and offers similar formatting options to FORM.PAGE.

- FORM.BREAK*n*: There are six of these panels, one for each of the six control break levels. Multiple heading and footing lines are allowed for each level; they are positioned using formatting options similar to those on FORM.PAGE. One further option controls whether column headings are to be repeated at each new control break.

- FORM.DETAIL: Controls more precisely where retrieved data, constants, and calculated values (see FORM.CALC below) are to appear in the report. This form provides more flexibility in defining report layouts than the rather rigid FORM.MAIN panel does.

- FORM.CALC: Allows the user to specify arithmetic and string operations to be performed on retrieved data. Each calculation is given a unique identifier so that it can be referenced in other FORM panels. A calculation with the identifier 5, for example, can be referenced on FORM.MAIN by specifying the USAGE code CALC5. This feature allows the result of the calculation to be included in the final report.

- FORM.CONDITIONS: Allows the user to specify a conditional expression (coded in the REXX language) to be performed on retrieved and calculated data. The result of the expression must be *true* or *false*; if it is *true*, the data is displayed in the report, otherwise it is omitted. Each condition is given a unique identifier so that it can be referenced in the FORM.DETAIL panel.

- FORM.OPTIONS: Controls such matters as detail line spacing, line wrapping, final and break text width, the use of aggregate function names in column headings, page renumbering, column heading separators, and so forth.

These panels work in conjunction with FORM.MAIN to let the user construct more elaborate reports. Everything entered on FORM.MAIN is automatically reflected in a corresponding detailed form panel. Each of the detailed panels can be reached by selecting the appropriate PF key from FORM.MAIN (see the PF keys in Fig. 20.5 or Fig. 20.9).

Creating a Chart

The foregoing subsections have given some idea as to what is involved in creating a QMF report. However, a report (as described above) is only one way of displaying a query result; a chart or graph is another. QMF uses the Interactive Chart Utility (ICU) to create and display charts. Although most aspects of such charts are controlled by QMF, users can specify and save certain chart format options of their own in the ICU.

The QMF command syntax to display a chart is

```
DISPLAY CHART ( ICUFORM = name )
```

The chart is formatted and displayed in accordance with the chart format identified by "name"—either one of the builtin chart formats provided by QMF or a user-defined chart format previously saved in the ICU. For example, to display a pie chart using a QMF-provided format called PIE, the user would enter

```
DISPLAY CHART ( ICUFORM = PIE )
```

Similarly, to display a chart saved in the ICU with the name MYPIE, the command

```
DISPLAY CHART ( ICUFORM = MYPIE )
```

would be used.

As already indicated, several builtin ICU chart formats are provided by QMF to reduce the need for users to create and save their own chart formats. The builtin formats are BAR, PIE, LINE, TOWER, TABLE, POLAR, HISTOGRAM, SURFACE, and SCATTER (these names are intended to be self-explanatory). By default, QMF formats data into a bar chart.

In general, the rules used by QMF for constructing a chart from a given report are as follows:

- For report forms without any GROUP or BREAKn columns, the X-axis data is taken from the leftmost data column. For report forms that include one or more GROUP or BREAKn columns, the X-axis data is taken from those columns.

- The Y-axis data is taken from the remaining numeric columns of the report.

Charts can be printed using the PRINT CHART command.

Commands

So far in our discussions we have shown the use of QMF commands to create, execute, and save queries, and to display and print reports and charts. Many additional commands are also available. For purposes of reference, we present below a summary of the main ones:

- BATCH: Run a query or procedure as a batch job.
- CICS: Enter a CICS command without leaving QMF.
- CONVERT: Translate a QBE or relational prompted query into executable SQL form. The converted query can be saved, edited, run, exported, or transferred into an application program.
- DISPLAY: Display a query, form, report, chart, procedure, profile, or table. The table option provides a quick way to display some specified table (it is shorthand for coding and executing the SQL statement "SELECT * FROM table").
- DPRE: Display a report as it would appear on a printer.
- DRAW: Create a skeleton query (SQL SELECT, INSERT, or UPDATE).
- EDIT: Edit a QMF procedure or SQL query, using an editor of the user's choice instead of the builtin QMF editor.
- EDIT TABLE: Modify the contents of a specified table. This command invokes the QMF table editor, which displays a formatted panel that can be used to insert, update, or delete table data, one row at a time.
- ERASE: Erase a query, form, procedure, or table from the system (the table option is shorthand for coding and executing the SQL statement "DROP TABLE table").
- EXPORT: Transfer data, a query, form, procedure, table, report, or chart to a TSO data set.
- EXTRACT: Access the Data Extract (DXT) Dialogs or send an extract request to DXT (see Section 20.3).
- GETQMF: Insert a QMF report into a document during editing. Options exist to add SCRIPT/VS control words to the inserted report. *Note*: GETQMF is really an edit macro, not a QMF command per se.
- HELP: Get online information about using QMF.

- IMPORT: Transfer data, a query, form, table, or procedure from a TSO data set into QMF.

- IRM: Access the Repository Manager Dialogs.

- ISPF: Invoke the Interactive System Product Facility (ISPF).

- LIST: List the names of saved QMF queries, forms, and procedures, and local and remote tables.

- MESSAGE: Used in a QMF procedure or in the QMF Command Interface to display a message at the terminal. QMF procedures and the QMF Command Interface are discussed below.

- PRINT: Print a query, form, report, chart, procedure, profile, or table.

- RESET: Clear the current panel.

- RETRIEVE: Retrieve and redisplay previously entered QMF commands.

- RUN: Execute a query or procedure.

- SAVE: Save the current query, form, procedure, profile, or data for future use (the data option is equivalent to executing the SQL statement "CREATE TABLE," followed by a statement to populate that newly created table).

- SET GLOBAL: Define values for variables used in QMF queries and procedures.

- SET PROFILE: Change the values in a user profile.

- SHOW: Display the specified panel.

- TSO: Enter a TSO command without leaving QMF.

Procedures

There will frequently be situations in which the same set of commands needs to be executed repeatedly on some regular basis. In such a situation, it is obviously convenient to be able to execute the complete set via a single command. QMF therefore allows commands to be grouped together to form a QMF *procedure*. Such a procedure can be invoked by means of the QMF RUN command. Like queries, procedures are created using an editor; they can be saved for later reuse using the SAVE command, and—again like queries—can contain variables (i.e., parameters), values for which must be supplied when the procedure is executed.

Procedures can consist either of QMF commands only ("linear procedures") or of QMF commands together with procedural code ("procedures with logic"). In the latter case, the procedural code (which is written in

REXX) can be used to handle flow of control, to carry out calculations, to build strings, to pass commands to the host environment, and so forth. Procedures with logic would usually be developed by data processing staff, rather than business users. Linear procedures and procedures with logic can call each other in any combination. *Note*: Procedures with logic are not supported with QMF under CICS.

Here is an example of a linear procedure. *Note*: Lines beginning with a double hyphen are comment lines.

```
-- Run the stored query called CITYQUERY.
-- CITYNAME is a variable contained in CITYQUERY.
-- Other variables are for use with the procedure itself.
--
RUN CITYQUERY ( FORM = &FORMN  &&CITYNAME = &CITY )
--
-- Create a new table containing the result data:
--
SAVE DATA AS &NEWTAB
--
-- Print report using a page length of 55 lines:
--
PRINT REPORT ( LENGTH = 55 )
```

The following is an equivalent procedure with logic.

```
/* Run the stored query called CITYQUERY              */
/* CITYNAME is a variable contained in CITYQUERY      */
/* Other variables are for use with the procedure itself */
/*                                                    */
signal on error_rtn
"RUN CITYQUERY ( FORM = &FORMN  &&CITYNAME = &CITY )"
/*                                                    */
/* Create a new table containing the result data      */
/*                                                    */
"SAVE DATA AS &NEWTAB"
/*                                                    */
/* Print report using a page length of 55 lines       */
/*                                                    */
"PRINT REPORT ( LENGTH = 55 )"
exit 0
/* Error handling code                                */
error_rtn:
"MESSAGE (TEXT='"dsq_message_text"'"
exit rc
```

Procedures can be saved by executing a SAVE command—for example:

```
SAVE PROC AS CITYPROC
```

—and can be executed using a RUN command. For example:

```
RUN CITYPROC ( &FORMN=CITYFORM &CITY='London' &NEWTAB=CITYDATA )
```

Application Support Facilities

In addition to all of the end-user facilities discussed so far, QMF also provides a set of facilities specifically intended for the professional programmer. Those facilities consist of:

- The QMF *Command Interface*, which allows TSO ISPF applications to pass commands to QMF for execution. These commands are executed in a similar fashion to those entered from the QMF command line or QMF procedures. This interface requires QMF to be started before the TSO ISPF application is run.

- The QMF *Callable Interface*, which allows 3GL programs to invoke QMF functions using the SAA Common Programming Interface (see Section 18.2). Unlike the Command Interface, this interface does not require ISPF, and does not require QMF to be active before running the application.

- *Application Support Commands*, which are a special set of commands for use by application programs. These commands make it possible for applications to behave just like QMF commands in their style of interaction with the end-user.

- *PF Key Customization*, which can be used to reassign QMF commands to different PF keys and to add installation-defined commands to PF keys.

- *EXPORT and IMPORT Commands* (see "Commands" above), which allow QMF objects (e.g., queries, forms, reports, charts, procedures) to be used outside the QMF environment.

Conclusion

This brings us to the end of our survey of the capabilities of QMF. To summarize briefly: QMF provides a set of easy-to-use facilities by which end-users can create their own queries and produce reports and charts (graphs) from the results of those queries. It also provides a set of application support facilities and a set of interfaces to certain other IBM products, all of which can be useful to the DP professional in constructing highly customized applications that make use of the features of QMF.

20.3 DATA EXTRACT

Overview

Data Extract (DXT) is a program for extracting data from operational databases and files. The extracted data is in a suitable format for loading (via the appropriate load utility) into a DB2 or SQL/DS table on the same or a different computer system. *Note*: The extracted data can also be used to create an Integration Exchange Format (IXF) file; IXF is an IBM self-defining file format that is used as a basis for transferring data between IBM products such as QMF, DXT, and AS.

DXT users can use either or both of the following:

- *Relational Data Extract Feature*, for extracting data from DB2 (MVS) or SQL/DS (VM) databases
- *General Data Extract Feature*, for extracting data from IMS databases, VSAM or sequential files, or nonIBM data sources (e.g., nonIBM SQL databases)

Note: DXT can also be used in conjunction with another product called DXT/D1 to extract data from files and databases on DEC systems (e.g., RMS files and Rdb/VMS, ORACLE, and INGRES databases). Details of DXT/D1 are beyond the scope of this book; the reader is referred to the IBM manuals for more information.

The main components of DXT are as follows (refer to Fig. 20.11):

- End User and Administrative Dialogs
- Online Commands
- Relational Extract Manager
- User Input Manager
- Data Extract Manager

Of these components, the Dialogs and Online Commands constitute the DXT base product, the Relational Extract Manager constitutes the Relational Data Extract Feature, and the User Input Manager and the Data Extract Manager constitute the General Data Extract Feature.

Dialogs and Online Commands

- The *End User Dialogs* allow users to submit existing extract requests or construct new ones. (*Note*: QMF provides commands to invoke these dialogs directly.) In the case of a new request, prompt screens allow the user to specify the source of the data, the specific data required (i.e.,

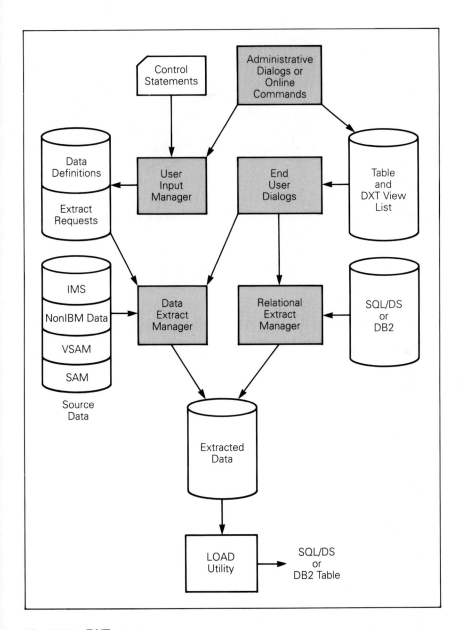

Fig. 20.11 DXT structure

the selection criteria), and the target DB2 or SQL/DS table into which the extracted data is to be loaded. The data source is identified by selecting the required item(s) from a list of tables and *DXT Views* (a DXT View is a "flat file" view of fields that may be accessed from nonrelational files and databases). Up to 16 different data sources can be referenced in an extract request. The source data and target table do not have to reside on the system where the dialog is executed.

- The *Administrative Dialogs* are used to define and maintain extract requests, to create DXT Views and other data descriptions, and to build information about the DB2 and SQL/DS tables accessible by individual users.

- The *Online Commands* are TSO REXX EXECs that provide similar capabilities to the Administrative Dialogs. Unlike the Administrative Dialogs they do not require TSO ISPF.

Relational Extract Manager

The Relational Extract Manager (REM) is the component that performs the actual data extraction when the source is a DB2 or SQL/DS database. Thus, it extracts data from DB2 and SQL/DS tables in accordance with SQL extract requests generated by the DXT End User Dialogs. The extracted data is written to a sequential file or an IXF file or is placed in a spool file for routing back to the submitting location. The extract request can optionally invoke a batch job to load the extracted data into a DB2 or SQL/DS table, using the applicable load utility.

User Input Manager

The User Input Manager (UIM) maintains data descriptions and extract requests for nonrelational files and databases. Data descriptions are stored in the File Description Table Library (FDTLIB); extract requests are stored in the Extract Request Library (EXTLIB).

A *data description* specifies the structure and organization of the source data to DXT. The main types of description used by the UIM are:

- *DXT file*, which describes a nonIMS file. Such files can be "simple" (with one record type) or "structured" (with multiple record types or one record type with repeating fields).

- *DXT PSB*, which describes an IMS database.

- *DXT User Type*, which describes data formats not directly supported by DXT. Such descriptions are used by the DXT *Generic Data Interface* (GDI), which extracts data from nonIBM data sources by means of installation-defined exit routines.
- *DXT View*, which describes a view of a DXT file or DXT PSB.

There are five possible sources for UIM input:

1. A card image file of DXT commands (i.e., data descriptions and/or extract requests) and job control statements, which is submitted as a batch job to MVS for processing. Job control statements describe a job to the operating system for the routing and final processing of extracted data.

2. The DXT Administrative Dialogs, which allow the equivalent of the card image input file to be created interactively.

3. The Online DXT Commands, which allow DXT requests to be built and run immediately instead of submitting a card image file for batch processing.

4. Output from the DXT *Dictionary Access Program* (DAP), which creates data descriptions from existing information stored in the IBM DB/DC Data Dictionary.

5. Output from the DXT *Structures Access Program* (SAP), which creates data descriptions from existing IMS database definitions and PL/I and COBOL structures.

Data Extract Manager

The Data Extract Manager (DEM) is the component that performs the actual data extraction when the source is something other than a DB2 or SQL/DS database. In other words, the DEM extracts data from IMS databases, VSAM and sequential files, and nonIBM data sources using extract requests stored in the Extract Request Library (EXTLIB). The DEM can either process all outstanding requests and then terminate, or it can execute continuously, processing requests as they appear in the EXTLIB. Facilities exist to process a batch of requests in a single pass and to control the priority in which requests are processed. (By contrast, the REM simply executes each request as it is submitted.) Extracted data is handled exactly as with the REM.

So much for the basic components of DXT. In the rest of this section, we consider what is involved in using DXT to extract data from a DB2 table, basing our discussion (as usual) on the suppliers-and-parts database.

Creating and Executing an Extract Request

We now consider what is involved in creating and executing a DXT request. By way of example, we create a request to extract supplier number, name, and city information for all suppliers. We begin with the main *DXT End User Dialogs* screen shown in Fig. 20.12. The options on that screen lead us to further screens which allow us to specify all aspects of the request in detail. In general, to create a request we must do all of the following (refer to the figure):

- Select the names of the tables (and/or DXT Views) from which data is to be extracted (Option 1, TABLES)
- Specify the columns to be extracted (Option 2, COLUMNS)
- Specify the search criteria to be used (Option 3, CONDITIONS)
- Specify the joining condition when extracting data from multiple tables and/or DXT Views (Option 4, JOIN)
- Identify the target DB2 or SQL/DS table and the system on which it resides (Option 5, TARGET)
- Specify control information for the source and target systems (Option 6, DB ACCESS)

```
                        DXT END USER DIALOGS

Select ONE of the following options,
  or use the PF Keys:

       1     TABLES        - Display table and DXT View
                             names available for extract
       2     COLUMNS       - Display  column  names  of
                             tables or DXT Views selected
       3     CONDITIONS    - Specify conditions on the
                             columns
       4     JOIN          - Specify join condition if more
                             than one table or DXT view selected
       5     TARGET        - Specify the target for loading
                             extracted data
       6     DB ACCESS     - Specify data base access information

       7     PROFILE REVIEW - Change Profile settings

Available Commands:  Send, Save, Display, Status, Cancel, Reset, Check, Erase

OPTION ===> 1
PF 1=HELP       2=SEND       3=END       4=TABLES    5=COLUMNS   6=CONDTION
PF 7=BACKWARD   8=FORWARD    9=JOIN      10=TARGET   11=EXT LIST 12=ACCESS
```

Fig. 20.12 Main DXT End User Dialogs screen

If the request already exists, we can execute it by selecting its name from the "extract list" obtained by pressing PF key 11. In our example, however, we want to create a new request, so we choose Option 1 (TABLES). That choice leads us to the *Select Tables/DXT Views for Extract* screen (Fig. 20.13), which displays the name of each table or DXT View we are allowed to access, the ID of its creator, the name of the system (i.e., node ID) on which it is located, its file type, and a short description of its use. All of this information is maintained by the *DXT administrator* using the DXT Administrative Dialogs.

```
                    SELECT TABLES/DXT VIEWS FOR EXTRACT

Enter an S under SELECT to select table(s) or dxt view(s) you wish to extract
from. Remember to select items from the same LOCATION and of the same TYPE.
To view additional table information, scroll RIGHT.


SELECT   TABLE/DXTVIEW      CREATOR    LOCATION    TYPE     DESCRIPTION
   S         NAME

=> S     S                  CJDATE     SANJOSE1    DB2      SUPPLIERS TABLE
=>       SP                 CJDATE     SANJOSE1    DB2      SUPPLIERS/PARTS TABLE
=>       P                  CJDATE     SANJOSE1    DB2      PARTS TABLE
=>       EDUC               DXT        SANJOSE2    DXT      IMS EDUCATION DB
****************************** BOTTOM OF DATA  ********************************






COMMAND ===>                                     SCROLL ===> HALF
PF 1=HELP       2=SEND      3=END       4=TABLES    5=COLUMNS   6=CONDTION
PF 7=BACKWARD   8=FORWARD   9=JOIN      10=TARGET   11=LEFT     12=RIGHT
```

Fig. 20.13 DXT Select Tables/DXT Views for Extract screen

According to Fig. 20.13, we are allowed to extract data from any or all of the suppliers (S), shipments (SP), and parts (P) tables, also from a DXT View called EDUC (introduced purely for the sake of the example). We enter an "S" ("select") alongside the suppliers table name. Pressing PF key 5 will now display the *Select Columns for Extract* screen (Fig. 20.14), which is used to specify the columns we want to extract. In our example, the screen contains a list of the columns of the supplier table. We select the S#, SNAME, and CITY columns by entering an "S" alongside those column names, and we then press PF key 10, which takes us to the *Name Target for Extract Output* screen. See Fig. 20.15.

```
                        SELECT COLUMNS FOR EXTRACT

Do you wish to select ALL columns for extract, Yes or No?    ===> N


If not, enter an S under SELECT to select specific columns for extract
and enter any FUNCTIONs for the columns. Press HELP for a list of functions.

SELECT  FUNCTION COLUMN                 TABLE               CREATOR
  S               NAME                  NAME

=> S  =>          S#                    S                   CJDATE
=> S  =>          SNAME                 S                   CJDATE
=>    =>          STATUS                S                   CJDATE
=> S  =>          CITY                  S                   CJDATE
****************************** BOTTOM OF DATA *******************************




COMMAND ===>                                          SCROLL ==> HALF
PF 1=HELP      2=SEND     3=END      4=TABLES    5=COLUMNS   6=CONDITION
PF 7=BACKWARD  8=FORWARD  9=JOIN     10=TARGET   11=EXT LIST 12=ACCESS
```

Fig. 20.14 DXT Select Columns for Extract screen

```
                  NAME TARGET FOR EXTRACT OUTPUT              ROW 2 OF 7

Target Nickname      ===> CJW1            Specify nickname of target system
Target Table Name    ===> SNEW           Specify for DB2, SQL/DS  & IXF
  Table Qualifier    ===> CJWHITE        Prefix for target table name
Specify when Target is SQL/DS or DB2:
Target Table Option ===>                 C / R / blank

Change the TARGET COLUMN NAMEs where appropriate.

INPUT COLUMN             ACCEPTS NULL    TARGET COLUMN
    NAME                 (Y,N, or D)        NAME

S#                          => N         ==> "S#"
SNAME                       => Y         ==> "SNAME"
CITY                        => Y         ==> "CITY"
****************************** BOTTOM OF DATA *******************************




COMMAND ===>                                          SCROLL ===> HALF
PF 1=HELP      2=SEND     3=END      4=TABLES    5=COLUMNS   6=CONDTION
PF 7=BACKWARD  8=FORWARD  9=JOIN     10=TARGET   11=LEFT     12=RIGHT
```

Fig. 20.15 DXT Name Target for Extract Output screen

To specify the extract target, we first give the "nickname" (CJW1 in our example) for the target system. Nicknames are intended to make it easy for the user to identify individual (source or target) systems. They are maintained by the DXT administrator. In general, a nickname is shorthand for the combination of all of the following:

- System node ID
- File name (the name of a file containing the job control statements to be used in building the extract job stream)
- File type (e.g., DB2, SQL/DS, IXF, DXT View)

After entering the nickname we specify:

- The target table name (SNEW)
- The target table owner (CJWHITE)
- Option "C" ("create a new table")
- The mapping of source columns to target columns
- Whether nulls are allowed in the target columns (in the example, we have specified "nulls not allowed" for the S# column)

Once all this information has been entered, we press PF key 3 to save our extract request and return to the main DXT End User Dialog screen.

The next task is to specify data access information to verify that we are authorized to read from the source table. To do this we press PF key 12 to reach the *Database Access* screen shown in Fig. 20.16.

The Database Access screen is in two parts. The top part is used to specify necessary control information to be used to access the source system (node ID, user ID, and password); this information will be used in constructing the data extract job stream. The bottom part (required only if the source system is SQL/DS) specifies similar information for the target system. (Remember that, in general, the source system, target system, and system running the DXT dialogs can all be different.) In practice, most of the information on the Database Access screen will be completed automatically using information supplied by the DXT administrator.

Our extract request is now complete. If we press PF key 2 the extract job will be submitted for execution. DXT will route the extract job to the source system, extract the data, and then route the extracted data to the target system. On the target system it will invoke the appropriate load utility and load the extracted data into the table specified. We will be notified when the data extract job completes and when the load of the target table is finished.

```
                        DATABASE ACCESS


Source information:

Location        ===> SANJOSE1          Location of table(s) to be extracted
User ID         ===> CJDATE            User ID to access source table(s).
Password        ===>                   Access password of above User ID.
VM Execution ID ===>                   User ID to execute VM extract request

Target information when source is SQL/DS:

User ID         ===>                   User ID to execute the job that
                                       processes the extracted output.
Network ID      ===> RSCS              Net ID to route extracted output.
Target Node ID  ===>                   Location for extracted output.



Press ENTER to save the required information.


COMMAND ===>
PF 1=HELP       2=SEND      3=END       4=TABLES    5=COLUMNS   6=CONDTION
PF 7=BACKWARD   8=FORWARD   9=JOIN      10=TARGET   11=EXT LIST 12=ACCESS
```

Fig. 20.16 DXT Database Access screen

Conclusion

Copy management is a complex task, particularly when extracting data from nonrelational files and databases. End-users will typically not set up and maintain their own copy management schemes, but will instead rely on the DP department to perform this function for them. The DXT Administrative Dialogs are designed to assist the DP department in this task. End-users can use the DXT End User Dialogs to code and submit extract requests to extract both relational and nonrelational data for loading into DB2 and SQL/DS tables. However, strict management of this process is required in practice.

20.4 DATA PROPAGATOR

Overview

It is often desirable in practice to be able to maintain multiple copies of "the same" data in multiple databases under multiple database managers. Typically, an organization might need to keep one copy of the data in its operational database for use in the day-to-day activity of running the business, and another, separate copy in what is sometimes called an "informational" database for use in business analysis and decision support activities. In Section 20.3 above, we saw how IBM's DXT product can be used to support this requirement by allowing data to be copied from an operational database maintained under IMS (say) to an informational database maintained under DB2 (say).

With DXT, however, the informational database is (obviously) always a little out of date, because it reflects the operational data as it was at the time when the copy was taken. In other words, the informational database contains historical data, not current data. But there will always be some situations in which this lack of synchronization is unacceptable, i.e., situations in which the informational and operational databases are required to be "in synch." If as suggested above the operational and informational databases are indeed maintained under IMS and DB2, respectively, then IBM's Data Propagator product (DPROP) can be used to satisfy this more demanding requirement.

DPROP operates by capturing updates to the IMS database as they occur and applying them to the DB2 database, a process that IBM calls *data propagation*. *Note*: If the two databases are to be kept truly in synch, of course, then this propagation process must effectively be "instantaneous"—i.e., both databases must be updated at the same time (*synchronous* propagation); however, DPROP actually supports both synchronous and asynchronous propagation, as we shall see.

DPROP thus allows the installation to develop DB2 applications that require access to data residing in IMS databases, without having to migrate those IMS databases—and, more importantly, without having to migrate existing IMS applications that use those databases—to the DB2 environment. Note, however, that such DB2 applications must be read-only with respect to that IMS data;* if updates were permitted, they would not be propagated back to IMS, and the DB2 and IMS data would no longer be in synch.

DPROP Operation

Note: The reader will need at least a basic familiarity with IMS in order to understand some of the detailed explanations in the remainder of this section.

As indicated above, DPROP supports the propagation of updates made to IMS databases to the DB2 environment. It supports IMS HISAM,

---

*More precisely, with respect to the DB2 copy of that IMS data.

HDAM, HIDAM, SHISAM, and DEDB databases,* and both batch and online IMS regions (MPP, BMP, and IFP). Its operation is logically transparent to existing IMS applications (though there may be a performance impact—see below). All updates made to designated IMS data by such applications are captured and sent to an IBM-supplied DB2 application called the *Relational Update Program* (see below). The capturing and copying of IMS updates is done in accordance with installation-supplied *mapping definitions* (discussed in the next subsection).

Fig. 20.17 shows the basic DPROP components. We explain that figure as follows. First, let *S* be an IMS segment type for which data propagation is required. When an update occurs to an instance of *S*, the IMS Data Capture Facility invokes an exit routine, namely the Relational Update Program referred to above (the name of this routine must have been supplied as part of the definition of *S* in the IMS database definition). The Relational Update Program is invoked for each update made to any instance of *S*, also for updates to other segment instances caused by IMS cascading deletes. It accesses the mapping definitions in the DPROP *directory* (which is maintained under DB2) to determine what propagation is required; it then invokes a DB2 SQL program to apply the required updates to the relevant DB2 tables. *Note*: That DB2 program—which uses static SQL, incidentally—is generated by DPROP itself from the mapping definitions.

In order to ensure the consistency of the two databases, the IMS update is not considered to have completed until the corresponding DB2 update has been applied as well. From DB2's point of view, the situation is exactly the same as it is with any application that updates both DB2 and IMS data—that is, transaction atomicity and DB2/IMS data consistency are guaranteed by means of the DB2/IMS *two-phase commit process* (as mentioned in Chapter 13). Because the two-phase commit process for IMS and DB2 does not currently operate across multiple distinct sites, the IMS and DB2 databases must reside on the same MVS system.

As suggested under the "Overview" subsection above, the process discussed so far, in which IMS updates cannot complete until all propagated DB2 updates have been done as well, is known as *synchronous* propagation. Synchronous propagation has the obvious advantage that the DB2 copy of the data always reflects the current state of the IMS original, but it does also have the disadvantage that it might negatively affect the performance of IMS applications (because the DB2 updates are done "inline"). For this reason, DPROP also supports *asynchronous* propagation (see Fig. 20.18 on page 428).

---

*DEDB sequential dependent segments are not supported.

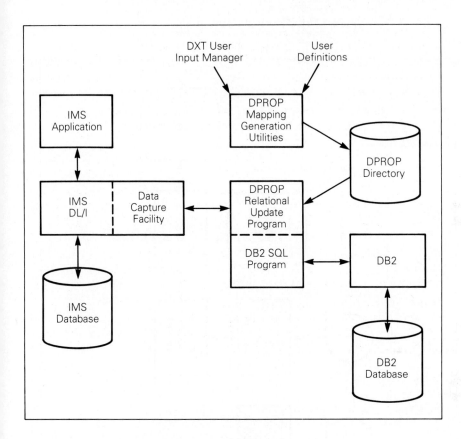

Fig. 20.17 DPROP synchronous propagation

Under aysnchronous propagation, the IMS Data Capture Facility invokes a installation-supplied exit routine (instead of the Relational Update
Program), passing it details of the IMS changes made. The exit routine can
then save those changes by (e.g.) writing them to an MVS file or an IMS
database or the IMS log; later, another installation-supplied routine can
read them back and pass them to the Relational Update Program for applying to the appropriate DB2 tables. Alternatively, the two routines could be
at different sites and could communicate directly over a network. *Note*:
The two installation-supplied routines are sometimes referred to as the
changed data sender and the *changed data receiver*, respectively.

There are several points to note regarding asynchronous propagation.
On the debit side:

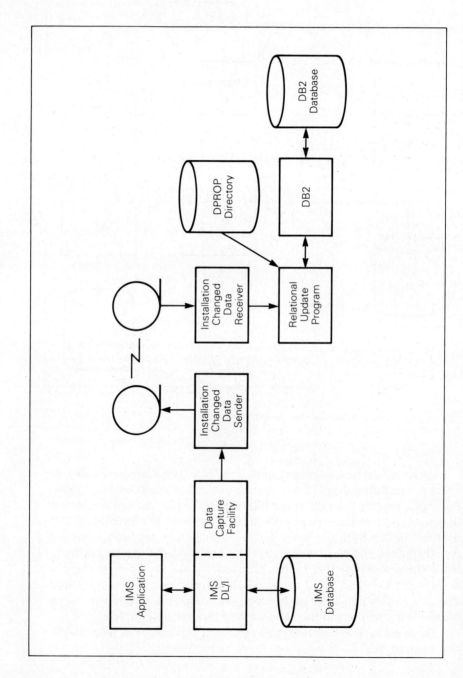

Fig. 20.18 DPROP asynchronous propagation

- First of all, of course, there is the obvious point that the DB2 and IMS databases are no longer being kept in synch. In other words, the DB2 tables now contain historical data, not current data.

- Also, the installation has much more work to do than it does with synchronous propagation.

On the other hand, there are several benefits too:

- The impact on IMS performance should be less than with synchronous propagation, because IMS updates do not have to wait for the DB2 tables to be updated before they can complete.

- The DB2 and IMS databases can now reside on different MVS systems.

- DPROP with asynchronous propagation provides an alternative to DXT as a mechanism for creating informational DB2 databases from operational IMS databases. Compared with DXT, it has the advantage that data that has not been updated does not need to be copied from one database to the other.

- DPROP with asynchronous propagation also supports CICS as a transaction manager.

Using DPROP

Data propagation in DPROP is done according to installation-supplied mapping definitions (also known as *propagation requests*) stored in the DPROP directory. These definitions specify which IMS segment types and fields map to which DB2 tables and columns, and how the mapping is to be done. There are two ways in which the mapping definitions can be created:

- *Using data extract requests created by DXT.* Note first that before DPROP can be used to propagate data from IMS to DB2, an initial one-time *extract* of the IMS data to DB2 must be done, in order to initialize the DB2 database appropriately (i.e., to ensure that the DB2 and IMS databases start off in synch with each other). One way of performing this initial extract is by means of DXT (the other is by means of a user-written application). If DXT is used, then clearly the DXT mapping process that has to be performed during that initial extract is very similar to the DPROP mapping process that has to be performed during data propagation. Thus, it is a comparatively straightforward matter for DPROP to generate the mapping definitions it requires from the DXT definitions used to do the initial extract. DPROP supplies an exit routine to be invoked from the DXT User Input Manager in order to perform this task (refer to Section 20.3 if you need to refresh your memory regarding the User Input Manager).

- *By entering propagation requests directly into DPROP tables.* These requests can be created using an ad hoc query tool such as QMF, or by an installation-supplied SQL application. The requests are entered into the tables in source form and then converted to the internal form needed by DPROP by a DPROP utility.

DPROP supports two types of IMS-to-DB2 mapping (note, however, that the first can be regarded as effectively just a special case of the second). Refer to Fig. 20.19.

1. One IMS segment type to one DB2 table. The DB2 table can include any or all of the fields (including key fields) from the IMS segment type. It can also include the keys of all of the ancestor segment types in the IMS hierarchy.

2. One IMS parent segment type, together with one or more immediate child segment types of that parent, to one DB2 table. The parent is called an *entity* segment type and the children *extension* segment types. Each extension segment type must have a maximum of one instance per instance of the entity segment type. The DB2 table can include any or all of the fields (including key fields) from each of the segment types involved; it can also include the keys of all of the ancestor segment types in the IMS hierarchy.

Note: DPROP provides a set of generalized mappings (similar to those used in DXT) from IMS data types to their DB2 counterparts. However, the installation has the option of performing its own more specific mappings (see below).

At execution time, the DPROP Relational Update Program can optionally invoke any of the following installation-supplied routines:

- An IMS segment exit routine (e.g., to handle IMS fields that have variable start positions within their containing segment)
- An IMS field exit routine (e.g., to handle IMS fields that have special formats not supported by DPROP)
- A DPROP exit routine for doing installation-defined mapping of IMS data to DB2 formats

Once the propagation requests have been created and the initial extract of the IMS data to DB2 done, data propagation can begin. IBM provides several utilities to aid in DPROP operation:

- *Status Change Utility*: This utility is used to control DPROP operations (e.g., to suspend and resume data propagation, activate and deactivate DPROP traces, and so forth). *Note*: DPROP traces are used for such

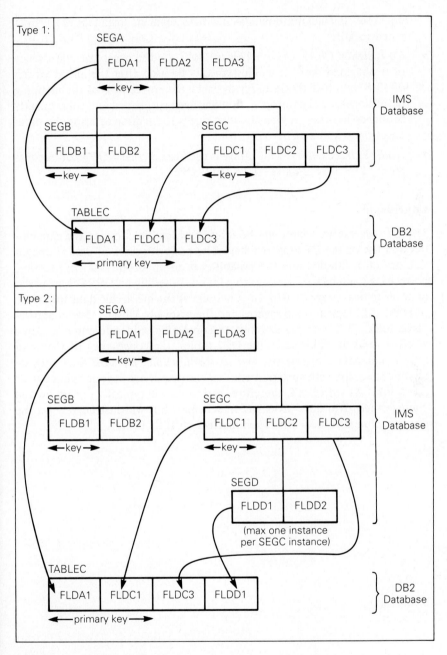

Fig. 20.19 DPROP mapping types (examples)

purposes as tracking how specific IMS segment instances are propagated to DB2.

- *Consistency Check Utility*: This utility is used to check the consistency of propagated data. It would typically be used after the initial extract of IMS data to DB2 (in order to check the correctness of the mapping definitions), or after propagation has been suspended and subsequently resumed (in order to identify what needs to be done to bring the databases back into synch).

- *Audit Extract Utility*: This utility is used to copy DPROP audit records from MVS SMF data sets into DB2 tables.

Conclusion

This has necessarily been only the briefest of introductions to the capabilities and use of the DPROP product. The basic concepts of data propagation are fairly simple, and the capability is an important one. In practice, however, a great deal of care has to be taken in setting up DPROP properly, in order to deal properly with such matters as the hierarchic data structures of IMS, IMS logical relationships and the associated insert, delete, and replace rules, DB2 referential integrity constraints and referential actions, whether nulls are allowed in the DB2 tables, the consistency of IMS and DB2 uniqueness declarations, and so forth. (*Note*: DPROP does provide facilities to assist with such matters, but the details are beyond the scope of this book.) As with DXT, therefore, end-users will typically not set up and manage their own data propagation schemes, but will instead rely on the DP department to deal with such matters on their behalf.

APPENDIXES

The Relational Model

A.1 INTRODUCTION

DB2 is a relational DBMS ("relational system" for short); in other words, it is a system that is constructed in accordance with the principles of the *relational model* (or the major principles, at any rate). The relational model, in turn, is *a way of looking at data*—that is, it is a prescription for how to represent data (namely, by means of "tables"), and a prescription for how to manipulate that representation (namely, by means of operators such as join). More precisely, the relational model is concerned with three aspects of data: data *structure*, data *integrity*, and data *manipulation*. The purpose of this appendix is to explain these three aspects in a little more detail. Section A.2 is concerned with relational data structure, Section A.3 with relational integrity rules, and Section A.4 with relational data manipulation.

A few preliminary remarks before we start getting into details:

1. First, in this appendix we will (for the most part) be using formal relational terminology. For convenience, Fig. A.1 repeats from Chapter 1 certain major relational terms and their informal equivalents.

2. Our treatment of the model in this appendix is necessarily somewhat terse and superficial, for reasons of space. A more extensive description can be found in the book *An Introduction to Database Systems: Volume I*, by C. J. Date (5th edition, Addison-Wesley, 1990).

3. Finally, we should also make the point that the relational model is not a static thing, but rather has evolved (and continues to evolve) over time. The version described in this appendix might be called the "original" or "basic" model; however, many new features have been added since that original version was first defined.* This appendix is concerned only with the original version.

Formal relational term	Informal equivalent(s)
relation tuple attribute primary key	table row, (logical) record column, field unique identifier

Fig. A.1 Some terminology

A.2 RELATIONAL DATA STRUCTURE

The smallest unit of data in the relational model is the individual data value. Such values are assumed to be *atomic*—that is, they have no internal structure so far as the model is concerned. A *domain* is the set of all possible data values of some particular type. For example, the domain of supplier numbers is the set of all valid supplier numbers; the domain of shipment quantities is the set of all integers greater than zero and less than 10,000 (say). Thus domains are *pools of values*, from which the actual values appearing in attributes (columns) are drawn.

The domain concept is significant for a number of reasons. In particular, it has implications for comparisons, and hence for operations such as join, union, etc., that directly or indirectly involve such comparisons. If two attributes draw their values from the same domain, then compari-

---

*Such matters are discussed in detail in the book *Relational Database Writings 1989–1991* (especially Chapters 15 and 16), by C. J. Date and Hugh Darwen (Addison-Wesley, 1992).

sons—and therefore joins, unions, etc.—involving those two attributes probably make sense, because they are comparing like with like. Conversely, if two attributes draw their values from different domains, then comparisons (etc.) involving those two attributes probably do not make sense. In SQL terms, for example, the query

```
SELECT  P.*, SP.*
FROM    P, SP
WHERE   P.P# = SP.P# ;
```

probably does make sense, whereas the query

```
SELECT  P.*, SP.*
FROM    P, SP
WHERE   P.P# = SP.S# ;
```

probably does not. (SQL, however, has no notion of domains per se. Both of the foregoing SELECT statements are legal in SQL today.)

Note that domains are primarily conceptual in nature. They may or may not be explicitly stored in the database as actual sets of values. But they should be specified as part of the database definition (in a system that supports the concept at all—but most systems currently do not); and then each attribute definition should include a reference to the corresponding domain. A given attribute may have the same name as the corresponding domain or a different name. Obviously it must have a different name if any ambiguity would otherwise result (in particular, if two attributes in the same relation are both based on the same domain; see the definition of relation below, and note the phrase "not necessarily all distinct").

We are now in a position to define the term "relation." A *relation* on domains D1, D2, . . . , Dn (not necessarily all distinct) consists of a *heading* and a *body*. The heading consists of a fixed set of distinct *attributes* A1, A2, . . ., An, such that each attribute Ai corresponds to exactly one of the underlying domains Di (i = 1,2, . . . ,n). The body consists of a time-varying set of *tuples*, where each tuple in turn consists of a set of attribute-value pairs (Ai:vi) (i = 1,2, . . . ,n), one such pair for each attribute Ai in the heading. For any given attribute-value pair (Ai:vi), vi is a value from the unique domain Di that is associated with the attribute Ai.

As an example, let us see how the supplier relation S measures up to this definition (see Fig. 1.2 in Chapter 1). The underlying domains are the domain of supplier numbers (D1, say), the domain of supplier names (D2), the domain of supplier status values (D3), and the domain of city names (D4). The heading of S consists of the attributes S# (underlying domain D1), SNAME (domain D2), STATUS (domain D3), and CITY (domain D4). The body of S consists of a set of tuples (five tuples in Fig. 1.2, but this set varies with time as updates are made to the relation); and each tuple consists of a set of four attribute-value pairs, one such pair for each of the four attributes in the heading. For example, the tuple for supplier S1 consists of the pairs

```
( S#      : 'S1'     )
( SNAME   : 'Smith'  )
( STATUS  :  20      )
( CITY    : 'London' )
```

(though it is normal to elide the attribute names in informal contexts). And of course each attribute value does indeed come from the appropriate underlying domain; the value "S1", for example, does come from the supplier number domain D1. So S is indeed a relation according to the definition.

Note carefully that when we draw a relation such as relation S as a table, as we did in Fig. 1.2, we are merely making use of a convenient method for representing the relation on paper. A table and a relation are not really the same thing, though for most of this book we have assumed that they are. For example, the rows of a table clearly have an ordering (from top to bottom), whereas the tuples of a relation do not (the body of a relation is a mathematical *set*, and sets do not have any ordering in mathematics). Likewise, the columns of a table also have an ordering (from left to right), whereas the attributes of a relation do not.

Notice also that the underlying domains of a relation are "not necessarily all distinct." Many examples have already been given in which they are not; see, e.g., the result relation in Example 5.3.1 (Chapter 5), which includes two attributes both defined on the domain of city names.

The value n (the number of attributes in the relation, or equivalently the number of underlying domains) is called the *degree* of the relation. A relation of degree one is called *unary*, a relation of degree two *binary*, a relation of degree three *ternary*, . . . , and a relation of degree n *n-ary*. In the suppliers-and-parts database, relations S, P, and SP have degrees 4, 5, and 3, respectively. The number of tuples in the relation is called the *cardinality* of that relation; the cardinalities of relations S, P, and SP of Fig. 1.2 are 5, 6, and 12, respectively. The cardinality of a relation changes with time, whereas the degree does not.

A.3   RELATIONAL DATA INTEGRITY

One important consequence of the definitions in the previous section is that *every relation has at least one candidate key*. Since the body of a relation is a set, and sets by definition do not contain duplicate elements, it follows that (at any given time) no two tuples of a relation can be duplicates of each other. Let R be a relation with attributes A1, A2, . . . , An. The set of attributes K = (A*i*,A*j*, . . . ,A*k*) of R is said to be a *candidate key* of R if and only if it satisfies the following two time-independent properties:

1. *Uniqueness*:

   At any given time, no two distinct tuples of R have the same value for A*i*, the same value for A*j*, . . . , and the same value for A*k*.

2. *Minimality*:

   No proper subset of the set (A*i*,A*j*, . . . ,A*k*) has the uniqueness property.

Every relation has at least one candidate key, because at least the combination of all of its attributes has the uniqueness property. In the case of base relations, at least, one candidate key is designated as the *primary* key; the remaining candidate keys (if any) are called *alternate* keys.* *Note*: The rationale by which one candidate key is chosen as the primary key (in cases where there is a choice) is outside the framework of the relational model per se. In practice the choice is usually straightforward.

Example: Suppose that supplier names and supplier numbers are both unique (at any given time, no two suppliers have the same number or the same name). Then relation S has two candidate keys, S# and SNAME. We choose S# as the primary key; SNAME then becomes an alternate key.

Continuing with the example, consider attribute S# of relation SP. It is clear that a given value for that attribute, say the supplier number S1, should be permitted to appear in the database only if that same value also appears as a value of the primary key S# of relation S (for otherwise the database cannot be considered to be in a state of integrity). An attribute such as SP.S# is said to be a *foreign key*. In general, a foreign key is an attribute (or attribute combination) of one relation R2 whose values are required to match those of the primary key of some relation R1 (R1 and R2 not necessarily distinct). Note that a foreign key and the corresponding primary key should be defined on the same underlying domain.

We can now state the two integrity rules of the relational model. *Note*: These rules are *general*, in the sense that any database that conforms to the model is required to satisfy them. However, any specific database will have a set of additional specific rules that apply to it alone. For example, the suppliers-and-parts database may have a specific rule to the effect that shipment quantities must be a multiple of 100, say. But such specific rules are outside the scope of the basic relational model per se.

---

*A base relation corresponds to what we have been calling a base table in the body of this book; i.e., it is an autonomous, named relation. See Chapter 4 for further discussion.

1. *Entity integrity*:

   No attribute participating in the primary key of a base relation is allowed to contain any nulls.

2. *Referential integrity*:

   If base relation R2 includes a foreign key FK matching the primary key PK of some base relation R1, then every value of FK in R2 must either (a) be equal to the value of PK in some tuple of R1 or (b) be wholly null (i.e., each attribute value participating in that FK value must be null). R1 and R2 are not necessarily distinct.

   > *A couple of asides*: Please note that, although the two rules are framed in terms of "nulls," we do not necessarily assume the rather peculiar kind of null found in SQL today. Please note too that each of the two rules is the subject of a certain amount of controversy, details of which are beyond the scope of this short appendix, however. *End of asides*.

   The justification for the entity integrity rule is as follows:

1. Base relations correspond to entities in the real world. For example, base relation S corresponds to a set of suppliers in the real world.

2. By definition, entities in the real world are distinguishable—i.e., they have a unique identification of some kind.

3. Primary keys perform the unique identification function in the relational model.

4. Thus, a null primary key value within a base relation would be a contradiction in terms—in effect, it would be saying that there was some entity that had no known *id*entity. An entity that cannot be identified is a contradiction in terms. Hence the name "entity integrity."

To put it another way: *In a relational database, we never record information about something we cannot identify.*

As for the second rule ("referential integrity"), it is clear that a given foreign key value must have a matching primary key value in some tuple of the referenced relation if that foreign key value is nonnull. Sometimes, however, it is necessary to permit the foreign key to accept nulls. (We remark, however, that nulls in a foreign key position are likely to be of the "value does not exist" variety, rather than the "value unknown" variety.) For example, suppose that in a given company it is legal for some employee to be currently assigned to no department at all. For such an employee, the department number attribute (which is a foreign key) would have to be null in the tuple representing that employee in the database.

A.4 RELATIONAL DATA MANIPULATION

The manipulative part of the relational model consists of a set of operators known collectively as the *relational algebra*, together with a *relational assignment* operator which assigns the value of some arbitrary expression of the algebra to another relation. We discuss the algebra first.

Each operator of the relational algebra takes either one or two relations as its input and produces a new relation as its output. Codd originally defined eight such operators, two groups of four each: (1) the traditional set operations union, intersection, difference, and Cartesian product (all modified slightly to take account of the fact that their operands are specifically relations, as opposed to arbitrary sets); and (2) the special relational operations restrict (also known as select), project, join, and divide. The eight operations are shown symbolically in Fig. A.2 (overleaf). We give a brief definition of each operation below; for simplicity, we assume in those definitions that the left-to-right order of attributes within a relation *is* significant—not because it is necessary to do so, but because it simplifies the discussion.*

Traditional Set Operations

Each of the traditional set operations takes two operands. For all except Cartesian product, the two operand relations must be "union-compatible"—that is, they must be of the same degree, *n* say, and the *i*th attribute of each (*i* = 1,2, . . . ,*n*) must be based on the same domain.

- Union

    The union of two union-compatible relations A and B is the set of all tuples *t* belonging to either A or B (or both).
    SQL example:

    ```
    SELECT S.S# FROM S
    UNION
    SELECT SP.S# FROM SP ;
    ```

- Intersection

    The intersection of two union-compatible relations A and B is the set of all tuples *t* belonging to both A and B.

---

*A "clean" version of the algebra that does not rely on this attribute ordering assumption is described in the book mentioned earlier, *An Introduction to Database Systems: Volume I*, by C. J. Date.

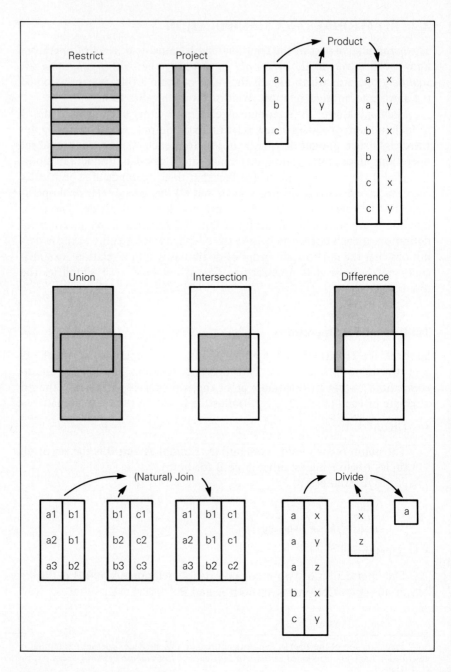

Fig. A.2 The relational algebra

SQL example:

```
SELECT S.S# FROM S
WHERE  EXISTS
       ( SELECT SP.S# FROM SP
         WHERE  SP.S# = S.S# ) ;
```

- Difference

  The difference between two union-compatible relations A and B—in
  that order—is the set of all tuples *t* belonging to A and not to B.
  SQL example:

```
SELECT S.S# FROM S
WHERE  NOT EXISTS
       ( SELECT SP.S# FROM SP
         WHERE  SP.S# = S.S# ) ;
```

- Product

  The product of two relations A and B is the set of all tuples *t* such that
  t is the concatenation of a tuple *a* belonging to A and a tuple *b* belonging to B.
  SQL example:

```
SELECT S.*, SP.*
FROM   S, SP ;
```

Special Relational Operations

- Restriction (also known as selection)

  Let *theta* represent any valid scalar comparison operator (for example,
  $=$, $\neg=$, $>$, $>=$, etc.). The theta-restriction of relation A on attributes X and Y is the set of all tuples *t* of A such that the condition "*t*.X
  theta t.Y" evaluates to *true*. (Attributes X and Y should be defined on
  the same domain, and the operation *theta* must make sense for that
  domain.) A literal value may be specified instead of attribute Y. Thus,
  the theta-restriction operator yields a "horizontal" subset of a given
  relation—that is, that subset of the tuples of the given relation for
  which a specified condition is satisfied. *Note*: "Theta-restriction" is
  usually abbreviated to just "restriction." Also, as mentioned above,
  this operator is often referred to as "theta-selection," or simply "selection," but note that the operation is certainly not identical to the
  SELECT operator of SQL.
  SQL example:

```
SELECT S.*
FROM   S
WHERE  CITY ¬= 'London' ;
```

- Projection

  The projection operator yields a "vertical" subset of a given relation—
  that is, that subset obtained by selecting specified attributes and then
  eliminating redundant duplicate tuples (if any) within the attributes selected.
    SQL example:

  ```
  SELECT DISTINCT P.COLOR, P.CITY
  FROM    P ;
  ```

- Join

  Let *theta* be as defined under "Restriction" above. The theta-join of
  relation A on attribute X with relation B on attribute Y is the set of all
  tuples *t* such that *t* is the concatenation of a tuple *a* belonging to A and
  a tuple *b* belonging to B and the condition "*a*.X *theta b*.Y" evaluates
  to *true*. (Attributes B.X and B.Y should be defined on the same domain, and the operation *theta* must make sense for that domain.)
    SQL example:

  ```
  SELECT S.*, P.*
  FROM    S, P
  WHERE   S.CITY > P.CITY ;
  ```

  If *theta* is equality, the join is called an equijoin. It follows from
  the definition that the result of an equijoin must include two identical
  attributes. If one of those two attributes is eliminated (by means of a
  projection), the result is called the *natural* join. The unqualified term
  "join" is usually taken to mean the natural join specifically.

- Division

  In its simplest form (which is all that we consider here), the division
  operator divides a relation of degree two (the dividend) by a relation
  of degree one (the divisor), and produces a result relation of degree one
  (the quotient). Let the dividend (A) have attributes X and Y, and let
  the divisor (B) have attribute Y. Attributes A.Y and B.Y should be
  defined on the same domain. The result of dividing A by B is the relation C, with sole attribute X, such that every value *x* of C.X appears
  as a value of A.X, and the pair of values (*x*,*y*) appears in A for *all*
  values *y* appearing in B.
    SQL example:

  ```
  SELECT DISTINCT SPX.S# FROM SP SPX
  WHERE   NOT EXISTS
      ( SELECT P.P# FROM P
        WHERE   NOT EXISTS
            ( SELECT SPY.* FROM SP SPY
              WHERE   SPY.S# = SPX.S# AND SPY.P# = P.P# ) ) ;
  ```

Here we are assuming for simplicity that (a) relation SP has only two attributes, namely S# and P# (we are ignoring QTY), and (b) relation P has only one attribute, namely P# (we are ignoring PNAME, COLOR, WEIGHT, and CITY). We divide the first of these two relations by the second and obtain a result, namely a relation with one attribute (S#) that lists supplier numbers for suppliers that supply all parts.*

It is worth mentioning that this set of eight operations is not (and was never intended to be) a *minimal* set. A minimal set—i.e., a set of *primitive* operations—would be the set consisting of restriction, projection, product, union, and difference; the other three operations can be defined in terms of those five. For example, the natural join is a projection of a restriction of a product. In practice, however, those other three operations (especially join) are so useful that a good case can be made for supporting them directly.

Turning now to the relational assignment operation, the purpose of that operation is simply to allow the value of some algebraic expression—say a join—to be saved in some more or less permanent place. It can be simulated in SQL by means of the INSERT . . . SELECT operation. For example, suppose relation XYZ has two attributes, S# and P#, and suppose also that it is currently empty (i.e., contains no tuples). The SQL statement

```
INSERT INTO XYZ ( S#, P# )
       SELECT S.S#, P.P#
       FROM   S, P
       WHERE  S.CITY = P.CITY ;
```

assigns the result of the SELECT (namely, a projection of a join) to the relation XYZ.

By way of conclusion, Fig. A.3 (overleaf) summarizes the major components of the relational model.

---

*More precisely, supplier numbers for suppliers who (a) supply *at least one part* and (b) in fact supply all parts. Just why this apparently redundant emendation is needed is beyond the scope of this appendix, but the reader might like to meditate on the case in which there are no parts at all in the database (i.e., table P is empty).

```
Data structure
  domains (values)
  keys (candidate, primary, alternate, foreign)

Data integrity
  1. primary key values must not be null
  2. foreign key values must match primary key values
     (or be null)

Data manipulation
  relational algebra
    union, intersection, difference, product
    restrict, project, join, divide
  relational assignment
```

Fig. A.3   The relational model

APPENDIX

◆ B ◆

Date and Time Support

B.1 INTRODUCTION

The date and time support in DB2 is quite extensive (and quite complicated—unduly so, in this writer's opinion). Rather than discussing that support in full detail in the main part of the text, therefore, and thereby interfering with the overall flow of the presentation, it seemed better to relegate
any such discussion to some less obtrusive position in the book; hence this
appendix. *Note*: In order to make the appendix reasonably self-contained,
we do repeat some of the details (regarding, e.g., "date/time literals" and
date/time functions) from the body of the book.

One preliminary note on terminology: Throughout this appendix, we
use the term "date/time" to mean "date or time or timestamp." For example, the expression "date/time data types" means the three data types
DATE and TIME and TIMESTAMP, considered collectively.

B.2   DATA TYPES

As indicated at the end of the previous section, there are three date/time data types in DB2:

DATE
: Date, represented as a sequence of eight unsigned packed decimal digits (*yyyymmdd*), occupying four bytes; permitted values are legal dates in the range January 1st, 1 A.D., to December 31st, 9999 A.D., inclusive

TIME
: Time, represented as a sequence of six unsigned packed decimal digits (*hhmmss*), occupying three bytes; permitted values are legal times in the range midnight to midnight, i.e., 000000 to 240000, inclusive

TIMESTAMP
: "Timestamp" (combination of date and time, accurate to the nearest microsecond), represented as a sequence of 20 unsigned packed decimal digits (*yyyymmddhhmmssnnnnnn*), occupying ten bytes; permitted values are legal timestamps in the range 00010101000000000000 to 99991231240000000000, inclusive

By the term "legal dates" in the foregoing, we mean that DB2 will not permit invalid dates such as 19960431 ("April 31st, 1996") or 19970229 ("February 29th, 1997"). Similarly for times and timestamps, of course.

B.3   LITERALS

As explained in Chapter 3, strictly speaking there is no such thing as a date/time literal. Instead, there are *interpreted character string literals*. If a character string literal appears in a context that requires a date/time value,* then that character string will be interpreted as a date/time value, provided of course that it is of the appropriate form (a conversion error will occur if it is not). We will use the term "date/time string" to refer to a character string that represents a legal date/time value.

"Date/time string" literals, then, take the following forms (except as noted below):

---

*More generally, of course, any character string *expression* can appear in such a context (see Section B.6).

date
string

Written as a character string literal of the form
mm/dd/yyyy, enclosed in single quotes

Examples: `'1/18/1941'`
`'12/25/1999'`

time
string

Written as a character string literal of the form
hh:mm AM or *hh:mm* PM, enclosed in single
quotes

Examples: `'10:00 AM'`
`'9:30 PM'`

timestamp
string

Written as a character string literal of the form
yyyy-mm-dd-hh.mm.ss.nnnnnn, enclosed in single quotes

Examples: `'1998-4-28-12.00.00.000000'`
`'1944-10-17-18.30.45'`

Note: Actually, several different date/time string formats are supported: US style (USA), European style (EUR), International Standards Organization style (ISO), Japanese Industrial Standard Christian Era style (JIS), and installation-defined (LOCAL). A variety of methods (installation options, Precompiler options, etc.) are available for specifying the particular style to be used in any particular context. In this appendix we will always assume US style, barring any explicit statement to the contrary. As pointed out in Chapter 3, a peculiarity of US-style time string literals is that they do not include a seconds component. Nevertheless, the internal representation of a time value always does include such a component.

To repeat some syntactic details from Chapter 3: Leading zeros can be omitted from the month and day portions of a date or timestamp string literal and from the hours portion of a time or timestamp string literal. The seconds portion (including the preceding colon or period) can be omitted entirely from a time string literal (in fact, it must be so omitted in US style); an implicit specification of zero is assumed. Trailing zeros can be omitted from the microseconds portion of a timestamp string literal; the microseconds portion (including the preceding period) can also be omitted entirely, in which case an implicit specification of zero is assumed.

B.4 COLUMN DEFINITIONS

Date/time column definitions of course use the conventional DB2 syntax—

```
column data-type [ NOT NULL [ WITH DEFAULT | UNIQUE ] ]
```

—where "data-type" is DATE or TIME or TIMESTAMP. As mentioned in Section B.2, date/time values are represented internally as unsigned sequences of packed decimal digits, 2 digits to a byte, with a width of 4 bytes (DATE), 3 bytes (TIME), or 10 bytes (TIMESTAMP). *Note*: Adding a new column to an existing base table will invalidate packages and/or plans that refer to that table, if the data type of the new column is DATE or TIME or TIMESTAMP.

Default values for columns defined WITH DEFAULT are the value of CURRENT DATE or CURRENT TIME or CURRENT TIMESTAMP, as applicable (see Section B.7). Note, therefore, that if table T has a date/time column C defined WITH DEFAULT, then two consecutive INSERTs to T that both omit a value for C will cause two different values to be placed in the C position. This feature could be useful in situations in which there is no "natural" primary key—for example, given a table of temperature readings, which are not necessarily (or naturally) all distinct, we might define a TIMESTAMP column WITH DEFAULT to act as the primary key:

```
CREATE TABLE TEMP_READINGS
      ( READING_TIME   TIMESTAMP NOT NULL WITH DEFAULT,
        READING        DECIMAL(4,1),
        PRIMARY KEY ( READING_TIME ) ) ;
```

In effect, DB2 will then generate unique primary key values automatically (assuming of course that no explicit value is ever specified by the user on INSERT). Note, however, that a UNIQUE (primary) index will still be required on READING_TIME.

Note: The foregoing explanation of default values tacitly assumed that the column in question was defined via CREATE TABLE, not ALTER TABLE. The explanation requires some slight revision in the ALTER case. For rows inserted into the table after the ALTER is executed, the CURRENT defaults apply as discussed above. For rows already existing in the table at ALTER time, however, the defaults are defined as follows:

- DATE   --   '01/01/0001'

- TIME   --   '00:00 AM'

- TIMESTAMP   --   '0001-01-01-00.00.00.000000'

The reason for the difference has to do with the way adding columns via ALTER TABLE is implemented in DB2. As explained in Chapter 4, existing rows are not physically extended at ALTER time. Instead, DB2 simply materializes the necessary default value (for the column in question) each time such a row is retrieved. Materializing a (different) "current" value on each retrieval would obviously be inappropriate.

B.5 DURATIONS

DB2 supports the notion of a *duration*. A duration is an interval of time, such as "3 years" or "90 days" or "5 minutes 30 seconds." For example, subtracting the time "9:00 AM" from the time "10:15 AM" yields the duration "1 hour 15 minutes." *Note carefully, however, that there is no duration data type.* Instead, durations are *interpreted decimal integers*. For example, suppose we are given the following data definition:

```
CREATE TABLE T
    ( ... ,
      START_TIME   TIME,
      ... ,
      WAIT_TIME    DECIMAL(6),
      ... ) ;
```

Now consider the expression:

```
START_TIME + WAIT_TIME
```

If START_TIME and WAIT_TIME happen to have the values "9:00 AM" and 50000, respectively, then this expression will evaluate to "2:00 PM"; in other words, the value 50000 will be interpreted to mean "5 hours." Likewise, if they have the values "9:00 AM" and −50000, respectively, then the expression will evaluate to "4:00 AM."

It follows from the foregoing that durations can be stored in the database, but only in the form of DECIMAL values. DB2 is not aware that the column in question (i.e., WAIT_TIME, in the example) is really being used to hold duration values.

Durations are of three basic kinds: date durations, time durations, and timestamp durations. *Note:* A fourth kind, "microsecond durations," also exists but seems to have no official classifying name; see the discussion of "labeled durations" below.

- A date duration is a signed decimal integer of 8 digits (5 bytes) of the form *yyyymmdd*, where *yyyy* is the number of years (0–9999), *mm* is the number of months (0–99), and *dd* is the number of days (0–99).

- A time duration is a signed decimal integer of 6 digits (4 bytes) of the form *hhmmss*, where *hh* is the number of hours (0–99), *mm* is the number of minutes (0–99), and *ss* is the number of seconds (0–99).

- A timestamp duration is a signed decimal integer of 20 digits (11 bytes) of the form *yyyymmddhhmmssnnnnnn*, where *yyyy*, *mm*, and *dd* are as for date durations, *hh*, *mm*, and *ss* are as for time durations, and *nnnnnn* is the number of microseconds (0–999999).

- A "microsecond duration" is a signed decimal integer of 6 digits (4 bytes) of the form *nnnnnn*, representing *nnnnnn* microseconds.

Note that a duration such as "90 days" or "25 hours" is legal; i.e., "days" is not restricted to a maximum of 31, nor "hours" to a maximum of 23 (etc.). To return to the example discussed earlier: If START_TIME and WAIT_TIME have the values "9:00 AM" and 250000, respectively, then the expression

```
START_TIME + WAIT_TIME
```

evaluates to "10:00 AM"; the overflow in the hours position is ignored (see Section B.8).

Since "duration" is not really a data type but is instead just an interpreted decimal integer, there is strictly speaking no such thing as a "duration literal." Instead, decimal integers (of the appropriate format) can be used, as in (e.g.) the expression

```
START_TIME + 050000.
```

(Note that the decimal literal must have *exactly* the right precision and scale.)

However, DB2 does also include the notion of a *labeled duration*. Labeled durations are a special kind of scalar expression, whose value is a decimal integer that is to be interpreted as a duration (date, time, or "microsecond," but not, however, timestamp). Such expressions can be used to play the role of "duration literals" (among other things). Labeled durations take the form "n units", where "n" is any numeric expression (it is converted to a decimal integer if necessary), and "units" is any of the following:

```
YEAR[S]
MONTH[S]
DAY[S]
HOUR[S]
MINUTE[S]
SECOND[S]
MICROSECOND[S]
```

Examples:

```
3 YEARS
90 DAYS
1 MINUTE
47 MICROSECONDS
```

Of the seven possible "units" specifications listed above, the first three identify the duration as a date duration, the next three as a time duration, and the last one as a "microsecond duration" (not an official DB2 term). *Note*: Observe that date durations in general involve years *and* months *and* days, but *labeled* date durations involve years *or* months *or* days (not a mixture). Similarly, time durations in general involve hours *and* minutes *and* seconds, but labeled time durations involve hours *or* minutes *or* seconds, not a mixture.

Note: The IBM manuals classify durations differently, into date, time, timestamp, and labeled durations (i.e., a labeled duration is not the same thing as a date, time, or timestamp duration). This classification is somewhat counterintuitive, however, since a labeled duration clearly does represent a "duration" (in the ordinary English sense) of years or days or hours or . . . (etc.). In this appendix we will stay with our own classification.

Here are some examples of the use of labeled durations:

```
UPDATE  T
SET     START_TIME = START_TIME + 15 MINUTES
WHERE   ... ;

SELECT ...
FROM    T
WHERE   END_TIME < START_TIME + 1 HOUR + 30 MINUTES ;

UPDATE  SCHEDULE
SET     FINISH = FINISH + :SLIPPAGE MONTHS
WHERE   ... ;
```

SLIPPAGE here is a (numeric) host variable.

Note finally that the *only* context in which a labeled duration can appear is in an expression involving infix " + " or " − ", in which one operand is the labeled duration in question and the other is a date/time value. See Section B.8 for further discussion.

B.6 CONVERSIONS

DB2 includes a number of scalar builtin functions for performing explicit conversions involving date/time data.

Extraction of Date/Time Components

- YEAR, MONTH, DAY:

  Convert the year or month or day portion (as applicable) of a specified date or timestamp or date duration or timestamp duration to a binary integer.

- HOUR, MINUTE, SECOND:

  Convert the hours or minutes or seconds portion (as applicable) of a specified time or timestamp or time duration or timestamp duration to a binary integer.

- MICROSECOND:

  Converts the microseconds portion of a specified timestamp or time-stamp duration to a binary integer.

Examples:

```
MONTH ( END_DATE )
DAY ( DEPART - ARRIVE )
SECOND ( CURRENT TIME )
```

Conversions To/From Other Data Types

- DATE, TIME, TIMESTAMP:

  Convert a specified scalar value to a date or time or timestamp (as applicable). In the case of TIMESTAMP, the scalar value can be specified as a pair of values, representing a date and a time, respectively.

- CHAR

  Converts a specified date/time value to its character string representation in USA, EUR, ISO, JIS, or LOCAL format (as specified either by an argument to the function or, if that argument is omitted, either by the DATE Precompiler option or by the DATE FORMAT installation option).

- DAYS

  Converts a specified date or timestamp to a binary integer, representing the number of days since December 31st, 1 B.C. (Note that there is no "0 B.C."; December 31st, 1 B.C., is immediately followed by January 1st, 1 A.D.)

Examples:

```
DATE ('6/7/87')
TIME ( CURRENT TIMESTAMP )
CHAR ( START_DATE, USA )
DAYS ( '1/18/1941' )
```

Implicit Conversions

In certain circumstances DB2 will also perform implicit date/time conversions:

1. If a character string value occurs in a position where the language requires a date/time value, then the string will be interpreted as a date/time if possible.

2. If a decimal value occurs in a position where the language requires a duration, then the decimal value will be interpreted as a duration if possible.

3. If a date/time value occurs in a position where the language requires a character string value, then the date/time will be converted to its character string representation.

Examples:

1.
```
UPDATE  T
SET     START_DATE = :XM || '/' || :XD || '/' || :XY
WHERE   ... ;
```

   Here XM, XD, and XY are character string variables of two, two, and four characters, respectively. The character string expression is evaluated and then interpreted as a date string.

2.
```
UPDATE  T
SET     START_TIME = START_TIME + 050000.
WHERE   ... ;
```

   In this example the decimal value is interpreted as a time duration of 5 hours.

3.
```
SELECT START_DATE
INTO   :HOST_CHAR_FIELD
FROM   T
WHERE  ... ;
```

   Here START_DATE will be converted to its character string representation.

Note, however, that DB2 does not always permit a date/time value to appear in place of a character string value (Case 3 above). For example, the argument to LIKE is required to be a string—it cannot be a date/time value. On the other hand, the converse situations (Cases 1 and 2) are apparently always legal—that is, a character string or decimal value can always appear in place of a date/time value or duration, respectively—although actually even this is not totally clear from the documentation. In fact, the precise rules as to exactly what is permitted do not seem to be very well defined. On the whole, the best practice would seem to be to avoid implicit conversions by always using the explicit functions DATE (etc.). We refer the reader to the IBM manuals for further clarification.

There are no implicit conversions between dates and timestamps, or times and timestamps, or dates and times.

B.7 SPECIAL REGISTERS

DB2 supports a number of date/time "special registers" (as explained in Chapter 3, this is the official DB2 term, although "zero-argument builtin scalar functions" would be closer to the mark). The date/time special registers are CURRENT TIMEZONE, CURRENT DATE, CURRENT TIME, and CURRENT TIMESTAMP. A reference to one of these registers returns a scalar value, as follows:

- CURRENT TIMEZONE

  Returns a time duration representing (typically) the displacement of the local time zone from Greenwich Mean Time (GMT).* The value returned by each of CURRENT DATE, CURRENT TIME, and CURRENT TIMESTAMP (see below) is based on a reading of the CPU clock, incremented in each case by the value of CURRENT TIMEZONE. In the case of Pacific Standard Time, for example, if the CPU clock is set to GMT and CURRENT TIMEZONE to " − 8 hours," then CURRENT DATE, CURRENT TIME, and CURRENT TIMESTAMP would each return the true local value. If, on the other hand, the CPU clock is in fact set to the local value, then CURRENT TIMEZONE should probably be set to zero.

- CURRENT DATE

  Returns the current date, i.e., the date "today" (but see CURRENT TIMEZONE above).

- CURRENT TIME

  Returns the current time, i.e., the time "now" (but see CURRENT TIMEZONE above).

- CURRENT TIMESTAMP

  Returns the current timestamp, i.e., the date "today" concatenated with the time "now" (but see CURRENT TIMEZONE above).

When any given SQL data manipulation statement is executed, all references to CURRENT DATE and/or CURRENT TIME and/or CURRENT TIMESTAMP are based on a single reading of the local clock. Thus, for example, the WHERE clause "WHERE CURRENT TIME = CURRENT TIME" is guaranteed always to evaluate to *true*.

---

*The actual value of CURRENT TIMEZONE is established by an installation-defined MVS system parameter. Note too that (as mentioned in Chapter 3) in the standards world, at least, the term Greenwich Mean Time (GMT) has recently been dropped, and GMT-based times have been replaced by "UTC" times (where UTC stands for "Universal Coordinated Time").

B.8 EXPRESSIONS

The infix arithmetic operators " + " and " − " (only) can be used with date/
times. For example, a date and a date duration can be added to yield
another date. The reader is warned, however, that not all operations that
would appear to make sense are in fact permitted. Here is a complete list
of the legal possibilities in DB2:

First operand	Operator	Second operand	Result
date	+	date duration	date
date duration	+	date	date
date	−	date	date duration
date	−	date duration	date
time	+	time duration	time
time duration	+	time	time
time	−	time	time duration
time	−	time duration	time
timestamp	+	duration	timestamp
duration	+	timestamp	timestamp
timestamp	−	duration	timestamp
timestamp	−	timestamp	timestamp duration

In other words:

- For addition (infix " + ")
  - if one operand is a date, the other must be a date or a date duration
  - if one operand is a time, the other must be a time or a time duration
  - if one operand is a timestamp, the other must be a duration
- For subtraction (infix " − ")
  - if the first operand is a date, the second must be a date or a date duration
  - if the first operand is a time, the second must be a time or a time duration
  - if the first operand is a timestamp, the second must be a timestamp or a duration
  - if the second operand is a date, the first must be a date
  - if the second operand is a time, the first must be a time
  - if the second operand is a timestamp, the first must be a timestamp

Labeled durations are subject to an additional (and very major) constraint, namely as follows: They are permitted *only* as operands of infix

"+" or "−", and *only* if the other operand is a date/time value—*not* another duration (labeled or otherwise). Thus the following operations are all *** ILLEGAL *** if either of the duration operands is labeled (the "Result" column thus shows what might be expected in each case, *not* what DB2 will actually produce).

First operand	*Operator*	*Second operand*	*"Result"*
date duration	+	date duration	date duration
date duration	−	date duration	date duration
time duration	+	time duration	time duration
time duration	−	time duration	time duration
microsec duration	+	microsec duration	microsec duration
microsec duration	−	microsec duration	microsec duration

The aggregate functions COUNT, MAX, and MIN (but not SUM or AVG) can be applied to date/time arguments; the result is an integer for COUNT, a date/time value of the appropriate type for MAX and MIN.

Examples:

Note that some of the following expressions are not legal. We leave it as an exercise for the reader to determine why not.

```
DATE ('8/17/1972') - DATE ('10/28/1969')
DATE ('8/17/1972') -      '10/28/1969'
     '8/17/1972'  - DATE ('10/28/1969')
     '8/17/1972'  -      '10/28/1969'          *** ILLEGAL ***

START_DATE +   1 YEAR   +  6 MONTHS
1 YEAR     +   6 MONTHS +  START_DATE          *** ILLEGAL ***
               1 YEAR   +  6 MONTHS            *** ILLEGAL ***
( START_DATE +  1 YEAR ) +  6 MONTHS
START_DATE + ( 1 YEAR   +  6 MONTHS )          *** ILLEGAL ***
START_DATE +   6 WEEKS                         *** ILLEGAL ***
START_DATE +   4 HOURS                         *** ILLEGAL ***

START_TIME + WAIT_TIME
START_TIME + HOUR(WAIT_TIME) HOURS
START_TIME + 120000.
TIME('9:00 AM')  + 120000.
'9:00 AM'  + 120000.                           *** ILLEGAL ***
9 HOURS    + 120000.                           *** ILLEGAL ***

CURRENT TIMESTAMP + 1 SECOND + 500000 MICROSECONDS
CURRENT TIME - CURRENT TIMEZONE
ETA - ( CURRENT TIME - CURRENT TIMEZONE )
```

Date/time arithmetic is performed in accordance with the calendar and permissible date/time values. Thus, for example, the expression

```
DATE('5/31/1988') + 1 MONTH
```

yields the result "6/30/1988" (*not* "6/31/1988"—i.e., "June 30th, 1988," not "June 31st, 1988"). On the other hand, the expression

```
DATE('6/30/1988') - 1 MONTH
```

yields the result "5/30/1988" (not "5/31/1988"—i.e., "May 30th, 1988," not "May 31st, 1988"). In other words, the expression

```
DATE('5/31/1988') + 1 MONTH - 1 MONTH
```

does not yield "5/31/1988"! More generally, if we add a date duration d to some date and then subtract that same duration d from the result, we are not guaranteed to end up with the date we started with. By contrast, the expression

```
DATE('5/31/1988') + 30 DAYS - 30 DAYS
```

will indeed yield "5/31/1988"—i.e., we do end up with the date we started with in this case.

Another potential trap for the unwary is illustrated by the following example: What is the value of each of the following two expressions? We leave the details as an exercise for the reader. (Hint: Which value is the greater?)

```
TIME('9:00 AM') + 000100.
TIME('9:00 AM') + 000099.
```

Date/time arithmetic can cause overflow or underflow. The rules are as follows (for brevity, we use the term "overflow" to include both overflow and underflow):

- For dates:
  - overflow in the days position affects the months
  - overflow in the months position affects the years
  - overflow in the years position is an error
- For times:
  - overflow in the seconds position affects the minutes
  - overflow in the minutes position affects the hours
  - overflow in the hours position is ignored
- For timestamps:
  - same as above, except that overflow in the hours position affects the days

B.9 ASSIGNMENTS

Assignments occur on database update and retrieval operations. We consider the DATE data type first. On update:

- If the source is of type DATE, the target must be either of type DATE or of type character string. In the latter case, the date is implicitly converted to its string representation (a date string).

- If the target is of type DATE, the source must be either an expression that evaluates to a date or a character string that can legally be interpreted as a date (a date string). In the latter case, the string is implicitly converted to a date.

On retrieval:

- If the source is of type DATE, the target must be of type character string. The date is implicitly converted to its string representation (a date string).

Analogous rules apply to TIMEs and TIMESTAMPs, of course.

The fact that character strings are considered to be compatible with date/times for assignment purposes permits us to transfer date/time values to and from and programs written in languages such as PL/I that do not support any date/time data types.

Note that it is not possible to assign a value to an individual component (such as the days portion) of a date/time value. Note too that there are no explicit assignment rules for durations, because there is no duration data type; a "duration assignment" is merely a special kind of numeric assignment.

Examples:

```
SELECT  START_DATE
INTO    :HOST_CHAR_VBLE
FROM    T
WHERE   ... ;

INSERT
INTO    T ( ..., START_TIME, ... )
VALUES  ( ....., '10:30 AM', ... ) ;

UPDATE  T
SET     START_TIME = :HOST_CHAR_VBLE + 25 MINUTES
WHERE   ... ;
```

An example of a "duration assignment":

```
UPDATE  T
SET     WAIT_TIME = 030000.
WHERE   ... ;
```

Note that in this example no harm would result if the leading zero and the decimal point were dropped from the literal; DB2's ordinary numeric conversion rules would take care of everything satisfactorily.

B.10 COMPARISONS

Comparisons can be performed between

1. a DATE, TIME, or TIMESTAMP value, on the one hand, and
2. either another value of the same type or a character string that can legally be interpreted as a value of the same type (i.e., an appropriate date/time string), on the other.

Comparisons are performed in accordance with chronologic ordering. Note that the fact that character strings are considered to be compatible with date/times for comparison purposes permits us to compare date/time values with values from programs written in languages such as PL/I that do not support any date/time data types. Note too that there are no explicit comparison rules for durations, because there is no duration data type; a "duration comparison" is merely a special kind of numeric comparison.

Examples:

```
SELECT ...
FROM    T
WHERE   START_TIME > '9:00 AM'
AND     END_TIME   < '5:00 PM' ;

SELECT ...
FROM    FLIGHTS
WHERE   ETA > CURRENT TIME - CURRENT TIMEZONE ;
```

Here is an example of a "duration comparison":

```
SELECT ...
FROM    T
WHERE   START_TIME - END_TIME < 080000. ;
```

And here are two examples involving date/time functions:

```
SELECT ...
FROM    T
WHERE   MINUTE ( START_TIME ) = 0 ;

SELECT ...
FROM    T
WHERE   HOUR ( START_TIME ) NOT BETWEEN 9 AND 17 ;
```

One possible surprise that can occur in connection with TIME and TIMESTAMP comparisons is the following: A time value (*hhmmss*) of 240000 is considered to be greater than a time value of 000000, even though logically they both represent the same time (i.e., midnight). Note that these two representations are both legal; refer back to Section B.2.

APPENDIX

· C ·

Syntax of SQL Data Manipulation Operations

C.1 INTRODUCTION

We present a simplified BNF grammar for the four data manipulation operations of SQL (SELECT, INSERT, UPDATE, and DELETE) described in this book. The grammar makes use of the following convenient shorthand:

- If "xyz" is a syntactic category, then "xyz-commalist" is a syntactic category consisting of a list of one or more "xyz"s in which each pair of adjacent "xyz"s is separated by a sequence of characters consisting of zero or more spaces, followed by a comma, followed by zero or more spaces.

We also make use of some simplifying abbreviations, namely "exp" for expression, "ref" for reference, and "spec" for specification. The following are terminal categories with respect to this grammar (i.e., they are not defined further in the production rules):

```
identifier
literal
integer
```

Note: In the interests of clarity and brevity, we ignore the complexities of naming introduced by synonyms, aliases, and the possibility of remote data access. Also, please note that our grammar does not accurately reflect all of the syntactic limitations of SQL but is instead rather permissive, in the sense that it allows the generation of certain constructs that are not legal in SQL. For example, it allows the argument to an aggregate function such as AVG to consist of a reference to another such function, which SQL does not in fact permit (see Chapter 6, Section 6.4). It also makes no attempt to distinguish between the different types of scalar expression (numeric expressions, character string expressions, etc.). See Chapter 3, also Appendix B, for the details of such distinctions. (Our reason for making all of these simplifications is that SQL is a very context-sensitive language, and attempts to reflect context sensitivity in BNF tend to lead to a rather unwieldy set of production rules.)

C.2 BASIC ELEMENTS

```
table-spec
   ::=    table-ref [ range-variable ]

table-ref
   ::=    base-table | view

base-table
   ::=    [ user . ] identifier

user
   ::=    authorization-identifier

authorization-identifier
   ::=    identifier

view
   ::=    [ user . ] identifier

range-variable
   ::=    identifier

column-ref
   ::=    [ column-qualifier . ] column

column-qualifier
   ::=    table-ref
        | range-variable

column
   ::=    identifier
```

C.3 SCALAR EXPRESSIONS

```
scalar-exp
   ::=    scalar-term
        | scalar-exp + scalar-term
        | scalar-exp - scalar-term
        | scalar-exp CONCAT scalar-term
```

Note: The concatenation operator CONCAT can also be written as two adjacent vertical bars, thus: ‖.

```
scalar-term
   ::=    scalar-factor
        | scalar-term * scalar-factor
        | scalar-term / scalar-factor

scalar-factor
   ::=  [ + | - ] scalar-primary

scalar-primary
   ::=    literal
        | labeled-duration
        | column-ref
        | special-register
        | scalar-function-ref
        | aggregate-function-ref
        | ( scalar-exp )

labeled-duration
   ::=    scalar-exp units

units
   ::=    YEAR[S]
        | MONTH[S]
        | DAY[S]
        | HOUR[S]
        | MINUTE[S]
        | SECOND[S]
        | MICROSECOND[S]

special-register
   ::=    USER
        | CURRENT SQLID
        | CURRENT SERVER
        | CURRENT PACKAGESET
        | CURRENT TIMEZONE
        | CURRENT DATE
        | CURRENT TIME
        | CURRENT TIMESTAMP

scalar-function-ref
   ::=    scalar-function ( scalar-exp-commalist )
```

```
scalar-function
```

CHAR	DATE	DAY	DAYS	DECIMAL
DIGITS	FLOAT	HEX	HOUR	INTEGER
LENGTH	MICROSECOND	MINUTE	MONTH	SECOND
SUBSTR	TIME	TIMESTAMP	VALUE	VARGRAPHIC
YEAR				

Note: Each of these scalar functions takes just a single scalar-expression argument, except (a) CHAR and TIMESTAMP, which take two,

(b) DECIMAL and SUBSTR, which take three, and (c) VALUE, which takes an arbitrary number (at least two).

```
aggregate-function-ref
    ::=     COUNT ( * )
          | aggregate-function ( [ ALL | DISTINCT ] scalar-exp )

aggregate-function
    ::=     COUNT | SUM | AVG | MAX | MIN
```

C.4 SELECT-EXPRESSIONS

```
select-exp
    ::=     select-clause
            from-clause
          [ where-clause ]
          [ grouping-clause ]
          [ having-clause ]

select-clause
    ::=     SELECT [ ALL | DISTINCT ] select-spec

select-spec
    ::=     * | selection-commalist

selection
    ::=     table-ref . *
          | scalar-exp

from-clause
    ::=     FROM table-spec-commalist

where-clause
    ::=     WHERE condition

grouping-clause
    ::=     GROUP BY column-ref-commalist

having-clause
    ::=     HAVING condition
```

C.5 CONDITIONS

```
condition
    ::=     condition-term
          | condition OR condition-term

condition-term
    ::=     condition-factor
          | condition-term AND condition-factor

condition-factor
    ::=     [ NOT ] condition-primary

condition-primary
    ::=     simple-condition
          | ( condition )
```

```
simple-condition
    ::=     compare-condition
          | between-condition
          | like-condition
          | in-condition
          | test-for-null
          | existence-test

compare-condition
    ::=     scalar-exp comparison scalar-exp
          | scalar-exp comparison [ ALL | ANY ] ( column-select-exp )

comparison
    ::=     = | ¬= | <> | < | ¬< | <= | > | ¬> | >=

column-select-exp
    ::=     column-select-clause
            from-clause
          [ where-clause ]
          [ grouping-clause ]
          [ having-clause ] ]

column-select-clause
    ::=     SELECT [ ALL | DISTINCT ] scalar-exp

between-condition
    ::=     column-ref [ NOT ] BETWEEN scalar-exp AND scalar-exp

like-condition
    ::=     scalar-exp [ NOT ] LIKE literal [ ESCAPE literal ]

in-condition
    ::=     scalar-exp [ NOT ] IN ( list-of-scalars )

list-of-scalars
    ::=     literal-commalist
          | column-select-exp

test-for-null
    ::=     scalar-exp IS [ NOT ] NULL

existence-test
    ::=     EXISTS ( select-exp )
```

C.6 STATEMENTS

```
statement
    ::=     select-statement
          | insert-statement
          | update-statement
          | delete-statement

select-statement
    ::=     union-exp [ ordering-clause ] ;

union-exp
    ::=     union-term
          | union-exp UNION [ ALL ] union-term
```

```
union-term
   ::=     select-exp
         | ( union-exp )

ordering-clause
   ::=     ORDER BY order-item-commalist

order-item
   ::=     ordering-column [ ASC | DESC ]

ordering-column
   ::=     column-ref | integer

insert-statement
   ::=     INSERT INTO table-ref [ ( column-commalist ) ]
                     source-values ;

source-values
   ::=     VALUES ( insert-item-commalist )
         | select-exp

insert-item
   ::=     literal | NULL | special-register

update-statement
   ::=     UPDATE table-spec
           SET column-assignment-commalist
         [ where-clause ] ;

column-assignment
   ::=     column = scalar-exp
         | column = NULL

delete-statement
   ::=     DELETE FROM table-spec [ where-clause ] ;
```

A P P E N D I X

DB2 System Tables

As explained in Chapter 8, the DB2 catalog consists of a set of predefined tables, called system tables. In this appendix we present a brief summary of the content of those tables, in order to give some idea of the control information that DB2 maintains therein and hence some idea of the kinds of SQL queries that are possible against the catalog. We also briefly describe the Communications Database, which contains some additional system tables for use in conjunction with the Distributed Data Facility.

Note: All system tables have an "owner" of SYSIBM. The fully qualified name of the SYSTABLES table, for example, is SYSIBM.SYSTABLES (ignoring the optional high-end "location" qualifier—see Chapter 17).

The Catalog

- SYSCOLAUTH

  Shows which authorization IDs have UPDATE privileges on which columns of which tables (see Chapter 10).

- SYSCOLUMNS

  Contains one row for each column of each table (see Chapter 8).

- SYSCOPY

  Contains recovery information (see Chapter 16).

- SYSDATABASE

  Contains one row for each database.*

- SYSDBAUTH

  Shows which authorization IDs have which privileges on which databases (see Chapter 10).

- SYSDBRM

  Contains one row for each DBRM in each application plan (see Chapter 2).

- SYSFIELDS

  Contains one row for each column that has a FIELDPROC (see Chapter 15), plus additional rows containing RUNSTATS information for certain indexed columns (see Chapter 16).

- SYSFOREIGNKEYS

  Contains one row for each column of each foreign key (see Chapter 11).

- SYSINDEXES

  Contains one row for each index (see Chapter 8).

- SYSINDEXPART

  Contains one row for each partition of each partitioned index space and one row for each simple index space (see Chapter 15).

- SYSKEYS

  Contains one row for each indexed column for each index (note that this has nothing to do with keys in the relational sense—the "keys" in question are "index keys," not necessarily primary or foreign keys).

- SYSLINKS

  Contains one row for each parent/child link in the catalog (as explained at the end of Chapter 15, the catalog itself makes use of certain storage structures, including in particular parent/child links, that DB2 databases in general do not).

---

*Except for a special system database called DSNDB01.

- **SYSPACKAGE**

  Contains one row for each package.

- **SYSPACKAUTH**

  Shows which authorization IDs have which privileges on which packages (see Chapter 10).

- **SYSPACKDEP**

  Shows which packages are dependent on which objects.

- **SYSPACKLIST**

  Shows which packages are involved in which application plans (see Chapter 2).

- **SYSPACKSTMT**

  Contains one or more rows for each SQL statement in each package.

- **SYSPKSYSTEM**

  Shows which environments are enabled or disabled for which packages (see Chapters 10 and 16).

- **SYSPLAN**

  Contains one row for each application plan.

- **SYSPLANAUTH**

  Shows which authorization IDs have which privileges on which application plans (see Chapter 10).

- **SYSPLANDEP**

  Shows which application plans are dependent on which objects.

- **SYSPLSYSTEM**

  Shows which environments are enabled or disabled for which plans (see Chapters 10 and 16).

- **SYSRELS**

  Contains a row for each "relationship" (i.e., referential constraint).

- **SYSRESAUTH**

  Shows which authorization IDs have which privileges on which collections, storage groups, tablespaces, and buffer pools (see Chapter 10).

- **SYSSTMT**

  Contains the source form of the SQL statements corresponding to the DBRMs listed in SYSDBRM (see above).

- **SYSSTOGROUP**

  Contains one row for each storage group.

- SYSSTRINGS

  Contains one row for each possible conversion between coded character sets.

- SYSSYNONYMS

  Contains one row for each synonym.

- SYSTABAUTH

  Shows which authorization IDs have which privileges on which tables (see Chapter 10).

- SYSTABLEPART

  Contains one row for each partition of each partitioned table space and one row for each simple or segmented table space (see Chapter 15).

- SYSTABLES

  Contains one row for each table and each alias (see Chapter 8).

- SYSTABLESPACE

  Contains one row for each table space.

- SYSUSERAUTH

  Shows which authorization IDs have which system privileges (see Chapter 10).

- SYSVIEWDEP

  Shows which views depend on which tables.

- SYSVIEWS

  Contains the source form of the SQL definition of each view.

- SYSVLTREE

  Contains the rest (if any) of the parse tree representation for each view (see SYSVTREE below).

- SYSVOLUMES

  Contains one row for each volume of each storage group.

- SYSVTREE

  Contains the first 4000 bytes of the parse tree representation for each view.

The Communications Database

The Communications Database (CDB) describes valid connections between the local DB2 system and other accessible systems (which may or may not be DB2 systems in turn). *Note*: A knowledge of VTAM is required in order to understand the contents of the CDB in detail.

- SYSLUNAMES

  Contains one row for each "logical unit" associated with each accessible system, giving security information.

- SYSLOCATIONS

  Contains one row for each accessible system.

- SYSLUMODES

  Defines the maximum number of "active conversations" permitted for each logical unit for each "logon mode."

- SYSMODESELECT

  Defines a logon mode for each conversation created to support a remote SQL request.

- SYSUSERNAMES

  Defines mappings between local and remote authorization IDs.

APPENDIX

· E ·

DB2 and the SQL Standard

E.1 INTRODUCTION

A highlight of the DB2 Version 2.3 announcement was "compliance with
SQL standards ANSI X3.135–1989 and X3.168–1989, FIPS 127-1, and ISO
standard 9075:1989 (without the optional Integrity Enhancement Feature)." The announcement went on to say that "compliance . . . includes
full SQL compliance at Level 2 for both DML and DDL . . . Support is
provided for embedded SQL COBOL, embedded SQL FORTRAN, embedded SQL PL/I, and embedded SQL C. The Integrity Enhancement Feature,
which is an optional feature of the standards, is not fully implemented. A
formal validation . . . by the National Institute of Standards and Technology will be completed shortly." The purpose of this appendix is to explain
and analyze these claims.

First we give a brief explanation of the various different standards (and
standards documents) mentioned in the IBM announcement:

- ANSI X3.135-1989 is the American National Standards Institute (ANSI) definition of the American national standard *Database Language SQL*, known informally as "SQL/89." SQL/89 consists of the original SQL standard (known informally as "SQL/86") plus an optional extension called the Integrity Enhancement Feature. *Note*: SQL/89 is the standard in effect at the time of writing, but it will probably have been superseded by "SQL2" by the time this book appears in print (see below).

- ANSI X3.168-1989 is the American National Standards Institute definition of the American national standard *Database Language Embedded SQL*. This standard defines the rules for embedding SQL in Ada, C, COBOL, FORTRAN, Pascal, and PL/I. Note that it is a national standard only, not an international standard.

- FIPS 127-1 effectively defines the specifications of ANSI X3.135-1989 (minus the Integrity Enhancement Feature) as a US Federal Information Processing Standard. The National Institute of Standards and Technology (a US federal body) has prepared a test suite for testing compliance with FIPS 127-1.

- ISO 9075:1989 (which is effectively identical to ANSI X3.135-1989) is the International Organization for Standardization (ISO) definition of the international standard *Database Language SQL*.

In addition to the foregoing, the reader should also be aware of the following:

- SQL/89 and its predecessor SQL/86 are both defined at two *levels*. Loosely speaking, Level 2 is the full standard, and Level 1 is a subset of Level 2 (Level 2 has been described, perhaps a little unkindly, as "the intersection of existing implementations"). IBM is claiming full compliance at Level 2.

- There are at least two additional SQL standards currently in existence, of which at least one is highly relevant to DB2. First, there is the X/OPEN standard, which is a standard for SQL in the UNIX environment. Second, there is IBM's own SAA ("Systems Application Architecture") standard.

- Finally, it is virtually certain that this year (1992) will see the ratification of a new joint national (ANSI) and international (ISO) standard that will supersede all three of X3.135-1989, X3.168-1989, and ISO 9075:1989. This new standard, which has been under development for several years, is known informally as "SQL2" (after ratification it will probably be known informally as "SQL/92").

For a thorough description of SQL/86 and SQL/89, the reader is referred to the book *A Guide to the SQL Standard*, 2nd edition, by C. J. Date (Addison-Wesley, 1989). The third edition of this book, with Hugh Darwen as coauthor, is due to appear later this year (1992) and will cover SQL2 (or SQL/92).

The remainder of this appendix is structured as follows. Section E.2 describes the various Precompiler options that are relevant to standards compliance. Section E.3 discusses the *schema processor* (a new feature of DB2 Version 2.3). The remaining three sections summarize all known differences between the DB2 dialect of SQL and the existing ISO/ANSI standard dialect. In an attempt to structure the discussion, the material is divided into three sections—Section E.4, "Standard Features Not Supported in DB2," Section E.5, "DB2 Features Not Supported in the Standard," and Section E.6, "Incompatibilities" (i.e., features supported in both but treated differently). However, the assignment of items to these three sections is sometimes a little arbitrary.

E.2 PRECOMPILER OPTIONS

The Precompiler options that are most directly relevant to standards compliance are STDSQL and SQLFLAG.

STDSQL

We mentioned this option in Chapter 12. To review, the possible specifications are NO and 86 (where "86," of course, stands for SQL/86, meaning SQL/89 without the Integrity Enhancement Feature). If 86 is specified:

- SQL-style comments are permitted.
- Explicit BEGIN DECLARE SECTION and END DECLARE SECTION statements are required (and all declarations of host variables that will be used in SQL statements must appear within a declare section).
- The program must not contain (or INCLUDE) a declaration for the SQLCA. Instead, it must contain an explicit SQLCODE declaration (and that declaration must not be part of a structure, nor factored in with other declarations).
- If the argument to an aggregate function such as SUM includes DISTINCT and the function reference in turn appears as an operand in a larger arithmetic expression, as in (e.g.) the expression SUM

(DISTINCT X) + 3, the overall expression is accepted but a warning message is produced.

We also remind the reader of the Precompiler option NOFOR. If this option is specified, the FOR UPDATE clause is not required on cursor declarations, even if UPDATE CURRENT statements will be used.* NOFOR is implied by STDSQL(86), since the FOR UPDATE clause is not part of SQL/86 (or SQL/89).

SQLFLAG

The purpose of the SQLFLAG option is to request the Precompiler to flag any SQL statements that deviate from the rules for whichever standard is specified in the option. The possible specifications are SAA and 86 ("86" also has a couple of additional variants that need not concern us here). If SAA is specified, the Precompiler will flag deviations from IBM's own SAA standard; if 86 is specified, it will flag deviations from SQL/86—and hence, more significantly, from FIPS 127-1; we say "more significantly," because one of the requirements of FIPS 127-1 is that the implementation "shall provide an option to flag nonconforming SQL language" (this is usually known as the *FIPS flagger* requirement).

E.3   THE SCHEMA PROCESSOR

SQL/86 and SQL/89 differ from DB2 (and from most other commercial SQL implementations, come to that) in one very important respect: They do not permit data definition language (DDL) statements to be interspersed with data manipulation language (DML) statements and executed from an application program; instead, they require all data definition to be done in a special "schema language." Accordingly, they provide a special statement called CREATE SCHEMA. All data definition operations are supposed to be specified as suboperations within such a CREATE SCHEMA operation, and the implementation is supposed to provide a *schema processor* to process them. For standards compliance reasons, therefore, DB2 Version 2.3 does indeed provide such a processor.

Here first is the syntax of CREATE SCHEMA:

```
CREATE SCHEMA AUTHORIZATION user
      [ schema-element [, schema-element ] ... ]
```

---

*By contrast, dynamically prepared SELECTs must include an appropriate FOR UPDATE clause if UPDATE CURRENT statements will be used, even if NOFOR is specified. Also, if NOFOR is specified but some cursor declaration nevertheless includes a FOR UPDATE clause, the effect of that clause will be exactly as if NOFOR had not been specified.

Each "schema-element" is a CREATE TABLE statement, a CREATE VIEW statement, or a GRANT statement (note that these are the *only* "data definition" operations in SQL/89). EXEC SQL prefixes and semicolon terminators must not be specified.

DB2's schema processor operates by first setting the current SQLID to the "user" value specified in the AUTHORIZATION clause. It then uses the facilities of dynamic SQL to execute the various data definition operations in the schema, one at a time. *Note*: The sequence of those operations within the containing CREATE SCHEMA is significant; none of those operations can refer to an object that does not yet exist. Thus, e.g., a CREATE VIEW cannot precede the CREATE TABLE for the base table on which the view is defined.

The DB2 CREATE SCHEMA statement is not regarded as part of SQL and cannot appear anywhere other than as input to the DB2 schema processor. Note that there is no DROP SCHEMA statement.

E.4 STANDARD FEATURES NOT SUPPORTED IN DB2

The only aspects of SQL/89 not supported by DB2 are certain elements of the Integrity Enhancement Feature, IEF. To be specific:

- IEF supports user-defined default values. DB2 does not.
- IEF supports CHECK constraints on base tables (and columns thereof). DB2 does not.
- If a primary key is single-column, IEF permits that primary key to be defined by means of a PRIMARY KEY specification within that column's individual column definition. DB2 requires all primary keys to be defined by means of a separate PRIMARY KEY clause.
- The IEF REFERENCES specification (as part of an individual column definition) is not supported in DB2; FOREIGN KEY specifications are supported in DB2 only by means of a separate FOREIGN KEY clause.
- IEF permits a foreign key to reference any candidate key; DB2 requires a foreign key to reference a primary key specifically.
- DB2 does not support the REFERENCES privilege (it uses the ALTER privilege for the purpose instead).

E.5 DB2 FEATURES NOT SUPPORTED IN THE STANDARD

- The standard does not allow any characters to appear in identifiers other than the uppercase letters A–Z, the digits 0–9, and the underscore character. DB2 allows the characters #, @, and $ to appear in an identifier wherever a letter can appear. DB2 also allows double-byte characters to appear in identifiers and supports "delimited identifiers" (see the IBM manuals for details of these latter two cases).

- DB2 allows consecutive underscore characters to appear in an identifier. The standard does not.

- The following DB2 data types are not supported in the standard:

```
VARCHAR (and LONG VARCHAR)
GRAPHIC
VARGRAPHIC (and LONG VARGRAPHIC)
DATE
TIME
TIMESTAMP
```

The concept of "durations" also does not exist in the standard.

- The DB2 concept of system-defined default values does not exist in the standard; the specification NOT NULL WITH DEFAULT on CREATE (or ALTER) TABLE is a DB2 extension.

- DB2's support for foreign keys includes (a) "constraint names" for foreign key constraints, (b) delete rules (CASCADE, SET NULL, and RESTRICT), and (c) support for constraint cycles. None of these items is included in the standard, except (implicitly) the RESTRICT delete rule. (*Note*: The DB2 support for primary and foreign keys is broadly but not totally compatible with the SQL2 proposals.)

- DB2 allows a value of approximate numeric type (FLOAT, REAL, or DOUBLE PRECISION) to be assigned to an object of exact numeric type (SMALLINT, INTEGER, or DECIMAL). The standard does not.

- The standard does not include any date/time support at all. Thus everything discussed in Appendix B of this book is a DB2 extension.

- DB2 supports hexadecimal literals.

- DB2 supports a concatenate operator (‖ or CONCAT).

- The standard does not include any scalar builtin functions. Thus the functions discussed in Section 3.4 of this book (SUBSTR, LENGTH, etc., etc.) are all DB2 extensions.

- In the standard, if the argument to an aggregate function such as SUM includes DISTINCT, then the function reference must appear in isolation—i.e., it cannot be an operand in a larger arithmetic expression such as SUM (DISTINCT X) + 3. This restriction does not exist in DB2.

- In the standard, if the argument to an aggregate function such as SUM includes DISTINCT, then the argument must consist of a simple column reference—i.e., it cannot be a more general arithmetic expression such as $X + 3$. This restriction does not exist in DB2.

- DB2 supports the scalar comparison operators $\neg =$, $\neg <$, and $\neg >$ as alternative representations of $< >$, $> =$, and $< =$, respectively.

- DB2 allows qualified references of the form "R.*" (where R is a range variable) in a SELECT clause. DB2 also allows references of the form "*" (or "R.*") in a SELECT clause to appear in conjunction with other items. Both of these possibilities are prohibited in the standard.

- In DB2, the commalist of literals in an IN condition (first format—see Example 5.2.8) must contain at least one literal; in the standard, it must contain at least two.

- The standard includes a much more restrictive definition of "union-compatibility" than DB2 does (so much so, in fact, that UNION in the standard is virtually unusable).

- UNION (with or without ALL) is strictly a binary operation in the standard. That is, an expression such as x UNION y UNION z is not permitted; it must be replaced by one of the two expressions (x UNION y) UNION z or x UNION (y UNION z).

- DB2 supports the use of explicitly defined range variables in UPDATE and DELETE as well as in SELECT.

- The standard does not include any definition of catalog tables (SYSTABLES, SYSCOLUMNS, etc.).

- The standard does not support the COMMENT or LABEL statements.

- The standard does not support synonyms (CREATE SYNONYM, DROP SYNONYM).

- The standard does not support aliases (CREATE ALIAS, DROP ALIAS).

- The only privileges defined in the standard are SELECT, INSERT, UPDATE (possibly column-specific), DELETE, REFERENCES (possibly column-specific), and ALL. As already noted in Section E.4, DB2 does not support the REFERENCES privilege; however, it does support numerous additional privileges (see the IBM manuals for details). In addition, the DB2 GRANT statement allows a commalist of table names (not just one, as in the standard) to be specified in the ON clause, and allows that commalist to be optionally preceded by the noiseword TABLE (not permitted in the standard). DB2 also allows privileges to be REVOKEd (the standard does not include a REVOKE statement).

- The standard does not support the statements SET CURRENT SQLID, SET CURRENT PACKAGESET, SET host variable, and CONNECT.

- The keyword WORK in COMMIT and ROLLBACK is required in the standard but optional in DB2.

- Certain view retrieval operations that fail in the standard succeed in DB2. For example, if column C of view V is derived from an expression such as SUM (X), then in the standard an retrieval of the form SELECT AVG (C) FROM V . . . is (tacitly) illegal. In DB2, however, it is legal. Refer to the discussion of "view materialization" in Chapter 9 for further discussion.

- DB2's rules regarding view updatability (see Section 9.4) are slightly more permissive than those of the standard, as follows:

(a) In DB2, if a column of the view is derived from a literal or an expression that does not involve an aggregate function, then INSERT operations are not allowed, and UPDATE operations are not allowed on that column, but DELETE operations are allowed, and so are UPDATE operations on other columns. In the standard, such a view cannot be updated at all.

(b) In DB2, if the WHERE clause in the view definition includes a subquery *and the FROM clause in that subquery refers to the base table on which the view is defined*, then the view is not updatable. In the standard, a view cannot be updated if its definition involves any subquery whatsoever.

- The FOR UPDATE clause on a cursor definition is not included in the standard; nor is the FOR FETCH ONLY clause.

- The WITH HOLD clause on a cursor definition is not included in the standard.

- The OPTIMIZE FOR *n* ROWS clause on a cursor definition is not included in the standard.

- The SQLWARNING condition on WHENEVER is not included in the standard.

- The embedded SQL statement DECLARE TABLE is not included in the standard.

- The standard requires host variables that will be used within embedded SQL statements to be defined within an "embedded SQL declare section," bracketed by BEGIN and END DECLARE SECTION statements. DB2 does not have this requirement, unless C is the host language or STDSQL(86) is in effect.

- DB2 allows host variables to be elements of a structure, and also supports the use of structure variables where a commalist of scalars is required (e.g., in the VALUES clause on INSERT).

- The colon marker (":") on host variables can be omitted in DB2 in contexts where no ambiguity can arise* (e.g., on the INTO clause in FETCH). It is always required in the standard.

- The SQL Communication Area (SQLCA) is not included in the standard, except for the single feedback parameter SQLCODE; there is therefore no INCLUDE SQLCA statement in the standard either. SQLCODE values are explicitly stated in the standard to be implementation-defined, except for the special values 0 and +100, so DB2 does conform to the standard in this respect even though other implementations will generate different SQLCODEs.

- The standard does not (yet) support SQLSTATE. (Moreover, the specific SQLSTATE values supported by DB2 are sometimes not the same as those proposed for SQL2.)

- The standard does not support an explicit LOCK TABLE statement.

- All dynamic SQL features—the statements PREPARE, DESCRIBE, and EXECUTE, the SQL Descriptor Area (SQLDA), the special INCLUDE statement for incorporating the SQLDA into host programs, the miscellaneous associated facilities (DECLARE STATEMENT, special form of OPEN, etc.)—are excluded from the standard.

- The standard does not include any ALTER or DROP statements at all. Therefore, the statements ALTER TABLE, DROP TABLE, and DROP VIEW are all DB2 extensions.

- The standard does not include any of the more "physical" data definition statements that are supported in DB2—CREATE/DROP INDEX, CREATE/DROP DATABASE, CREATE/DROP TABLESPACE, CREATE/DROP STOGROUP, etc. The standard also does not include

---

*Such omission will raise a warning, however.

any of the more "physical" operands on CREATE TABLE, such as EDITPROC, FIELDPROC, VALIDPROC, "IN tablespace," etc.

- DB2 does not require SQL definitional statements to be executed only within the context of CREATE SCHEMA; instead, such statements (like all others) can be executed both interactively and—in the form of embedded SQL—from within a program.

- DB2 supports partitioned tables. The standard does not.

- The standard does not support the EXPLAIN statement.

- The standard defines host language interfaces for Ada, C, COBOL, FORTRAN, Pascal, and PL/I; DB2, by contrast, supports C, COBOL, FORTRAN, PL/I, and System/370 Assembler Language (also, through the dynamic SQL facility, Ada, APL2, BASIC, LISP, and Prolog).

- The standard restricts the range of data types accessible from each host language; for example, according to the standard, INTEGER data is not accessible from PL/I (of course, this is probably an error in the standard). DB2 does not have such restrictions.

E.6   INCOMPATIBILITIES

- The standard and DB2 have different sets of reserved words. (In fact, DB2 allows "reserved" words to be used as identifiers in contexts where the reserved meaning does not apply, and so this point might arguably be seen as a DB2 extension rather than an incompatibility.)

- Authorization identifiers are limited to a maximum of 8 characters in DB2.

- String literals are varying length in DB2 but fixed length in the standard.

- In DB2, updates against a view V are checked against the check option (if any) specified for V and also against the check option (if any) specified for each view W (if any) on which V is defined. In other words, the check option is inheritable in DB2. This is not the case with the standard (of course, this is probably an error in the standard); nor was it with DB2, prior to Version 1 Release 3.

- The DB2 concept that there is an implicit WHENEVER statement for each condition—NOT FOUND, SQLERROR, also SQLWARNING— at the start of the program text, specifying CONTINUE in each case, is not supported in the standard.

- The standard does not explicitly permit the possibility that an error on retrieval might generate a null and set the indicator variable to −2. Whether it forbids it is unclear.

- The DB2 rules determining the binding of range variables to their corresponding table are not identical to those of the standard (though it is probably fair to say that they are the same if DB2 is used "sensibly"). The details are beyond the scope of this appendix; we merely observe that the behavior of DB2 may be unpredictable—and in some cases is certainly incorrect—if a FROM clause (a) mentions the same table twice and introduces an explicit range variable in one of the two mentions only (e.g., FROM S, S SX), or (b) mentions two tables and introduces explicit range variables for both, each having the same name as the other table (e.g., FROM S P, P S). The standard handles these cases (and all others like them) correctly.

- The COMMIT and ROLLBACK statements are illegal in DB2 under IMS batch, IMS/DC, and CICS.

- The standard requires all concurrent executions of interleaved transactions to be serializable (i.e., equivalent to some serial execution of those same transactions, running them one at a time). DB2 cannot provide such a guarantee if any of the transactions in question executes under CS isolation level.

APPENDIX

Bibliography

We present a short list of selected further reading (including in particular those IBM manuals consulted most heavily during the writing of this book).

IBM Manuals

1. IBM DATABASE 2 Version 2 General Information Release 3. IBM Document No. GC26-4373-03.

2. IBM DATABASE 2 Version 2 Administration Guide Release 3 (three volumes). IBM Document No. SC26-4374-02.

3. IBM DATABASE 2 Version 2 SQL Reference Release 3. IBM Document No. SC26-4380-02.

4. IBM DATABASE 2 Version 2 Application Programming and SQL Guide Release 3. IBM Document No. SC26-4377-02.

5. IBM DATABASE 2 Version 2 Command and Utility Reference Release 3. IBM Document No. SC26-4378-02.

System R

6. M. M. Astrahan et al.: "System R: Relational Approach to Database Management." *ACM Transactions on Database Systems 1*, No. 2 (June 1976).

The paper that first described the overall architecture of System R, the prototype forerunner of DB2 (and SQL/DS).

7. M. W. Blasgen et al.: "System R: An Architectural Overview." *IBM Systems Journal 20*, No. 1 (February 1981).

Describes the architecture of System R as it became by the time the system had been fully implemented.

8. D. D. Chamberlin et al.: "A History and Evaluation of System R." *Communications of the ACM 24*, No. 10 (October 1981).

Discusses the lessons learned from the System R prototype.

9. D. D. Chamberlin, A. M. Gilbert, and R. A. Yost: "A History of System R and SQL/Data System." *Proceedings of the 7th International Conference on Very Large Data Bases* (September 1981). Obtainable from ACM, IEEE, and INRIA.

Includes a description of the major differences between System R and SQL/DS (and, by extension, DB2).

DB2

10. Gabrielle Wiorkowski and David Kull: *DB2 Design and Development Guide* (3rd edition, Addison-Wesley, 1992).

A detailed guide to the use of DB2 in practice; describes proven strategies and techniques for designing and developing DB2 applications, with the emphasis on good performance. An ideal complement to the present book.

SQL

11. International Organization for Standardization: *Database Language SQL*. Document ISO/IEC 9075:1987. Also available as American National Standards Institute (ANSI) Document ANSI X3.135–1986.

Defines the original SQL standard (i.e., "SQL/86").

12. International Organization for Standardization: *Database Language SQL*. Document ISO/IEC 9075:1989. Also available as American National Standards Institute (ANSI) Document ANSI X3.135–1989.

Defines the original SQL standard as extended to include the Integrity Enhancement Feature IEF (i.e., "SQL/89").

13. American National Standards Institute: *Database Language Embedded SQL*. Document ANSI X3.168–1989.

Defines the ANSI embedded SQL standard.

14. U.S. Department of Commerce, National Institute of Standards and Technology: *Database Language SQL*. FIPS PUB 127–1 (2nd February 1990).

Defines the Federal Information Processing SQL standard.

15. International Organization for Standardization (ISO): *Database Language SQL*. Document ISO/IEC 9075:1992. Also available as American National Standards Institute (ANSI) Document ANSI X3.135–1992.

> Defines the new SQL standard ("SQL2").

16. IBM Corp.: *Systems Application Architecture Common Programming Interface*: *Database Reference*. IBM Document No. SC26-4348.

> Defines the IBM SAA SQL standard.

17. C. J. Date: *A Guide to the SQL Standard* (2nd edition, Addison-Wesley, 1989).

> An indepth discussion of "SQL/89."

18. C. J. Date and Hugh Darwen: *A Guide to the SQL Standard* (3rd edition, Addison-Wesley, to appear 1992).

> An indepth discussion of "SQL2."

19. Raymond A. Lorie and Jean-Jacques Daudenarde: *SQL and Its Applications* (Prentice-Hall, 1991).

Database Technology

20. C. J. Date: *An Introduction to Database Systems*: *Volume I* (5th edition, Addison-Wesley, 1990); *Volume II* (1st edition, Addison-Wesley, 1983).

> These two books between them provide the basis for a comprehensive education in most aspects of database technology. In particular, they include a very detailed tutorial on the relational approach.

Relational Technology

21. E. F. Codd: "A Relational Model of Data for Large Shared Data Banks." *Communications of the ACM 13*, No. 6 (June 1970). Reprinted in *Communications of the ACM 26*, No. 1 (January 1983).

> This was the paper that (apart from some internal IBM documents) first proposed the ideas of the relational model.

22. E. F. Codd: *The Relational Model for Database Management Version 2* (Addison-Wesley, 1990).

> A proposal for a vastly extended version of the relational model, by the creator of the original model.

23. C. J. Date: *Relational Database*: *Selected Writings* (Addison-Wesley, 1986); *Relational Database Writings 1985–1989* (Addison-Wesley, 1990); (with Hugh Darwen) *Relational Database Writings 1989–1991* (Addison-Wesley, 1992).

> These three books consist of a collection of papers on various aspects of relational technology. They include several papers on the SQL language and one (rather long) on a relational database design methodology that is directly applicable to DB2. The third book in the series also includes an analysis and critique of Codd's relational model, Versions 1 and 2 (see the previous item in this bibliography).

Other SQL Products

24. C. J. Date and Colin J. White: *A Guide to SQL/DS* (Addison-Wesley, 1989).

25. C. J. Date: *A Guide to INGRES* (Addison-Wesley, 1987).
    INGRES originally supported a different relational language, called QUEL, but SQL support was added later, and SQL has replaced QUEL as the primary INGRES language.

26. Jonathan Leffler: *Using INFORMIX-SQL* (Addison-Wesley, 1989).

27. David McGoveran and C. J. Date: *A Guide to SYBASE and SQL Server* (Addison-Wesley, 1992).

· G ·

Abbreviations and Acronyms

We list below some of the more important abbreviations and acronyms introduced in the text, together with their meanings.

ANSI	American National Standards Institute
API	application programming interface
APPC	Advanced Program-to-Program Communication
AS	Application System
BNF	Backus-Naur Form
BSDS	Boot Strap Data Set
CASE	Computer-Aided Software Engineering
CDB	Communications Database
CICS	Customer Information Control System
CLIST	command list (TSO)
CS	cursor stability (isolation level)
CSP	Cross System Product
DB/DC	database/data communications
DBA	database administrator

DBADM	database administration (privilege)
DBCTRL	database control (privilege)
DBMAINT	database maintenance (privilege)
DBMS	database management system
DBRM	Database Request Module
DB2	IBM DATABASE 2
DB2I	DB2 Interactive
DB2PM	DB2 Performance Monitor
DCLGEN	Declarations Generator
DDCS/2	Data Distribution Control System/2
DDF	Distributed Data Facility
DEM	Data Extract Manager (DXT)
DIS	Data Interpretation System
DPROP	Data Propagator
DRDA	Distributed Relational Data Architecture
DUW	distributed unit of work
DXT	Data Extract
EDA/SQL	Enterprise Data Access/SQL
EDITPROC	edit procedure
ESF	External Source Format
FAPs	Formats and Protocols
FIELDPROC	field procedure
GTF	Generalized Trace Facility
GUI	graphical user interface
I/O	input/output
ICU	Interactive Chart Utility
IMS	Information Management System
IMS/DB	IMS Database Manager
IMS/DC	IMS Data Communications Manager
IRLM	IMS Resource Lock Manager
ISO	International Organization for Standardization
IXF	Integration Exchange Format
LAN	local area network
LU	logical unit
MSL	Member Specification Library (CSP)
OSI	Open Systems Interconnection
PACKADM	package administration (privilege)
PAS	Personal AS
PF key	program function key
QBE	Query-By-Example
QMF	Query Management Facility
RDS	Relational Data System
REM	Relational Extract Manager (DXT)
RID	record ID
RR	repeatable read (isolation level)
RUW	remote unit of work

S lock	shared lock
SAA	Systems Application Architecture
SMF	System Management Facility
SPUFI	SQL Processor Using File Input
SQL	Structured Query Language
SQL/DS	Structured Query Language/Data System
SQLCA	SQL Communication Area
SQLDA	SQL Descriptor Area
SYSADM	system administration (privilege)
SYSCTRL	system control (privilege)
SYSOPR	system operation (privilege)
TCP/IP	Transmission Control Protocol/Internet Protocol
TSO	Time Sharing Option
U lock	update lock
UIM	User Input Manager (DXT)
VALIDPROC	validation procedure
VSAM	Virtual Storage Access Method
VTAM	Virtual Telecommunications Access Method
X lock	exclusive lock

Index